McCLARIN HIGH
3605 MAIN STREET
COLLEGE PARK   GA   30337

Billie Clinton

Billie Clinton

Be

World Literature

AGS®

American Guidance Service, Inc.
Circle Pines, Minnesota 55014-1796
800-328-2560

Literature Consultant

Jack Cassidy, Ph.D.
Texas A&M University
Corpus Christi, Texas

Original Cover Art

Connie Hayes

Printed in the United States of America

ISBN 0-7854-1828-8

Product Number 93030

A 0 9 8 7 6 5 4 3 2 1

Contents

Unit 2 Nonfiction **139**

The Stronger

Appendixes

Handbook of Literary Terms

Glossary

Indexes

Acknowledgments

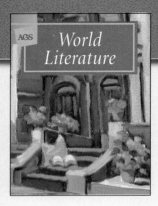

How to Use This Book

This book is an anthology of world literature. An anthology is a collection of literary selections written by different authors. The selections can be poems, plays, short stories, essays, parts of novels, folktales, legends, or myths. Sometimes, an anthology is organized around selections from a certain country or continent. For example, you might have an anthology with great literature from America. The first section of an American literature anthology could include a section with early American Indian poetry or Puritan diaries. Sometimes, anthologies are organized around different types of literature (genres). Then, you might have sections on poems, short stories, plays, essays, or folktales.

Why is a literature anthology important?

This anthology contains many enjoyable literary selections. An anthology helps you understand yourself and other people. You will read about people from other countries. Sometimes, you will read about people who lived in the past. Try to relate what the author is saying to your own life. Have I ever felt this way? Have I known anyone like this person? Have I seen anything like this?

A literature anthology can also help you appreciate the beauty of language. As you read, find phrases or sentences that you particularly like. You may want to start a notebook of these. You could also include words that are difficult.

This anthology is also important because it introduces you to great works of literature. Many times, you will find references to these works in everyday life. You will sometimes hear a quotation on TV or read it in the newspaper. Reading great literature helps you to become more literate. Generally, literate people are more likely to get better paying jobs.

What is in this book?

This book is filled with interesting works of literature. Great literature can come in many forms. On the next page are definitions of some kinds of literature genres in an anthology.

Genre Definitions

autobiography A person's life story written by that person.

biography The story of a person's life written by someone else. You will find many biographies in this book.

diary A record of personal events, thoughts, or private feelings. People usually write in a diary every day or weekly. Mostly, people write diaries for themselves. Sometimes an author will create a fictional diary.

drama A play that often involves intense emotional conflict. Usually, a drama is serious.

essay A written work that expresses a writer's opinions on some basic or current issue.

fable A short story or poem with a moral, often with animals who act like humans. Aesop was a famous author of fables.

fiction Writing that is made up and often intended to entertain. Fiction is usually in prose form. Short stories, novels, folktales, myths, legends, and most plays are works of fiction.

folktale A story that has been handed down from one generation to another. The characters are usually either good or bad. Folktales make use of rhyme and repetitive phrases. Sometimes, they are called tall tales, particularly if they are humorous and exaggerated. They are also called folklore.

journal Writing that expresses an author's feelings or first impressions about a subject. A journal is like a diary, but it expresses more of the author's feelings. Sometimes, students keep journals to record their feelings about what they have read.

legend A traditional story that at one time was told orally and handed down from one generation to another. Legends are like myths, but they do not have as many supernatural forces. Usually, they have some historical base.

myth A story designed to explain the mysteries of life. A myth explains natural events, such as the change of seasons. Like fables and folktales, myths were first oral stories. Most early cultures have myths.

nonfiction Writing about real people and events. Nonfiction is usually designed to explain, argue, or describe. Essays, speeches, diaries, journals, autobiographies, and biographies are all usually nonfiction.

novel Fiction that is book-length and has more plot and character details than a short story.

poem A short piece of literature that usually has rhythm and paints powerful or beautiful impressions with words. Poems often have sound patterns such as rhyme. Songs are poetry set to music. Prose is the opposite of poetry.

prose Written language that is not verse. Short stories, novels, autobiographies, biographies, diaries, journals, and essays are examples of prose.

science fiction A type of literature that deals with people, places, and events that could not happen in our reality. However, science fiction is sometimes based on projected scientific developments. Most stories are set in the future. Stories about space are examples of science fiction. Jules Verne was one of the first science fiction authors.

short story A brief prose narrative. Short stories are designed to create unified impressions forcefully. Edgar Allan Poe was a great writer of short stories.

What is a literary term?

Literary terms are words or phrases used to study and discuss works of literature. These terms describe the devices that an author uses to help us enjoy and understand what we are reading. Some of the terms also describe a genre. In this anthology, you will see shaded boxes on the side of the Introducing the Selection pages that define some literary terms. These terms are important in understanding and discussing the selection being read. By understanding these literary terms, you can appreciate the author's craft.

The following are literary terms that apply to all works of literature. You should be familiar with these terms as you read this anthology. All of the literary terms used in this book can be found on page 436 in the Handbook of Literary Terms.

Literary Terms

autobiography a story about a person's life written by that person

setting the place and time in a story

Glossary of Key Literary Terms

characterization The devices authors use to reveal characters. Characters are revealed by their actions, speech, appearance, others' comments, or the author's comments.

conflict The struggle the main character of a story faces. Conflict is an important part of the plot of a short story or novel. Main characters can struggle against themselves, other people, society, or nature. The four types of conflict are defined as person-against-person, person-against-self, person-against-society, and person-against-nature.

plot The series of events in a story. The plot shows what happens to the characters. Plots have conflict and resolutions to that conflict. Plots are very important in stories. Plots should have rising action, foreshadowing, a climax, and falling action.

setting The time and place in a story. Sometimes authors describe the setting in detail. Sometimes, the setting is left unclear so the reader can imagine it. A setting can even be a person's mind.

theme The idea that holds the whole piece of literature together. A theme is a generalization about humankind that the author wants to make. Themes are underlying statements about a topic. A theme is the topic of a piece of literature and the author's opinion about that topic.

How do I read this book?

Different works of literature can be read in different ways. However, you can use some strategies with all works of literature.

Before beginning a unit:
- Read the unit title and selection titles.
- Read any introductory paragraphs about the unit.
- Look at the pictures and other graphics in the unit. There may be maps to help you.
- Think about the unit's main topic.
- Think about what you want to learn about this topic.
- Think about what you already know about the unit.
- Develop questions in your mind that you think will be answered in this unit.

Before beginning the reading of a selection:
- Read the selection's title.
- Look at the pictures and other visuals.
- Read the background material included in About the Author and About the Selection.
- Predict what you think the selection is going to be about.
- Ask yourself questions about the material.

As you read the selections:
- Think about the predictions that you made before reading. Were they right?
- Make new predictions as you read.
- Read the notes in the side columns. These will help you understand and think about the main concepts.
- Think of people or events in your own life that are similar to those described.
- Reread sentences or paragraphs that you do not understand.
- Refer to the definitions at the bottom of the page for words you do not know.
- In a notebook or on note cards, record definitions of words that you do not know. Also, record words defined in the text that you find interesting or unusual.

| affirm to state positively | miseries things that cause one to suffer | tedious tiresome; boring |

After reading the selections:

■ Think about the questions that you asked yourself before you read. Were your answers to these questions right?

■ Reread interesting or difficult parts of the selection.

■ Reflect on what you have learned.

■ Write the answers to the review questions in Reviewing the Selection.

■ Use graphic organizers to help you organize and remember information. (See "What is a graphic organizer?" on page 15 to get some ideas.)

How do I read specific types of literature?

The strategies already described will work for all kinds of literature, but some types of literature need specific strategies.

When reading poetry:

■ Read the poem aloud.

■ Listen to the sounds of the words.

■ Picture the images the author is describing.

■ Reread poems over and over again to appreciate the author's use of language.

When reading essays:

■ Review the questions in Reviewing the Selection before you begin reading.

■ Use the questions to help you make your own predictions before reading.

■ Remember that essays usually express an author's opinions. Try to understand how the author arrived at these opinions.

When reading plays:

■ Picture the setting of the play. There is usually not much description. Try to relate it to what you have seen before.

■ Pay attention to the dialogue. How does the dialogue reveal the characters' personality? Have you ever known anyone like this? Are you like this?

What is a graphic organizer?

A graphic organizer is a visual representation of information. It can help you see how ideas are related to each other. A graphic organizer can help you study for a test or organize information before writing an essay. Following are some examples.

Character Analysis Guide

The graphic organizer below can help you better understand characters in a story or real people in a biography or autobiography. Fill in the character trait on the ray and then list events in the story or in the person's life that demonstrate that character trait.

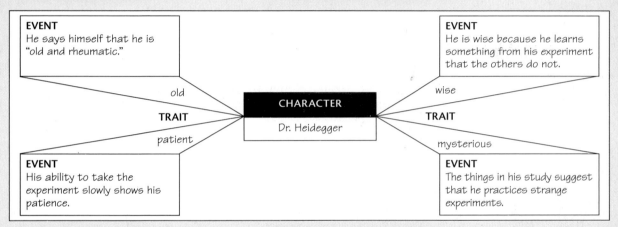

EVENT
He says himself that he is "old and rheumatic."

EVENT
He is wise because he learns something from his experiment that the others do not.

old
TRAIT
patient

wise
TRAIT
mysterious

CHARACTER
Dr. Heidegger

EVENT
His ability to take the experiment slowly shows his patience.

EVENT
The things in his study suggest that he practices strange experiments.

Venn Diagram

The Venn Diagram can help you compare and contrast two characters, two authors, or two pieces of literature. List the similarities on the overlap between the circles. List the differences on the parts of the circles that do not overlap.

Remember that all graphic organizers can be used in various ways. They can be used to help you organize your writing. They can be used to help you analyze your thoughts, and they can be used to help you study for a test. You can even create your own graphic organizer.

Wrote about faith in God
Lived away from others
Never married
Writings were popular after her death

Wrote poetry
Wrote about loss
Wrote about death
Used stanzas and symbols

Wrote short stories
Wrote horror stories
Was married
Lived in poverty
Was famous as a writer in his lifetime

Emily Dickinson

Edgar Allan Poe

What strategies should I use when I encounter a word that I don't know?

- If the word is boldface, look for the definition of the word at the bottom of the page.
- If the word is not boldface, read to the end of the sentence and maybe the next sentence. Can you determine the unknown word now?
- If your teacher has given you a Selection Glossary, use it to look up additional terms that are not boldface.
- Look at the beginning sound of the unknown word.
- Ask yourself, "What word would make sense here that begins with this sound?"
- Sound out the syllables of the word.
- If you still cannot determine the unknown word, see if you know any parts of the word: prefixes, suffixes, or roots.
- If this does not work, write the word on a note card or in a vocabulary notebook and look it up in the dictionary after you have finished reading the selection.
- If the word is necessary to understand the passage, look it up in a dictionary or glossary immediately.

Word Study Tip
- Start a vocabulary file with note cards to use for review.
- Write one word on the front of each card. Write the unit number, selection title, and the definition on the other side.
- You can use these cards as flash cards by yourself or with a study partner to test your knowledge.

Detract

Unit 5

The Gettysburg Address

To lessen the importance or value of

What should I know about taking a test on literature?

Before the test day:
- Read all the works assigned.
- Review your class notes, the Unit Summary, and the Unit Review.
- Ask your teacher what kinds of questions will be on the test.
- Review any notes that you have taken or graphic organizers you have developed.
- Try to predict what questions will be asked and develop answers to those questions.
- Review the Test-Taking Tips at the bottom of the Unit Review pages in this book.

UNIT 1 SUMMARY

Unit 1 covers 1620 to 1849. The development of new colonies, the struggle between Europeans and American Indians, and the American Revolution took place during this time.

Four styles of literature—native, colonial, revolutionary, and early national—represent early America. Native literature in this unit includes American Indian poems and a myth that had been passed down orally. Colonial literature in this unit includes the works of William Bradford, Anne Dudley Bradstreet, and Benjamin Franklin. These writings copied European styles. The revolutionary literature in this unit is by Thomas Paine, a writer during the American Revolution. Early national literature came about in the 1800s. Two professional writers, Washington Irving and Edgar Allan Poe, were part of this movement. They studied the inner workings of people and society. Early national literature began to replace letters, essays, and speeches that were popular in the past.

- "To My Dear and Loving Husband" by Anne Dudley Bradstreet is a love poem from a wife to her husband.
- The selection from *Poor Richard's Almanac* by Benjamin Franklin is a list of aphorisms, or clever sayings.
- *The American Crisis, Number 1* by Thomas Paine is a pamphlet that expresses the desire for freedom and urges Americans to continue their struggle against England.
- "Wouter Van Twiller" by Washington Irving is a sketch that uses satire and exaggeration to poke fun at a man's undeserved fame.
- Three American Indian poems by the Omaha, Sioux, and Chippewa express American Indian attitudes toward death and love for the land.
- "The Origin of Plumage" is an Iroquois myth, or story that explains how something in the natural world came to be. This myth explains how all birds got their feathers.
- "The Black Cat" by Edgar Allan Poe is a horror short story about one man's madness and his cat.
- "Annabel Lee" by Edgar Allan Poe is a poem about the grief caused by the death of a lover.

UNIT 1 REVIEW

Directions Write the answers to these questions using complete sentences.

Comprehension: Identifying Facts
1. Why did the Puritans and Pilgrims leave England?
2. What was established in the South?
3. Who were three political leaders of the 1700s?
4. Which two authors in this unit represent the time after the American Revolution?
5. Who were the very first people to live in America?

Comprehension: Understanding Main Ideas
6. What similarities and differences can you see in the works of Washington Irving and Edgar Allan Poe? How did each writer's background affect his works?
7. Describe the similarities and differences found in the poetry of Anne Dudley Bradstreet and Edgar Allan Poe.

8. How does Benjamin Franklin's writing differ from William Bradford's? Are their writings similar in any way? Explain your answer.
9. In what ways are the American Indian poems in this unit similar to and different from the other poetry in this unit?
10. What are three common themes of the selections in this unit?

Understanding Literature: Fiction and Nonfiction
Most early American literature is nonfiction and based on writing styles used in Europe. Nonfiction describes actual people and real events. Toward the middle of the nineteenth century, fiction was introduced. Fiction describes imaginary characters and made-up events. An American style of writing also developed.
11. Identify each selection in Unit 1 by genre (poem, short story, essay, etc.). If the work is not a poem, tell whether the selection is fiction or nonfiction.
12. Choose two works from Unit 1. How are these two works different? Compare these two selections for language, style, content, and characters.

13. Write the name of the selection from Unit 1 that surprised you the most. Explain the reasons for your choice.
14. Which selection from this unit describes life in America best? Why?
15. Is it important for a nation to have its own style of writing? Explain.

Critical Thinking
16. Anne Dudley Bradstreet is the only woman represented in this unit. Do you think she would be admired today? Explain your answer.
17. Do you like the early American literature from this unit? Why or why not?
18. Explain what you think is most important about early American literature.
19. Which author from this unit did you like best? Why?
20. Which poem from this unit did you like best? Why?

Speak and Listen
Think how society has changed since the 1800s. What are some ways in which modern life is different from the life of a young person who lived 150 to 200 years ago? What is the one thing that you would miss most if you were to go back

in time to the 1800s? For your class, prepare a brief speech that answers these questions. Think about what you will say. Make a few notes to help you remember what to say. Practice by giving your speech to a partner. Listen to your partner's speech and give each other suggestions. Then you are ready to give your speech to the class.

Beyond Words
Review the selections included in Unit 1. Think about how you might illustrate one poem or story. Draw a picture or poster that illustrates some selection in this unit.

> **Writing on Your Own** Write an essay describing your favorite selection from Unit 1. Explain why you liked the selection, how it made you feel, and what you learned by reading it. Include an introductory sentence, a body, and a conclusion.

> **Test-Taking Tip** Avoid waiting until the night before a test to study. Plan your time so that you can get a good night's sleep the night before a test.

During the test:
- Come to the test with a positive attitude.
- Preview the test and read the directions carefully.
- Plan your time.
- Answer the essay questions and the questions that you know first.
- Go back and answer the more difficult questions.
- Allow time to reread all of the questions and your answers.
- Put your name on the paper.

"You know that fiction...is possibly the roughest trade of all in writing....You have the sheet of blank paper, the pencil, and the obligation to invent truer than things can be true."

—Ernest Hemingway

"It is not a bad thing in a tale that you understand only half of it."

—Isak Dinesen

UNIT 1 *Fiction*

How long have people told stories? Probably as long as they have been able to talk. People made up stories to explain things like why the sky is blue or ducks have webbed feet. They created stories to entertain themselves. Some stories are scary. Some are funny. Some are short. Others are very long. No matter where in the world you go, people tell stories and have always told stories. In this unit, you will enjoy stories from the nine different countries shown on the map on the next page.

Writing about events that did not really happen is called fiction. Some fiction is realistic and may seem like it is from a newspaper. Other fictional stories describe far-off planets, alien life forms, or the future.

All works of fiction share three elements: character, setting, and plot. Characters perform the action. They are usually people, but they can be animals or even objects. Some examples of nonhuman characters are the magic mirror in *Snow White* and the rabbits Hazel and Fiver in *Watership Down*. Plot is the action in a story. As characters act and react, they move the plot along. Plot changes the characters and reveals their true nature and hidden feelings. The plot of *A Christmas Carol*, for instance, is about Ebenezer Scrooge. He changes from being cheap and lonely to generous and friendly. Setting is a country or the special place or time in which a story happens. For example, the setting of *Star Wars* is "a long time ago in a galaxy far, far away."

Fiction can be grouped by the length of the work. Short stories are short enough to read in one sitting. They usually center on one character or situation. Novels are longer works. They can explore more than one character or situation over a longer period of time.

Fiction can also be grouped by where the stories take place or where the authors come from. Gabriela Mistral, Pablo Neruda, and Gabriel García Márquez are from different countries. But all may be discussed as Latin American writers.

The fiction in Unit 1 is arranged by genre, or type of story. The authors use setting, character, and plot to create many kinds of stories. Libraries often place the stories they have in special sections so you can find them easily. Look for sections of detective stories, science fiction, or other genres. You may also find the complete work from which a selection in this unit was taken.

The following countries are represented in this unit: Great Britain, the United States, Germany, Russia, Colombia, Zimbabwe, Nigeria, and Korea.

Detective Stories

- "A really good detective never gets married." —Raymond Chandler
- "What the detective story is about is not murder but the restoration of order." —P. D. James

Detective stories are sometimes called mysteries or "whodunits." They present a crime and a protagonist, or main character. The protagonist is usually a detective. He or she watches and questions the other characters. The detective finds clues and reveals the criminal.

Detectives originally observed and commented without being part of the plot. Today, they are right in the middle of the action. V. I. Warshawski, with her hard Chicago attitude, or the English busybody Miss Marple are detectives with strong personalities. Over a cup of tea or a glass of something stronger they reveal the "bad guy."

Detectives dodge bullets and plunge into fights. Sometimes they take the place of the law. They may protect the innocent or punish the guilty. All this action often attracts any handsome or beautiful person involved in the crime. Modern detectives do not always stay away from such temptations. Characters like Easy Rawlins of Los Angeles are much like their antagonists, or opponents. Only their sense of decency and justice separates them from the criminals. Much of the fun in reading a detective story is in spotting the criminal before the detective explains everything.

The Adventure of the Speckled Band
Arthur Conan Doyle

Arthur Conan Doyle
(1859–1930)
British

Literary Terms

character a person, animal, or object who performs the action in a fictional work

first-person using "I" to tell a story; told from the narrator's point of view

narrator the person telling the story

About the Author

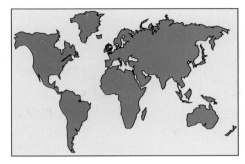

Sir Arthur Conan Doyle was trained as a doctor. He quit medicine to write. The first Sherlock Holmes story was "A Study in Scarlet," which came out in 1887. From 1891 on, Doyle wrote many more Holmes stories. To many, the **characters** of Holmes and his friend Dr. John Watson seemed real. Characters are people or objects in a story who do the action. The Sherlock Holmes stories have been made into films and television shows. You can even find fan clubs such as the "Baker Street Irregulars," named for Holmes's London address, 221-B Baker Street. "The Hounds of the Internet" are on the World Wide Web. Doyle wrote other books, too. In fact, he grew very tired of Holmes. He killed off the detective in an 1893 story. People were so upset that Doyle had to bring him back to life. A final book of Holmes stories came out in 1927. Doyle was made a knight in 1902 for his work during the Boer War.

About the Selection

Sherlock Holmes is one of the greatest fictional detectives. He lived and worked in the city of London in the late 1800s. When many people think of detectives, they think of Holmes. He is usually shown with deerstalker cap, a pipe, and a magnifying glass. The admiring Dr. Watson is the **narrator** for almost all the adventures. He writes in the **first-person**. This means Watson writes as "I," as though he is watching the action. In the following selection, Holmes looks into a mysterious death. Notice his attention to details.

The Adventure of the Speckled Band

Arthur Conan Doyle

As you read, watch for clues that lead to a solution.

This story takes place in April 1883.

To *knock up* is British slang for *to wake by knocking at the door.*

Mrs. Hudson is the landlady and housekeeper for Holmes and Watson.

It was early in April in the year '83 that I woke one morning to find Sherlock Holmes standing, fully dressed, by the side of my bed. He was a late riser, as a rule, and as the clock on the mantelpiece showed me that it was only a quarter-past seven, I blinked up at him in some surprise, and perhaps just a little resentment, for I was myself regular in my habits.

"Very sorry to knock you up, Watson," he said, "but it's the common lot this morning. Mrs. Hudson has been knocked up, she retorted upon me, and I on you."

"What is it, then—a fire?"

"No; a **client**. It seems that a young lady has arrived in a considerable state of excitement, who insists upon seeing me. She is waiting now in the sitting-room. Now, when young ladies wander about the **metropolis** at this hour of the morning, and knock sleepy people up out of their beds, I presume that it is something very pressing which they have to communicate. Should it prove to be an interesting case, you would, I am sure, wish to follow it from the **outset**. I thought, at any rate, that I should call you and give you the chance."

"My dear fellow, I would not miss it for anything."

I had no keener pleasure than in following Holmes in his professional **investigations**, and in admiring the rapid **deductions**, as swift as **intuitions**, and yet always founded on a **logical** basis, with which he unravelled the problems which were submitted to him. I rapidly threw on my clothes and was ready in a few minutes to accompany my friend down to the sitting-room. A lady dressed in black and heavily veiled, who had been sitting in the window, rose as we entered.

---

client a customer; a person for whom one does a professional service

deduction an answer found by reasoning

intuition a way of knowing without proof

investigation a study to get facts

logical reasonable

metropolis a city

outset the beginning

"Good-morning, madam," said Holmes cheerily. "My name is Sherlock Holmes. This is my intimate friend and associate, Dr. Watson, before whom you can speak as freely as before myself. Ha! I am glad to see that Mrs. Hudson has had the good sense to light the fire. Pray draw up to it, and I shall order you a cup of hot coffee, for I observe that you are shivering."

"It is not cold which makes me shiver," said the woman in a low voice, changing her seat as requested.

"What, then?"

"It is fear, Mr. Holmes. It is terror." She raised her veil as she spoke, and we could see that she was indeed in a **pitiable** state of **agitation**, her face all drawn and gray, with restless, frightened eyes, like those of some hunted animal. Her features and figure were those of a woman of thirty, but her hair was shot with **premature** gray, and her expression was weary and **haggard**. Sherlock Holmes ran her over with one of his quick, all-**comprehensive** glances.

"You must not fear," said he soothingly, bending forward and patting her forearm. "We shall soon set matters right, I have no doubt. You have come in by train this morning, I see."

"You know me, then?"

"No, but I observe the second half of a return ticket in the palm of your left glove. You must have started early, and yet you had a good drive in a **dog-cart**, along heavy roads, before you reached the station."

A *dog-cart* is a small, horse-drawn wagon.

The lady gave a violent start and stared in bewilderment at my companion.

"There is no mystery, my dear madam," said he, smiling. "The left arm of your jacket is **spattered** with mud in no less than seven places. The marks are perfectly fresh. There is no vehicle save a dog-cart which throws up mud in that way, and then only when you sit on the left-hand side of the driver."

This is an example of Holmes's amazing deductions.

"Whatever your reasons may be, you are perfectly correct," said she. "I started from home before six, reached Leatherhead at twenty past, and came in by the first train to Waterloo. Sir, I can stand this strain no longer; I shall go mad if it continues. I have no one to turn to—none, save only one, who cares for me, and he, poor fellow, can be of little aid. I have heard of you, Mr. Holmes; I have heard of you from Mrs. Farintosh, whom you helped in the hour of her sore

Leatherhead is a town south of London. *Waterloo* is a train station in London.

agitation strong emotion; disturbance	**dog-cart** a cart pulled by one horse with room for two passengers	**pitiable** causing a feeling of pity
comprehensive knowing	**haggard** looking worn because of worry	**premature** earlier than expected
		spatter to splash

need. It was from her that I had your address. Oh, sir, do you not think that you could help me, too, and at least throw a little light through the dense darkness which surrounds me? At present it is out of my power to reward you for your services, but in a month or six weeks I shall be married, with the control of my own income, and then at least you shall not find me ungrateful."

Holmes turned to his desk and, unlocking it, drew out a small case-book, which he consulted.

"Farintosh," said he. "Ah yes, I recall the case; it was concerned with an opal **tiara**. I think it was before your time, Watson. I can only say, madam, that I shall be happy to devote the same care to your case as I did to that of your friend. As to reward, my profession is its own reward; but you are at liberty to **defray** whatever expenses I may be put to, at the time which suits you best. And now I beg that you will lay before us everything that may help us in forming an opinion upon the matter."

"Alas!" replied our visitor, "the very horror of my situation lies in the fact that my fears are so vague, and my suspicions depend so entirely upon small points, which might seem **trivial** to another, that even he to whom of all others I have a right to look for help and advice looks upon all that I tell him about it as the fancies of a nervous woman. He does not say so, but I can read it from his soothing answers and **averted** eyes. But I have heard, Mr. Holmes, that you can see deeply into the **manifold** wickedness of the human heart. You may advise me how to walk amid the dangers which encompass me."

"I am all attention, madam."

"My name is Helen Stoner, and I am living with my stepfather, who is the last survivor of one of the oldest Saxon families in England, the Roylotts of Stoke Moran, on the western border of Surrey."

Holmes nodded his head. "The name is familiar to me," said he.

"The family was at one time among the richest in England, and the estates extended over the borders into Berkshire in the north, and Hampshire in the west. In the last century, however, four **successive** heirs were of a **dissolute** and wasteful disposition, and the family ruin was eventually completed by a gambler in the days of the Regency. Nothing was left save a few acres of ground, and the two-hundred-year-old house, which is itself crushed under a

Miss Stoner is speaking of her fiancé here.

About 1,500 years ago, Germanic people from Europe conquered and settled parts of England. They were *Angles* and *Saxons*.

In English history, the *Regency* lasted 1811–1820. In this period, King George III had a mental illness. His son ruled as *regent* in his place.

averted looking away	**manifold** of many kinds	**tiara** a small crown
defray to pay the costs		**trivial** not important
dissolute wicked; of bad character	**successive** following	

heavy mortgage. The last squire dragged out his existence there, living the horrible life of an **aristocratic** pauper; but his only son, my stepfather, seeing that he must adapt himself to the new conditions, obtained an advance from a relative, which enabled him to take a medical degree and went out to Calcutta, where, by his professional skill and his force of character, he established a large practice. In a fit of anger, however, caused by some robberies which had been **perpetrated** in the house, he beat his native butler to death and narrowly escaped a capital sentence. As it was, he suffered a long term of imprisonment and afterwards returned to England a **morose** and disappointed man.

Calcutta is a large city in India. India was a colony of Britain when this story was written.

"When Dr. Roylott was in India he married my mother, Mrs. Stoner, the young widow of Major-General Stoner, of the Bengal **Artillery**. My sister Julia and I were twins, and we were only two years old at the time of my mother's re-marriage. She had a considerable sum of money—not less than £1000 a year—and this she **bequeathed** to Dr. Roylott entirely while we resided with him, with a provision that a certain annual sum should be allowed to each of us in the event of our marriage. Shortly after our return to England my mother died—she was killed eight years ago in a railway accident near Crewe. Dr. Roylott then abandoned his attempts to establish himself in practice in London and took us to live with him in the old ancestral house at Stoke Moran. The money which my mother had left was enough for all our wants, and there seemed to be no obstacle to our happiness.

The unit of money in Great Britain is the pound. Its symbol is £.

"But a terrible change came over our stepfather about this time. Instead of making friends and exchanging visits with our neighbours, who had at first been overjoyed to see a Roylott of Stoke Moran back in the old family seat, he shut himself up in his house and seldom came out save to indulge in ferocious quarrels with whoever might cross his path. Violence of temper approaching to **mania** has been hereditary in the men of the family, and in my stepfather's case it had, I believe, been **intensified** by his long residence in the tropics. A series of disgraceful brawls took place, two of which ended in the police-court, until at last he became the terror of the village, and the folks would fly at his approach, for he is a man of immense strength, and absolutely uncontrollable in his anger.

Neighbour is a British spelling of the American word *neighbor.* Do you see other British spellings in this story?

aristocratic of high social class	**bequeath** to give to, as in a will	**mania** an intense, almost insane, excitement
artillery branch of the military armed with large guns	**intensify** to become stronger	**morose** gloomy
		perpetrate to carry out

Why would the villagers be afraid of a *cheetah* and a *baboon*?

Why do you think the hair of the two women turned white so early?

"Last week he hurled the local blacksmith over a **parapet** into a stream, and it was only by paying over all the money which I could gather together that I was able to avert another public exposure. He had no friends at all save the wandering gypsies, and he would give these vagabonds leave to encamp upon the few acres of bramble-covered land which represent the family estate, and would accept in return the **hospitality** of their tents, wandering away with them sometimes for weeks on end. He has a passion also for Indian animals, which are sent over to him by a correspondent, and he has at this moment a **cheetah** and a **baboon**, which wander freely over his grounds and are feared by the villagers almost as much as their master.

"You can imagine from what I say that my poor sister Julia and I had no great pleasure in our lives. No servant would stay with us, and for a long time we did all the work of the house. She was but thirty at the time of her death, and yet her hair had already begun to whiten, even as mine has."

"Your sister is dead, then?"

"She died just two years ago, and it is of her death that I wish to speak to you. You can understand that, living the life which I have described, we were little likely to see anyone of our own age and position. We had, however, an aunt, my mother's maiden sister, Miss Honoria Westphail, who lives near Harrow, and we were occasionally allowed to pay short visits at this lady's house. Julia went there at Christmas two years ago, and met there a half-pay major of marines, to whom she became engaged. My stepfather learned of the engagement when my sister returned and offered no objection to the marriage; but within a **fortnight** of the day which had been fixed for the wedding, the terrible event occurred which has deprived me of my only companion."

Sherlock Holmes had been leaning back in his chair with his eyes closed and his head sunk in a cushion, but he half opened his lids now and glanced across at his visitor.

"Pray be precise as to details," said he.

"It is easy for me to be so, for every event of that dreadful time is **seared** into my memory. The **manor**-house is, as I have already said, very old, and only one wing is now inhabited. The bedrooms in this wing are on the ground floor, the sitting-rooms being in the

baboon a large monkey	**fortnight** a period of two weeks	**manor** the main house on an estate
cheetah a wild spotted cat	**hospitality** the friendly treatment of guests	**parapet** a railing along the edge of a roof or wall
		sear to burn

central block of the buildings. Of these bedrooms the first is Dr. Roylott's, the second my sister's, and the third my own. There is no communication between them, but they all open out into the same corridor. Do I make myself plain?"

"Perfectly so."

"The windows of the three rooms open out upon the lawn. That fatal night Dr. Roylott had gone to his room early, though we knew that he had not retired to rest, for my sister was troubled by the smell of the strong Indian cigars which it was his custom to smoke. She left her room, therefore, and came into mine, where she sat for some time, chatting about her approaching wedding. At eleven o'clock she rose to leave me, but she paused at the door and looked back.

"'Tell me, Helen,' said she, 'have you ever heard anyone whistle in the dead of the night?'

"'Never,' said I.

"'I suppose that you could not possibly whistle, yourself, in your sleep?'

"'Certainly not. But why?'

"'Because during the last few nights I have always, about three in the morning, heard a low, clear whistle. I am a light sleeper, and it has awakened me. I cannot tell where it came from—perhaps from the next room, perhaps from the lawn. I thought that I would just ask you whether you had heard it.'

"'No, I have not. It must be those **wretched** gypsies in the plantation.'

"'Very likely. And yet if it were on the lawn, I wonder that you did not hear it also.'

"'Ah, but I sleep more heavily than you.'

"'Well, it is of no great **consequence**, at any rate.' She smiled back at me, closed my door, and a few moments later I heard her key turn in the lock."

"Indeed," said Holmes. "Was it your custom always to lock yourselves in at night?"

"Always."

"And why?"

"I think that I mentioned to you that the doctor kept a cheetah and a baboon. We had no feeling of **security** unless our doors were locked."

consequence importance	**security** safety	**wretched** worthless; seen with scorn

"Quite so. Pray proceed with your statement."

"I could not sleep that night. A vague feeling of **impending** misfortune impressed me. My sister and I, you will recollect, were twins, and you know how subtle are the links which bind two souls which are so closely allied. It was a wild night. The wind was howling outside, and the rain was beating and splashing against the windows. Suddenly, amid all the **hubbub** of the gale, there burst forth the wild scream of a terrified woman. I knew that it was my sister's voice. I sprang from my bed, wrapped a shawl round me, and rushed into the corridor. As I opened my door I seemed to hear a low whistle, such as my sister described, and a few moments later a **clanging** sound, as if a mass of metal had fallen. As I ran down the passage, my sister's door was unlocked, and revolved slowly upon its hinges. I stared at it horror-**stricken**, not knowing what was about to issue from it. By the light of the corridor-lamp I saw my sister appear at the opening, her face **blanched** with terror, her hands groping for help, her whole figure swaying to and fro like that of a drunkard. I ran to her and threw my arms around her, but at that moment her knees seemed to give way and she fell to the ground. She **writhed** as one who is in terrible pain, and her limbs were dreadfully **convulsed**. At first I thought that she had not recognized me, but as I bent over her she suddenly shrieked out in a voice which I shall never forget, 'Oh, my God! Helen! It was the band! The speckled band!' There was something else which she would fain have said, and she stabbed with her finger into the air in the direction of the doctor's room, but a fresh convulsion seized her and choked her words. I rushed out, calling loudly for my stepfather, and I met him hastening from his room in his dressing-gown. When he reached my sister's side she was unconscious, and though he poured brandy down her throat and sent for medical aid from the village, all efforts were in vain, for she slowly sank and died without having recovered her consciousness. Such was the dreadful end of my beloved sister."...

[Holmes takes the case. Holmes and Watson travel to the house and examine Miss Stoner's rooms. At night, they are waiting in the dark in the room where her sister died. Holmes has not told Watson why. Suddenly they see a small light and hear a very gentle sound. Holmes jumps up and yells.]

"You see it, Watson?" he yelled. "You see it?"

What do you think happened to Julia?

blanch to turn pale	**hubbub** confusion	**stricken** struck; strongly affected
clanging ringing	**impending** about to happen	**writhe** to twist as in pain
convulsed shaken or pulled jerkily		

But I saw nothing. At the moment when Holmes struck the light I heard a low, clear whistle, but the sudden glare flashing into my weary eyes made it impossible for me to tell what it was at which my friend lashed so savagely. I could, however, see that his face was deadly pale and filled with horror and **loathing**.

He had ceased to strike and was gazing up at the **ventilator** when suddenly there broke from the silence of the night the most horrible cry to which I have ever listened. It swelled up louder and louder, a hoarse yell of pain and fear and anger all mingled in the one dreadful shriek. They say that away down in the village, and even in the distant **parsonage**, that cry raised the sleepers from their beds. It struck cold to our hearts, and I stood gazing at Holmes, and he at me, until the last echoes of it had died away into the silence from which it rose.

"What can it mean?" I gasped.

"It means that it is all over," Holmes answered. "And perhaps, after all, it is for the best. Take your pistol, and we will enter Dr. Roylott's room."...

On the wooden chair, sat Dr. Grimesby Roylott, clad in a long gray dressing-gown, his bare ankles **protruding** beneath, and his feet thrust into red heelless Turkish slippers. Across his lap lay the short stock with the long lash which we had noticed during the day. His chin was cocked upward and his eyes were fixed in a dreadful, rigid stare at the corner of the ceiling. Round his brow he had a peculiar yellow band, with brownish speckles, which seemed to be bound tightly round his head. As we entered he made neither sound nor motion.

"The band! the speckled band!" whispered Holmes.

I took a step forward. In an instant his strange headgear began to move, and there reared itself from among his hair the squat diamond-shaped head and puffed neck of a **loathsome** serpent.

"It is a swamp *adder*!" cried Holmes; "the deadliest snake in India. He has died within ten seconds of being bitten."

[Later Holmes explained,] "It became clear to me that whatever danger threatened an **occupant** of the room could not come either from the window or the door. My attention was **speedily** drawn, as I have already remarked to you, to this ventilator, and to the bell-rope which hung down to the bed. The discovery that this was a dummy,

Adders are highly poisonous snakes in the viper family.

loathing intense dislike	**parsonage** a house where a church minister lives	**speedily** quickly
loathsome disgusting		**ventilator** a passage in a house that air is blown through
occupant a person who lives or stays in a certain place	**protruding** sticking out	

and that the bed was clamped to the floor, instantly gave rise to the suspicion that the rope was there as a bridge for something passing through the hole and coming to the bed. The idea of a snake instantly occurred to me, and when I coupled it with my knowledge that the doctor was furnished with a supply of creatures from India, I felt that I was probably on the right track. The idea of using a form of poison which could not possibly be discovered by any chemical test was just such a one as would occur to a clever and **ruthless** man who had had an Eastern training. The **rapidity** with which such a poison would take effect would also, from his point of view, be an advantage. It would be a sharp-eyed **coroner**, indeed, who could distinguish the two little dark **punctures** which would show where the poison fangs had done their work. Then I thought of the whistle. Of course he must **recall** the snake before the morning light **revealed** it to the victim. He had trained it, probably by the use of the milk which we saw, to return to him when summoned. He would put it through this ventilator at the hour that he thought best, with the certainty that it would crawl down the rope and land on the bed. It might or might not bite the occupant, perhaps she might escape every night for a week, but sooner or later she must fall a victim.

"I had come to these conclusions before ever I had entered his room. An inspection of his chair showed me that he had been in the habit of standing on it, which of course would be necessary in order that he should reach the ventilator. The sight of the safe, the saucer of milk, and the loop of whipcord were enough to finally **dispel** any doubts which may have remained. The metallic clang heard by Miss Stoner was obviously caused by her stepfather hastily closing the door of his safe upon its terrible occupant. Having once made up my mind, you know the steps which I took in order to put the matter to the proof. I heard the creature hiss as I have no doubt that you did also, and I instantly lit the light and attacked it."

"With the result of driving it through the ventilator."

"And also with the result of causing it to turn upon its master at the other side. Some of the blows of my cane came home and roused its snakish temper, so that it flew upon the first person it saw. In this way I am no doubt indirectly responsible for Dr. Grimesby Roylott's death, and I cannot say that it is likely to weigh very heavily upon my conscience."

coroner the official who decides the cause of death	puncture a small hole caused by a sharp object	recall to call back; remember
dispel to make disappear	rapidity speed	reveal to show
		ruthless cruel

Directions Write the answers to these questions using complete sentences.

Comprehension: Identifying Facts

1. How did Helen Stoner travel to London?

2. Who does Helen Stoner live with when she comes to see Sherlock Holmes?

3. How long has her sister been dead when Helen Stoner comes to see Holmes?

4. What change had happened in Julia's life a few weeks before she died?

5. What sound did Julia tell her sister she heard in the night?

6. What words did Julia say just before she died?

7. What wild animals roam the estate?

8. What is the speckled band?

9. How did the speckled band get into Julia's room?

10. Who is the speckled band's final victim?

Comprehension: Understanding Main Ideas

11. What facts about Helen Stoner does Holmes learn just by observing her?

12. How do you know that the story takes place in the 1800s?

13. Why does Helen Stoner look tired and older than her age?

14. Why does Helen think she can trust only Holmes?

15. What happened to Dr. Roylott before his return to England?

16. Where did the family's money come from?

17. What causes Dr. Roylott's terrible temper?

18. Why didn't the Stoner sisters ever have company?

19. Why was Julia Stoner killed?

20. How does Holmes feel about Dr. Roylott's death?

Review Continued on Next Page

Understanding Literature: First-Person

A story told in first-person uses pronouns such as *I, me, my,* and *we.* It is told from the point of view of the narrator—the person telling the story. In the Sherlock Holmes stories, the narrator is his friend Watson. We know only what Watson knows. We do not know what Sherlock Holmes is thinking. We can be as puzzled as Watson is during the case.

21. Watson tells us a little bit about himself. Describe one thing about Watson.

22. How does Holmes explain to the woman why Watson is in the room?

23. Would the story work as well if Holmes were the narrator? Explain.

24. Imagine the story told in the third-person. A third-person narrator knows the thoughts and acts of all the characters. What role would Watson have? Explain.

25. Think of other stories you have read. Do you prefer first-person stories or third-person stories? Explain.

Critical Thinking

26. What do you think life was like for Helen Stoner after Dr. Roylott's death?

27. Do you think you could be a detective like Sherlock Holmes? Why or why not?

28. Is "The Adventure of the Speckled Band" a good title for this story? Why or why not?

29. What was the scariest part of the story for you?

30. Did you like this story? Why or why not?

Writing on Your Own Imagine you are writing the text for a paperback book cover to attract readers. Write two paragraphs about the mysterious murder of Julia Stoker without giving the story away.

Death Arrives on Schedule
Hansjörg Martin (translated by Charles E. Pederson)

Hansjörg Martin
(1920–)
German

Literary Terms

detective story a story in which the main character usually solves a crime

novel a literary work of fiction having more plot and character details than a short story

theme the main idea of a literary work

About the Author

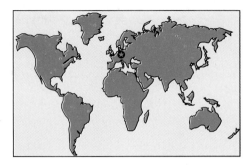

Hansjörg Martin was born in 1920 in Leipzig, Germany. He served in the German army during World War II. After the war he held many jobs. He was an artist, clown, decorator, stage set builder, editor, and teacher. In 1962, he became a full-time writer. He moved with his family to a province in northern Germany, where he still lives.

Martin has been called the "founder of the modern German **detective story.**" A detective story is one in which the main character usually solves a crime. Martin's work has several **themes,** or main ideas. One is that crime is not entirely a person's own fault. It is also a result of social pressure. Martin's mysteries may not always have a careful plot or well-developed characters. But he always presents a problem in an entertaining way. He has written more than seventy **novels** and books of short stories. A novel is fiction with more plot and character details than a short story has. His books have been translated into at least fourteen languages, with millions of copies sold. His writing has also won many awards.

About the Selection

One of Martin's idols is Raymond Chandler, a well-known American mystery writer. Martin especially loves Chandler's use of natural language. The following selection uses similarly short sentences and everyday language. Martin's theme of social pressure appears, as well. But the story does not have the usual dead body, with no clues about "whodunnit." Instead, it follows the criminal as he plans and commits his crime. But the luck of this bad guy is about to run out. "Death Arrives on Schedule" was first published in 1974.

Death Arrives on Schedule

Hansjörg Martin

As you read, think about why the characters act as they do.

At a time in his life when he possessed almost everything a man could want, Alfred Algernissen's eyes fell on Loni Leisegang. And his heart beat as it never had before. His wealth, his luxury limousine, his **exclusive bungalow** home, everything became unimportant—everything but Loni Leisegang, whose looks (and this must be said both to explain and to defend Alfred Algernissen's behavior) had already caused many other men to lose their heads in the same way. Besides, it's understandable why men might lose their heads over Loni. After all, chestnut-red hair and green eyes like Loni's are the best guarantee of **masculine** head loss. And when such hair and eyes crown a **regally** curvy shape, men might even become **aggressive**. Alfred Algernissen became aggressive.

It was not Loni Leisegang's fault (or **merit**, if you prefer) that she met Alfred Algernissen at a party. It's not her fault that she led him to understand that she certainly was not against aggressiveness, or at least not against

---

aggressive ready to do combat

bungalow a low, one-story house

exclusive not letting others participate

masculine relating to men

merit a positive quality

regally in a royal way

---

certain *kinds* of aggressiveness—and especially not against rich **aggressors** such as Alfred Algernissen obviously was. In any case, it cannot be proven whether Loni's **inclination** toward violence included at this point the idea of her becoming a widow.

Financial broker Helfried Leisegang, Loni's husband, was far too healthy for thoughts of widowhood, anyway.

Do you think Loni wants her husband to be killed?

aggressor an aggressive person	**financial broker** one who helps others invest money	**inclination** a way of thinking

Herr Leisegang's only real **passion** was whiskey. Because of this passion, he had lost his driver's license several months before. That his passion had put him on the quickest path to losing his wife, too, had not yet become clear to him. And that shortly, he would lose his life— well, he could hardly **foresee** that.

Fourteen days after that first party, however, the fate of the whiskey lover Herr Leisegang was sealed. In those two weeks Alfred Algernissen had found three opportunities to test whether he and Loni were suited to each other. They found themselves so well suited, in fact, that Algernissen decided to win his lover completely. It was certain that Leisegang would never freely release his Loni. So Algernissen began to forge a plan that would help him sweep away, risk free, the only **barrier** to Loni's release: Helfried Leisegang himself. And because Algernissen was a self-confident and clear-thinking man, and because he had no taste for a years-long visit to jail, the plan grew slowly, was altered, rethought, and improved. Finally, it was so good that it led to an almost-perfect **murder**. And this is what happened:

Do you think Algernissen will get away with his plan?

Alfred Algernissen knew that Leisegang's company (Leisegang & Co., Building Contractors) provided Helfried Leisegang enough profits that he wanted to **invest** in property. So one beautiful evening, Algernissen called up the **hale** and healthy husband and said he had

barrier something that blocks

foresee to know in advance

hale healthy

invest to use money for later profit

murder a killing of another

passion an object of deep interest

available 12,000 square meters of land to sell. Prime land for **development**. **Favorable** location in the country. Cheap. Inside tip.

Leisegang was extremely interested.

Algernissen gave him a few other tempting **tidbits**. The very healthy candidate for death promptly took the bait.

They agreed to take a look at the property the day after tomorrow. Algernissen told Leisegang that it lay near Nienburg, about a hundred kilometers, or an hour's drive, outside the city. Naturally, Leisegang swore himself to **absolute secrecy**—if only in his own interest. Algernissen offered to pick him up by car—yes, early in the morning, how did seven-thirty sound? That's okay with you? Great, thank you!

The evening before the meeting, Algernissen called again: "Sorry, Leisegang, slight problem. This afternoon I went out to the property and . . ."

"What has happened?" Leisegang interrupted, shocked. "Has the property been sold?"

"No, no, of course not. It's just that—well, my car went on strike! Something with the **ignition**. I don't know anything about cars. I just dropped it off at the repair shop. They said they'll drive it over to the Nienburg train station by tomorrow morning. I have a second key. We'll have to—if you're still interested, as I assume you

> *12,000 square meters* is about three acres.

> Why is Leisegang called a *very healthy candidate for death?*

> *100 kilometers* is about 60 miles.

> Do you think Algernissen's car is really *at the repair shop?*

---

absolute complete

development an area prepared for commercial use

favorable promoting success

ignition a car's starter

secrecy the condition of being hidden

tidbit a small bit of knowledge

Hamburg is a large seaport in northern Germany.

are?—we'll have to take the train over, and then drive back to Hamburg in my car. Sorry about the **inconvenience** . . ."

"Don't worry about it," said Leisegang, "it's no trouble at all. Maybe taking a **rental** car to pick up your car would be best . . .?"

"I can't drive two cars at once," Algernissen patiently explained. "And you have no driver's license, if I remember correctly."

"That's right," Leisegang said with a curse. "Then we'll take the train. Have you already looked into connections, or should I?"

Algernissen had already done so. In fact, he had found a fine connection. He had sat for almost two hours studying the timetables until he had found exactly the right train—or rather, the right trains. He told Leisegang that a train left the central Hamburg train **terminal**, track 11, at 8:24 the next morning, arriving in Nienburg at 9:58. They could meet on the track 11 platform.

Leisegang had three more whiskeys—the last ones in this life—and went to sleep next to Loni about eleven. He fell asleep right away while she read. It can be assumed that she knew nothing, though perhaps she had a feeling something was going to happen.

Do you think Loni really *knew nothing?*

inconvenience trouble or annoyance	**rental** available to be rented	**terminal** station

Algernissen, meanwhile, had packed a small suitcase and laid out and rechecked his train tickets and schedule. He loaded his small pistol, set the safety, and pocketed it in his loose, double-sided jacket. He had bought the gun a week earlier from a dealer in Frankfurt. In the morning, shortly before eight, Algernissen boarded the express train for Munich, which **originated** in Hamburg, and which—as he had found out by asking careful questions—was always ready a half hour before departure.

Frankfurt is a large city in central Germany. *Munich* is far to the south.

He walked down the corridor of the still-empty train, said a few friendly words to the conductor, and finally found a second-class **compartment** in which an **elderly** couple sat. They were full of travel fever.

Algernissen lifted his suitcase into the luggage rack above the vacant third seat and chatted with the elderly couple. He made fun of himself for always being too early, always too excited at the prospect of traveling, and now they had a half hour before departure—but better thirty minutes too early than thirty minutes too late, right? Ha ha!

Algernissen is "proving" he will be on the train.

He asked the elderly pair to watch his suitcase, saying he was just going to slip out for a quick smoke and a magazine, then head over to the dining car for a bit of breakfast. "At the latest, I'm sure I'll be back by the time we reach Hannover, full and contented," he said after hearing that they were going only as far as Würzburg.

On its way to Munich, the train will stop in *Hannover.* Nienburg is about twenty miles away. *Würzburg* is farther south.

compartment an enclosed space	**elderly** old	**originate** to start

At 8:13, twenty minutes before the express was to depart, he stepped off the train. He crossed to track 11, putting on sunglasses as he went—although even outside there was no sun to speak of, and certainly none inside the train terminal. He greeted Leisegang, who was already nervously waiting for him. They climbed aboard this train, which was bound for Nienburg. That train left the terminal three minutes later, with him and Leisegang on board. Crossing from the express train to the Nienburg train, Algernissen had turned his jacket inside out—now the light-colored side faced in and the dark side faced out. And he was still wearing the same dark jacket and sunglasses as he got off the train again with Leisegang at the end of the line.

Why does Algernissen turn *his jacket inside out* and put on sunglasses?

Five minutes later they sat in a car.

Ten minutes later they were leaving the village of Nienburg.

Algernissen rented this car. His own car is parked in Hamburg, as you will see.

Fourteen minutes later Algernissen turned the car off the highway into a small woods, drove a couple hundred meters along a small forest path among the beech trees, birches, and firs, and stopped the car.

"Here?" Leisegang sounded **irritated**. "But this is certainly not 'prime land for development,' Herr Algernissen, is it?"

"Of course it is," said Algernissen. "Get out. I'll show you."

irritated annoyed

Leisegang hesitated—maybe it was an instinct that warned him of danger, or maybe he felt a sudden distrust of Algernissen. But finally he got out.

Algernissen had also left the car. He now approached Leisegang and smoothly drew his pistol, shooting Leisegang twice. He was surprised that it was not louder. He had feared it would be much worse. In the basement of his lovely home, where he had practiced for so many hours, it had seemed almost to roar.

Leisegang had no time for any other doubts. He died immediately.

Algernissen pulled him beneath a bushy blue spruce tree, hurriedly brushing over the tracks they had made as he dragged the body. He got back in the car and quickly drove back to the highway, which was empty— and from the highway to the freeway, where he got from the car everything its motor was capable of. He reached the Hannover train station at the same time a voice on the loudspeaker announced, "Attention on track 3. The express train for Munich will arrive in several minutes. Stand back on the platform, please."

Algernissen grinned. He stood behind a pillar on the platform until the train had arrived. Then he stepped up into the dining car, took off the jacket—which he had reversed again so that the light side was facing out—and sat down at an empty table.

He took a deep breath, ordered an egg, coffee, and cold cuts with double butter on the bread—and with a start

Algernissen wants to reach Hannover before the Hamburg-to-Munich train arrives.

He must have returned the rental car.

saw a fir needle stuck to the leg of his pants. He discovered it as he bent to **retrieve** his lighter, which had fallen from his pocket. He quickly picked the needle from his pants.

The *fir needle* comes from the spot where he killed Leisegang. Why might he be startled?

After a good, relatively hasty breakfast, he strolled back to the compartment where he had left his suitcase in the care of the elderly married couple.

The woman slept. The man gave a **curt** nod to his greeting and to his "Thanks very much for watching my things" and then went on reading the thick book he held in his hands.

Algernissen carefully hung up his double-sided jacket and settled himself comfortably in his corner. He would have liked to sleep too, but he couldn't. After ten minutes, he stood, went to the toilet, and then remained standing in the corridor to smoke a cigarette.

Why can't Algernissen sleep?

The married couple left the train in Würzburg with friendly good-byes. In Munich, Alfred Algernissen climbed from the train. There he experienced a severe shock: his pistol had disappeared. He could have sworn that after using it on Leisegang, he had stuck it back in his jacket pocket. But it was not there now.

He forced himself to calm down. It was probably in his car, which stood in the parking lot at the Hamburg train terminal. He would find it when he went back tomorrow.

---

curt short   **retrieve** to pick up

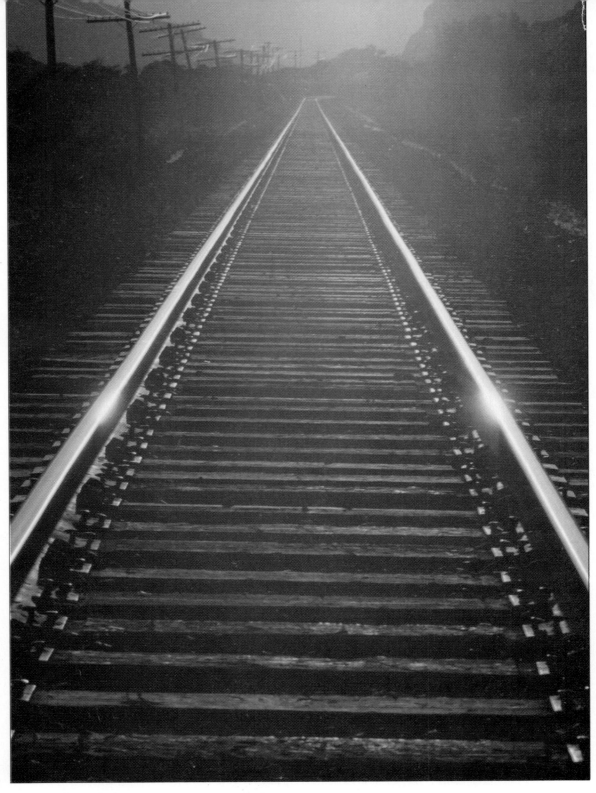

The next afternoon in Hamburg, as Algernissen unlocked his car, he was arrested.

The following police **deposition** had led to his arrest:

> I happened to follow the man, since I wanted a newspaper before our express for Munich left. I was surprised that he put on sunglasses and took off the light-colored jacket to put it on again with the dark side out. It also surprised me that he did not go to the newsstand, as he had said he was going to, but instead ran over to a different platform. There he greeted another man and to my astonishment climbed with him into another train, which left immediately. As our train pulled in to Hannover, the man was standing on the platform. He wore the jacket with the light side facing out again and no sunglasses, although the sun was brightly shining there. He got into the dining car and half an hour after that returned to our compartment. He acted as though he had been in the train the entire time. The man was not calm. When he left for the toilet, I searched his jacket. I found his car's **registration** papers, including its license number and, in the left-hand inside pocket a 7.65 caliber Smith and Wesson revolver. I was able to **ascertain** that it had been fired shortly before then. Along with that I found a train ticket for Nienburg.

ascertain to find out   **deposition** a statement   **registration** an official document

The deposition, dated at Würzburg on May 26, 19————, was given into the criminal records, signed by the elderly man from the train: Heinrich Hafermass, Criminal Inspector (retired).

Hafermass is the *elderly man*. Bad luck for Algernissen to meet a retired policeman.

Leisegang's body was found and shown to Alfred Algernissen. In light of the pistol, the train ticket, and the statement of the retired criminal inspector, Algernissen confessed to the killing. He was convicted and sentenced to life in prison.

Nothing could be proven against the attractive Loni L., and a short time later she married a film producer who promised to make her a movie star. Instead, he wasted her fortune before dying of a heart attack.

Did this ending surprise you?

Directions Write the answers to these questions using complete sentences.

Comprehension: Identifying Facts

1. Why is everything suddenly unimportant to Algernissen?

2. What is Herr Leisegang's passion?

3. Why does Herr Leisegang have no driver's license?

4. What kind of danger is Leisegang in?

5. There are two trains. Which cities are they bound for?

6. How does Algernissen change his looks when going to track 11?

7. Why does Leisegang hesitate to get out of the car?

8. In the dining car, what does Algernissen find that startles him?

9. What does the elderly man find in Algernissen's jacket pocket?

10. Describe Algernissen's plan to kill Leisegang.

Comprehension: Understanding Main Ideas

11. Describe Loni Leisegang.

12. There are two trains. How does Algernissen use them?

13. Why does Algernissen ask the elderly couple to watch his bags?

14. Where is Algernissen arrested?

15. Why does he confess when shown Leisegang's body?

16. What was Heinrich Hafermass's profession before retiring?

17. Does Hafermass follow Algernissen on purpose?

18. Name the three things that surprise Hafermass.

19. What prison sentence does Algernissen receive?

20. Whom does Loni Leisegang marry?

Review Continued on Next Page

Understanding Literature: Detective Story

Detective stories are also called mysteries. There is a good reason for that name. If the writer is clever enough, the reader will find it hard to solve the puzzle. The answer will be a mystery for most of the story. Detective stories also have good guys and bad guys. The good guys win in the end, but not before facing danger.

21. Who is the good guy in this story?

22. Who is the bad guy or bad guys?

23. Is the main character a good guy or bad guy?

24. What are the elderly man's reasons for having the police arrest Algernissen? Does he have good reason to suspect Algernissen of a crime?

25. Is the elderly man's police deposition believable? Why or why not?

Critical Thinking

26. How does the title of the story apply to the story's action?

27. What is Algernissen's real reason for swearing Leisegang to secrecy?

28. Why does Hafermass, the elderly man, decide to become involved?

29. Do you think Loni Leisegang knows her husband will be killed? Explain your answer.

30. Did you like the ending to this story? Why or why not?

Writing on Your Own Which detective story did you prefer, "The Adventure of the Speckled Band" or "Death Arrives on Schedule"? Write a sentence telling which story you liked better. Then, write at least three sentences about why you prefer that story.

Science Fiction

- "If science fiction is the mythology of modern technology, then its myth is tragic."
  —Ursula K. Le Guin

- "Space or science fiction has become a dialect for our time." —Doris Lessing

Science fiction deals with people, places, and events that didn't happen. Not only that, but they couldn't—at least in life as we know it. Science fiction is often divided into "sci-fi" and fantasy. Sci-fi may try to tell exactly what the world will be like. Fantasy includes tales in which objects can talk or characters save the day with powerful words. Each describes a world with certain rules. The characters in these stories help us understand our world more clearly. That is because good, evil, power, love, stupidity, and fear affect these imaginary beings and places. They affect us here and now in the same way.

Writers view their imaginary settings in many ways. Some science fiction is hopeful. Arthur C. Clarke (the *Space Odyssey* books) and Isaac Asimov believe that humanity will improve. The future will be a better place. Work will be less boring. There will be more excitement and challenge. Other writers, though, see a loss of personal freedom. George Orwell's *1984* shows such a grim world. C. J. Cherryh in her *Alien* series and Frank Herbert in *Dune* see the future as a mixture of challenge and danger. They raise thought-provoking and entertaining questions. These writers write about good and evil and excite our imaginations. As you sample science fiction, you may find authors who share your view of the future. Many libraries and bookstores have special science fiction sections. Look there to find more stories like these.

The Feeling of Power
Isaac Asimov

Isaac Asimov
(1920–1992)
American

Literary Terms

autobiography a story about a person's life written by that person

irony the use of words that seem to say one thing but mean the opposite

parody an exaggerated look at a situation

science fiction literature that deals with people, places, and events that could not happen in our reality

About the Author

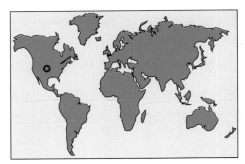

Born in Russia, Isaac Asimov came to America when he was a small child. As a teenager, he began to write **science fiction** stories for magazines. He earned a Ph.D. in chemistry and taught at Boston University. Later, he became a full-time writer of both fact and fiction. Asimov wrote hundreds of books on every subject from Shakespeare to the Bible. One of the most famous is his *Foundation Trilogy*. It is a series of science fiction stories and novels. They trace the history of a space empire started by earth people. Asimov wrote many stories about robots. One collection is *I, Robot* (1950). It is the fictional **autobiography** of a designer of robots. (An autobiography is a person's life story told by that person.) In it, Asimov sets up three "laws of robotics." This set of rules seems to control the behavior of most artificial life forms in modern science fiction.

About the Selection

"The Feeling of Power" is a humorous look at the future. Society is so advanced and technical that it depends completely on computers. People find human abilities strange. This story is also a **parody** of the arms race between the United States and the former Soviet Union. Parody is an exaggerated look at a situation. The arms race was a major issue in 1957, when the story was written. The story uses **irony** to point out the humor of the situation. Irony is using an idea or image in the opposite way from its ordinary meaning.

THE FEELING OF POWER

Isaac Asimov

Jehan Shuman was used to dealing with the men in authority on long-**embattled** Earth. He was only a civilian but he **originated** programming patterns that resulted in self-directing war computers of the highest sort. Generals **consequently** listened to him. Heads of congressional committees, too.

There was one of each in the special **lounge** of New Pentagon. General Weider was space-burnt and had a small mouth puckered almost into a **cipher**. Congressman Brant was smooth-cheeked and clear-eyed. He smoked Denebian tobacco with the air of one whose patriotism was so notorious, he could be allowed such liberties.

Shuman, tall, distinguished, and Programmer-first-class, faced them fearlessly.

He said, "This, gentlemen, is Myron Aub."

"The one with the unusual gift that you discovered quite by accident," said Congressman Brant **placidly**. "Ah." He inspected the little man with the egg-bald head with **amiable** curiosity.

The little man, in return, twisted the fingers of his hands anxiously. He had never been near such great men before. He was only an aging low-grade Technician who had long ago failed all tests designed to smoke out the gifted ones among mankind and had settled into the rut of unskilled labor. There was just this hobby of his that the great Programmer had found out about and was now making such a frightening fuss over.

> As you read, watch for ways in which the author uses irony.

> The story takes place on earth in the future. Earth is at war with *Deneb*, a planet the author has invented. The war is being carried on by computers.

> Consider how important a *Programmer-first-class* would be in a world run by computers.

---

amiable friendly

cipher a zero

consequently as a result

embattled locked in a struggle

lounge a room in which to wait or relax

originate to begin

placidly calmly

General Weider said, "I find this atmosphere of mystery childish."

"You won't in a moment," said Shuman. "This is not something we can leak to the firstcomer. — Aub!" There was something **imperative** about his manner of biting off that one-syllable name, but then he was a great Programmer speaking to a mere Technician. "Aub! How much is nine times seven?"

Aub hesitated a moment. His pale eyes **glimmered** with a feeble anxiety. "Sixty-three," he said.

Congressman Brant lifted his eyebrows. "Is that right?"

"Check it for yourself, Congressman."

Why do you think these people needed a computer to do simple multiplication?

The congressman took out his pocket computer, nudged the milled edges twice, looked at its face as it lay there in the palm of his hand, and put it back. He said, "Is this the gift you brought us here to demonstrate. An **illusionist**?"

"More than that, sir. Aub has memorized a few operations and with them he **computes** on paper."

"A paper computer?" said the general. He looked pained.

"No, sir," said Shuman patiently. "Not a paper computer. Simply a sheet of paper. General, would you be so kind as to suggest a number?"

"Seventeen," said the general.

"And you, Congressman?"

"Twenty-three."

"Good! Aub, multiply those numbers and please show the gentlemen your manner of doing it."

"Yes, Programmer," said Aub, ducking his head. He fished a small pad out of one shirt pocket and an artist's hairline **stylus** out of the

smoke out to find; to make known	**compute** to find a number; to work mathematical problems	**glimmer** to give off a dim light
		illusionist a magician

other. His forehead **corrugated** as he made **painstaking** marks on the paper.

General Weider interrupted him sharply. "Let's see that."

Aub passed him the paper, and Weider said, "Well, it looks like the figure seventeen."

Congressman Brant nodded and said, "So it does, but I suppose anyone can copy figures off a computer. I think I could make a passable seventeen myself, even without practice."

"If you will let Aub continue, gentlemen," said Shuman without heat.

Aub continued, his hand trembling a little. Finally he said in a low voice, "The answer is three hundred and ninety-one."

Congressman Brant took out his computer a second time and flicked it, "By Godfrey, so it is. How did he guess?"

"No guess, Congressman," said Shuman. "He computed that result. He did it on this sheet of paper."

Do you think earthlings used computers for all writing as well as all mathematics?

"Humbug," said the general impatiently. "A computer is one thing and marks on paper are another."

"Explain, Aub," said Shuman.

"Yes, Programmer. —Well, gentlemen, I write down seventeen and just underneath it, I write twenty-three. Next, I say to myself: seven times three—"

The congressman interrupted smoothly, "Now, Aub, the problem is seventeen times twenty-three."

"Yes, I know," said the little Technician earnestly, "but I start by saying seven times three because that's the way it works. Now seven times three is twenty-one."

"And how do you know that?" asked the congressman.

"I just remember it. It's always twenty-one on the computer. I've checked it any number of times."

"That doesn't mean it always will be, though, does it?" said the congressman.

imperative commanding	**corrugate** to wrinkle	**painstaking** very careful
stylus a sharp pointed tool		

"Maybe not," stammered Aub. "I'm not a mathematician. But I always get the right answers, you see."

"Go on."

"Seven times three is twenty-one, so I write down twenty-one. Then one times three is three, so I write down a three under the two of the twenty-one."

"Why under the two?" asked Congressman Brant at once.

"Because—" Aub looked helplessly at his superior for support. "It's difficult to explain."

Shuman said, "If you will accept his work for the moment, we can leave the details for the mathematicians."

Brant **subsided**.

Why do you think the author makes a parody of the process of multiplying?

Aub said, "Three plus two makes five, you see, so the twenty-one become a fifty-one. Now you let that go for a while and start fresh. You multiply seven and two, that's fourteen, and one and two, that's two. Put them down like this and it adds up to thirty-four. Now if you put the thirty-four under the fifty-one this way and add them, you get three hundred and ninety-one and that's the answer."

There was an instant's silence and then General Weider said, "I don't believe it. He goes through this **rigmarole** and makes up numbers and multiplies and adds them this way and that, but I don't believe it. It's too **complicated** to be anything but **hornswoggling**."

"Oh no, sir," said Aub in a sweat. "It only seems complicated because you're not used to it. Actually, the rules are quite simple and will work for any numbers."

GI stands for "Government Issue." It refers to a soldier or to equipment issued by the military.

"Any numbers, eh?" said the general. "Come then." He took out his own computer (a severely styled GI model) and struck it at **random**. "Make a five seven three eight on the paper. That's five thousand seven hundred and thirty-eight."

"Yes, sir," said Aub, taking a new sheet of paper.

"Now," (more punching of his computer), "seven two three nine. Seven thousand two hundred and thirty-nine."

"Yes, sir."

"And now multiply those two."

complicated not simple	**random** by chance; without purpose	**rigmarole** nonsense
hornswoggling tricking someone		**subside** to become quiet

"It will take some time," quavered Aub.

"Take the time," said the general.

"Go ahead, Aub," said Shuman crisply.

Aub set to work, bending low. He took another sheet of paper and another. The general took out his watch finally and stared at it. "Are you through with your magic-making, Technician?"

"I'm almost done, sir. —Here it is, sir. Forty-one million, five hundred and thirty-seven thousand, three hundred and eighty-two." He showed the scrawled figures of the result.

General Weider smiled bitterly. He pushed the multiplication contact on his computer and let the numbers whirl to a halt. And then he stared and said in a surprised squeak, "Great Galaxy, the fella's right."

The President of the **Terrestrial Federation** had grown **haggard** in office and, in private, he allowed a look of settled melancholy to appear on his sensitive features. The Denebian war, after its early start of vast movement and great popularity, had trickled down into a **sordid** matter of maneuver and countermaneuver, with discontent rising steadily on Earth. Possibly, it was rising on Deneb, too.

And now Congressman Brant, head of the important Committee on Military **Appropriations** was cheerfully and smoothly spending his half-hour appointment spouting nonsense.

"Computing without a computer," said the president impatiently, "is a **contradiction** in terms."

"Computing," said the congressman, "is only a system for handling **data**. A machine might do it, or the human brain might. Let me give you an example." And, using the new skills he had learned, he worked out sums and products until the president, despite himself, grew interested.

"Does this always work?"

"Every time, Mr. President. It is foolproof."

"Is it hard to learn?"

"It took me a week to get the real hang of it. I think you would do better."

appropriations public money to be spent on certain things	**data** information	**sordid** dirty; selfish
contradict saying both one thing and its opposite	**federation** an association of states	**terrestrial** referring to the earth and its people
	haggard looking thin and tired	

What is the irony here? Did some people once think that using computers was just for entertainment whereas using pencil and paper was more useful?

"Well," said the president, considering, "it's an interesting parlor game, but what is the use of it?"

"What is the use of a newborn baby, Mr. President? At the moment there is no use, but don't you see that this points the way toward liberation from the machine. Consider, Mr. President," the congressman rose and his deep voice automatically took on some of the **cadences** he used in public debate, "that the Denebian war is a war of computer against computer. Their computers forge an **impenetrable** shield of counter-missiles against our missiles, and ours forge one against theirs. If we advance the efficiency of our computers, so do they theirs, and for five years a **precarious** and profitless balance has existed.

"Now we have in our hands a method for going beyond the computer, leapfrogging it, passing through it. We will combine the mechanics of computation with human thought; we will have the **equivalent** of intelligent computers; billions of them. I can't predict what the consequences will be in detail but they will be **incalculable**. And if Deneb beats us to the punch, they may be unimaginably **catastrophic**."

The president said, troubled, "What would you have me do?"

"Put the power of the administration behind the establishment of a secret project on human computation. Call it Project Number, if you like. I can vouch for my committee, but I will need the administration behind me."

"But how far can human computation go?"

"There is no limit. According to Programmer Shuman, who first introduced me to this discovery—"

"I've heard of Shuman, of course."

"Yes. Well, Dr. Shuman tells me that in theory there is nothing the computer can do that the human mind cannot do. The computer merely takes a **finite** amount of data and performs a finite number of operations upon them. The human mind can duplicate the process."

The president considered that. He said, "If Shuman says this, I am inclined to believe him—in theory. But, in practice, how can anyone know how a computer works?"

cadence a rhythm of speech	**finite** limited	**incalculable** not possible to measure in advance
catastrophic terrible	**impenetrable** not able to be pierced or broken	
equivalent something that is equal		**precarious** dangerous

Brant laughed genially. "Well, Mr. President, I asked the same question. It seems that at one time computers were designed directly by human beings. Those were simple computers, of course, this being before the time of the **rational** use of computers to design more advanced computers had been established."

"Yes, yes. Go on."

"Technician Aub apparently had, as his hobby, the **reconstruction** of some of these ancient devices and in so doing he studied the details of their workings and found he could imitate them. The multiplication I just performed for you is an imitation of the workings of a computer."

"Amazing!"

The congressman coughed gently, "If I may make another point, Mr. President— The further we can develop this thing, the more we can **divert** our Federal effort from computer production and computer maintenance. As the human brain takes over, more of our energy can be directed into peacetime pursuits and the **impingement** of war on the ordinary man will be less. This will be most advantageous for the party in power, of course."

"Ah," said the president, "I see your point. Well, sit down, Congressman, sit down. I want some time to think about this. — But meanwhile, show me that multiplication trick again. Let's see if I can't catch the point of it."

Programmer Shuman did not try to hurry matters. Loesser was **conservative**, very conservative, and liked to deal with computers as his father and grandfather had. Still, he controlled the West European computer combine, and if he could be persuaded to join Project Number in full enthusiasm, a great deal would be accomplished.

But Loesser was holding back. He said, "I'm not sure I like the idea of relaxing our hold on computers. The human mind is a **capricious** thing. The computer will give the same answer to the same problem each time. What guarantee have we that the human mind will do the same?"

"The human mind, Computer Loesser, only **manipulates** facts. It doesn't matter whether the human mind or a machine does it.

capricious acting on impulse; hard to predict	**impingement** the act of intruding or disturbing	**rational** based on reason
conservative not liking change	**manipulate** to handle or manage	**reconstruction** the rebuilding of something
divert to turn aside		

They are just tools."

"Yes, yes. I've gone over your ingenious demonstration that the mind can duplicate the computer but it seems to me a little in the air. I'll grant the theory but what reason have we for thinking that theory can be converted to practice?"

"I think we have reason, sir. After all, computers have not always existed. The cave men with their **triremes**, stone axes, and railroads had no computers."

"And possibly they did not compute."

"You know better than that. Even the building of a railroad or a **ziggurat** called for some computing, and that must have been without computers as we know them."

"Do you suggest they computed in the fashion you demonstrate?"

What other words can you think of that are also based on the root *graph-*?

"Probably not. After all, this method—we call it 'graphitics,' by the way, from the old European word 'grapho' meaning 'to write'—is developed from the computers themselves so it cannot have **antedated** them. Still, the cave men must have had some method, eh?"

"Lost arts! If you're going to talk about lost arts—"

"No, no. I'm not a lost art enthusiast, though I don't say there may not be some. After all, man was eating grain before **hydroponics**, and if the primitives ate grain, they must have grown it in soil. What else could they have done?"

What does this tell you about life on earth during the time of this story?

"I don't know, but I'll believe in soil-growing when I see someone grow grain in soil. And I'll believe in making fire by rubbing two pieces of flint together when I see that, too."

Shuman grew **placative**. "Well, let's stick to graphitics. It's just part of the process of **etherealization**. Transportation by means of bulky **contrivances** is giving way to direct mass-transference. Communications devices become less massive and more efficient constantly. For that matter, compare your pocket computer with the massive jobs of a thousand years ago. Why not, then, the last step of doing away with computers altogether? Come, sir, Project Number is a going concern; progress is already headlong. But we

antedate to come before	**hydroponics** a method of growing plants in water	**trireme** an ancient Greek or Roman warship
contrivance a mechanical device		
etherealization making things lighter	**placative** calming; ready to ease another person's mind	**ziggurat** an ancient tower built something like a pyramid

want your help. If patriotism doesn't move you, consider the **intellectual** adventure involved."

Loesser said **skeptically**, "What progress? What can you do beyond multiplication? Can you integrate a transcendental function?"

"In time, sir. In time. In the last month I have learned to handle division. I can determine, and correctly, integral quotients and decimal quotients."

"Decimal quotients? To how many places?"

Programmer Shuman tried to keep his tone casual. "Any number!"

Loesser's jaw dropped. "Without a computer?"

"Set me a problem."

"Divide twenty-seven by thirteen. Take it to six places."

Five minutes later, Shuman said, "Two point oh seven six nine two three."

Loesser checked it. "Well, now, that's amazing. Multiplication didn't impress me too much because it involved **integers** after all, and I thought trick manipulation might do it. But decimals—"

"And that is not all. There is a new development that is, so far, top secret and which, strictly speaking, I ought not to mention. Still— We may have made a **breakthrough** on the square root front."

"Square roots?"

"It involves some tricky points and we haven't licked the bugs yet, but Technician Aub, the man who invented the science and who has an amazing **intuition** in connection with it, maintains he has the problem almost solved. And he is only a Technician. A man like yourself, a trained and talented mathematician, ought to have no difficulty."

"Square roots," muttered Loesser, attracted.

"Cube roots, too. Are you with us?"

Loesser's hand thrust out suddenly, "Count me in."

General Weider stumped his way back and forth at the head of the room and addressed his listeners after the fashion of a savage

This conversation is about various kinds of mathematical processes. A *quotient* is the answer in a division problem. It can be a whole number (*integral*) or a *decimal*.

breakthrough a major accomplishment	**intellectual** having to do with the mind	**intuition** a way of knowing without proof
integer a whole number such as 1, 2, 3		**skeptically** with doubt

teacher facing a group of **recalcitrant** students. It made no difference to the general that they were the civilian scientists heading Project Number. The general was the over-all head, and he so considered himself at every waking moment.

He said, "Now square roots are all fine. I can't do them myself and I don't understand the methods, but they're fine. Still, the Project will not be sidetracked into what some of you call the **fundamentals**. You can play with graphitics any way you want to after the war is over, but right now we have **specific** and very practical problems to solve."

In a far corner, Technician Aub listened with painful attention. He was no longer a Technician, of course, having been relieved of his duties and assigned to the project, with a fine-sounding title and good pay. But, of course, the social distinction remained and the highly placed scientific leaders could never bring themselves to admit him to their ranks on a footing of **equality**. Nor, to do Aub justice, did he, himself, wish it. He was as uncomfortable with them as they with him.

The general was saying, "Our goal is a simple one, gentlemen; the replacement of the computer. A ship that can navigate space without a computer on board can be constructed in one fifth the time and at one tenth the expense of a computer-**laden** ship. We could build fleets five times, ten times, as great as Deneb could if we could but **eliminate** the computer.

"And I see something even beyond this. It may be fantastic now; a mere dream; but in the future I see the manned missile!"

There was an instant murmur from the audience.

The general drove on. "At the present time, our chief **bottleneck** is the fact that missiles are limited in intelligence. The computer controlling them can only be so large, and for that reason they can meet the changing nature of anti-missile defenses in an unsatisfactory way. Few missiles, if any, accomplish their goal and missile warfare is coming to a dead end; for the enemy, fortunately, as well as for ourselves.

"On the other hand, a missile with a man or two within, controlling flight by graphitics, would be lighter, more mobile, more intelligent.

bottleneck something that slows progress	**fundamentals** the basics	**recalcitrant** stubborn; resisting authority
eliminate to get rid of	**laden** loaded with; heavy	**specific** particular
equality state of being equal		

It would give us a lead that might well mean the margin of victory. Besides which, gentlemen, the **exigencies** of war **compel** us to remember one thing. A man is much more **dispensable** than a computer. Manned missiles could be launched in numbers and under **circumstances** that no good general would care to undertake as far as computer-directed missiles are concerned—"

He said much more but Technician Aub did not wait.

Technician Aub, in the **privacy** of his quarters, labored long over the note he was leaving behind. It read finally as follows:

"When I began the study of what is now called graphitics, it was no more than a hobby. I saw no more in it than an interesting **amusement**, an exercise of mind.

"When Project Number began, I thought that others were wiser than I; that graphitics might be put to practical use as a benefit to mankind, to aid in the production of really practical mass-transference devices perhaps. But now I see it is to be used only for death and destruction.

"I cannot face the responsibility involved in having invented graphitics."

He then deliberately turned the focus of a protein-depolarizer on himself and fell instantly and painlessly dead.

They stood over the grave of the little Technician while tribute was paid to the greatness of his discovery.

Programmer Shuman bowed his head along with the rest of them, but remained unmoved. The Technician had done his share and was no longer needed, after all. He might have started graphitics, but now that it had started, it would carry on by itself **overwhelmingly**, triumphantly, until manned missiles were possible with who knew what else.

Nine times seven, thought Shuman with deep satisfaction, is sixty-three, and I don't need a computer to tell me so. The computer is in my own head.

And it was amazing the feeling of power that gave him.

What is the irony of saying that it is easier to lose a human than a computer?

The *protein-depolarizer* is a weapon of science fiction.

amusement entertainment	**dispensable** not necessary	**overwhelmingly** with strength impossible to resist
circumstances conditions	**exigency** something demanding immediate attention	**privacy** state of being alone, away from others
compel to force		

The Feeling of Power
Isaac Asimov

Directions Write the answers to these questions using complete sentences.

Comprehension: Identifying Facts

1. List the characters.

2. What unusual skill has Myron Aub developed?

3. By the end of the story, what has Jehan Shuman learned to do?

4. What is doing math with pencil and paper called in this story?

5. How does the general want to use Aub's skill?

6. What kind of job does Myron Aub have?

7. How does Aub find the answer to 23 times 17? What do we call the process he used?

8. With whom is earth at war?

9. When General Weider first sees Aub at work, what does he say Aub is doing?

10. What finally happens to Aub?

Comprehension: Understanding Main Ideas

11. Name one point that tells you the story takes place in the future.

12. How important is Aub compared with the other characters?

13. What is Project Number?

14. What does Congressman Brant have to do with the military?

15. Why does Shuman's job make him so important in the government?

16. What does Aub hope that graphitics would be used for?

17. Why are the congressman and the general amazed that Aub can solve multiplication problems?

18. Why aren't humans making new computers at the time of the story?

19. Why does Shuman think that at one time grains were grown in soil?

20. Why do the leaders want to put humans into missiles?

Understanding Literature: Irony

Irony is using an idea or image in the opposite way from its ordinary meaning. For instance, we depend on computers to do what we can't. It is irony when General Weider wants to use people to do what computers can't. It is also irony that officials would rather lose a human life than a computer.

21. Find one statement about graphitics in which you could substitute the word *computers* to sound like today's attitudes.

22. What is ironic about Brant's statement that multiplication is an imitation of how a computer works?

23. What is ironic about General Weider's wanting to replace the computers on missiles?

24. Why is Aub's fate ironic?

25. Shuman feels powerful because he can multiply. What is ironic about that?

Critical Thinking

26. Which person in this story did you like best? Explain.

27. Choose one of the characters. List some of the emotions he shows.

28. Does the author think that everything about technology is good? Explain.

29. Choose one of the characters who has to be persuaded to support Project Number. Tell what arguments win him over.

30. Would you want to live during this time? Why or why not?

Writing on Your Own Write at least two sentences explaining why you think Aub doesn't want his skills to become Project Number.

The Expedition
Rudolf Lorenzen (translated by Charles E. Pederson)

About the Author

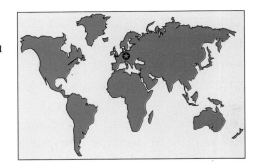

Rudolf Lorenzen was born in 1922 in Lübeck, a seaport in northern Germany. His first jobs were in the shipping industry. He wrote many short stories and newspaper articles before publishing his best-known work, *Anything but a Hero*, in 1959. This book has been translated into English. It has also been made into a movie. "The Expedition" has also been translated into Japanese. Lorenzen has written novels, short stories, screen and television plays, and documentary movie scripts. He currently lives in Berlin, Germany, with his second wife, Bettina.

Literary Terms

conflict a struggle the main character of a story has

denouement the resolution to a story

protagonist the main character in a story

About the Selection

"The Expedition" was published in 1974. It tells the story of four astronauts on a space journey to Cerberus, an imaginary planet. The voyage will take about eighty years. The travelers expect to have children and die before their spaceship can return to earth. They depend on the children to take over. The characters experience **conflict** with each other and their children. Conflict is a struggle the **protagonist**, or main character, has. The group must also struggle against boredom and meaninglessness. The author avoids a real **denouement**, or resolution to the story.

THE EXPEDITION

RUDOLF LORENZEN

Part I

They came together for the experiment. Strictly speaking, visiting Cerberus, the outermost of the known planets, was no longer an experiment. The result of an exact **calculation** had already assured success. Both men and the two women who had come together were good calculators.

They met at the space station *Halifax*. One of the men was an engineer, the other, a chemist. They had known each other since they were schoolboys. Cerberus was thirteen light hours, eight minutes distant from earth. Nothing was known about its volume, density, or **rotation**. Leichrieder had discovered the planet two years ago. He expected to find methane and ammoniac gas on it. The two women came from Springfield. They were medical students in their eighth semester. They had become acquainted with their fellow travelers at a ball. They had danced well together. Now they wanted to go to Cerberus with the men.

All four **participants** were healthy. Knowing this fact was important, because the distance of Cerberus to earth was so great that there was almost no chance any of them would reach their goal. The trip depended on children, and those children depended on their children to bring back to earth the results of the expedition.

As you read, watch for *conflicts* among the people on the spaceship.

Cerberus is not a real planet. The most distant known planet in the solar system today is Pluto. Many other stars and planets mentioned in the story are real, however.

Frozen gases surround the biggest planets in the solar system—Jupiter, Saturn, Neptune. They are mainly helium, hydrogen, *methane,* and *ammonia.*

How does the trip depend on children?

calculation a mathematical process or answer	**participant** one who takes part in something	**rotation** the motion of a planet turning around its axis

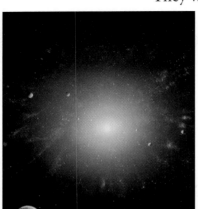

They went into the station bar before departing from Halifax. They were jolly. It made no difference to them that this was to be their last departure ever. To them, such expressions as "homesickness" and "Mother Earth" were foreign. They laughed at their parents, who were not **indifferent** where they died. "My father," said the engineer, "wants to die on the terrace of his summer home, with the sight of the Alps before his eyes." They all laughed. Even the barkeeper laughed. "Have you packed enough toothbrushes for eighty-six years?" he asked, but no one answered him. They had heard similar jokes ever since they had begun preparing for the trip. They had thought of everything. They even had plenty of diapers for the grandchildren. These had been placed in **sterile** packing, entered as Item 53 in the **inventory** list. Melanie, who was responsible for **administering** the supplies, knew the items by heart.

In this part of the story, who is the protagonist?

Their spaceship was named *Galaxis*. Bruno, the engineer, was commander. At the moment, he was being interviewed by two reporters who had entered the bar to report on the start of the *Galaxis* for Cerberus. Bruno was annoyed that it was only two reporters. In the old days, such events had received huge **coverage**.

"You are counting on dying before reaching Cerberus," said one reporter, the one who wrote for a news agency. Bruno answered, "That seems certain. Under such conditions, who could live longer than seventy?"

"Aren't you afraid of being bored until the day you die?" the reporter went on.

Bruno answered, "We won't be any more bored than we would be on earth. Aren't you a little bit bored?"

"Sometimes, yes," said the reporter. Then he turned to questions about technical **data** and amount of supplies.

administer to manage	**data** information	**inventory** the stock of supplies
coverage the way something is reported in newspapers or on television	**indifferent** not caring	**sterile** free from germs

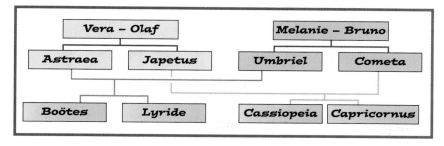

Vera – Olaf		Melanie – Bruno	
Astraea	Japetus	Umbriel	Cometa
Boötes	Lyride	Cassiopeia	Capricornus

Olaf, the chemist, was just dancing with Vera on the small dance floor. "As I left early this morning," said Vera, "my mother asked when I was coming back. I said, 'Read about it in tomorrow's paper.' Then she asked where she could write me."

"I would definitely never make such a trip," said the other reporter to Bruno. "Just thinking that I could never again lie on the beach in the sun makes me uncomfortable."

"Has lying in the sun on the beach ever made you happy?" asked Bruno.

The reporter considered. "Sometimes, yes," he said. "Sometimes, no."

"There you are then," said Bruno, adding that the time had come, and he paid their bar tab.

They went down Corridor C to the starting pad. The two reporters followed them. They noted that besides the technical inspector, the inspector general of space station *Halifax* accompanied them to take leave of the four adventurers as they started this journey, which after all was still uncommon. The inspector general shook the hand of each. As the rocket left the base, the reporters went to the radio station to file their reports with their home office.

The ship was large and comfortable. It had come from last year's production at the Clavenna Works. All difficulties with handling had been reduced to a minimum. Heat, air pressure, and **humidity** were **self-regulating**. It was hardly necessary to touch the instruments. Still, Bruno never neglected to make his **rounds** every eight hours, as recommended in the training

humidity the amount of moisture in the air	**rounds** a pattern of assigned duties	**self-regulating** making adjustments without outside help

course. During his rounds, he also checked for meteor damage. But meteor damage was rare.

Mostly, the company sat in the main room of the ship, played cards, and listened to music from earth's radio stations. They looked through the portholes only now and again. They had all seen the pictures of a space trip in countless films—the ever-shrinking earth, the **waning** earth, the half earth, the crescent earth, the orange of Mars, the green spots on its surface. There was nothing new to it. First-grade children made trips to Mars all the time during school film period.

At the far edge of the asteroid belt, Vera had a child. It was a girl, and the company named her Astraea, after the asteroid that was closest to them in the belt. Bruno entered the event in the logbook, along with the exact time and their universal position.

After four years, radio reception with earth was weakening, three-quarters of a year later it faded out altogether. The last news reports that they could hear, Melanie recorded in **calligraphy** on a piece of tinted cardboard. In Nepal, there was a temporary truce. The post office had raised its rates. An heir to the Bourbons had married an Ostrowski in San Sebastian. The couple had ridden in a coach drawn by horses, a spy was executed in the electric chair, European beer **consumption** continued to rise. Melanie framed the reports and hung them next to the ship's rules and regulations. She had good taste in such artistic matters.

As they crossed Neptune's orbit, Astraea had already passed astronautical mathematics. She had learned to make entries in the logbook and to read the instruments. For the past year, she had been responsible for the care of the test plants. Her mother had trained her, urging her to take **conscientious** care of the continued **pollination**. In the following year, her medical training would begin.

calligraphy fine handwriting	**consumption** the process of eating or drinking	**waning** growing smaller, as the visible part of the moon
conscientious careful to do things right	**pollination** transfer of pollen to make plants fertile	

Astraea's brother, Japetus, born in the vicinity of Saturn, had begun being able to read in his primer at this time.

"The planet is beautiful. The moons are beautiful too. Our rocket is fast. I like to live on a rocket."

Melanie and Bruno's son, named for Uranus's moon Umbriel, still lay next to the map cabinet in the bunk that had been **designated** for newborns. A fourth child, Melanie's daughter, was due to be born. But there was no doubt that it would come on time. There also was no doubt that it would be a girl. Birth control and the **predetermination** of **gender** were **reliable**. One used Ryders-Schelde's tables, which were the most dependable, being based on hundreds of experiments.

Six years after exiting the angle of the **ecliptic** of Pluto, Olaf died. The ship was shortly to cross the orbit of Monokeros, a small, **eccentrically** orbiting planet. Monokeros, like Cerberus, had been little researched. Its brightness varied. Melanie and Vera agreed about time and cause of death. Bruno had Astraea enter the death in the logbook. Astraea wrote, "At kilometer position 7,862,447,350, on 30 October 2145, at 0:43:15, Olaf Tyde died at the age of fifty-nine years. Cause of death: **dystrophy** of the liver. Nothing else to report. No meteor damage. He was a good husband, friend, and father to us all." Bruno judged that the last sentence did not belong in the logbook.

Olaf's body was released into space through the airlock in Opening D.

Neptune, Saturn, Uranus, and *Pluto* are the outer planets in the solar system. *Monokeros* is imaginary.

What conflict is developing among the characters here?

designate to select for a role	**eccentrically** oddly, not in an expected way	**gender** sex; male or female
dystrophy illness caused by poor nutrition	**ecliptic** circle formed where the plane of earth's orbit and another object cross	**predetermination** deciding in advance
		reliable to be trusted

After five years of elementary school, eight years of technical schooling, and six years of **internship**, Japetus was **certified** as an engineer. Bruno presented his diploma, which Japetus hung at the head of his bunk. The education of all the children on the trip was one-sided, but thorough in the specialties. They learned from their parents, and then from books in the various fields. At the end of their education, they knew somewhat more than their parents. They knew nothing of geography, history, or foreign languages. They had no experience of art, literature, or music. Even their parents had forgotten what they had known of literature, art, and music. But they did not miss it.

Do you think the children's education was better or worse than their parents' education?

When Cometa was born, they had only ten years until arrival at Cerberus. Umbriel and Astraea had been engaged for a year. They wanted to marry within the next year. Astraea was the oldest of the second-generation children. Bruno had looked forward to the day when he could hand over command of the ship to her. But Astraea seemed to lack the **aptitude** for the position. She was more inclined to dream. When she dreamed, she neglected her duty. One day, some of the test plants in her care died, and the cause was pinpointed as **negligence**. Bruno removed the duty from Astraea. The remaining plants came under Umbriel's care. In place of the plants, Astraea administered the wash, **disbursed** the dry soap, and distributed the vitamins. Only a pot of moss with boat-shaped leaves was left to her.

How is *Astraea* different from the others on the ship?

Sirius is also called the Dog Star. It is about the same size as our sun but gives off about 30 times as much light.

Cometa learned to recognize the sun as a tiny spot among the other stars. The sun lay in the **constellation** Great Dog (Canis Major) and was outshone by Sirius. Earth could no longer be seen with the ship's telescope. When Cometa asked what was happening on earth, her mother answered, "What does it matter? Everything is the same there as it is here on board, only larger. Be happy that we will be on Cerberus in a couple of years."

One day Bruno began to suffer from panic attacks, although they were not based in his **psychic** nature. He imagined he could not

aptitude an natural ability or talent	**constellation** a pattern of stars that form a picture	**internship** a time of supervised training
certify to confirm that standards have been met	**disburse** to pay out or hand out	**negligence** carelessness
		psychic having to do with mind and spirit

get his breath. Many times a day, he staggered to the instruments, stared at them. He pounded his fists against the glass of the air pressure monitor and screamed, "Air! I can't get any air. The instrument is broken." The instruments were **functioning** perfectly. It was guessed that Bruno had a mild heart condition; but the medicine that Vera gave him did not help. The fear of **suffocation** constantly grew in Bruno, until one day he dashed into the air lock and also into the lockless Exit A, to get some air. He had to be overpowered by Japetus and Umbriel.

When Bruno's condition did not improve and he threatened to become a general **hazard**, the company decided he had to be killed. Vera gave him an injection. Japetus oversaw removal of the body through Opening D. While entering the death into the logbook, Astraea was watched by her mother, so that no **extraneous** remarks would find their way into the official record. Astraea did not write that Bruno was a good husband, father, and friend, but only entered the position, time, and kilometer position. She wrote, "Bruno Perneder died at the age of seventy-one years. Cause of death: complications of **psychoneurotic** disturbances. No evidence of organic disease. Since early today, Cerberus clearly visible at 2° 12' to starboard. Nothing else to report."

When Melanie died eleven months later, Vera overtook sole command of the ship. She handed over complete technical supervision to her son, Japetus.

As you read, notice a change in the protagonist.

Four years before arrival at Cerberus, Japetus and Umbriel had begun daily preparations for the landing. They practiced the maneuvers, learned the regulations by heart. "Power units on. Approaching **tangential**. Rotate the machine. Stern forward. Check pressure suits before exiting ship." Every three days they held a general exercise to practice emergency **procedures**. Vera and little Cometa had to take part in these exercises too. Only Astraea was left in peace, with her logbook and her pot of moss. She was expecting a child.

extraneous not necessary	**procedure** a way of doing something	**suffocation** suffering from not having enough air
function to work properly	**psychoneurotic** having mental problems	
hazard something dangerous		**tangential** a point or line that touches, but doesn't cross, another

Boötes is the name of a constellation.

The child that Astraea had was a boy. She called him Boötes. He lay in the bunk next to the map cabinet. Every twenty-four hours Astraea prayed with him, "Deliver us from meteors. And protect our equipment. Let us not suffer lack of oxygen, moisture, and vitamins. Lead us not into false calculations. And turn your eyes to us when we land."

As *Galaxis* reached Cerberus, Boötes was three years old. As the stay on the planet was to last two years and the child couldn't be denied a chance to go outside the ship and play a little, his mother made a little protective suit for him. With a small oxygen tank on his back, he sat in it at the foot of a **pumice** hill, building little **pyramids** of stones. Now and then his mother called him when it was time to eat his pills or his oxygen should be topped up. She said, "Be careful of your spacesuit! If you tear it, poison gas will come in and make you very sick!" At the same time, the two men undertook **excursions** over a wide area. They made measurements and tested the rocks and atmosphere. Leichrieder had been correct about methane and ammoniac gas on the planet. The period of rotation was one and a half days, the angle of the elliptic was nineteen degrees. These results had no practical value, as their distance from the sun was so great that day and night, summer and winter were unnoticeable. The test plants that were exposed to Cerberus died.

Does the work on Cerberus seem interesting or valuable?

Only in the afternoons would Cometa watch the measurements. In the mornings she had school. She solved simple astronautical problems, studied scientific laws, and wrote compositions. Astraea gave her the topic "A Beautiful Day in My Life." Cometa wrote:

"A beautiful day in my life was when we landed on Cerberus. My father and mother gave a me holiday from school on this day, and I did not have to study. When our ship stood firmly on the ground, I was allowed to put on my new protective suit and breathe oxygen from a bottle. That was very fun. Then I

excursion a trip	**pumice** a light rock from a volcano	**pyramid** a figure with four triangles for sides

was allowed to jump outside through Exit D. I held little Boötes's hand. I played outside all day long, until Mother called and I had to go to bed. That was a beautiful day. When I get big, I will tell my children about it."

Part II

Almost two years later, the time that Bruno had calculated arrived. It was the best time to leave Cerberus and begin the return trip. Japetus followed Uncle Bruno's instructions to the letter, laid out in many carefully **compiled** notebooks. On the day before liftoff, little Boötes celebrated his fifth birthday. His parents gave him building blocks and puzzles. From Grandma Vera he received a picture book, "Hansi and Möpsi in the Milky Way." For the evening meal, Boötes got $C_6H_{12}O_6$ tablets—as many as he wanted. He was allowed to stay up two hours past his bedtime.

The writer gives the chemical formula for fructose, a sugar. Why do you suppose he doesn't just say "sugar"?

Ten years later, at his fifteenth birthday, Boötes's father gave him a do-it-yourself electric motor and a biography of explorers, called *Look Forward!* But Boötes did not like to read, and he also disliked building things, and was definitely not a stay-at-home type. His favorite thing was to play ball in the forward cabin of the ship with Lyride, his little sister, who had been born eight years earlier, and little Cassiopeia, Cometa's daughter.

Sometimes, when the children were too loud, Japetus came to the forward cabin and scolded them, "Pay a little more attention to your lessons. What will you do when we are all gone? Boötes, you don't even know how to regulate the heat and measure the air pressure!" But the children did not listen, they had no technical interests, they preferred to play ball. "What would your grandmother say if she saw you," said Cometa. But Grandmother Vera did not see them. She had been dead seven years. She had died shortly before the start of the return trip. No

compile to put together information into a record

one was left alive of the first generation that had planned the expedition fifty-four years ago back on earth.

The company's worries about the children grew. Little Cassiopeia could not even understand the multiplication table, and Lyride refused even the simplest task her parents set her. She messed the supply rooms and mixed up their **vital** pills. At fourteen she still chewed her fingernails. Her brother Boötes was not expected ever to pass the engineering tests.

So all hopes came to rest on Capricornus, the youngest, born to Cometa sixteen years after leaving Cerberus. Capricornus was a strong baby, and his father, Japetus, often sat for hours at the infant's bunk next to the map cabinet, speaking to the newborn. "Your parents," he said, "live only for you. They have never seen earth, and never will. When our ship arrives there, we will all be dead. Only you will be alive, and your sister, and Boötes and Lyride. But they are all ungrateful and can't see that we live only for all of you, they don't understand the sacrifice that we have made for you. We take on ourselves the gloomy, disgusting life of this miserable steel casing, the **monotonous** days on this pointless trip, the uselessness of our daily **manipulations**, so that all of you can one day land on earth. Boötes, Lyride, and your sister Cassiopeia do not understand that. So we live only for you, Capricornus."

What conflicts do Japetus's words show?

Six years later, Japetus was still saying the same things to Capricornus. He sat at his son's bunk and said, "Our daily activities are useless, our life is disgusting, and this trip makes no sense." But Capricornus did not understand his father. He understood nothing, took in nothing that happened around him, did not speak, only made little gurgling sounds. His look was numb. If he did move around the ship, he crawled on all fours. Capricornus was one spoon short of a silverware drawer.

What does this phrase tell you about Capricornus?

When there clearly was no hope of improvement for his son, Japetus killed himself. He injected himself with a poison **serum**.

manipulation the action of controlling or operating	**monotonous** dull, boring	**vital** very important and necessary
	serum a liquid containing medicine	

He felt no pain. Umbriel dispatched the body through the air lock. Boötes **sullenly** helped him with this procedure.

Astraea entered her brother's death in the logbook. Making entries in the logbook was one of the few duties that had been left to her. She was the oldest on board, but the company was **reluctant** to give her other assignments. Her **tendency** to dream, which she had shown early in life, became stronger with every passing year. She was now sixty-four years old. In her youth, there had still been light outside the porthole, the sun was a small, glowing ball, one could see earth through the telescope. Astraea remembered hearing the radio when she was four years old. The programs from earth had sometimes come weakly and unclearly, often accompanied by static. On other days, clear and pure, came music. Sometimes someone spoke on the radio and reported happenings on earth. The last reports, which had been received sixty years ago on the outward voyage, Aunt Melanie had **transcribed** in calligraphy, framed, and hung next to the house rules and regulations. The document still hung there. A Bourbon had married an Ostrowski. That was in San Sebastian, and the couple had ridden in a coach pulled by horses. Truce in Nepal, higher rates at the post office. In Europe, beer consumption continued to rise, and a spy was sent to the electric chair.

Astraea sat at her place near the porthole, looking into the darkness and the stars. She dreamed that the sun was a small glowing ball, and outside, everything shone with brightness. She dreamed of stepping up to the telescope and seeing the earth as a big, round disk, half dark, half lighted by the sun. She dreamed that music came from the radio, and that a voice on the radio said postage rates had gone down again and that the spy had been pardoned. She sat at the porthole, looking into the darkness. The moss with the boat-shaped leaves, which her Uncle Bruno had given her as a present, had died thirty years ago. The empty pot still stood next to her bunk.

Are Astraea's feelings about life different from the others' feelings?

reluctant not willing	**sullenly** in a gloomy or sulky way	**transcribe** make a copy of
	tendency a pattern of doing things a certain way	

One day Astraea surprised the company with the news that **precisely** at this point on the outward trip, her father had died and been **dispatched** into space. Umbriel and Cometa were not able to convince Astraea that their Uncle Olaf had not died on this spot. "We have taken a completely different return path," said Umbriel, and Cometa added, "Dear Astraea, you're wrong, your father died six years beyond Pluto. And we are now a year and a half inside Pluto's orbit." Astraea would not listen to reason. She sat at the porthole, looked out, and waited to meet her father's body. But she saw nothing.

Between the orbits of Pluto and Neptune, Cometa contracted a lung infection. She had chills, fever, and chest pains. Her **sputum** left no doubt about the diagnosis, and everyone wondered where such germs had come from. In twelve days, Cometa was dead. Umbriel took care of **disinfection**, and in the logbook, Astraea wrote, "Cometa died at age thirty-nine. She always had weak health. She was a good mother, sister, sister-in-law, and aunt to us all." When, only a few years later, Astraea's husband, Umbriel, followed his sister in death, she added a similar line in the logbook. No one stopped her from such personal entries anymore. Her children, Boötes and Lyride, and her niece, Cassiopeia, did not care what she did. Making entries in the logbook seemed **superfluous** to the young people. They left such games to Astraea, who had reached the age of seventy-one.

With the third generation, a new era came to *Galaxis.* The youngsters did not possess the strict outlook that their parents had, nor the sporting spirit of their grandparents. They lived only for the moment, expecting nothing of the future. Mostly the three of them sat in the main room of the ship and played cards. Astraea, watching them, was surprised at how **primitive** their card-playing was. The players constantly chose several random cards from the pile, threw them down on the table, and laughed. It was nothing compared to the **complicated** games with which

complicated not easy to understand	**dispatch** to send out	**sputum** spit
disinfection getting rid of germs that can cause diseases	**precisely** exactly	**superfluous** more than needed
	primitive simple or crude	

their grandparents had occupied themselves, back in the days of the outward trip. But Astraea said nothing, stayed out of it, was happy that her children and nieces left her in peace.

She sat at the porthole, watching the stars. Capricornus chewed at her feet. He still could not speak, could not run. This year he turned fourteen. Slowly over years, the sun emerged from the constellation Hydra. It became larger, gave light, soon was the size of a screw head, DIN M 8. "Day by day, I feel it getting warmer," Astraea said, but her children laughed. "The inside temperature is always the same," they said. "You're imagining things." But Astraea was not to be talked out of what she felt. "For seventy years, I've frozen," she said. "Finally, I feel better."

A couple of years later, it was possible to receive radio signals from earth. But the company made no use of the privilege. The music hurt their ears, the news was meaningless to them. Only Astraea would have liked to listen now and then, but her hearing was failing. Soon she would be eighty. She was also unable to see earth's disk through the telescope, her eyes were too weak. She sat at the porthole again, watching the sun through the protective glass and imagining that she could feel the warmth on her skin.

At Jupiter's orbit, the company gradually considered it might become necessary to learn how to land the ship. Lyride looked in her grandfather's papers and found a notebook that precisely described the landing **maneuvers** and all possible dangers that came with it. It is true that the notes were for landing on Cerberus; but Boötes thought that the difference of landing on earth couldn't be that much. They practiced the necessary manipulations and also **improvised** a way to use the radio. When they believed they had mastered everything, they went back to playing cards until they reached earth's vicinity.

The *Galaxis* landed, following radioed commands, at space station *Wellington*. At touchdown, there was some slight

Hydra is a constellation of stars in the southern sky of earth.

DIN M 8 is an industrial measurement.

Why do they realize they are nearing the earth?

Think about the ways in which Astraea is the protagonist in the story. Why do you think she decides to stay on the ship?

Would the company have gone back to playing cards if Bruno or Japetus were in command?

maneuver a change in course or position	**improvise** to invent or put together on the spur of the moment

damage, but the company did not bother about it. They left the ship and followed the directions of the ground crew, who sent them down Corridor C to register. Boötes carried his cousin Capricornus on his shoulders, Lyride and Cassiopeia carried the crates of rock samples from Cerberus and the test tube samples of its atmosphere. They carried all the papers that had been issued almost ninety years ago: permission to depart, Bruno's commission, their grandparents' health certificates, and the logbook kept by Astraea. They were uncertain what might be asked of them. They had no experience with the **formalities** of a space station on earth.

Astraea remained behind in the ship. She had no wish to climb out and make acquaintance with the ground that her parents had left. A few years ago she had often thought, while sitting in her place at the porthole, what a space station might be like, or even how earth itself might look. She had looked at the sun and dreamed that she walked down corridor after endless corridor.

Think of how Astraea is the protagonist. Why does she stay on the ship?

But the dream had ceased, and with the dream, her last wishes had disappeared. Astraea was eighty-four years old. As her children **debarked**, she said, "Leave me at my place. From here I've seen everything. I've seen all the stars, and I've seen the sun as it disappeared and came back again. As a child I saw the earth as a tiny point, and now as a great round disk. What else is there? What else don't know I about?"

The doctor does not understand how long the *Galaxis* has been gone. Does anyone on earth seem to understand this expedition?

So the children went without mother and aunt. At the end of Corridor C they found the registration office. They heard that their papers were no longer valid and if they wished to renew them, a certain fee was required. From registration they were sent for a technical inspection, and from the technical inspection to a physical inspection. The doctor gave them trouble about Capricornus. "How could you make a space journey with a mentally retarded boy?" the doctor scolded them, and Boötes had

debark to get off, as from a ship

formalities official rules; customs

to describe in detail that the *Galaxis* had just finished a long journey and that his cousin had been born underway.

With the formalities taken care of, the four of them went to Counter G, where they could buy shuttle tickets for earth. Counter G was busy, a tour group had just arrived from the moon. The people stood in a long line before the counter. They had been underway for several days and were in a hurry because after the Easter holiday, they had to be at their workplaces promptly the next day. Joining the line, the crew of the *Galaxis* briefly attracted the attention of these Easter vacationers. The tourists poked each other and laughed. They joked about Lyride and Cassiopeia, about their hairstyles and clothes. The tour group also joked about Capricornus, who sat drooling on the floor.

Meanwhile, a mechanic entered the *Galaxis*. He had been sent to inspect the damage done at landing. He met Astraea in the main room. "Well, Grandma, did you have a nice trip?" But Astraea did not understand him. The mechanic repeated his question. "Yes, yes," said Astraea. "The sun is getting warmer. I've frozen for eighty years." The mechanic laughed, tapping his forehead behind Astraea's back as he left.

Not long afterward, an inspector arrived at the *Galaxis*'s landing place. The mechanic reported the damage he had found. "An old grandma is sitting inside," he added. "She must be older than eighty. I always wonder what use these old people have with flying around in space."

"Yeah," answered the inspector. "I always think the same thing. We live in crazy times."

The mechanic said, "You're right about that, sir. Crazy times." Then he took a pencil and the pad of forms to write down the damage he had found.

Why don't the inspector and the mechanic know that Astraea was born in space?

This story stops without following the characters to an end. In the conflict with boredom, what has won?

The Expedition
Rudolf Lorenzen

Directions Write the answers to these questions using complete sentences.

Comprehension: Identifying Facts

1. How long will the expedition to Cerberus take?

2. What does Bruno check for on his daily rounds?

3. Who is the first person to die on board?

4. Who takes over control of the ship after Melanie dies?

5. What does Astraea do when the ship first returns to earth?

6. List the four people who start the trip. What are their professions?

7. Who gives birth to the first child?

8. Who is Bruno and Melanie's son?

9. Who are Boötes's parents?

10. What does Bruno suffer from?

Comprehension: Understanding Main Ideas

11. Why doesn't Bruno want to include the words about Olaf being a good husband, friend, and father in the logbook?

12. What is one way in which Boötes is different from his uncle Japetus?

13. Why does Japetus kill himself?

14. How are the grandchildren born on the trip different from their parents?

15. Why do the grandchildren finally learn how to make landings?

16. Why could Astraea put personal information about Cometa in the logbook?

17. Why does the company have to kill Bruno?

18. Would Boötes's birthday presents be up to date? Explain.

19. Give examples of the forms that Astraea's daydreaming takes.

20. What is strange about Cometa's death?

Understanding Literature: Conflict

Conflict is the struggle that the main character in the story has. (In this story, the main character changes from time to time.) The conflict may force the character to grow or change. The conflict may be with something outside the character. It may take place in the character's head or heart.

21. Think about the four who started the expedition. Do they seem to have conflicts between the adventure and what they will leave behind? Give an example to support your answer.

22. What conflict arises over what should be put in the logbook?

23. What is the conflict between what Bruno wants for Astraea and Astraea's ways?

24. What is the conflict between Japetus and Boötes?

25. Give an example of conflict between Astraea and the younger people.

Critical Thinking

26. Why do Vera and Melanie make the expedition? Do you think this is a good reason?

27. Does this story make living in a spaceship sound like something you would like to do? Why or why not?

28. Is it wise for the parents not to teach their children about art, literature, and music? Why or why not?

29. Which group would you rather be in: parents, children, or grandchildren? Explain your reasons.

30. Was the trip worth it for anyone? Why or why not?

Writing on Your Own Think about the people who do get back to earth. Write a paragraph about one of them telling what life will be like later for him or her.

Adventure

- "The price of hating other human beings is loving oneself less." —Eldridge Cleaver
- "Send me out into another life. But get me back for supper." —Faith Popcorn

Adventure stories are like those you have read so far, but their appeal comes from plot. Exciting, fast-paced, dangerous events are the trademark of certain authors. For instance, John Grisham makes sure someone tries to kill his main characters at least once in every book. Plot rather than symbolism defines each character. Symbolism gives places, people, and objects a larger meaning.

The action in adventures rarely changes the characters. They may go broke, fall in love, or betray friends. Danger brings out the protagonist's basic strengths and values. For this reason, adventures often make effective TV or film series—even computer games. You can always count on Captain Picard and the trusty crew of the starship *Enterprise* or "Tomb Raider" Lara Croft to save the day. They might even have to die and come back to life to finish the job. Westerns, spy stories, and war stories all appeal to readers of adventures.

The selections in this section all include other elements besides adventure. Each story has brave, clever protagonists. They try to survive by using their wits as well as their strength.

About the Author

Robert D. San Souci
(1946–)
American

Robert D. San Souci has written more than fifty books and has won many awards. *The Talking Eggs* won both a Caldecott Honor and a Coretta Scott King Honor. He also won an award from the Smithsonian. San Souci lives in the San Francisco Bay area of California.

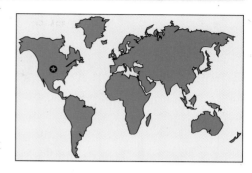

About the Selection

In this story from Costa Rica, a young man is traveling alone on horseback. He is warned about a terrible monster—the Cegua. It lures careless travelers into giving it a ride and then kills the rider or drives him mad. The story takes place in the rural countryside near San José, the capital city of Costa Rica, which is its **setting**. The author uses **regionalisms**, or words that are found in that area. These words help set the mood for the **action**. The action is what happens in the story. The traveler has a terrifying trip. Did it really happen? You decide.

Literary Terms

action what goes on in a story

regionalism a word or phrase that comes from a particular area

setting the time and place in a story

The Cegua

Robert D. San Souci

As you read, picture the settings in your mind.

One evening, a young man from San José, the capital of Costa Rica, rode into a small town north of the city. He was on his way to visit the ranch of a friend situated in a lonely area, but he wasn't sure which road to take out of the town.

The word *cantina* is Spanish for a tavern.

He decided to stop in the local *cantina* to **quench** his thirst and ask directions.

When the **proprietor** brought him a mug of beer, he told the traveler he still had a fair distance to cover. "But," the proprietor warned, "no one travels these roads after dark. Stay here: I have a room I will let for a few *pesos*—then you can finish your journey in the morning."

A *peso* is a unit of money.

The young man shook his head. "I have to reach my friend's ranch tonight."

The older man shook his head. "Only a fool would risk meeting the *Cegua*."

"The *Cegua!*" the traveler exclaimed. "What kind of creature is *that?*"

Señor means "mister" in Spanish.

The *cantina* owner smiled, as if he was unable to believe such ignorance existed. "*Señor,*" he said, "don't folks in San José know

proprietor the owner of a business	**quench** to satisfy; to put out

what the *Cegua* is? She is a demon—and heaven keep you from meeting her on the road!"

"I've never heard of such a thing," said the young man. "Bring me another mug of beer, and please explain what you know about this *Cegua*."

When the older man returned with the beer the traveler had ordered, he brought a second mug for himself. He sat down across the **rude** wooden table and said, "No one who sees the *Cegua* is left with a sound mind. Strong men, in the peak of health, have gone mad from the sight. Some have even died of fright." He began to rattle off the names of locals who had lost their minds or lives because of this monster.

But the younger man interrupted him, saying, "If she is such a terrible devil, why haven't I heard of her before?"

"She prefers certain parts of our country; we have the misfortune to be one such place," explained the proprietor patiently. "For that reason, no one here rides alone after dark. If someone must travel after nightfall, he always goes with a companion."

"Why? Doesn't she like crowds?" laughed the young man, who was beginning to feel the effects of his long ride and the beer.

"The *Cegua* only appears to someone who travels alone," said the older man gravely, finishing his own beer and starting to rise. "She appears as a beautiful *señorita*, smiling sadly and fluttering her eyes, pleading for a ride—but **woe** to the traveler who stops to help her! If the **unsuspecting** rider sits her in front, she turns her head. If he has placed her behind him, she will make him turn to look at her. In either case, his doom is sealed."

"How so?" traveler asked.

The name of the *Cegua* is an example of a regionalism. The term—and the legend—are found only in certain places.

A *señorita* is a young woman.

rude rough; crudely made	**unsuspecting** trusting; not suspicious	**woe** misfortune; great sorrow

Sulfur is often associated with the devil. It has a smell like rotten eggs.

"When he looks, the beautiful *señorita* is gone. The creature riding with him has a huge horse's head, with monstrous fangs. Her eyes burn fiery red, like hot coals, and her breath stinks like *sulfur*. With a hiss, she will bury her claws in the shoulders of the rider and hang on like a wild animal. A horse, sensing that he is being ridden by a demon, will bolt in such a **frenzy** that no one can stop him."

"What then?" asked the younger man, no longer smiling quite so broadly.

"Those who are found the next day, if they are still alive, will have gone mad from the sight of her."

"Nonsense," said the traveler, suddenly standing up and tossing down a few *pesos* to pay for the beer. "I must be on my way, if I'm to reach my friend's ranch tonight."

The older man shrugged, gathered up the coins, and turned away. Clearly, he thought to himself, there is no arguing with a fool.

The little town square was deserted. The traveler untied his horse from the hitching post and set out along the road the *cantina*'s proprietor had pointed out to him earlier.

It was a warm night. Not a breath of wind stirred the leaves in the trees on either side of the road. Nothing disturbed the silence, except the *clop-clop* of his horse's hoofs on stones in the roadway.

As you read, note the action.

Suddenly, around the bend, when the town was out of sight behind him and no other building was visible, he saw a slender figure standing in the thick shadows where the trees overhung the road.

Slowing his horse, the young man discovered a beautiful girl, with a pale face framed by the black-lace *mantilla* that covered her head, and which she held under her chin with her left hand. In the moonlight he could see she had curly black hair, huge dark eyes, and deep red lips.

A *mantilla* is a scarf worn over the head.

"*Señor*," she began. Her voice was sweet, but so weak and weary that he feared she must be near fainting. "I am so tired, but I must go to see my mother, who is ill. Would you take me to Bagaces?"

"Of course," he said, bringing his horse to a stop and climbing down. Bowing slightly and removing his hat, he said, "My friend's

frenzy a wild excitement

ranch is just south of that town. You can spend the night there. In the morning I will escort you the rest of the way."

"You are very kind, *señor*," she said, in such a faint whisper that he had to lean close to make out her words. Then he helped her onto the horse—which had grown **restive** during their halt—behind his saddle. He mounted himself, and they took off at a good trot.

A breeze had arisen to freshen the still air and flutter the leaves on the nearby trees. The moon and stars tinted the **landscape** pale silver. Several times the traveler tried to make conversation with the woman, but she didn't answer. She only leaned her head against his back and clung to his shoulders with her hands, as if she were afraid of fainting and tumbling from his horse.

Abruptly his horse, without any prodding, broke into a gallop. The woman dug her fingers into his shoulder, clearly afraid of falling. The young man was too polite to tell her that her nails were digging into his skin.

The horse gave a cry and charged down the dark road as though something terrible were pursuing them. The traveler pulled back on the reins and shouted, but it did no good. His horse only galloped faster.

Suddenly he felt **razor**-sharp teeth lock onto his neck so that only the collar of his coat saved his skin. An instant later, he heard a cry that came from no human throat as the awful teeth suddenly pulled away a mouthful of his coat collar.

He wrapped the ends of the reins around the fingers of one hand, and with his free hand he struggled to pry loose the fingers that were clamped on his shoulder. As shadow, then moonlight, then shadow again, washed over the horse and its two riders, the young man saw that the fingers clutching him were too pale—they were the white of bone, rather than fair skin.

---

abruptly suddenly

landscape a stretch of land forming a single scene

razor an instrument used for shaving

restive hard to handle

He heard another screech and smelled the creature's foul breath. He felt his strength giving out, while the bony fingers pulling at him seemed to grow stronger. The jaws snapped at the back of his neck, this time drawing blood.

Then, ahead, he could see his friend's ranch. He thought he could hear dogs barking, to signal his arrival. Lights were burning in the *hacienda.* There were figures running up the road toward him, carrying torches.

A *hacienda* is a ranch house.

There was a final, ear-splitting scream from the demon behind him. He felt his whole body jerked backward. The hand that was tangled in the reins pulled backward suddenly, causing his horse to rear up, then fall sideways. Both riders fell with the animal.

The traveler was knocked senseless for a moment. When he came to, his friend, holding a torch, was staring at him, asking if he was all right. He nodded, still shaking from his near-brush with death. When he touched his hand to the stinging at the back of his neck, his fingers came away bloody. He looked around **hastily**, but all he saw was a crowd of friendly-looking *campesinos,* countrymen, watching him. One was calming his horse, which was on its feet again.

"Where is it—the creature?" he asked his friend.

"What creature?"

"The *Cegua.*"

"My friend," laughed the other man, "you stayed too long at some *cantina,* I think. The *Cegua* is a story to frighten children, nothing more. Still, next time you ride at night, be sure you travel with a companion. These lonely roads can be dangerous in the dark."

What do you think really happened?

The young man said nothing, but he shivered just a little when the night breeze brought the **lingering** odor of sulfur to his nostrils.

---

hastily quickly

lingering lasting a long time; staying on

The Cegua
Robert D. San Souci

Directions Write the answers to these questions using complete sentences.

Comprehension: Identifying Facts

1. Where is the young man from?

2. Where is the young man traveling to?

3. Where does he stop to ask directions?

Comprehension: Understanding Main Ideas

4. Why does the proprietor tell the young man not to travel alone after dark?

5. The young man tries to talk to the woman. What happens?

6. What is the traveler's experience on the road?

Understanding Literature: Regionalism

A regionalism is a word or term used in a certain region or area. Regionalisms can include a region's habits, folk tales, and customs. Regionalisms help give a story a local flavor. They help us understand the setting and the characters.

7. How does the writer give us an idea of the language of the region?

8. How is the *Cegua* an example of regionalism?

Critical Thinking

9. Do you think the traveler actually met the Cegua? Why or why not?

10. Would you have stayed the night at the cantina? Why or why not?

Writing on Your Own Think of a time in your life when you were afraid of something. Write a paragraph about that event. Was it really something scary or did it turn out to be nothing to fear?

Master and Man
Leo Tolstoy (translated by Paul Foote)

Leo Tolstoy
(1828–1910)
Russian

Literary Term

naturalism a literary movement focused on the survival of the fittest against nature. It features helpless characters against events beyond human control and understanding

About the Author

Count Leo Tolstoy was born at Yasnaya Polyana, his wealthy family's estate south of Moscow. Tolstoy's parents died when he was nine and he then lived with relatives. He attended but did not finish college. Tolstoy later became a soldier and took part in the Crimean War. He began to write stories after the war. Tolstoy married in 1896 and had a large family. While managing his estates, he wrote two of the greatest modern novels. *War and Peace* was written in 1865–1868; *Anna Karenina* was written about eight years later. Tolstoy worked to make life better for the peasants on his land. In later life, he wrote about morals and religion.

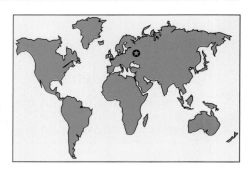

About the Selection

Master and Man takes place in 1870's Russia. The "master" is Vasilii Andreich and the "man" is his servant, Nikita. Vasilii Andreich is a rich businessman who will let nothing stop him from gaining more money. On a winter's day, Vasilii Andreich takes a horse-drawn sleigh to see a piece of valuable property he wants to buy. Nikita goes with him. Master and man both become lost in a severe snowstorm. Money does not matter to the storm. Tolstoy uses **naturalism** in this story, his characters are helpless against nature. Events are beyond human control. In the following selection, Vasilii Andreich takes the horse to try to find help.

Master and Man
Leo Tolstoy

Meanwhile Vasilii Andreich was driving the horse on with feet and reins towards where for some reason he supposed the forest and the keeper's hut to be. He was blinded by the snow, the wind seemed anxious to hold him back, but **relentlessly** he drove the horse on, crouching forward and continually drawing his coat across him and tucking it between himself and the small cold saddle which stopped him sitting properly. Though with difficulty, the horse obediently went at an **ambling** pace along the way he was made to go.

For some five minutes Vasilii Andreich rode as he thought in a straight line, seeing nothing but the horse's head and the white wilderness, hearing nothing but the wind whistling past the horse's ears and the collar of his fur top-coat.

There was suddenly something dark ahead. His heart thumped with joy and he headed towards this dark something, already seeing it as the walls of houses in the village. But the dark shape did not keep still, it kept

As you read, watch how *Vasilii Andreich* struggles against nature.

---

ambling slow-moving

relentlessly without yielding

Wormwood is a tall weedy plant that has a bitter flavor.

moving, and it was not the village but a tall patch of wormwood that had grown up along the edge of a field and stood up clear of the snow, frantically tossing in the wind, which bent it over and whistled through it. For some reason the sight of this wormwood tormented by the **merciless** wind made Vasilii Andreich shudder and he hastily urged the horse on, not noticing that in going towards the wormwood he had completely changed course and was now pointing the horse in a quite different direction, though he still supposed he was heading for where the keeper's hut should be. But the horse kept pulling to the right and Vasilii Andreich continually had to make him go left.

Which do you think knows the way, the man or the horse?

Once more there was something dark ahead. He was **overjoyed**, certain that this really must now be the village. But again it was a field-boundary with wormwood growing along it. The tall dry weeds tossed and swayed as frantically as ever and **unaccountably** terrified Vasilii Andreich. But it was not only that the weeds were the same— alongside ran hoof-prints partly covered with blown snow. Vasilii Andreich stopped and bent to take a closer look: it was the lightly covered tracks of a horse and it could be no one else's but his own. He had evidently been going in a circle and in quite a small **compass**. This way I'm done for! he thought, but so as not to give way to his fear he drove the horse on more urgently than before, peering ahead into the snowy white gloom in which shining dots seemed to appear, only to vanish the moment he tried to focus on them. Once

What do the *hoof-prints* tell Vasilii Andreich

compass limited area	**merciless** cruel; without mercy	**unaccountably** mysteriously; without explanation
	overjoyed delighted; very happy	

he thought he heard the bark of a dog or the howl of a wolf, but the sound was so faint and **indistinct** that he could not tell if he had actually heard it or if it was just his **fancy**, so he stopped to listen.

All at once there was a terrible deafening cry right in his ears and everything shuddered and shook beneath him. Vasilii Andreich grabbed the horse's neck, but that too was shuddering and the terrible cry was more terrifying than before. For some seconds Vasilii Andreich could not collect himself and realize what it was. In fact all that had happened was that Dapple—for good cheer or as a cry for help—had let out a loud, well-tuned neigh. 'Cursed horse! Proper put the wind up me!' said Vasilii Andreich to himself. But even though he now knew what had caused his fear he could not shake it off.

To *put the wind up* is to be startled or alarmed.

I've got to come to and get a grip on myself, he thought, but still he could not help himself and pressed the horse on, without noticing that he now had the wind behind him and not in his face. His body, especially in the crutch, where it was exposed and touched the saddle, was chilled through and aching, his arms and legs trembled, his breath came in gasps. He could see that he would perish in this awful waste of snow and saw no way of escape.

Suddenly the horse collapsed under him. It was deep in a drift and began to struggle, falling over on its side. Vasilii Andreich sprang off. In doing so he pulled over the **breeching** which supported his foot and twisted **askew** the saddle to which he held while jumping off. No sooner had Vasilii Andreich sprung clear than the horse found its feet again and plunged ahead. It gave a couple of leaps, let out another neigh and disappeared from sight, trailing the

| **askew** to one side | **breeching** strap of harness behind a horse's rear legs | **fancy** imagination |
| | | **indistinct** not clear |

sackcloth and breeching behind and leaving Vasilii Andreich alone in the snowdrift. Vasilii Andreich dashed after it, but the snow was so deep and his fur coats so heavy that with every step he sank in over his knees and after running some twenty yards he was out of breath and stopped. What will become of it all? he thought. The **coppice**, the **wethers**, the **leasehold**, my shop and taverns, my metal-roofed house and barn, my son and heir? What's going on? It just can't be true! And for some reason he remembered the wormwood tossing in the wind which he had twice passed and experienced such a feeling of terror that he did not believe that this was actually happening to him. He thought it must all be a dream and tried to wake up, but there was no other, waking world. It was real snow which lashed his face and settled on him and numbed his right hand whose glove he had lost; and this was a real wilderness, this place where he was now alone, like the wormwood, waiting for death, **inevitable**, swift and pointless.

Mother of Heaven, Holy Father Nicholas, thou who teachest the way of **abstinence**... he recalled the prayers said the day before, and the icon with the black face framed in the golden riza, [robe] and the candles he sold for lighting to this icon which were then promptly returned to him and stored away in a bin, scarcely used. And he begged this same Nicholas the miracle-worker to save him, and promised to offer prayers and candles to him. But at the same time he realized clearly and certainly that the face on the icon, the frame, the candles, the priest and the prayers were all very important and necessary *there,* in church, but that where he was they could do nothing for him, and that there was not and could not be any possible connection between these candles and prayers and his present desperate **plight**. I must not despair,

Vasilii Andreich is thinking of his wealth and property.

Icons are religious paintings, usually of Jesus or saints. They are considered holy images in Eastern Orthodox churches.

abstinence stopping oneself from doing something; self-denial	**inevitable** sure to happen	**sackcloth** rough, coarse cloth
coppice a dense growth of bushes; a small wood	**leasehold** property held by lease	**wethers** sheep
	plight a serious problem	**aright** correctly

he thought. And he had an idea. I must follow the tracks of the horse before they get covered. The horse will lead me **aright**. I might even catch him. The great thing is not to hurry or I'll get tired out and be worse off still. But despite his **intention** to go slowly, he hurried on and ran, continually falling and getting up and falling again. The horse tracks were already hard to see where there was no depth of snow. I'm done for, thought Vasilii Andreich. I can't follow the tracks and I'll never catch up with the horse. But at that very moment as he looked ahead he saw something black. It was Dapple—and not only Dapple, but also the sledge and the upright shafts with his kerchief. With the breeching and sackcloth pulled over to one side Dapple now stood where he had been before, only nearer the shafts; he was shaking his head, which was held down by the reins caught up in his leg. It turned out that Vasilii Andreich had got stuck in the same gully where he and Nikita had got stuck earlier; the horse was taking him back to the sledge and where he had jumped off was no more than fifty yards away from it.

Kerchief is another form of *handkerchief.*

intention aim; plan

Master and Man
Leo Tolstoy

Directions Write the answers to these questions using complete sentences.

Comprehension: Identifying Facts

1. What is Vasilii Andreich trying to reach?

2. What is the loud cry that he hears?

3. Whom does Vasilii Andreich beg to save him?

Comprehension: Understanding Main Ideas

4. Why isn't Vasilii Andreich getting where he wants to go?

5. Where does Vasilii Andreich finally find himself?

6. What does Vasilii Andreich think is going to happen?

Understanding Literature: Naturalism

Naturalism is a form of literature that deals with life's realities. Characters struggle against forces of nature. The strong survive and the weak do not. In some fiction of this type, the characters are helpless against events that are beyond their control. Nature is more powerful than humans.

7. What natural event is the setting for this story?

8. Point out an action showing how Vasilii Andreich struggles against nature.

Critical Thinking

9. What do you think of Vasilii Andreich as a person?

10. How does this story make you feel about the power of nature?

> **Writing on Your Own** Think of a real natural disaster you know about or have been through. (It might be a flood, storm, or hurricane.) Write a paragraph about the power of the event.

Just Lather, That's All

Hernando Téllez (translated by Donald A. Yates)

Hernando Téllez
(1908–1966)
Colombian

About the Author

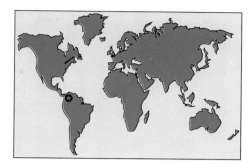

Hernando Téllez was born in Bogotá, Colombia, in 1908. He worked for several magazines and newspapers. Téllez also was active in the politics of Colombia. He served as a diplomat and a senator. As a writer, he is best known for a book of short stories *Ashes for the Wind and Other Tales* published in 1950. Téllez also wrote essays. "Just Lather, That's All" was made into a movie with the name "Just Lather, Please."

Literary Term

rising action the buildup of excitement in a story

About the Selection

The following story is set during a civil war. Captain Torres leads soldiers who hunt down rebels. He executes them in public. The barber is a secret member of the rebel group. He gets the perfect chance to kill his enemy, Captain Torres. The adventure takes place in the barber's mind. The **rising action** builds with every stroke of his razor against the captain's unprotected neck. The suspense builds and the reader feels the mood of violence in the town. Will the barber let the captain go? Will he kill him? What will happen if he does? What will happen if he doesn't?

Just Lather, That's All

Hernando Téllez

As you read, notice how the suspense builds. That is the rising action.

Is this story being told in first person or third person?

He said nothing when he entered. I was passing the best of my **razors** back and forth on a **strop**. When I recognized him I started to tremble. But he didn't notice. Hoping to conceal my emotion, I continued sharpening the razor. I tested it on the meat of my thumb, and then held it up to the light.

At that moment he took off the bullet-studded belt that his gun **holster** dangled from. He hung it up on a wall hook and placed his military cap over it. Then he turned to me, loosening the knot of his tie, and said, "It's hot as hell. Give me a shave." He sat in the chair.

I estimated he had a four-day beard—the four days taken up by the latest expedition in search of our troops. His face seemed reddened, burned by the sun. Carefully, I began to prepare the soap. I cut off a few slices, dropped them into the cup, mixed in a bit of warm water, and began to stir with the brush. Immediately the foam began to rise. "The other boys in the group should have this much beard, too," he remarked. I continued stirring the lather.

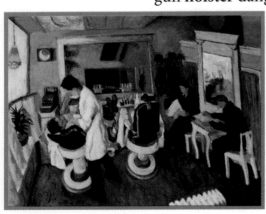

In the Barbershop, Ilya Bolotowsky, 1934. Estate of Ilya Bolotowsky/Licensed by VAGA, New York, NY.

holster a case for a pistol	**razor** an instrument used for shaving	**strop** a strip of leather used for sharpening razors

"But we did all right, you know. We got the main ones. We brought back some dead, and we got some others still alive. But pretty soon they'll all be dead."

"How many did you catch?" I asked.

"Fourteen. We had to go pretty deep into the woods to find them. But we'll get even. Not one of them comes out of this alive, not one."

He leaned back on the chair when he saw me with the lather-covered brush in my hand. I still had to put the sheet on him. No doubt about it, I was upset. I took a sheet out of a drawer and knotted it around his neck. He wouldn't stop talking. He probably thought I was in sympathy with his party.

"The town must have learned a lesson from what we did," he said.

"Yes," I replied, securing the knot at the base of his dark, sweaty neck.

"That was a fine show, eh?"

"Very good," I answered, turning back for the brush.

The man closed his eyes with a gesture of fatigue and sat waiting for the cool **caress** of the soap. I had never had him so close to me. The day he ordered the whole town to file into the patio of the school to see the four rebels hanging there, I came face to face with him for an instant. But the sight of the **mutilated** bodies kept me from noticing the face of the man who had directed it all, the face I was now about to take into my hands.

It was not an unpleasant face, and the beard, which made him look a bit older than he was, didn't suit him badly at all. His name was Torres—Captain Torres. A man of imagination, because who else would have thought of hanging the naked rebels and then holding target practice on their bodies?

Why was the barber upset? Who were the people the other man been hunting?

What does this detail tell you about *Captain Torres*?

caress a gentle touch	**mutilated** cut up; badly damaged

I began to apply the first layer of soap. With his eyes closed, he continued. "Without any effort I could go straight to sleep," he said, "but there's plenty to do this afternoon."

I stopped the lathering and asked with a **feigned** lack of interest, "A firing squad?"

"Something like that, but a little slower."

What problem is the barber facing?

I got on with the job of lathering his beard. My hands started trembling again. The man could not possibly realize it, and this was in my favor. But I would have preferred that he hadn't come. It was likely that many of our faction had seen him enter. And an enemy under one's roof imposes certain conditions.

I would be obliged to shave that beard like any other one, carefully, gently, like that of any customer, taking pains to see that no single pore **emitted** a drop of blood. Being careful to see that the little **tufts** of hair did not lead the blade astray. Seeing that his skin ended up clean, soft, and healthy, so that passing the back of my hand over it I couldn't feel a hair. Yes, I was secretly a rebel, but I was also a **conscientious** barber, and proud of the **precision** required of my profession.

I took the razor, opened up the two protective arms, exposed the blade, and began the job—from one of the sideburns downward. The razor responded beautifully. His beard was **inflexible** and hard, not too long, but thick. Bit by bit the skin emerged. The razor **rasped** along, making its customary sound as fluffs of lather, mixed with bits of hair, gathered along the blade.

I paused a moment to clean it, then took up the strop again to sharpen the razor, because I'm a barber who does things properly. The man, who had kept his eyes closed, opened them now, removed one of his hands from under the sheet, felt the spot on his face where the soap had been cleared off, and said, "Come to the school today at six o'clock."

conscientious careful to do things right	**feign** to pretend	**rasp** scrape with a harsh sound
emit send out	**inflexible** stiff; rigid	**tuft** a small clump of hair
	precision exactness	

"The same thing as the other day?" I asked, horrified.

"It could be even better," he said.

"What do you plan to do?"

"I don't know yet. But we'll amuse ourselves." Once more he leaned back and closed his eyes. I approached with the razor **poised**.

"Do you plan to punish them all?" I ventured timidly.

"All."

The soap was drying on his face. I had to hurry. In the mirror I looked towards the street. It was the same as ever—the grocery store with two or three customers in it. Then I glanced at the clock— 2:20 in the afternoon.

The razor continued on its downward stroke. Now from the other sideburn down. A thick, blue beard. He should have let it grow like some poets or priests do. It would suit him well. A lot of people wouldn't recognize him. Much to his benefit, I thought, as I attempted to cover the neck areas smoothly.

Why might Torres not want to be recognized?

There, surely, the razor had to be handled masterfully, since the hair, although softer, grew into little swirls. A curly beard. One of the tiny pores could open up and issue forth its pearl of blood, but a good barber prides himself on never allowing this to happen to a customer.

How many of us had he ordered shot? How many of us had he ordered mutilated? It was better not to think about it. Torres did not know that I was his enemy. He did not know it

poised held up; balanced

nor did the rest. It was a secret shared by very few, precisely so that I could inform the revolutionaries of what Torres was doing in the town and of what he was planning each time he undertook a rebel-hunting **excursion**.

So it was going to be very difficult to explain that I had him right in my hands and let him go peacefully—alive and shaved.

The beard was now almost completely gone. He seemed younger, less burdened by years than when he had arrived. I suppose this always happens with men who visit barber shops. Under the stroke of my razor Torres was being **rejuvenated**—rejuvenated because I am a good barber, the best in the town, if I may say so.

How hot it is getting! Torres must be sweating as much as I. But he is a calm man, who is not even thinking about what he is going to do with the prisoners this afternoon. On the other hand I, with this razor in my hands—I stroking and restroking this skin, can't even think clearly.

Damn him for coming! I'm a revolutionary, not a **murderer**. And how easy it would be to kill him. And he deserves it. Does he? No! What the devil! No one deserves to have someone else make the sacrifice of becoming a murderer. What do you gain by it? Nothing. Others come along and still others, and the first ones kill the second ones, and they the next ones—and it goes on like this until everything is a sea of blood.

I could cut this throat just so—*zip, zip!* I wouldn't give him time to resist and since he has his eyes closed he wouldn't see the glistening blade or my glistening eyes. But I'm trembling like a real murderer. Out of his neck a gush of blood would sprout onto the sheet, on the chair, on my hands, on the floor. I would have to close the door. And the blood would keep inching along the floor, warm, **ineradicable**, uncontainable, until it reached the street, like a little scarlet stream.

---

excursion a trip; an expedition

ineradicable impossible to erase or remove

murderer someone who kills another person

rejuvenate to restore youth or energy

I'm sure that one solid stroke, one deep **incision**, would prevent any pain. He wouldn't suffer. But what would I do with the body? Where would I hide it? I would have to flee, leaving all I have behind, and take refuge far away. But they would follow until they found me. "Captain Torres' murderer. He slit his throat while he was shaving him—a coward."

And then on the other side. "The avenger of us all. A name to remember. He was the town barber. No one knew he was defending our cause."

Murderer or hero? My **destiny** depends on the edge of this blade. I can turn my hand a bit more, press a little harder on the razor, and sink it in. The skin would give way like silk, like rubber. There is nothing more tender than human skin and the blood is always there, ready to pour forth.

But I don't want to be a murderer. You came to me for a shave. And I perform my work honorably...I don't want blood on my hands. Just lather, that's all. You are an executioner and I am only a barber. Each person has his own place in the scheme of things.

Now his chin had been stroked clean and smooth. The man sat up and looked into the mirror. He rubbed his hands over his skin and felt it fresh, like new.

"Thanks," he said. He went to the hanger for his belt, pistol, and cap. I must have been very pale; my shirt felt soaked. Torres finished adjusting the buckle, straightened his pistol in the holster, and after automatically smoothing down his hair, he put on the cap. From his pants pocket he took out several coins to pay me for my services and then headed for the door.

In the doorway he paused for a moment and said, "They told me that you'd kill me. I came to find out. But killing isn't easy. You can take my word for it." And he turned and walked away.

Why does the barber decide not to kill the captain?

Does the ending surprise you?

destiny fate	**incision** a thin cut

Directions Write the answers to these questions using complete sentences.

Comprehension: Identifying Facts

1. What does Captain Torres want in the barber shop?

2. What has Captain Torres done to the barber's political friends?

3. Where has he been for four days?

Comprehension: Understanding Main Ideas

4. What does the barber have to decide?

5. What will happen at the school at six o'clock?

6. Why does the barber make the decision he makes?

Understanding Literature: Rising Action

Rising action is the build-up of excitement in the story. It takes place as the story introduces a conflict. The action then builds to a climax or turning point.

7. What is the conflict in this story?

8. What is the turning point in this story?

Critical Thinking

9. Do you think the barber did the right thing? Why or why not?

10. What does Captain Torres say as he leaves? What do you think he means?

Writing on Your Own What if the barber had killed Torres? Write a paragraph telling what might have happened.

Turning Points

- "Youth was serious, but not entirely fatal." —Rosario Castellanos
- "Now it seems to me...that one can *choose* to become an adult, but only at given moments."
  —Nick Hornby

The experiences of characters often move the plot toward an exciting ending, or denouement. Or an experience may show an important part of their personalities. When an experience changes a character's life, the story belongs to a genre called turning points.

Turning points are often events that, at the time, seem frightening or confusing. The character does not understand the event's importance right away; only later does he or she understand. For this reason, the narrator's point of view is important in these stories. Point of view refers to who is telling the story. If the events happen to the narrator, the first-person point of view is used. This point of view has limits, such as the narrator's age or intelligence. Sometimes a story is told by someone who is not part of it. This known as the third-person point of view.

Turning points seem to have the most effect on young people. For that reason, turning points about young people are sometimes called "coming of age" or "initiation" stories. Only as adults can these characters finally see what a childhood experience meant. They can then understand and explain it.

Nervous Conditions
Tsitsi Dangarembga

Tsitsi Dangarembga
(1959–)
Zimbabwean

Literary Term

coming-of-age story
a story that tells how a
young person matures

About the Author

Tsitsi Dangarembga was born in 1959 in Zimbabwe (then called Rhodesia.) She spent her childhood in England, where her parents were studying. In 1965, she returned to Zimbabwe and

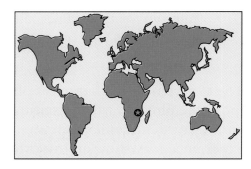

went to a mission school. Dangarembga went back to England to study medicine at Cambridge University. She also studied psychology at the University of Zimbabwe. She then became a full-time writer. *Nervous Conditions* was written when Dangarembga was twenty-five years old. It was not published immediately. It won the Commonwealth Writers Prize in 1989. She has also written three plays. Dangarembga now lives in Germany. She is studying film and working on another novel.

About the Selection

This **coming-of-age story** is about Tambudzai, a young black girl who lives in 1960's Rhodesia. Babamukuru, her rich uncle, offers her a chance to go to school. She wants a better education. But each step weakens her ties to her family and way of life. The story explores many themes. One theme is power. In her family, some members have power over others. In the culture, men have power over women. Colonial schools conflict with traditional ways.

In the following selection, Tambudzai is talking with her cousin Nyasha. Nyasha's parents lived in England, where Nyasha grew up. Now Nyasha feels at home nowhere. She seems too English to be accepted by her relatives at home. White society does not accept her either. Nyasha warns Tambudzai against going to a school run by whites. Her uncle has some doubts. Tambudzai must decide what to do.

NERVOUS CONDITIONS
TSITSI DANGAREMBGA

Of course, I did not appreciate the gravity of my situation at that time, my only experience of those people having been with **charitable** Doris and the **fervent** missionaries on the mission. But Nyasha knew them and was alarmed. She could not hide, did not even try to hide, her disappointment when I told her how thrilled I was, what an experience I would have, what an opportunity it was, how I intended to put that opportunity to **maximum** use. She thought there were more evils than advantages to be reaped from such an opportunity. It would be a marvellous opportunity, she said **sarcastically**, to forget. To forget who you were, what you were and why you were that. The process, she said, was called **assimilation**, and that was what was intended for the **precocious** few who might prove a nuisance if left to themselves, **whereas** the others—well really, who cared about the others? So they made a little space into which you were assimilated, an honorary space in which you could join them and they could make sure that you behaved yourself. I would be comfortable in such a position, she remarked nastily, because look how well I had got on with Babamukuru. But, she insisted, one ought not to occupy that space. Really, one ought to refuse. In my case that meant not going to the nun's mission. "You'll fall for their

As you read, watch for ways in which Tambudzai grows up.

Marvellous is the British spelling of *marvelous*. Look for other British spellings.

Nyasha is speaking from her own experience.

---

assimilation being taken in by a group

charitable generous

fervent showing deep feeling

maximum the greatest possible amount

precocious showing ability at an earlier age than usual

sarcastically mockingly

whereas while at the same time

Tambudzai's uncle also runs a *mission* with a school. It is for black children only.

tricks," she said, pointing out that I would obtain a much more useful education at the mission.

If she hadn't said that, that last bit about education at the mission, I might have believed her, but everybody knew that

the European schools had better equipment, better teachers, better furniture, better food, better everything. The idea that anything about our mission could be better than theirs was clearly ridiculous. Besides, once you were given a place at one of their schools, you went on and on until you'd finished your "A" levels. You didn't have to worry about eliminating exams at every stage of the way. That was how it was. That was how it would be. If you were clever, you slipped through any **loophole** you could find. I for one was going to take any opportunity that came my way. I was quite sure about that; I was very determined. The latest opportunity was this one of going to the **convent**. I would go. I was sure of myself. I was not **sceptical** like Nyasha. How could I possibly forget my brother and the mealies, my mother and the **latrine** and the wedding? These were all evidence of the burdens my mother had **succumbed** to.

In some schools, students had to take exams at certain grades. If they failed, they could not go higher.

Mealies is corn that can be eaten.

convent a community of nuns	**loophole** a way out of a difficult situation	**succumb** to give in to
latrine an outdoor toilet	**sceptical** (Amer. skeptical) doubting	

Going to the convent was a chance to lighten those burdens by entering a world where burdens were light. I would take the chance. I would lighten my burdens. I would go. If Babamukuru would let me.

Still Nyasha was not impressed. "Really, Tambudzai," she said severely when I had finished **glorifying** my interests, "there'll always be brothers and mealies and mothers too tired to clean latrines. Whether you go to the convent or not. There's more to be done than that." This was typical of Nyasha, this **obstinate idealism**. But she could afford it, being my **affluent** uncle's daughter. Whereas I, I had to take whatever chances came my way.

Babamukuru was of the opinion that enough chances had come my way, and on another level he agreed with Nyasha that the experience would not be good for me. From his armchair opposite the fireplace he told me why I could not go to the convent.

"It is not a question of money," he assured me. "Although there would still be a lot of expense on my part, you have your scholarship, so the major **financial** burden would be lifted. But I feel that even that little money could be better used. For one thing, there is now the small boy at home. Every month I put away a little bit, a very little bit, a very little bit every month, so that when he is of school-going age everything will be provided for. As you know, he is the only boy in your family, so he must be provided for. As for you, we think we are providing for you quite well. By the time you have finished your Form Four you will be able to take

Boys and girls were not treated equally at this time and this place.

affluent rich; having plenty of money	**glorify** to give honor or high praise	**obstinate** stubborn
financial having to do with money	**idealism** belief that things can be perfect	

your course, whatever it is that you choose. In time you will be earning money. You will be in a position to be married by a decent man and set up a decent home. In all that we are doing for you, we are preparing you for this future life of yours, and I have observed from my own daughter's behaviour that it is not a good thing for a young girl to associate too much with these white people, to have too much freedom. I have seen that girls who do that do not develop into decent women."

Marriage. I had nothing against it in principle. In an **abstract** way I thought it was a very good idea. But it was **irritating** the way it always cropped up in one form or another, stretching its tentacles back to bind me before I had even begun to think about it seriously, threatening to **disrupt** my life before I could even call it my own. Babamukuru had lost me with his talk of marriage. I inspected my dressing-gown for fluff, waiting for the session to end. "This," continued my uncle, "is what I shall tell your father: if he wishes to send you there to that school, he may do so if he can find the money. Myself, I would not consider it money well spent. Mai," he concluded, turning to my aunt, "is there anything that you would wish to say?"

Why is Tambudzai surprised when her aunt chooses to speak?

"Yes, Baba," Maiguru spoke up softly from the sofa. My inspection came to an abrupt end. I listened **incredulously**.

"You do!" exclaimed Babamukuru and, recovering himself, invited her to continue. "Speak freely, Mai. Say whatever you are thinking."

There was a pause during which Maiguru folded her arms and leant back in the sofa. "I don't think," she began easily in her soft, soothing voice, "that Tambudzai will be **corrupted** by going to that school. Don't you remember, when we went to

abstract not practical; not related to real life	**disrupt** to upset or interfere	**incredulously** in surprise; not believing
corrupt spoil; to make less honest or moral		**irritating** annoying

South Africa everybody was saying that we, the women, were loose." Babamukuru winced at this **explicitness**. Maiguru continued. "It wasn't a question of **associating** with this race or that race at that time. People were **prejudiced** against educated women. Prejudiced. That's why they said we weren't decent. That was in the fifties. Now we are into the seventies. I am disappointed that people still believe the same things. After all this time and when we have seen nothing to say it is true. I don't know what people mean by a loose woman—sometimes she is someone who walks the streets, sometimes she is an educated woman, sometimes she is a successful man's daughter or she is simply beautiful. Loose or decent, I don't know. All I know is that if our daughter Tambudzai is not a decent person now, she never will be, no matter where she goes to school. And if she is decent, then this convent should not change her. As for money, you have said yourself that she has a full scholarship. It is possible that you have other reasons why she should not go there, Babawa Chido, but these—the question of decency and the question of money—are the ones I have heard and so these are the ones I have talked of."

There was another pause during which Maiguru unfolded her arms and clasped her hands in her lap.

Babamukuru cleared his throat. "Er, Tambudzai," he asked **tentatively**, "do you have anything to say?"...

It was on New Year's Eve that my uncle and my father discussed my future. The discussion took place in the house. I was obliged to **eavesdrop**.

"It may change her character for the worse...these Whites, you know...you never know," mused Babamukuru.

"No," agreed my father. "How could you know with these ones? You never know. With Whites! No. You never know."

Is Nyasha included in this description of *loose women*?

associating being with; keeping company	**explicitness** a very frank or clear statement	**tentatively** with hesitation
eavesdrop to listen secretly	**prejudice** an unfair strong feeling toward a group	

"On the other hand," continued my uncle, "she would receive a first-class education."

"Ah, ya, Mukoma, first class. First class," my father **enthused**.

"I did not want her to go to that school..." said Babamukuru.

"What for, Mukoma? Why should she go there? Your mission is first class."

"...because of the reasons I have told you," continued my uncle. "But then, considering that this is a fine opportunity for the girl to receive the finest education in Rhodesia, I think she must not be denied the opportunity. I have decided to let her go."

My father went down on one knee. Bo-bo-bo. "We thank you, Chirandu, we thank you, Muera bonga, Chihwa" he **intoned**. "Truly, we would not **survive** without you. Our children would not survive without you. Head of the family, princeling, we thank you."

This is how it was settled. I was to take another step upwards in the direction of my freedom. Another step away from the flies, the smells, the fields and the rags; from stomachs which were seldom full, from dirt and disease, from my father's **abject obeisance** to Babamukuru and my mother's **chronic lethargy**. Also from Nyamarira that I loved.

Rhodesia is now called Zimbabwe.

abject humble; without self-respect	**enthuse** to show excitement or interest	**lethargy** drowsiness; slowness
chronic constant; continuing	**intone** to speak in a chant	**obeisance** a respectful gesture or attitude
		survive to stay alive

Nervous Conditions
Tsitsi Dangarembga

Directions Write the answers to these questions using complete sentences.

Comprehension: Identifying Facts

1. Who runs the school Tambudzai wants to go to?

2. Who is Babamukuru?

3. Who speaks up in favor of the school?

Comprehension: Understanding Main Ideas

4. What is Tambudzai's family discussing?

5. Why does Tambudzai want to go away to school?

6. Why does Nyasha think Tambudzai should not go to the convent school?

Understanding Literature: Coming-of-Age Story

This is a coming-of-age story. The main character, Tambudzai, experiences new events that help her grow up. She learns that choosing a school is not just about whether her family can afford it. She learns about the power of those who make decisions. She also learns about prejudice.

7. How does Tambudzai find out what the family is saying about her and the school?

8. What does Tambudzai learn about herself when her uncle talks about marriage?

Critical Thinking

9. Why is it Babamukuru who makes the decision about the school?

10. Why does Babamukuru finally say Tambudzai can go to the convent school?

Writing on Your Own Write a brief description of a person who learns something important. This can be the beginning of a coming-of-age story. It might be about yourself or someone you know. Or, it can be entirely made up. Think about how the character will change because of the experience.

Marriage Is a Private Affair
Chinua Achebe

**Chinua Achebe
(1930–)
Nigerian**

Literary Term

third-person a point of view that refers to characters as "he" or "she" and expresses some characters' thoughts

About the Author

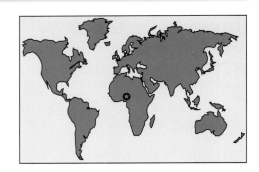

Chinua Achebe is one of Nigeria's most popular writers. He was born in Ogidi, Nigeria, on November 16, 1930. He graduated from the University College at Ibadan in 1953. He was a teacher and has worked in radio. Achebe often writes about a conflict between traditional African culture and new ideas. His first novel, in 1958, was *Things Fall Apart*. Others are *No Longer at Ease* and *A Man of the People*. He also writes poems and short stories. Achebe writes in English. His books have been translated into many other languages.

About the Selection

Achebe looks at conflicts between customs. A young Nigerian, Nnaemeka, plans to marry Nene. She is city-bred and from another tribe. Back in his home town, Nnaemeka's father Okeke has already chosen a wife for Nnaemeka. Nnaemeka still marries Nene. Okeke believes in tradition and is angry when his son defies his wishes. He will have nothing to do with the new wife. The son and father in this story are Ibos, which is one of Nigeria's many large tribal groups. (The author is also Ibo.) The story reveals how old customs continue. It is told in **third-person**.

Marriage Is a Private Affair

Chinua Achebe

"Have you written to your dad yet?" asked Nene one afternoon as she sat with Nnaemeka in her room at 16 Kasanga Street, Lagos.

"No. I've been thinking about it. I think it's better to tell him when I get home on **leave!**"

"But why? Your leave is such a long way off yet—six whole weeks. He should be let into our happiness now."

Nnaemeka was silent for a while, and then began very slowly as if he groped for his words: "I wish I were sure it would be happiness to him."

"Of course it must," replied Nene, a little surprised. "Why shouldn't it?"

"You have lived in Lagos all your life, and you know very little about people in remote parts of the country."

"That's what you always say. But I don't believe anybody will be so unlike other people that they will be unhappy when their sons are engaged to marry."

"Yes. They are most unhappy if the engagement is not arranged by them. In our case it's worse—you are not even an Ibo."

This was said so seriously and so bluntly that Nene could not find speech immediately. In the **cosmopolitan** atmosphere of the city it had always seemed to her something of a joke that a person's tribe could determine whom he married.

cosmopolitan including people from many places

leave a vacation; permission to be away from work

At last she said, "You don't really mean that he will object to your marrying me simply on that account? I had always thought you Ibos were kindly disposed to other people."

"So we are. But when it comes to marriage, well, it's not quite so simple. And this," he added, "is not peculiar to the Ibos. If your father were alive and lived in the heart of Ibibio-land he would be exactly like my father."

"I don't know. But anyway, as your father is so fond of you, I'm sure he will forgive you soon enough. Come on then, be a good boy and send him a nice lovely letter..."

In Nnaemeka's tribe, parents chose marriage partners for their children. This is called an arranged marriage.

"It would not be wise to break the news to him by writing. A letter will bring it upon him with a shock. I'm quite sure about that."

"All right, honey, suit yourself. You know your father."

As Nnaemeka walked home that evening he turned over in his mind the different ways of overcoming his father's opposition, especially now that he had gone and found a girl for him. He had thought of showing his letter to Nene but decided on second thoughts not to, at least for the moment. He read it again when he got home and couldn't help smiling to himself. He remembered Ugoye quite well, an Amazon of a girl who used to beat up all the boys, himself included, on the way to the stream, a complete **dunce** at school.

In Greek mythology, an *Amazon* was a woman warrior.

I have found a girl who will suit you admirably—Ugoye Nweke, the eldest daughter of our neighbour, Jacob Nweke. She has a proper Christian upbringing. When she stopped schooling some years ago her father (a man of sound judgment) sent her to live in the house of a **pastor** *where she has received all the training a wife could need. Her Sunday School teacher has told me that she reads her Bible very*

dunce a stupid person   **pastor** a Christian minister *fluently. I hope we shall begin **negotiations** when you come home in December.*

On the second evening of his return from Lagos Nnaemeka sat with his father under a cassia tree. This was the old man's retreat where he went to read his Bible when the **parching** December sun had set and a fresh, reviving wind blew on the leaves.

"Father," began Nnaemeka suddenly, "I have come to ask forgiveness."

"Forgiveness? For what, my son?" he asked in amazement.

"It's about this marriage question."

"Which marriage question?"

"I can't—we must—I mean it is impossible for me to marry Nweke's daughter."

"Impossible? Why?" asked his father.

"I don't love her."

"Nobody said you did. Why should you?" he asked.

"Marriage today is different..."

"Look here, my son," interrupted his father, "nothing is different. What one looks for in a wife are a good character and a Christian background."

Nnaemeka saw there was no hope along the present line of argument.

"Moreover," he said, "I am engaged to marry another girl who has all of Ugoye's good qualities, and who . . ."

His father did not believe his ears. "What did you say?" he asked slowly and **disconcertingly**.

"She is a good Christian," his son went on, "and a teacher in a Girls' School in Lagos."

"Teacher, did you say? If you consider that a **qualification** for a good wife I should like to point out to you, Emeka, that no Christian woman should teach. St. Paul in his letter to the Corinthians says that women should keep silence." He rose slowly from his seat and paced forwards and backwards. This was his pet

St. Paul wrote letters to the church at Corinth. They make up two books of the New Testament of the Christian Bible.

disconcertingly in an upsetting way	**negotiations** discussions leading to an agreement	**qualification** an ability that suits a person for a certain task
fluently using language easily	**parching** very dry	

subject, and he condemned **vehemently** those church leaders who encouraged women to teach in their schools. After he had spent his emotion on a long **homily** he at last came back to his son's engagement, in a seemingly milder tone.

Note that the father is not interested in the woman herself. He only wants to know about her family.

"Whose daughter is she, anyway?"

"She is Nene Atang."

"What!" All the mildness was gone again. "Did you say Neneataga, what does that mean?"

"Nene Atang from Calabar. She is the only girl I can marry." This was a very **rash** reply and Nnaemeka expected the storm to burst. But it did not. His father merely walked away into his room. This was most unexpected and perplexed Nnaemeka. His father's silence was **infinitely** more menacing than a flood of threatening speech. That night the old man did not eat.

When he sent for Nnaemeka a day later he applied all possible ways of **dissuasion**. But the young man's heart was hardened, and his father eventually gave him up as lost.

"I owe it to you, my son, as a duty to show you what is right and what is wrong. Whoever put this idea into your head might as well have cut your throat. It is Satan's work." He waved his son away.

"You will change your mind, Father, when you know Nene."

"I shall never see her," was the reply. From that night the father scarcely spoke to his son. He did not, however, cease hoping that he would realize how serious was the danger he was heading for. Day and night he put him in his prayers.

Nnaemeka, for his own part, was very deeply affected by his father's grief. But he kept hoping that it would pass away. It if had occurred to him that never in the history of his people had a man married a woman who spoke a different tongue, he might have been less optimistic. "It has never been heard," was the verdict of an old man speaking a few weeks later. In that short sentence he spoke for all of his people. This man had come with others to **commiserate** with Okeke when news went round about his son's behaviour. By that time the son had gone back to Lagos.

commiserate to express sorrow and sympathy	**dissuasion** discouraging someone from an action	**infinitely** without any limits
	homily a sermon	**rash** bold; hasty
		vehemently with strong emotion

"It has never been heard," said the old man again with a sad shake of his head.

Note that the entire village is concerned.

"What did Our Lord say?" asked another gentleman. "Sons shall rise against their Fathers; it is there in the Holy Book."

"It is the beginning of the end," said another.

The discussion thus tending to become **theological**, Madubogwu, a highly practical man, brought it down once more to the ordinary level.

"Have you thought of consulting a native doctor about your son?" he asked Nnaemeka's father.

"He isn't sick," was the reply.

"What is he then? The boy's mind is diseased and only a good **herbalist** can bring him back to his right senses. The medicine he requires is *Amalile,* the same that women apply with success to recapture their husbands' straying affection."

"Madubogwu is right," said another gentleman. "This thing calls for medicine."

"I shall not call in a native doctor." Nnaemeka's father was known to be **obstinately** ahead of his more superstitious neighbours in these matters. "I will not be another Mrs. Ochuba. If my son wants to kill himself let him do it with his own hands. It is not for me to help him."

Nnaemeka's father does not hold with every tradition among the Ibo.

"But it was her fault," said Madubogwu. "She ought to have gone to an honest herbalist. She was a clever woman, **nevertheless**."

"She was a wicked **murderess**," said Jonathan who rarely argued with his neighbours because, he often said, they were **incapable** of reasoning. "The medicine was prepared for her husband, it was his name they called in its preparation and I am sure it would have been perfectly **beneficial** to him. It was wicked to put it into the herbalist's food, and say you were only trying it out."

Six months later, Nnaemeka was showing his young wife a short letter from his father:

beneficial doing good; helpful	**incapable** without the ability	**nevertheless** all the same
herbalist a person who makes medicines from herbs	**murderess** a woman who kills someone	**obstinately** stubbornly
		theological related to the study of religion

It amazes me that you could be so unfeeling as to send me your wedding picture. I would have sent it back. But on further thought I decided just to cut off your wife and send it back to you because I have nothing to do with her. How I wish that I had nothing to do with you either.

When Nene read through this letter and looked at the **mutilated** picture her eyes filled with tears, and she began to sob.

"Don't cry, my darling," said her husband. "He is essentially good-natured and will one day look more kindly on our marriage." But years passed and that one day did not come.

For eight years, Okeke would have nothing to do with his son, Nnaemeka. Only three times (when Nnaemeka asked to come home and spend his leave) did he write to him.

"I can't have you in my house," he replied on one occasion. "It can be of no interest to me where or how you spend your leave—or your life, for that matter."

The prejudice against Nnaemeka's marriage was not confined to his little village. In Lagos, especially among his people who worked there, it showed itself in a different way. Their women, when they met at their village meeting were not **hostile** to Nene. Rather, they paid her such **excessive deference** as to make her feel she was not one of them. But as time went on, Nene gradually broke through some of this prejudice and even began to make friends among them. Slowly and **grudgingly** they began to admit that she kept her home much better than most of them.

Do you think that Nnaemeka and Nene are strong people? Why or why not?

The story eventually got to the little village in the heart of the Ibo country that Nnaemeka and his young wife were a most happy couple. But his father was one of the few people who knew nothing about this. He always displayed so much temper whenever his son's name was mentioned that everyone avoided it in his presence. By a tremendous effort of will he had succeeded in pushing his son to the back of his mind. The strain had nearly killed him but he had **persevered**, and won.

Then one day he received a letter from Nene, and in spite of himself he began to glance through it **perfunctorily** until all of a

deference courteous respect	**hostile** angrily opposed to	**perfunctorily** without thought or care
excessive too much	**mutilated** cut up; damaged	**persevere** to carry on in spite of difficulties
grudgingly unwillingly		

sudden the expression on his face changed and he began to read more carefully.

*...Our two sons, from the day they learnt that they have a grandfather, have insisted on being taken to him. I find it impossible to tell them that you will not see them. I **implore** you to allow Nnaemeka to bring them home for a short time during his leave next month. I shall remain here in Lagos....*

The old man at once felt the resolution he had built up over so many years falling in. He was telling himself that he must not give in. He tried to steel his heart against all emotional appeals. It was a **re-enactment** of that other struggle. He leaned against a window and looked out. The sky was overcast with heavy black clouds and a high wind began to blow filling the air with dust and dry leaves. It was one of those rare occasions when even Nature takes a hand in a human fight. Very soon it began to rain, the first rain in the year. It came down in large sharp drops and was accompanied by the lightning and thunder which mark a change of season. Okeke was trying hard not to think of his two grandsons. But he knew he was now fighting a losing battle. He tried to hum a favourite hymn but the pattering of large rain drops on the roof broke up the tune. His mind immediately returned to the children. How could he shut his door against them? By a curious mental process he imagined them standing, sad and **forsaken,** under the harsh angry weather—shut out from his house.

That night he hardly slept, from **remorse**—and a vague fear that he might die without making it up to them.

How is the weather like what is going on in Okeke's heart?

---

forsaken abandoned; left alone

implore to beg

re-enactment acting out something that happened once before

remorse regret for having done something harmful

Marriage Is a Private Affair
Chinua Achebe

Directions Write the answers to these questions using complete sentences.

Comprehension: Identifying Facts

1. Where do Nnaemeka and Nene live? Have they always lived there?

2. What is Nnaemeka's tribe?

3. Why does Nnaemeka want to tell his father about their engagement in person?

4. Whom does Nnaemeka's father want him to marry?

5. What two things does the father say are important in a wife?

6. What does Okeke, the father, do with the wedding picture?

7. What story gets back to the village about Nene and Nnaemeka?

8. Why doesn't Okeke know about the story?

9. Why does Nene write to Okeke?

10. What does Okeke worry about that night?

Comprehension: Understanding Main Ideas

11. Why does Nene think Nnaemeka should write to his father?

12. Why does Nene think the tribal difference won't matter?

13. How does Okeke expect his son to get a wife?

14. Why does Nnaemeka ask for his father's forgiveness?

15. Why does Okeke object to women being teachers?

16. How does Nnaemeka react to his father's grief?

17. How do the other men in the village feel about Nnaemeka's marriage?

18. In what way is Okeke less traditional than other men in the village?

19. How does Nene get along with the Ibo women in Lagos?

20. What changes Okeke's mind about the marriage?

Understanding Literature: Third-Person

"Marriage Is a Private Affair" is a third-person story. The writer speaks of all the characters as "he" or "she." The reader knows the thoughts and actions of the major characters. A third-person story can show what is going on in Lagos with Nene and Nnaemeka. It can also show what is going on in the village with Okeke and his friends. The ideas of all the main characters are clear. So are the ideas of some less important characters.

21. Whose thoughts does the reader know about?

22. Who is the first person whose thoughts the reader knows? Who is the last?

23. How does the reader know what the villagers think?

24. If the story were told in the first-person, who would the narrator probably be? Explain.

25. Who writes the letters in the story?

Critical Thinking

26. How was Nnaemeka's boyhood different from the way Nene grew up?

27. How does Nnaemeka feel about the letter from his father?

28. In what way is Nnaemeka surprised by his father's reaction?

29. What happened when the village woman consulted the herbalist?

30. How does Okeke feel at the end of the story?

Writing on Your Own Write the beginning of a story. Use the third-person. In your beginning, show that there will be several characters and situations. Share your story beginning with a partner.

Cranes

Hwang Sun-won (translated by J. Martin Holman)

Hwang Sun-won
(1915–)
Korean

Literary Terms

style an author's way of writing

symbol a person, place, or thing that represents an idea or thought

About the Author

Hwang Sun-won was born near Pyongyang, Korea. After World War II, Korea was divided. In 1946, his family moved from the Soviet-occupied north to South Korea. Hwang Sun-won lived through the Korean War in the 1950s. These wartime experiences affected his writing. Hwang Sun-won is a major figure in modern Korean literature. From 1957 to 1993, he taught Korean literature at Kyung Hee University in Seoul, South Korea. He is known as a master of the short story. He has also written novels and poems. His novel *Trees on the Cliff* won a major award in Korea. It has been published in English. Hwang Sun-won lives in Seoul with his wife.

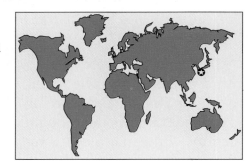

About the Selection

"Cranes" is the story of friends divided by war. Its setting is divided Korea. One man, Tok-jae, is a North Korean communist. He has been taken prisoner by the South Korean army. The other is a South Korean soldier, Song-sam. Song-sam is to take Tok-jae for questioning. But he recognizes an old childhood friend. The two grew up together, but the war separated them. Song-sam is full of hatred toward his old friend.

"Cranes" has many **symbols**. Think about the divided country and the Demilitarized Zone. Notice the symbol of the captured crane and its flight. Also pay attention to the author's **style**. It is simple but says much more than the words. Hwang Sun-won's understanding of people comes through clearly.

CRANES

HWANG SUN-WON

The village just north of the thirty-eighth parallel was quiet beneath the clear, **lofty** autumn sky.

A white **gourd** lay where it had tumbled, leaning against another on the dirt-floored space between the rooms of an **abandoned** house.

An old man Song-sam happened to meet put his long tobacco pipe behind his back. The children, as children would, had already fled from the street to keep their distance. Everyone's face was masked with fear.

Overall, the village showed few signs of the **conflict** that had just ended. Still, it did not seem to Song-sam to be the same village where he had grown up.

He stopped walking at a grove of **chestnut** trees on the hill behind the village. He climbed one of the trees. In his mind, from far away, he could hear the shouts of the old man with a **wen**. Are you kids climbing my chestnut tree again?

Had that old man died during Song-sam's absence? He had not seen him among the men he had met so far in the village. Hanging onto the

As you read, notice the author's style, or way of writing.

The *thirty-eighth parallel,* or line of latitude, is the dividing line between North and South Korea.

abandoned no longer lived in

chestnut a type of tree that has nuts enclosed in a prickly casing

conflict a battle; the fighting

gourd a kind of vegetable that grows on a vine

lofty high

wen a small growth on the skin

Read on to see why *Song-sam* has been away from the village.

tree, Song-sam looked up at the clear autumn sky. Though he did not shake the branch, some of the remaining chestnut **burrs** burst open, and the nuts fell to the ground.

When he reached the house that was being used temporarily as the Public Peace Office, he found someone there bound tightly with rope. This was the first young man he had seen in the village. As Song-sam drew closer and examined his face, he was **taken aback**. It was none other than his boyhood friend Tok-jae.

Song-sam asked one of the security guards from his **detachment** who had accompanied him from Ch'ont'ae what the situation was. The guard answered that the prisoner had been vice-chairman of the Communist Farmers' Alliance and that he had just been captured while hiding in his own house here in the village.

Song-sam squatted by the house and lit a cigarette. Tok-jae was to be escorted to Ch'ongdan by one of the young security guards.

After a while Song-sam lit a cigarette from the one he had been smoking, then stood up.

"I'll take the guy myself."

Tok-jae kept his face turned away; he did not even glance at Song-sam.

They left the village.

Song-sam kept smoking, but he could not taste the tobacco. He just sucked and puffed. He suddenly realized that Tok-jae might like a smoke. He **recalled** when they were boys how they had shared a smoke of dried pumpkin leaves, hiding from the adults in the corner of the wall around the house. But how could he offer a guy like this a cigarette?

Why does Song-sam think of Tok-jae as *a guy like this*?

Once, when they were boys, he had gone with Tok-jae to steal chestnuts from the old man with the wen. Song-sam was taking his turn climbing the tree when suddenly they heard the old man shouting. Song-sam slid down the tree and got chestnut burrs stuck in his rear end. Yet he **dashed** off without doing anything about them. Once they had run far enough that the old man could

burr a rough or prickly covering around a nut	**detachment** a small military unit of soldiers	**recall** to remember
dash to run quickly		**taken aback** startled

not catch them, he turned his backside toward Tok-jae. It hurt even more to have the prickly chestnut **spines** pulled out. Tears ran freely down Song-sam's face. Tok-jae held out a fistful of his own chestnuts, then thrust them into Song-sam's pocket.

Song-sam had just lit a cigarette from the last one he had smoked, but he tossed it away. He made up his mind not to smoke anymore while he was escorting...Tok-jae.

They reached the mountain ridge road. He had often come to the ridge with Tok-jae to cut **fodder** before Song-sam moved to the area around Ch'ont'ae, south of the thirty-eighth parallel, two years before the Liberation in 1945.

The 1945 *Liberation* freed Korea from Japanese rule. Japan had been defeated in World War II. American troops occupied the south, below the thirty-eighth parallel. Soviet troops occupied the north.

Song-sam felt an **inexplicable** urge. He burst out shouting. "...How many people have you killed?"

Tok-jae glanced toward Song-sam, then looked away again.

"How many people have you killed?"

Tok-jae turned his face toward Song-sam and glared. The light in his eyes grew fierce and his mouth, which was surrounded by a **stubble** beard, twitched.

"So, is that what you've been doing? Killing people?"

...Still, Song-sam felt a clearing in the center of his chest, as if something caught there had been released. But then he said, "Why wouldn't someone like the vice-chairman of the Farmers' Alliance try to escape? You must have been hiding out because you had been given some assignment."

Tok-jae did not respond.

"Well? Answer me. What kind of **mission** were you hiding out to do?"

Silent, Tok-jae just kept walking. The guy certainly seems **cowed**. At a time like this, it would be good to get a look at his face. But Tok-jae did not turn toward Song-sam again.

Song-sam took hold of the pistol in his belt.

"It's no use trying to explain your way out of it. You'll have to be shot anyway, so go ahead and tell the truth."

cowed frightened by threats

fodder dry food for farm animals

inexplicable not possible to explain

mission a task; an assignment

spine a thorn

stubble short, stiff growth

Tok-jae began to speak. "I'm not trying to get out of anything. First and last, I'm the son of a dirt farmer. I was made vice-chairman of the Farmers' Alliance because they said I was a hard worker. If that's a crime worthy of death, there is nothing I can do. The only skill I've got is **tilling** the ground." After a moment he continued. "My father is sick in bed at home. It's been six months now."

Do you think Sam-song believes Tok-jae?

Tok-jae's father was a **widower**, a poor farmer who had grown old with only his son by his side. Seven years ago his back had already been bent, and his face had dark age spots.

"Are you married?"

"Yes," Tok-jae answered after a moment.

"Who to?"

"To Shorty."

What does this sentence tell you about *Shorty's* personality?

Not Shorty! Now that's interesting. Shorty, a fat little girl who knew the **breadth** of the earth but not the height of the sky. Always such a **prig**. Song-sam and Tok-jae had hated that about her. They were always teasing and laughing at her. So that's who Tok-jae had married.

"And how many kids do you have?"

"Our first is due this fall."

Song-sam tried to **stifle** a smile that rose to his lips in spite of himself. Asking how many children Tok-jae had and having him answer that the first was due in autumn was so funny he could not stand it. Shorty—holding up her armload of a belly on that little body. But Song-sam realized that this was not the place to laugh or joke about such things.

"Anyway, don't you think it looks **suspicious** that you stayed behind and didn't flee?"

"I tried to go. They said if there was an **invasion** from the south, every last man who was a man would be captured and killed, so all the men between seventeen and forty were forced to head north. I really didn't have any choice. I thought I would carry my father on my back and go. But he wouldn't stand for it. He said if a farmer

breadth width; extent	**prig** a person who is easily offended	**till** to make land ready for growing crops
invasion an entering by force	**stifle** to hold back	**widower** a man whose wife has died
	suspicious arousing distrust	

leaves the fields he has already tilled and planted, where can he go? My father has always depended on me alone. He's grown old farming all these years, and I have to be the one to close his eyes when the end comes. The truth is, people like us who just till the ground wouldn't be any better off even if we *did* flee..."

Song-sam himself had fled the past June. One night he secretly spoke to his father about escaping, but his father had said the same thing as Tok-jae's. How could a farmer flee and leave his work behind? Song-sam fled alone. As he wandered along the strange roads through strange towns in the south, he never stopped thinking of the farm work he had left to his old parents and his wife and children. Fortunately, then as now, his family was healthy.

They crossed the ridge. Now, somehow, Song-sam was the one who kept his eyes **averted**. The autumn sun was hot on his forehead. What a perfect day this would be for harvesting, he thought.

Does Song-sam wonder whether he should have stayed with his family like Tok-jae did?

After they had gone down the far side of the ridge, Song-sam **hesitated**.

It looked like a group of people wearing white clothes were stooped over working in the middle of the field. It was actually a flock of cranes, here in the so-called Demilitarized Zone at the thirty-eighth parallel. Even though people were no longer living here, the cranes remained as before.

The *Demilitarized Zone* was a no-fighting zone on either side of the boundary dividing the two sides.

Once when Song-sam and Tok-jae were about twelve years old, they had secretly set a **snare** and caught a crane. They even bound its wings with a straw rope. The two boys came out to the place they kept the crane almost every day; they would hold the crane around the neck and raise a **ruckus** trying to ride on its back. Then one day they heard the adults in the village talking in whispers. Some people had come from Seoul to hunt cranes. They had special permission from the Japanese governor-general to collect **specimens** of some kind. When they heard this, the two boys raced off to the field. They were not worried about being caught by the adults and scolded. Now they had only one thought: their crane must not die. Without stopping to catch their breath, they

Korea was under Japanese rule until 1945.

averted turned away
hesitate to hold back

ruckus a noisy disturbance
snare a trap

specimen an example of a group of things

scrambled through the weeds. They took the snare off the crane's leg and loosened the straw rope from its wings. But the crane could hardly walk, probably because it had been tied up for so long. The boys held the crane up between them and tossed it into the air. They heard a gunshot. The bird flapped its wings two, three, four times, but fell back to the ground. It was hit! But in the next instant, another crane in the grass nearby spread its wings. Their own crane, which had been lying on the ground, stretched out its long neck, gave a cry, and rose into the sky, too. They circled over the boys' heads, then flew off into the distance. The boys could not take their eyes off the spot in the blue sky where the cranes had disappeared.

"Let's go catch a crane," Song-sam said **abruptly**.

Tok-jae was bewildered. He did not know what was going on.

"I'll make a snare out of this, and you drive the cranes this way." Song-sam untied Tok-jae's bonds and took the cord. Before Tok-jae knew it, Song-sam was crawling through the grass.

At once, Tok-jae's face went white. The words "you'll have to be shot" flashed through his mind. At any moment a bullet would come from wherever Song-sam had crawled.

Some distance away, Song-sam rose and turned toward Tok-jae. "What do you mean standing there like an idiot! Go drive some cranes this way!"

Only then did Tok-jae realize what was happening. He started crawling through the weeds.

What are the *cranes* a symbol of?

Above, two cranes were soaring, their vast wings spread against the high, blue autumn sky.

abruptly all of a sudden

Directions Write the answers to these questions using complete sentences.

Comprehension: Identifying Facts

1. Who are the two main characters? How do they know each other?

2. Why is Tok-jae tied up?

3. What is supposed to happen to Tok-jae in Ch'ongdan?

Comprehension: Understanding Main Ideas

4. What is Song-sam thinking about as he enters the village?

5. What does Song-sam remember about Tok-jae?

6. As boys, what did they do with the crane they had captured?

Understanding Literature: Style

The style in "Cranes" is simple but tells a powerful story. The style is matter-of-fact. The author does not describe the characters' feelings. He just states the actions and the words. He also draws on the power of visual symbols.

7. When in the story does the author tell about Song-sam crying? Describe the event.

8. The author gives strong, simple visual pictures of the village. Point one out.

Critical Thinking

9. How are Song-sam and Tok-jae alike?

10. Why do you think Song-sam releases Tok-jae?

Writing on Your Own This story contains some strong but simple pictures drawn with words. Look, for example, at the first two sentences. Write three sentences of your own in which you create a vivid word picture.

Plot

Plot is the action or the main events in a story. Each plot has a beginning, middle, and end. It might begin with a puzzle. Action starts when the characters learn about the puzzle. The middle tells the events as they try to solve the puzzle. The end solves the puzzle. For example:

Beginning
- a puzzle
- event: finding out about the puzzle

Middle
- event: trying to solve the puzzle
- event: characters face problems

End
- event: the puzzle is solved

Below is a list of events in "The Adventure of the Speckled Band." They are divided into parts of the plot:

Beginning
- Helen Stoner calls on Sherlock Holmes. She asks him to solve her sister's death.
- Holmes takes the case.

Middle
- Holmes and Watson visit the manor house. They wait in the dark.
- Holmes hears something. He hits at it with his cane.

- The stepfather screams. He is found dead. The "speckled band" around his head is a deadly snake.

End
- Holmes shows how the stepfather caused the snake to bite the sister. Holmes has scared the snake and sent it back through the air vent. Then the snake bit the stepfather.

- Holmes also explains why the stepfather wanted Julia Stoner dead.

Review

1. What is a plot?

2. Which part of a plot gives the puzzle to be solved?

3. In which part of the plot does Holmes figure out about the snake?

4. In which part does Holmes explain what he has learned?

5. Did Doyle use a plot that kept you interested? Why or why not?

Writing on Your Own Make up your own plot. What will be the beginning, middle, and end? Write two sentences for each part of the plot.

UNIT 1 SUMMARY

In Unit 1 you have read several types of fiction. They were detective, science fiction, adventure, and turning point stories. In a detective story, the protagonist looks for clues to solve a crime. Science fiction deals with unreal places and events. It is usually set in the future or in far-off places. The protagonist in an adventure story survives by wits and luck. Turning points are about experiences that change a character's life. Some turning points are "coming of age" stories. A young person makes a decision, only later does he or she understand its importance.

Selections

- "The Adventure of the Speckled Band" by Arthur Conan Doyle. Sherlock Holmes solves the murder of a young woman.

- "Death Arrives on Schedule" by Hansjörg Martin. A killer has bad luck with well-laid plans.

- "The Feeling of Power" by Isaac Asimov. In a world run by computers, a technician learns the power of the human mind.

- "The Expedition" by Rudolf Lorenzen. Four astronauts and their descendants make a space expedition but learn little from it.

- "The Cegua" by Robert D. San Souci. A lone traveler has a frightening experience on the road.

- *Master and Man* by Leo Tolstoy. A rich man looks for help after he and his servant are stranded in a snowstorm.

- "Just Lather, That's All" by Hernando Téllez. A barber, who is a secret rebel, has a chance to murder the captain whose soldiers have been killing his friends.

- *Nervous Conditions* by Tsitsi Dangarembga. A young girl in Zimbabwe makes a choice between tradition and the chance for a good education.

- "Marriage Is a Private Affair" by Chinua Achebe. A Nigerian family is split when a man marries a woman who is not of his tribe.

- "Cranes" by Hwang Sun-won. A South Korean soldier meets a boyhood friend who has been taken prisoner as an enemy.

Directions Write the answers to these questions using complete sentences.

Comprehension: Identifying Facts

1. What four types of fiction are in this unit?

2. Name two countries in which these stories take place.

3. Name one story whose setting is a long time ago.

4. Name one of the stories that is set in the future.

5. Name the protagonist of one story. Tell what story he or she is in.

Comprehension: Understanding Main Ideas

6. Explain at least one difference between a detective story and a science fiction story.

7. What is the turning point in "Marriage Is a Private Affair"?

8. What is the mystery that Sherlock Holmes solves?

9. "The Cegua" and "Just Lather, That's All" are adventure stories. How are they alike? How are they different?

10. Tambudzai in *Nervous Conditions* and the young couple in "Marriage Is a Private Affair" face similar conflicts. How are those conflicts alike?

Understanding Literature: Fiction

Stories that did not happen are called fiction. Some fiction seems very real. Other fiction is clearly not real. Science fiction, for example, is often set in the future. We know it could not have happened. Fiction is made up of characters, setting, and plot. Characters are the people, animals, or things in the story. They perform the action. Setting is the time and place where the story takes place. Plot is the action in the story.

11. Name a story from the unit in which the setting is very important. Tell why it is important.

12. Name one story that is realistic. Tell what makes it realistic.

13. Name a story that is not realistic. Tell why it is not.

14. Some of these stories show a change in the main character's feelings. Name one of these stories. Tell what the change was.

15. Choose one story. Briefly tell what happens in the plot.

Critical Thinking

16. Which genre of fiction do you like best? Why?

17. Which story did you like best? Why?

18. Name a story that has a moral, or lesson. Tell what the moral is.

19. Choose a character from this unit that you like. Tell why you like the person.

20. Choose a character from this unit that you do not like. Tell why.

Speak and Listen

Choose a story that has dialogue, or characters talking to each other. Work with a partner. Each of you will choose one of the characters. Practice reading each character's words aloud. Think about how that person would speak. Try to make your words sound like a real conversation. Read the dialogue for the class.

Beyond Words

Imagine that one of these stories has been made into a movie. Think of an exciting scene from the story. Think about its setting and action. What characters are in it? Draw a poster of that scene to advertise the movie version. Your poster should make people want to see the movie.

Writing on Your Own Endings can be very important to stories. Write an essay about why the ending of a story is often the most important part. Begin your essay with a general statement about endings. Add statements to support your idea. Use stories from this unit for examples.

Test-Taking Tip

Prepare for a test by making a set of flash cards. Write a word on the front of each card. Write the definition on the back. Use the flash cards in a game to test your knowledge.

"The challenge of nonfiction is to marry art and truth."

　　—Phyllis Rose

"Facts don't lie—not if you've got enough of 'em."

　　—John Stephen Strange

UNIT 2 *Nonfiction*

Nonfiction by authors all over the world gives us new perspectives. Their letters, autobiographies, biographies, and articles are a valuable resource for learning about our world.

Nonfiction literature is about real people, settings, and events. It can be divided into several genres. The most personal kinds of nonfiction are diaries, journals, and letters. Sometimes diaries or collected letters are published. A diary is more personal than a journal because the writer expresses feelings. Journals and letters record a writer's first impressions and reactions about places and events as well as emotions.

Nonfiction about a person's life can be an autobiography or a biography. When people tell their own stories they are autobiographies. An autobiography describes events, people, places, and feelings from the author's own life. It often gives a colorful picture of the author. Biographies are not written by the person whom the book is about. Instead, they are written by authors who are interested in that person. They don't talk about feelings as much as autobiographies.

Journalism is another type of nonfiction. It answers the "who," "what," "where," "when," and "how" of an event clearly and quickly. It tells readers what has happened. The first reports of journalists are news stories. These are the kind of stories you see on the front page or cover of newspapers and magazines. Feature stories come after the first reports. They analyze, explain, and judge the importance of the news. Sometimes feature stories grow into books as their authors collect information and opinion. The Internet is having an effect on journalism; some newspapers are putting their stories online. Two of the journalism selections in this unit were first published on the Internet.

The following countries are represented in this unit: the Netherlands, India, the United States, Vietnam, South Africa, Pakistan, Great Britain, and Poland.

Journals and Letters

- "A journal is a leap of faith. You write without knowing what the next day's entry will be—or when the last." —Violet Weingarten
- "I never even kept a journal. I thought, 'I want to live my life, not record it.'" —Jacqueline Kennedy Onassis

The most personal form of writing is the journal or diary. The diary is often like an imaginary friend. It gives the writer a chance to express anger, fear, or jealousy. These emotions might be embarrassing if told to the wrong person. Diaries are popular with people trying to sort out life and their feelings as they grow and change.

Journals are another personal writing form. They focus more on events than feelings. People may keep journals to remind themselves of interesting events, sights, or ideas. The ideas in journals, diaries, and letters may appear in later writing. But the events and people in them usually have been changed. This is because the author has thought about how to use the experiences effectively. These early looks into a personality can sometimes help a reader better understand the writer.

Letters also can discuss feelings or events, but they communicate with a real person. The writer keeps that person in mind while writing, which helps the letter "speak" effectively. Today, handwritten communication is less popular than it once was. Most people use telephones or computers to reach others. But perhaps you have discovered a packet of love letters or an old diary. You will agree that the written word holds a special charm and force that can't be reproduced electronically.

Anne Frank
(1929–1945)
Dutch

Literary Term

diary a record of personal events, thoughts, or private feelings

About the Author

Anne Frank was the younger of two daughters in a wealthy Dutch Jewish family. A month after she turned thirteen, Adolf Hitler began his campaign to destroy all Jews in

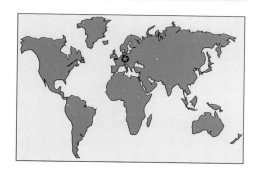

Europe. The Frank family and four others hid in a small apartment above her father's office. She called it the "secret annex." After two years, the Nazis discovered the group. They were all sent to concentration camps. In 1945, shortly before the end of World War II, Anne Frank died of typhus in the Bergen-Belsen camp. She was fifteen.

About the Selection

Anne Frank received a **diary** for her thirteenth birthday in 1942. A diary is a personal record. She thought of it as a secret friend. (She even called it "Kitty.") Her diary records the boredom of daytime silence. It tells of quarrels with her family. Anne dreams of a romance with Peter, a sixteen-year-old boy hiding with them. Through the diary we learn that she loves American movie stars and misses her friends.

After World War II, Anne Frank's father returned to Amsterdam. There he found his daughter's diary. He decided to share it with the world in a book. The book was later made into a play and a film. Here are selections from three entries in that diary.

Anne Frank: The Diary of a Young Girl

Anne Frank

As you read, remember that Anne Frank is writing in the small hiding place she shares with her family and several other people.

Thursday, 16 March 1944

Dear Kitty,

The weather is lovely, **superb,** I can't describe it; I'm going up to the attic in a minute.

Now I know why I'm so much more **restless** than Peter. He has his own room where he can work, dream, think, and sleep. I am shoved about from one corner to another. I hardly spend any time in my "double" room and yet it's something I long for so much. That is the reason too why I so frequently escape to the attic. There, and with you, I can be myself for a while, just a little while. Still, I don't want to moan about myself, on the contrary, I want to be brave. Thank goodness the others can't tell what my inward feelings are, except that I'm growing cooler towards Mummy daily, I'm not so **affectionate** to Daddy and don't tell Margot a single thing. I'm completely closed up. Above all, I must maintain my outward reserve, no one must know that war

---

affectionate showing loving, fond feelings for someone

restless never still or motionless

superb of unusually high quality

still **reigns incessantly** within. War between desire and common sense. The **latter** has won up till now; yet will the former prove to be the stronger of the two? Sometimes I fear that it will and sometimes I long for it to be!

Oh, it is so terribly difficult never to say anything to Peter, but I know that the first to begin must be he; there's so much I want to say and do, I've lived it all in my dreams, it is so hard to find that yet another day has gone by, and none of it comes true! Yes, Kitty, Anne is a crazy child, but I do live in crazy times and under still crazier **circumstances**.

But, still, the brightest spot of all is that at least I can write down my thoughts and feelings, otherwise I would be absolutely **stifled**! ...

Yours, Anne

The building that Anne Frank and her family lived in is now a museum.

Why does writing in her diary make Anne Frank feel better?

Friday, 17 March 1944

Dear Kitty, ...

Margot and I are getting a bit tired of our parents. Don't **misunderstand** me, I can't get on well with Mummy at the moment, as you know. I still love Daddy just as much, and Margot loves Daddy and Mummy, but when you are as old as we are, you do want to decide just a few things for yourself, you want to be independent sometimes.

Remember that *Kitty* is Anne's name for her diary, as if it were a friend.

circumstances the way someone lives	**latter** the second of two things mentioned	**reign** to rule or dominate
incessantly without stopping	**misunderstand** to fail to understand correctly	**stifled** choked or smothered

Remember that the Franks are living in a small space. How might this affect Anne and her sister's point of view?

If I go upstairs, then I'm asked what I'm going to do, I'm not allowed salt with my food, every evening regularly at a quarter past eight Mummy asks whether I ought not to start undressing, every book I read must be inspected. I must admit that they are not at all strict, and I'm allowed to read nearly everything, and yet we are both sick of all the remarks plus all the questioning that go on the whole day long.

Something else, especially about me, that doesn't please them: I don't feel like giving lots of kisses any more and I think fancy nicknames are terribly **affected.** In short, I'd really like to be rid of them for a while. Margot said last evening, "I think it's awfully annoying, the way they ask if you've got a headache, or whether you don't feel well, if you happen to give a sigh and put your hand to your head!"

It is a great blow to us both, suddenly to realize how little remains of the confidence and **harmony** that we used to have at home. And it's largely due to the fact that we're all "skew-wiff" here. By this I mean that we are treated as children over outward things, and we are much older than most girls of our age inwardly.

Although I'm only fourteen, I know quite well what I want, I know who is right and who is wrong, I have my opinions, my own ideas and principles, and although it may sound pretty mad from an **adolescent,** I feel more of a person than a child, I feel quite independent of anyone.

I know that I can discuss things and argue better than Mummy, I know I'm not so **prejudiced,** I don't **exaggerate** so much, I am more precise and adroit and because of this—you may laugh—I feel superior to her over a great

adolescent a teenager or young person	**exaggerate** to make something greater or more serious than it really is	**harmony** agreement
affected artificial; assumed to impress others		**prejudice** feeling of hatred for a particular group

many things. If I love anyone, above all I must have admiration for them, admiration and respect. Everything would be all right if only I had Peter, for I do admire him in many ways. He is such a nice, good-looking boy!

Yours, Anne

Saturday, 15 July 1944

Dear Kitty,

... "For in its **innermost** depths youth is lonelier than old age." I read this saying in some book and I've always remembered it, and found it to be true. Is it true then that grownups have a more difficult time here than we do? No. I know it isn't. Older people have formed their opinions about everything, and don't **waver** before they act. It's twice as hard for us young ones to hold our ground, and maintain our opinions, in a time when all ideals are being shattered and destroyed, when people are showing their worst side, and do not know whether to believe in truth and right and God.

Anyone who claims that the older ones have a more difficult time here certainly doesn't realize to what extent our problems weigh down on us, problems for which we are probably much too young, but which thrust themselves upon us continually, until, after a long time, we think we've found a solution, but the solution doesn't seem able to resist the facts which reduce it to nothing again. That's the difficulty in these times: ideals, dreams, and **cherished** hopes rise within us, only to meet the horrible truth and be shattered.

As a Jew during World War II, what might Anne mean about *the horrible truth*?

cherished kept fondly in mind	**innermost** most personal; deepest	**waver** to be unsure

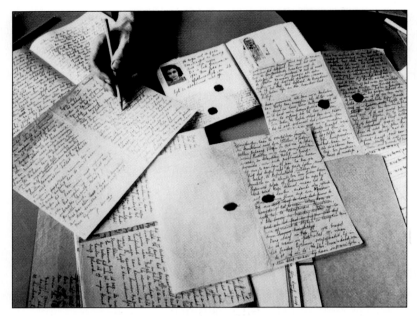

The actual pages from Anne Frank's diary are on view at the Anne Frank museum in Amsterdam.

It's really a wonder that I haven't dropped all my ideals, because they seem so absurd and impossible to carry out. Yet I keep them, because in spite of everything I still believe that people are really good at heart. I simply can't build up my hopes on a foundation consisting of confusion, **misery,** and death. I see the world gradually being turned into a wilderness, I hear the ever approaching thunder, which will destroy us too, I can feel the suffering of millions and yet, if I look up into the heavens, I think that it will all come right, that this **cruelty** too will end, and that peace and **tranquillity** will return again.

In the meantime, I must **uphold** my ideals, for perhaps the time will come when I shall be able to carry them out.

Yours, Anne

cruelty something that causes pain or suffering	**misery** great pain	**tranquillity** calm **uphold** to maintain; to keep

Anne Frank: The Diary of a Young Girl
Anne Frank

Directions Write the answers to these questions using complete sentences.

Comprehension: Identifying Facts

1. How has hiding changed Anne Frank?

2. Who else is getting tired of her parents?

3. What does Anne Frank think about Peter?

Comprehension: Understanding Main Ideas

For more than two years, Anne Frank lived in a small, crowded apartment. She could not leave for fear of being seen. Everyone had to be quiet during the day. People worked in the office below them during the day. They did not know there was a hiding place above the office.

4. Problems must have occurred in such a situation. List four.

5. Why do her parents' questions bother Anne Frank?

6. Why does Anne Frank write in her diary?

Understanding Literature: Diary

A diary holds people's private thoughts and feelings. Diaries are usually written in the form of a letter addressed to "Dear Diary." Anne Frank writes to an imaginary friend called "Kitty."

7. List one advantage of writing to a person rather than a book.

8. Did Anne Frank know that others would read what she wrote? Why do you think so?

Critical Thinking

On July 15, 1944, Anne Frank wondered about this question: "Is it true that grownups have a more difficult time here than we do?"

9. Do you agree with her answer? Why or why not?

10. List the most important problems Anne Frank faced.

Writing on Your Own The last two paragraphs of Anne Frank's July 15 entry explain her beliefs. They also predict what will happen in the future. Write a paragraph explaining which predictions came true and which parts were wrong.

Letter to Indira Tagore

Rabindranath Tagore (translated by Krishna Dutta and Andrew Robinson)

Rabindranath
Tagore
(1861–1941)
Indian

Literary Terms

letter impressions
and feelings written to
a specific person

personification
giving human
characteristics to a
nonhuman object

About the Author

Rabindranath Tagore was
born in Calcutta, India.
The Tagores were artists,
musicians, and social
reformers. Tagore was
brought up among books
and literature. He began

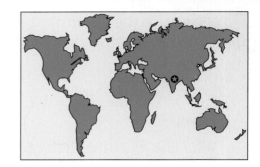

writing poems in the Bengali language when he was young.
Tagore greatly admired the English poets Shelley and Keats.

Tagore received the Nobel Prize for Literature in 1913. The
prize was for an English translation of *Gitanjali,* a collection
of his poetry. King George V of England knighted him in
1914. (Tagore later gave back his knighthood. He was angry
about Britain's treatment of Indians.)

Tagore wrote essays, novels, and short stories. Many of his
poems were set to music. In his last years he became a well-
known painter. Tagore also wanted to give Indian boys a
retreat from the modern world where they could learn
traditional ideals. So in 1901 he founded a "world university"
near Calcutta. This school was called *Shantiniketan,* or "The
Abode of Peace."

About the Selection

Tagore often wrote **letters** to his favorite niece, Indira
Tagore. She was a young woman in her twenties. His letters
show his gentleness and love of nature. The following
selection shows how Tagore reacts to the natural beauty of
moonlight. Notice how he describes the lamp he is using
and the book he is reading. He uses **personification** to
describe the moon and the night. Personification is giving
human characteristics to nonhuman things.

Letter to Indira Tagore
Rabindranath Tagore

Shelidah, East Bengal
12 December 1895

[Bibi]

The other evening an **insignificant** incident startled me. As I mentioned before, of late I have taken to lighting a lamp in the boat and sitting and reading till I feel sleepy...That evening I was reading a book of critical essays in English full of **contorted disputation** about poetry, art, beauty and so forth. As I plodded through these artificial discussions, my weary mind seemed to have strayed into a **mirage**, a land where things were constructed out of words. A **deadening** spirit seemed to dance before me like a **mocking** demon. The night was far advanced, so I shut the book with a snap and flung it on the table, intending to head for bed after blowing out the lamp. But the moment I **extinguished** the flame, moonlight burst through the open window and flooded the boat. It was like a shock to an infatuated man. The glare from a satanic little lamp had been mocking an infinite radiance. What on earth had I been hoping to find in the empty wordiness of that book? The heavens had been waiting for me soundlessly outside all the time. Had I chanced to miss them and gone off to bed in darkness, they would not have made the slightest protest. Had I never given them a glance during my mortal existence and remained unenlightened even on my death-bed, that lamp would have triumphed. But the moon would always have been there, silent and sweetly smiling, neither concealing nor advertising her presence.

Since then I have begun doing without the lamp in the evenings.

[Uncle Rabi]

As you read, think about how the author appreciates the beauty of nature.

Literary and art critics judge what others have written or drawn. Their opinions appear in critical essays.

contorted twisted; hard to follow	**disputation** a discussion or debate	**mirage** an optical illusion; something you see that is not really there
deadening making less intense or lively	**extinguish** to put out	**mocking** laughing in disgust and anger
	insignificant small; not important	

Directions Write the answers to these questions using complete sentences.

Comprehension: Identifying Facts

1. At what time of day do the events in the letter take place?

2. Where is Tagore when the events are taking place?

3. What is he doing?

Comprehension: Understanding Main Ideas

Tagore has been reading. He does not notice the moonlight until he blows out his lamp.

4. What is Tagore's first reaction to the moonlight?

5. How does the lamplight compare with the moonlight?

6. Tagore says this was "an insignificant incident." However, it clearly means a lot to him. Describe its significance in your own words.

Understanding Literature: Personification

Personification is giving human qualities to objects, animals, or ideas. Tagore's letter has several examples of this figure of speech. For instance, he writes "... that lamp would have triumphed." Can a lamp feel victory or failure? No, a lamp is an object. It cannot feel an emotion. Tagore is using personification to describe it.

7. Explain how Tagore uses personification to describe the moon.

8. Explain how he uses personification to describe the heavens.

Critical Thinking

9. What discovery does Tagore make?

10. What do you think Tagore wants his niece to do?

Writing on Your Own Think about something in nature that surprises or delights you. Use personification to describe its qualities. For example, you might write about a winter storm that cries and howls outside your window.

Letter to the Reverend J. H. Twichell
Mark Twain

Mark Twain
(1835–1910)
American

Literary Terms

pen name a false name used for writing

pun humorous use of words or phrases

satire humorous writing that makes fun of foolishness or evil

theme the main idea of a literary work

About the Author

Mark Twain was born Samuel L. Clemens in a small Missouri town. As a young man, he was a Mississippi riverboat pilot. Later he was a gold miner in Nevada and a printer.

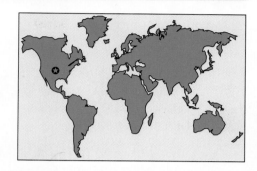

For his writing he chose the **pen name** "Mark Twain." A pen name is a false name used by an author. Twain's humorous stories about American life quickly made him popular. He is regarded as one of the first truly American writers. He uses **themes** (topics), language, and ideas gathered during his travels. His major works are *The Adventures of Tom Sawyer* and *The Adventures of Huckleberry Finn.* Both combine **satire** with fiction. Satire is humor that makes fun of foolishness or evil.

Late in life, Twain lost most of his wealth in bad investments. In 1895 he started a long lecture tour to earn money to repay debts. During the tour, one of his daughters died. Shortly after he returned, his wife and another daughter also died. These losses, as well as continuing disappointment in humans, affected his mood. Later satires like *The Mysterious Stranger* are more intense and serious than earlier works.

About the Selection

After his writing became popular, Twain married and moved to Connecticut. There he began a friendship with a local minister, the Reverend Joseph H. Twichell. Twain loved to travel. He went to Germany in the late 1870s. From Munich he wrote the following letter to Twichell. It is the kind you might enjoy getting from a friend who happens to be writer. It contains many funny images. Twain also used **puns**—humorous use of words or phrases.

Letter to the Rev J. H. Twichell

Mark Twain

To the Reverend J. H. Twichell

Munich, January 26, 1879

Dear Old Joe:

As you read, watch for clues to help you determine who *Livy* is.

Twain is referring to a story he read in a letter from Twichell.

Sunday. Your **delicious** letter arrived exactly at the right time. It was laid by my plate as I was finishing breakfast at 12 noon. Livy and Clara [Spaulding] arrived from church 5 minutes later. I took a pipe and spread myself out on the sofa and Livy sat by and read, and I warmed to that butcher the moment he began to swear. There is more than one way of praying and I like the butcher's way because the **petitioner** is so apt to be **in earnest**. I was peculiarly alive to his performance just at this time for another reason, **to wit:** Last night I awoke at 3 this morning and after raging to myself for 2 **interminable** hours, I gave it up. I rose, assumed a catlike **stealthiness**, to keep from waking Livy, and proceeded to dress in the **pitch** dark. Slowly but surely I got on garment after garment—all down to one sock; I had one slipper on and the other in my hand. Well, on my hands and knees I crept softly around, pawing and feeling and scooping along the carpet and among chair-legs for that missing sock;

delicious delightful	**petitioner** one who asks for help	**stealthiness** secretive actions
in earnest sincere	**pitch** completely black	**to wit** an expression meaning "that is to say"
interminable endless		

I kept that up;—and still kept it up and *kept* it up. At first I only said to myself "Blame that sock," but that soon ceased to answer; my **expletives** grew steadily stronger and stronger and at last, when I found I was *lost,* I had to sit flat down on the floor and take hold of something to keep from lifting the roof off with the **profane** explosion that was trying to get out of me. I could see the dim blur of the window, but of course it was in the wrong place and could give me no information as to where I was. But I had one comfort, I had not waked Livy; I believed I could find that sock in silence if the night lasted long enough. So I started again and softly pawed all over the place, and

Twain is writing in the late 1800s. The hotel room didn't have a bathroom or running water. Instead, they were given water in a pitcher and a bowl to pour it in. Both sat on the washstand.

sure enough at the end of half an hour I laid my hand on the missing article. I rose joyfully up and butted the wash-bowl and pitcher off the stand and simply raised - - - - so to speak. Livy screamed, then said, "Who is that? what *is* the matter? I said, "There ain't anything the matter—I'm hunting for my sock." She said, "Are you hunting for it with a club?"...

expletive a curse   **profane** not holy or sacred

Letter to the Reverend J. H. Twichell
Mark Twain

Directions Write the answers to these questions using complete sentences.

Comprehension: Identifying Facts

1. What is the first name of Twain's wife?

2. What time does Twain wake up?

3. Why is Twain trying to dress in the dark?

Comprehension: Understanding Main Ideas

4. Put these events in the correct order.

   ■ Twain bumps his head.

   ■ Livy wakes up.

   ■ Twain can't sleep.

   ■ Twain loses his temper.

Twain may have used bad language during the night he described, but he doesn't in this letter.

5. List one reason why he doesn't.

6. What does he use in the letter to show bad language?

Understanding Literature: Puns

A pun is a humorous play on words or phrases. The joke depends on different meanings. For instance, a film called *Family Plot* contains a pun on the word *plot*. The movie is about a plan to murder various relatives. (That's a plot to kill the family). They will then be buried in the family's section of the cemetery, which is called the family plot.)

7. What is the pun in the last line of Twain's letter?

8. Is Twain's use of "delicious" in the first sentence another pun?

Critical Thinking

Letters tell us much of what we know about life in earlier times. People from all walks of life wrote letters. They wrote to family members, and to friends. The telephone and low-cost long distance service has changed this. People now call instead of writing.

9. How has this change affected the type of information people exchange?

10. What effect will this have on recorded history?

> **Writing on Your Own** Write two paragraphs about one of these topics.
>
> ■ Explain what happens to Mark Twain during the night described in his letter.
>
> ■ Contrast the purpose of Twain's letter with that of Tagore's.

Autobiography

- "Few books are more thrilling than certain confessions, but they must be honest, and the author must have something to confess." —Simone de Beauvoir
- "Hiring someone to write your autobiography is like hiring someone to take a bath for you." —Mae West

Writing one's own life story is known as an autobiography. If talented enough, the person may write the story alone. Or the person may choose to write the book "as told to" someone. A ghost writer may be paid to write the book and let its subject take credit. In any case, the author shapes and arranges the life experiences. Some events will be pointed out, others ignored. This helps the reader share the author's view of his or her life.

Authors of autobiographies try to be honest, then write about all of their life, good and bad. Or they may look only at what they think is most important. Whatever the choice, these authors must leave out some personal experiences. They can talk about their life only from their own point of view.

An author's personal knowledge and viewpoint limit an autobiography. A good autobiography balances those limits. It does so by offering a personal glimpse at the author's mistakes and the decisions that shaped his or her life. In this section you will learn how people react to something in their lives. As you read, think about how these people are the same as or different from you.

When Heaven and Earth Changed Places
Le Ly Hayslip

Le Ly Hayslip
(1949–)
Vietnamese

Literary Terms

legend a traditional story that was told orally and handed down from one generation to another

sequence the order of events in a literary work

About the Author

Le Ly Hayslip was born in central Vietnam. She was the youngest girl in a peasant family. The country was a French colony, but some Vietnamese were fighting

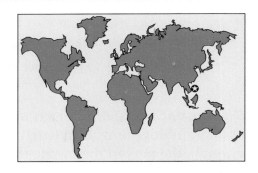

for independence. The fighters were led by Communists in the north. As a result, Americans later became involved. Villages like Ky La were caught between the armies. In 1969 Hayslip married an older American who worked in Vietnam. They moved to the United States. She became a citizen. In 1973 her husband died and Hayslip was left to make her own way. In 1987 she founded the East Meets West Foundation, which tries to help Vietnam rebuild from the war. Another goal of the foundation is to improve cultural relations between Vietnam and the United States.

About the Selection

When Heaven and Earth Changed Places is Hayslip's story of life in Vietnam. Her wartime life was full of love and hate and fear. This selection describes the hard work that goes into planting and harvesting rice.

The order of events in a story is called **sequence.** Hayslip's story carefully shows the sequence of work in raising a rice crop. Look for the steps in this sequence as you read.

Hayslip retells a Vietnamese legend in her story. A **legend** is a traditional story that was once told orally. It was handed down from one generation to another. Notice how the legend adds interest and humor to the story.

When Heaven and Earth Changed Places

Le Ly Hayslip

Twice a year, in May and October, we villagers prepared the land for planting. Because these months followed the winter and summer **monsoons**, it meant we had a variety of natural (as well as war-made) disasters to repair: from floods and high winds to **plagues** of grasshoppers and the wearing out of the soil itself.

Although we grew many crops around Ky La—sweet potatoes, peanuts, cinnamon, and **taro**—the most important by far was rice. Yet for all its long history as the staff of life in our country, rice was a **fickle** provider. First, the spot of ground on which the rice was thrown had to be just right for the seed to sprout. Then, it had to be protected from birds and animals who needed food as much as we did. As a child, I spent many hours with the other kids in Ky La acting like human scarecrows—making noise and waving our arms—just to keep the raven-like *se-se* birds away from our future supper.

According to legend, god did not mean for us to work so hard for our rice. My father told me the story of *ong trang bu hung,* the spirit messenger who had been entrusted by god to bring rice—the heavenly food—to earth for humans to enjoy. God gave the messenger two magic sacks. "The seeds in the first," god said, "will grow when they touch the ground and give a plentiful harvest, anywhere, with no effort. The seeds in the second sack, however, must be **nurtured**; but, if tended properly, will give the earth great beauty."

> As you read, notice that the author is telling about simple, everyday events. Even in wartime, they are essential to life in the village.

> About 200 to 400 pounds per person of rice is eaten per year in Asia, compared with 6 pounds per person in North America.

> The author uses words from the Vietnamese language throughout her story to remind you of the setting.

fickle not faithful; not reliable

monsoon seasonal winds that bring rain to southern Asia

nurture to care for

plague the sudden arrival of something destructive; a nuisance

taro a plant grown for its edible, starchy root

Of course, god meant for the first seeds to be rice, which would feed millions with little effort; and the second to be grass, which humans couldn't eat but would enjoy as a cover for bare ground. Unfortunately, the heavenly messenger got the sacks mixed up, and humans immediately paid for his error: finding that rice was hard to grow whereas grass grew easily everywhere, especially where it wasn't wanted.

When god learned of this mistake, he booted the messenger out of heaven and sent him to earth as a hard-shelled beetle, to crawl on the ground forever lost in the grass to dodge the feet of the people he had so carelessly injured. This harsh **karma**, however, did nothing to make life easier for farmers.

A rice *paddy* is a field, usually small, surrounded by banks of dirt that serve as dams to hold the water when the field is flooded.

When the seeds had grown into stalks, we would pull them up—*nho ma*—and replant them in the paddies—the place where the rice **matured** and our crop eventually would be harvested.

After the hard crust had been turned and the **clods** broken up with **mallets** to the size of gravel, we had to wet it down with water **conveyed** from nearby ponds or rivers. Once the field had been flooded, it was left to soak for several days, after which our

buffalo-powered plows could finish the job. In order to accept the seedling rice, however, the ground had to be *bua ruong*—even softer than the richest soil we used to grow vegetables. We knew the texture was right when a handful of watery mud would ooze through our fingers like soup.

Transplanting the rice stalks from their "nursery" to the field was primarily women's work. Although we labored as fast as we could, this chore involved bending over for hours in knee-deep, muddy water. No matter how practiced we

clod a lump or chunk of dirt	karma fate; destiny	mature to become fully grown
convey to bring or carry	mallet a short-handled, heavy hammer	transplant to lift and replant in another area

were, the constant search for a foothold in the sucking mud made the tedious work exhausting. Still, there was no other way to transplant the seedlings properly; and that **sensual** contact between our hands and feet, the baby rice, and the wet, **receptive** earth, is one of the things that preserved and **heightened** our connection with the land. While we worked, we sometimes sang to break the **monotony** and raise our spirits. One song my mother taught me went:

> We love the *hoa binh;*
> *Hoa binh* means peace—first *hoa,* then *binh:*
> *Hoa* means "together" and *binh* means "all the same."
> When we're all together, no one is parted.
> When we're the same, no one's at war.
> Peace means no more suffering,
> *Hoa binh* means no more war.

Why do you think the author included this song in her story?

When the planting was done, the ground had to be watered every other day and, because each **parcel** had supported our village for centuries, fertilized as well. Unless a family was very wealthy, it could not buy chemicals for this purpose, so we had to shovel **manure** from the animal pens and carry it in baskets to the fields where we would cast it evenly onto the growing plants. When animals became scarce later in the war, we sometimes had to add human waste collected from the latrines outside the village. And of course, wet, fertile ground breeds weeds and pulling them was the special task of the women and children. The first big weeding was called *lam co lua di,* followed a month later by a second "weeding party" called *lam co lua lai.* The standing water was also home for mosquitoes, **leeches**, snakes, and freshwater crabs and you were never too sure just what you would come up with in the next handful of weeds. It was backbreaking, unpleasant labor that ran fourteen hours a day for many days....

heighten to make more intense	**manure** animal waste used as fertilizer	**receptive** ready to accept
leech a blood-sucking worm	**monotony** sameness	**sensual** pleasing to the senses
	parcel an area of land	

But planting was only part of village life. Like daylight and darkness, wakefulness and sleep, the labors and **rituals** of harvest defined the other half of our existence.

The author refers back to the legend telling the story of how rice came to earth.

According to legend, human problems with rice didn't end with the forgetful beetle. When god saw that the mix-up in magic sacks had caused so much trouble on earth, he commanded the rice to "present itself for cooking" by rolling up to each home in a ball. Of course, the rice obeyed god and rolled into the first house it was supposed to serve. But the housewife, unprepared for such a sight, became frightened and hit it with a broom, scattering the rice ball into a thousand pieces. This so angered the rice that it went back outside and shouted, "See if I come back to let you cook me! Now you'll have to come out to the fields and bring me in if you want your supper!"

That was the closest any Vietnamese ever came to a free bowl of rice.

Beginning in March, and again in August, we would bring the mature rice in from the fields and process it for use during the rest of the year. In March, when the ground was dry, we cut the rice very close to the soil—*cat lua*—to keep the plant alive. In August, when the ground was wet, we cut the plant halfway up—*cat gat*—which made the job much easier.

The separation of stalk and rice was done outside in a special smooth area beside our house. Because the rice was freshly cut, it had to dry in the sun for several days. At this stage, we called it *phoi lua*—not-yet rice. The actual separation was done by our water buffalo, which walked in lazy circles over a heap of cuttings until the rice fell easily from the stalks. We gathered the stalks, tied them in bundles, and used them to fix roofs or to kindle our fires. The good, light-colored rice,

ritual a series of acts done in a traditional order

called *lua chet,* was separated from the bad, dark-colored rice—*lua lep*—and taken home for further processing. The very best rice, of course, we gave back to Mother Earth. This seed rice was called *lua giong* and we put it into great jars which we filled with water. The wet rice was then packed under a haystack to keep warm. The **nutrients**, moisture, and heat helped the rice seeds to sprout, and after three days (during which we watered and fertilized the seedbed like a garden), we recovered the jars and cast the fertile *geo ma* seeds onto the ground we had prepared. But this was rice we would enjoy another day...

We always blamed crop failures on ourselves—we had not worked hard enough or, if there was no other explanation, we had failed to **adequately** honor our ancestors. Our solution was to pray more and sacrifice more and eventually things always got better. Crops ruined by soldiers were another matter. We knew prayer was useless because soldiers were human beings, too, and the god of nature meant for them to work out their own karma just like us.

In any event, the journey from seedling to rice bowl was long and **laborious** and because each grain was a symbol of life, we never wasted any of it. Good rice was considered god's **gemstone**—*hot ngoc troi*—and was cared for accordingly on pain of **divine** punishment. Even today a peasant seeing lightning will crouch under the table and look for lost grains in order to escape the next bolt. And parents must never strike children, no matter how naughty they've been, while the child is eating rice, for that would interrupt the sacred **communion** between rice-eater and rice-maker. Like my brothers and sisters, I learned quickly the advantages of chewing my dinner slowly.

The villagers made use of everything they grew and harvested. The stalks were used to patch roofs, the best rice as seeds for replanting, and the rest of the rice for food.

adequately well enough

communion a sharing of feelings

divine coming from a god

gemstone a jewel

laborious requiring long, hard work

nutrient food needed for growth

Directions Write the answers to these questions using complete sentences.

Comprehension: Identifying Facts

1. When do the villagers plant rice? When do they harvest the crop?

2. How many crops of rice do they harvest in one year?

3. Whose job is it to transplant the rice stalks?

Comprehension: Understanding Main Ideas

4. Why do the villagers need to fertilize the rice paddies?

5. Why do they use water buffaloes instead of tractors to plow the paddies?

6. Why is the rice crop so important to the villagers?

Understanding Literature: Legend

Hayslip retells the legend of how rice came to earth. A legend is a traditional story. It is passed on, often orally, from one generation to another. This legend tells how a heavenly messenger mixed up the sacks of grass seeds and rice seeds.

7. How do humans have to pay for the messenger's mistake?

8. What happened to the messenger? Was it a punishment that fit his crime?

Critical Thinking

Planting, caring for, and harvesting a rice crop is hard work. It required the help and time of everyone in the village. Hayslip writes that it defined their existence.

9. Do you think the villagers are happy or unhappy about their life?

10. Hayslip includes humor, the funny side of things, in her story. Give two examples of humor from the story.

Writing on Your Own What do you think life was like for a child in Hayslip's village? Make a list of three advantages and three disadvantages of growing up in her village.

Santha Rama Rau
(1923–)
Indian

Literary Terms

autobiography a person's life story written by that person

first-person written as if the author is telling the story

point of view the position from which the author or storyteller tells the story

sketch a brief written work that often runs from subject to subject and is often humorous

About the Author

Santha Rama Rau was born in Madras, India in 1923. Her father held an important job in the British colonial government. His job took him many different places.

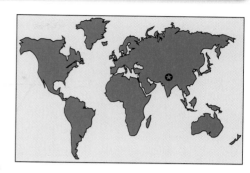

His family moved with him. As a child, Rau lived in many parts of India. She also lived in England and South Africa. Rau went to college in the United States. She attended Wellesley College in Massachusetts. In her early twenties, she wrote an **autobiography**, a story of her life. It was called *Home to India*. The book was about her childhood and growing-up years. She went on to write several more books of autobiography. She also wrote fiction and articles about her travels.

About the Selection

In 1961, Rau published a book titled *Gifts of Passage.* It was a collection of **sketches** about her life. A sketch is a short piece of writing. It moves from subject to subject. A sketch is often humorous. The next selection is one of those sketches. It is written from a **first-person point of view.** This means that Rau is telling her own story just as she saw it. She tells about her experiences as a new student in a British school.

BY ANY OTHER NAME
SANTHA RAMA RAU

As you read, think about when you were new in school.

The term *Anglo-Indian* usually meant a person from Britain living in India. It could also mean a person of English and Indian descent. This school is run by the British.

At the Anglo-Indian day school in Zorinabad to which my sister and I were sent when she was eight and I was five and a half, they changed our names. On the first day of school, a hot, windless morning of a north Indian September, we stood in the **headmistress's** study and she said, "Now you're the *new* girls. What are your names?"

My sister answered for us. "I am Premila, and she"—nodding in my direction—"is Santha."

The headmistress had been in India, I suppose, fifteen years or so, but she still smiled her helpless **inability** to **cope** with Indian names. Her rimless half-glasses glittered, and the **precarious** bun on the top of her head trembled as she shook her head. "Oh, my dears, those are much too hard for me. Suppose we give you pretty English names. Wouldn't that be more jolly? Let's see, now—Pamela for you, I think." She shrugged in a **baffled** way at my sister. "That's as close as I can get. And for *you*," she said to me, "how about Cynthia? Isn't that nice?"

My sister was always less easily **intimidated** than I was, and while she kept a stubborn silence, I said, "Thank you," in a very tiny voice.

We had been sent to that school because my father, among his responsibilities as an officer of the **civil service**, had a tour of duty to perform in the villages around that steamy little provincial town, where he had his headquarters at that time. He used to make his shorter inspection tours on horseback, and a week before, in the stale heat of a

baffled confused	**cope** to manage successfully	**inability** lack of ability
civil service civilian workers of the government	**headmistress** female principal of a school	**intimidated** frightened
		precarious insecure

typically **postmonsoon** day, we had waved good-by to him and a little procession—an assistant, a secretary, two bearers, and the man to look after the bedding rolls and luggage: They rode away through our large garden, still bright green from the rains, and we turned back into the twilight of the house and the sound of fans whispering in every room.

Up to then, my mother had refused to send Premila to school in the British-run establishments of that time, because, she used to say, "you can bury a dog's tail for seven years and it still comes out curly, and you can take a Britisher away from his home for a lifetime and he still remains **insular**." The examinations and degrees from entirely Indian schools were not, in those days, considered **valid.** In my case, the question had never come up, and probably never would have come up if Mother's **extraordinary** good health had not broken down. For the first time in my life, she was not able to continue the lessons she had been giving us every morning. So our **Hindi** books were put away, the stories of the Lord Krishna as a little boy were left in mid-air, and we were sent to the Anglo-Indian school.

The girls' mother believes that the British always act as if they were still in England although they are really living and working in India.

That first day at school is still, when I think of it, a remarkable one. At that age, if one's name is changed, one develops a curious form of dual personality. I remember having a certain detached and disbelieving concern in the actions of "Cynthia," but certainly no responsibility. Accordingly, I followed the thin, erect back of the headmistress down the **veranda** to my classroom feeling, at most, a passing interest in what was going to happen to me in this strange, new atmosphere of School.

Lord Krishna is revered as a Hindu deity or god. His triumph over a demon god is celebrated each year in a festival of lights.

The building was Indian in design, with wide verandas opening onto a central courtyard, but Indian verandas are usually whitewashed, with stone floors. These, in the tradition of British schools, were painted dark brown and had matting on the floors. It gave a feeling of extra intensity to the heat.

The dark paint and mats absorbed the heat from the sun. The whitewashed floors reflected it and were therefore cooler

I suppose there were about a dozen Indian children in the school—which contained perhaps forty children in all—and four of them were in my class. They were all sitting at the back of the room, and I went to join them. I sat next to a small, solemn girl who didn't smile at me. She had long, glossy-black braids and wore a cotton

extraordinary remarkable	**insular** limited in outlook and experience	**valid** completely acceptable; genuine
Hindi languages widely spoken in India	**postmonsoon** after the rainy season	**veranda** a roofed porch running along the outside of a building

dress, but she still kept on her Indian jewelry—a gold chain around her neck, thin gold bracelets, and tiny ruby studs in her ears. Like most Indian children, she had a rim of black **kohl** around her eyes. The cotton dress should have looked strange, but all I could think of was that I should ask my mother if I couldn't wear a dress to school, too, instead of my Indian clothes.

I can't remember too much about the **proceedings** in class that day, except for the beginning. The teacher pointed to me and asked me to stand up. "Now, dear, tell the class your name."

I said nothing.

"Come along," she said, frowning slightly. "What's your name, dear?"

"I don't know," I said, finally.

The English children in the front of the class—there were about eight or ten of them—giggled and twisted around in their chairs to look at me. I sat down quickly and opened my eyes very wide, hoping in that way to dry them off. The little girl with the braids put out her hand and very lightly touched my arm. She still didn't smile.

Most of that morning I was rather bored. I looked briefly at the children's drawings pinned to the wall, and then concentrated on a lizard clinging to the ledge of the high, barred window behind the teacher's head. Occasionally it would shoot out its long yellow tongue for a fly, and then it would rest, with its eyes closed and its belly **palpitating**, as though it were swallowing several times quickly. The lessons were mostly concerned with reading and writing and simple numbers—things that my mother had already taught me—and I paid very little attention. The teacher wrote on the easel blackboard words like "bat" and "cat," which seemed babyish to me; only "apple" was new and **incomprehensible**.

When it was time for the lunch recess, I followed the girl with braids out onto the veranda. There the children from the other classes were assembled. I saw Premila at once and ran over to her, as she had charge of our lunchbox. The children were all opening packages and sitting down to eat sandwiches. Premila and I were the only ones who had Indian food—thin wheat chapatties, some

Why didn't Santha know what an apple was? Why did the teacher present it as a word to learn?

Chapatties are delicate flatbreads served with almost every meal in India. They may be used in place of a fork or spoon to scoop up bites of food.

kohl dark powder used as eye makeup	**incomprehensible** not capable of being understood	**proceedings** series of events
	palpitate to beat rapidly	

vegetable **curry**, and a bottle of buttermilk. Premila thrust half of it into my hand and whispered fiercely that I should go and sit with my class, because that was what the others seemed to be doing.

The enormous black eyes of the little Indian girl from my class looked at my food longingly, so I offered her some. But she only shook her head and plowed her way solemnly through her sandwiches.

I was very sleepy after lunch, because at home we always took a **siesta**. It was usually a pleasant time of day, with the bedroom darkened against the harsh afternoon sun, the drifting off into sleep with the sound of Mother's voice reading a story in one's mind, and, finally, the shrill, fussy voice of the ayah waking one for tea.

At school, we rested for a short time on low, folding cots on the veranda, and then we were expected to play games. During the hot part of the afternoon we played indoors, and after the shadows had begun to lengthen and the slight breeze of the evening had come up we moved outside to the wide courtyard.

I had never really grasped the system of **competitive** games. At home, whenever we played tag or guessing games, I was always allowed to "win"—"because," Mother used to tell Premila, "she is the youngest, and we have to allow for that." I had often heard her say it, and it seemed quite reasonable to me, but the result was that I had no clear idea of what "winning" meant.

When we played twos-and-threes that afternoon at school, in **accordance** with my training, I let one of the small English boys catch me, but was naturally rather puzzled when the other children did not return the **courtesy**. I ran about for what seemed like hours without ever catching anyone, until it was time for school to close. Much later I learned that my attitude was called "not being a good sport," and I stopped allowing myself to be caught, but it was not for years that I really learned the spirit of the thing.

When I saw our car come up to the school gate, I broke away from my classmates and rushed toward it yelling, "Ayah! Ayah!" It seemed like an eternity since I had seen her that morning—a

An *ayah* in India is a person who cares for young children. In America, the person would be called a nanny.

accordance agreement

competitive involving the effort to win

courtesy an act of politeness

curry a food dish seasoned with curry powder

siesta a rest, usually taken after the noonday meal

wizened, affectionate figure in her white cotton **sari** giving me dozens of urgent and useless instructions on how to be a good girl at school. Premila followed more **sedately,** and she told me on the way home never to do that again in front of the other children.

Why did Premila criticize Santha's behavior?

When we got home we went straight to Mother's high, white room to have tea with her, and I immediately climbed onto the bed and bounced gently up and down on the springs. Mother asked how we had liked our first day in school. I was so pleased to be home and to have left that peculiar Cynthia behind that I had nothing whatever to say about school, except to ask what "apple" meant. But Premila told Mother about the classes, and added that in her class they had weekly tests to see if they had learned their lessons well.

I asked, "What's a test?"

Premila said, "You're too small to have them. You won't have them in your class for donkey's years." She had learned the expression that day and was using it for the first time. We all laughed enormously at her wit. She also told Mother, in an aside, that we should take sandwiches to school the next day. Not, she said, that *she* minded. But they would be simpler for me to handle.

Did Premila really want to take sandwiches because that's what all the other students ate? Did she want to do it in order to fit in?

That whole lovely evening I didn't think about school at all. I **sprinted** barefoot across the lawns with my favorite playmate, the cook's son, to the stream at the end of the garden. We quarreled in our usual way, waded in the **tepid** water under the lime trees, and waited for the night to bring out the smell of the **jasmine**. I listened with fascination to his stories of ghosts and demons, until I was too frightened to cross the garden alone in the semidarkness.

jasmine a vine or bush with fragrant flowers	**sedately** calmly; with dignity	**tepid** slightly warm
sari a draped outer garment of lightweight cloth traditionally worn by Indian women	**sprint** to run a short distance at top speed	**wizened** dried up; wrinkled

The ayah found me, shouted at the cook's son, scolded me, hurried me in to supper—it was an entirely usual, wonderful evening.

It was a week later, the day of Premila's first test, that our lives changed rather abruptly. I was sitting at the back of my class, in my usual inattentive way, only half listening to the teacher. I had started a rather guarded friendship with the girl with the braids, whose name turned out to be Nalini (Nancy, in school). The three other Indian children were already fast friends. Even at that age it was **apparent** to all of us that friendship with the English or Anglo-Indian children was out of the question. Occasionally, during the class, my new friend and I would draw pictures and show them to each other secretly.

Notice that Nalini has also been given an English name to use in school.

The door opened sharply and Premila marched in. At first, the teacher smiled at her in a kindly and encouraging way and said, "Now, you're little Cynthia's sister?"

Premila didn't even look at her. She stood with her feet planted firmly apart and her shoulders **rigid**, and addressed herself directly to me. "Get up," she said. "We're going home."

I didn't know what had happened, but I was aware that it was a crisis of some sort. I rose obediently and started to walk toward my sister.

"Bring your pencils and your notebook," she said.

I went back for them, and together we left the room. The teacher started to say something just as Premila closed the door, but we didn't wait to hear what it was.

In complete silence we left the school grounds and started to walk home. Then I asked Premila what the matter was. All she would say was "We're going home for good."

It was a very tiring walk for a child of five and a half, and I dragged along behind Premila with my pencils growing sticky in my hand. I can still remember looking at the dusty hedges, and the tangles of thorns in the ditches by the side of the road, smelling the faint **fragrance** from the **eucalyptus** trees and wondering whether we would ever reach home. Occasionally a horse-drawn **tonga** passed

apparent easily understood	**eucalyptus** a tall tree with strong-smelling leaves	**rigid** stiff
		tonga a wagon
	fragrance sweetness of smell	

us, and the women, in their pink or green silks, stared at Premila and me trudging along on the side of the road. A few **coolies** and a line of women carrying baskets of vegetables on their heads smiled at us. But it was nearing the hottest time of day, and the road was almost **deserted**. I walked more and more slowly, and shouted to Premila, from time to time, "Wait for me!" with increasing **peevishness**. She spoke to me only once, and that was to tell me to carry my notebook on my head, because of the sun.

When we got to our house the ayah was just taking a tray of lunch into Mother's room. She immediately started a long, worried questioning about what are you children doing back here at this hour of the day.

Mother looked very startled and very concerned, and asked Premila what had happened.

Premila said, "We had our test today, and She made me and the other Indians sit at the back of the room, with a desk between each one."

Mother said, "Why was that, darling?"

"She said it was because Indians cheat," Premila added. "So I don't think we should go back to that school."

What was Mother thinking? Remember what she said about the British earlier in the story.

Mother looked very distant, and was silent a long time. At last she said, "Of course not, darling." She sounded displeased.

We all shared the curry she was having for lunch, and afterward I was sent off to the beautifully familiar bedroom for my siesta. I could hear Mother and Premila talking through the open door.

Mother said, "Do you suppose she understood all that?"

Premila said, "I shouldn't think so. She's a baby."

Mother said, "Well, I hope it won't bother her."

Of course, they were both wrong. I understood it perfectly, and I remember it all very clearly. But I put it happily away, because it had all happened to a girl called Cynthia, and I never was really particularly interested in her.

---

coolie an unskilled worker who does odd jobs

deserted empty

peevishness annoyance; bad temper

By Any Other Name
Santha Rama Rau

Directions Write the answers to these questions using complete sentences.

Comprehension: Identifying Facts

1. Although Rau's school is in India, who runs the school?

2. Rau's sister has two names in the story. What are they?

3. What English name does the teacher give Santha Rama Rau?

4. What does Rau's father do for a living?

5. Why are Rau and her sister sent to school?

6. Are most of the children in the school English or Indian?

7. Why doesn't Rau pay attention in class on her first day?

8. How is the lunch that Rau and her sister brought different from the other childrens' lunches?

9. What kind of clothes does Rau wear to school?

10. How long do Rau and her sister go to this school?

Comprehension: Understanding Main Ideas

11. Rau's mother taught the girls at home instead of sending them to school. Why?

12. Rau says the new name gave her a dual personality. What does she mean?

13. What makes the school look like a British school?

14. The teacher asks Rau her name. She answers, "I don't know." Why?

15. Why doesn't Rau understand competitive games?

16. After her first day, Rau is happy to be home and "to have left that peculiar Cynthia behind." What does she mean when she says that?

17. Why does Rau's sister ask to take sandwiches for lunch? What is her real reason?

18. Does Rau make friends with the English students? Why or why not?

19. What happens to make Rau's sister decide to leave the school?

20. Why does Premila tell her sister to carry her notebook on her head?

Review Continued on Next Page

Understanding Literature: Autobiography and First-Person Point of View

"By Any Other Name" is an autobiographical sketch. Santha Rama Rau tells a brief story about one subject in her life. She tells it from the first-person point of view. This means the author is a character in the story. She uses the pronouns "I," "me," and "my" in telling the facts. This lets us know the story happened to the writer. It also tells how she felt about it.

21. "Most of that morning I was rather bored." How do you know from this sentence that the story is told from the first person point of view?

22. How do you know the story is an autobiography?

23. Find three examples from the story where Rau tells how she feels. List them.

24. If this story was told from another point of view, how would it be different?

25. Do you think the story is more effective because it is told in the first person? Why or why not?

Critical Thinking

In the Anglo-Indian school, the Indian students are expected to behave like the English students. However, they are not treated like the English students. For example, Rau is called by an English name. Yet she joins the Indian students sitting at the back of the classroom.

26. At first, how does Rau feel about being called by an English name? How does her sister feel about it?

27. Name two things Premila does to try to fit in.

28. What does the teacher's behavior show about her attitude toward Indians?

29. How does their mother react to the news of the teacher's treatment of the Indian children?

30. What lasting effect does this school experience have on Rau?

Writing on Your Own Write a sketch about a time when you were the new person in town, in class, or on the team. Tell about how others reacted to you and how you felt. Refer to the selections for ideas.

Kaffir Boy
Mark Mathabane

About the Author

White South Africans created a system called *apartheid*. It used the law to keep the different races apart. Apartheid was a government policy. Under it, blacks had few rights.

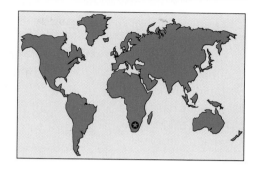

Many lived in dismal slums. Mark Mathabane was born in 1960 in Alexandra, which was one of Johannesburg's worst slums. His early life was full of gangs, police raids, and death. Then he found he had a talent for tennis. His playing continued to improve. He began to hope for a life outside Alexandra. Finally, he was allowed to play in tournaments for whites. Later, he received a tennis scholarship to an American college. In the United States, Mathabane became a fine tennis player. He also found the freedom to write about his life in the apartheid system.

About the Selection

Kaffir Boy is a remarkable story of courage. It tells how Mathabane survived eighteen years in Alexandra. He got his start with a good head on his shoulders. His mother and grandmother lent him their strength as well. They insisted that he go to school. Mathabane himself at first wanted to be a *tsotsi*. That was the term for a member of a South African gang. Mathabane believed his decision to attend school was a **turning point** in his life. A turning point is an experience that changes a character's life. In the following selection Mathabane is the **narrator.** He tells the story of his first visit to school at the age of seven and a half.

Kaffir Boy — Mark Mathabane

"Education will open doors where none seem to exist."

As you read, think about the quote at the beginning of the story. Mathabane has placed it there to tell you that it's what his story will be about.

When my mother began dropping hints that I would soon be going to school, I vowed never to go because school was a waste of time. She laughed and said, "We'll see. You don't know what you're talking about." My **philosophy** on school was that of a gang of ten-, eleven- and twelve-year-olds whom I so **revered** that their every word seemed that of an **oracle**.

These boys had long left their homes and were now living in various neighbourhood junkyards, making it their own. They slept in abandoned cars, smoked glue and **benzene**, ate **pilchards** and brown bread, sneaked into the white world to caddy and, if unsuccessful, came back to the township to steal beer and soda bottles from shebeens, or goods from the Indian traders on First Avenue. Their life-style was exciting, adventurous and full of surprises; and I was attracted to it. My mother told me that they were no-gooders, that they would amount to nothing, that I should not associate with them, but I paid no heed. What does she know? I used to tell myself. One thing she did not know was that the gang's way of life had **captivated** me wholly, particularly their philosophy on school: they hated it and considered an education a waste of time.

Shebeens were illegal drinking places. They made their own liquor and beer. That was illegal because it took business away from government-run beer halls.

They, like myself, had grown up in an environment where the value of an education was never emphasized, where the first thing a child learned was not how to read and write and spell, but how to fight and steal and rebel; where the money to send children to school was grossly lacking, for survival was first **priority**. I kept my membership in the gang, knowing that for as long as I was under its influence, I would never go to school.

benzene a colorless, flammable liquid	**oracle** a person who gives wise advice	**pilchard** a small fish related to the herring
captivate to fascinate; to interest deeply	**philosophy** a basic theory; a viewpoint	**priority** order of importance
		revere to honor and respect

One day my mother woke me up at four in the morning.

"Are they here? I didn't hear any noises," I asked in the usual way.

"No," my mother said. "I want you to get into that washtub over there."

"What!" I **balked**, upon hearing the word *washtub*. I feared taking baths like one feared the plague. Throughout seven years of **hectic** living the number of baths I had taken could be counted on one hand with several fingers missing. I simply had no natural inclination for water; cleanliness was a **trait** I still had to acquire. Besides, we had only one bathtub in the house, and it constantly sprung a leak.

Mathabane's family and others like them lived in fear of the police. They often treated blacks harshly while enforcing South Africa's apartheid laws.

"I said get into that tub!" My mother shook a finger in my face.

Reluctantly, I obeyed, yet wondered why all of a sudden I had to take a bath. My mother, armed with a **scropbrush** and a piece of Lifebuoy soap, **purged** me of years and years of grime till I ached

Granny holds a great-grandchild.

and bled. As I howled, feeling pain shoot through my limbs as the thistles of the brush encountered stubborn callouses, there was a loud knock at the door.

Instantly my mother leaped away from the tub and headed, on tiptoe, toward the bedroom. Fear seized me as I, too, thought of the police. I sat frozen in the bathtub, not knowing what to do.

"Open up, Mujaji [my mother's maiden name]," Granny's voice came shrilling through the door. "It's me."

balk to stop and refuse to go	**purge** to cleanse; to purify	**scropbrush** a brush to scrub with
hectic confused; full of fast activity	**reluctantly** unwillingly	**trait** a quality of character, a peculiarity

My mother heaved a sigh of relief; her tense **limbs** relaxed. She turned and headed to the kitchen door, unlatched it and in came Granny and Aunt Bushy.

"You scared me half to death," my mother said to Granny. "I had forgotten all about your coming."

"Are you ready?" Granny asked my mother.

"Yes—just about," my mother said, **beckoning** me to get out of the washtub.

She handed me a piece of cloth to dry myself. As I dried myself, questions raced through my mind: What's going on? What's Granny doing at our house this **ungodly** hour of the morning? And why did she ask my mother, "Are you ready?" While I stood debating, my mother went into the bedroom and came out with a stained white shirt and a pair of faded black shorts.

"Here," she said, handing me the **togs**, "put these on."

"Why?" I asked.

"Put them on I said!"

I put the shirt on; it was grossly loose-fitting. It reached all the way down to my ankles. Then I saw the reason why: it was my father's shirt!

"But this is Papa's shirt," I complained. "It don't fit me."

"Put it on," my mother insisted. "I'll make it fit."

"The pants don't fit me either," I said. "Whose are they anyway?"

"Put them on," my mother said. "I'll make them fit."

Moments later I had the garments on; I looked ridiculous. My mother started working on the pants and shirt to make them fit. She folded the shirt in so many **intricate** ways and stashed it inside the pants, they too having been folded several times at the waist. She then choked the pants at the waist with a piece of **sisal**

beckon to summon by gesturing	**limb** a leg or arm	**togs** clothes
intricate complex; difficult to arrange	**sisal** a long, strong durable white fiber used to make ropes and twine	**ungodly** wicked or outrageous

rope to hold them up. She then **lavishly** smeared my face, arms and legs with a mixture of pig's fat and Vaseline. "This will insulate you from the cold," she said. My skin gleamed like the morning star and I felt as hot as the centre of the sun and I smelled God knows like what. After **embalming** me, she headed to the bedroom.

"Where are we going, Gran'ma?" I said, hoping that she would tell me what my mother refused to tell me. I still had no idea I was about to be taken to school.

"Didn't your mother tell you?" Granny said with a smile. "You're going to start school."

"What!" I gasped, leaping from the chair where I was sitting as if it were made of hot lead. "I am not going to school!" I **blurted** out and raced toward the kitchen door.

My mother had just reappeared from the bedroom and guessing what I was up to, she yelled, "Someone get the door!"

Aunt Bushy immediately barred the door. I turned and headed for the window. As I leaped for the windowsill, my mother lunged at me and brought me down. I **tussled**, "Let go of me! I don't want to go to school! Let me go!" but my mother held fast onto me.

"It's no use now," she said, grinning triumphantly as she pinned me down. Turning her head in Granny's direction, she shouted, "Granny! Get a rope quickly!"

Granny grabbed a piece of rope nearby and came to my mother's aid. I bit and clawed every hand that grabbed me, and howled **protestations** against going to school; however, I was no match for the two determined **matriarchs**. In a jiffy they had me bound, hands and feet.

"What's the matter with him?" Granny, bewildered, asked my mother. "Why did he suddenly turn into an imp when I told him you're taking him to school?"

Centre is the British spelling for the word *center*. Look for other British spellings in this story.

blurt to say suddenly and without thinking

embalm to preserve

lavishly generously; using more than is necessary

matriarch a woman who rules a family

protestation a strong objection

tussle to struggle; to wrestle

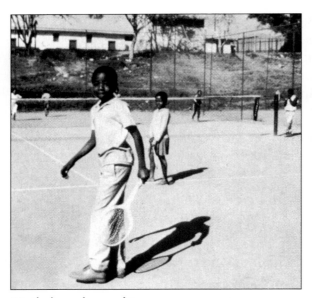

Mathabane learned to play tennis on a court like this in Alexandra.

Apartheid laws required black South Africans to carry a government-issued passbook with papers stating where they were assigned to live and work. The police often conducted *pass raids* during the night to look for people who were not where they were supposed to be.

"You shouldn't have told him that he's being taken to school," my mother said. "He doesn't want to go there. That's why I requested you come today, to help me take him there. Those boys in the streets have been a bad influence on him."

As the two matriarchs hauled me through the door, they told Aunt Bushy not to go to school but stay behind and mind the house and the children.

The sun was beginning to rise from beyond the **veld** when Granny and my mother dragged me to school. The streets were beginning to fill with their everyday traffic: old men and women, wizened, bent and ragged, were beginning to assemble in their usual **coteries** and head for shebeens in the backyards where they discussed how they escaped the morning pass raids and **contemplated** the conditions of life amidst intense beer drinking and vacant, uneasy laughter; young boys and girls, some as young as myself, were beginning their aimless wanderings along the narrow, dusty streets in search of food, carrying **bawling** infants piggyback.

As we went along some of the streets, boys and girls who shared the same fears about school as I were making their feelings known in a variety of ways. They were howling their protests and trying to escape. A few managed to break loose and make a mad dash for freedom, only to be recaptured in no time, **admonished** or whipped, or both, and ordered to march again.

As we made a turn into Sixteenth Avenue, the street leading to the tribal school I was being taken to, a short, chubby black woman came along from the opposite direction. She had a **scuttle** overflowing with coal on her *doek*-covered (cloth-

admonish warn; to scold with a warning	**coterie** a group of people who meet often	**veld** the South African grassland
bawling crying loudly	**scuttle** a pail for carrying coal	**wizened** dried up
contemplate to look at thoughtfully		

covered) head. An infant, bawling deafeningly, was loosely **swathed** with a piece of sheepskin onto her back. Following closely behind the woman, and picking up pieces of coal as they fell from the scuttle and placing them in a small plastic bag, was a half-naked, potbellied and thumb-sucking boy of about four. The woman stopped **abreast**. For some reason we stopped too.

"I wish I had done the same to my oldest son," the strange woman said in a **regretful** voice, gazing at me. I was **confounded** by her stopping and offering her **unsolicited** opinion.

"I wish I had done that to my oldest son," she repeated, and suddenly burst into tears; amidst sobs, she continued, "before ...the street claimed him ...and ...turned him into a *tsotsi*."

Granny and my mother offered consolatory remarks to the strange woman.

A *tsotsi* is a gang member.

"But it's too late now," the strange woman continued, tears now streaming freely down her puffy cheeks. She made no attempt to dry them. "It's too late now," she said for the second time, "he's beyond any help. I can't help him even if I wanted to. *Uswile* [He is dead]."

"How did he die?" my mother asked in a sympathetic voice.

"He shunned school and, instead, grew up to live by the knife. And the same knife he lived by ended his life. That's why whenever I see a boy-child refuse to go to school, I stop and tell the story of my dear little *mbitsini* [heartbreak]."

How did the strange woman's son die?

Having said that, the strange woman left as mysteriously as she had arrived.

"Did you hear what that woman said!" my mother screamed into my ears. "Do you want the same to happen to you?"

I dropped my eyes. I was confused.

"Poor woman," Granny said **ruefully**. "She must have truly loved her son."

abreast side by side; in an even line	**regretful** remembering with sorrow or grief	**swathe** to wrap with a band of material
confounded confused; puzzled	**ruefully** expressing regret or pity	**unsolicited** not requested

Finally, we reached the school and I was **ushered** into the principal's office, a tiny **cubicle** facing a row of **privies** and a patch of yellowed grass.

"So this is the rascal we'd been talking about," the principal, a tall, **wiry** man, **foppishly** dressed in a black pin-striped suit, said to my mother as we entered. His **austere**, shiny face, inscrutable and imposing, reminded me of my father. He was sitting behind a brown table upon which stood piles of dust and cobweb-covered books and papers. In one upper pocket of his jacket was arrayed a variety of pens and pencils; in the other nestled a lily-white handkerchief whose presence was more decorative than utilitarian. Alongside him stood a disproportionately portly black woman, fashionably dressed in a black skirt and a white blouse. She had but one pen, and this she held in her hand. The room was hot and stuffy and buzzing with flies.

"Yes, Principal," my mother answered, "this is he."

"I see he's living up to his notoriety," remarked the principal, noticing that I had been bound. "Did he give you too much trouble?"

"Trouble, Principal," my mother sighed. "He was like an imp."

"He's just like the rest of them, Principal," Granny sighed. "Once they get out into the streets, they become wild. They take to the many vices of the streets like an infant takes to its mother's milk. They begin to think that there's no other life but the one shown them by the *tsotsis*. They come to hate school and forget about the future."

"Well," the principal said. "We'll soon remedy all that. Untie him."

"He'll run away," my mother cried.

"I don't think he's that foolish to attempt that with all of us here."

austere stern and serious	**foppishly** vainly; overly proud of one's looks	**usher** to conduct; to escort
cubicle a small room	**privy** an outhouse	**wiry** slender yet muscular

"He *is* that foolish, Principal," my mother said as she and Granny began untying me. "He's tried it before. Getting him here was an ordeal in itself."

The principal rose from his seat, took two steps to the door and closed it. As the door swung closed, I spotted a row of canes of different lengths and thicknesses hanging behind it. The principal, seeing me staring at the canes, grinned and said, in a manner suggesting that he had wanted me to see them, "As long as you behave, I won't have to use any of those on you."

Use those canes on me? I gasped. I stared at my mother—she smiled; at Granny—she smiled too. That made me abandon any **inkling** of escaping.

"So they finally gave you the birth certificate and the papers," the principal addressed my mother as he returned to his chair.

"Yes, Principal," my mother said, "they finally did. But what a battle it was. It took me nearly a year to get all them papers together." She took out of her handbag a neatly wrapped package and handed it to the principal. "They've been running us around for so long that there were times when I thought he would never attend school, Principal," she said.

inkling a hint; a suggestion

South Africa has three capital cities. *Pretoria* is the administrative capital; Cape Town the legislative capital; and Bloemfontein the judicial capital.

Granny mispronounces the name *Pretoria*.

"That's pretty much standard procedure, Mrs. Mathabane," the principal said, unwrapping the package. "But you now have the papers and that's what's important.

"As long as we have the papers," he continued, **minutely perusing** the contents of the package, "we won't be breaking the law in admitting your son to this school, for we'll be in full **compliance** with the requirements set by the authorities in Pretoria."

"Sometimes I don't understand the laws from Pitori," Granny said. "They did the same to me with my Piet and Bushy. Why, Principal, should our children not be allowed to learn because of some piece of paper?"

"The piece of paper you're referring to, Mrs. Mabaso," the principal said to Granny, "is as important to our children as a pass is to us adults. We all hate passes; therefore, it's only natural we should hate the regulations our children are subjected to. But as we have to live with passes, so our children have to live with the regulations, Mrs. Mabaso. I hope you understand, that is the law of the country. We would have admitted your grandson a long time ago, as you well know, had it not been for the papers. I hope you understand."

"I understand, Principal," Granny said, "but I don't understand," she added **paradoxically**.

One of the papers caught the principal's eye and he turned to my mother and asked, "Is your husband a Shangaan, Mrs. Mathabane?"

The people of South Africa belong to many tribes and ethnic groups, which speak different languages.

"No, he's not, Principal," my mother said. "Is there anything wrong? He's Venda and I'm Shangaan."

The principal reflected for a moment or so and then said, concernedly, "No, there's nothing seriously wrong. Nothing that we can't take care of. You see, Mrs. Mathabane, technically, the fact that your child's father is a Venda makes him **ineligible** to

compliance yielding to a demand	**minutely** paying attention to small details	**peruse** to read carefully
ineligible not qualified	**paradoxically** self-contradictory	

attend this tribal school because it is only for children whose parents are of the Shangaan tribe. May I ask what language the children speak at home?"

"Both languages," my mother said worriedly, "Venda and Shangaan. Is there anything wrong?

The principal coughed, clearing his throat, then said, "I mean which language do they speak more?"

"It depends, Principal," my mother said, swallowing hard. "When their father is around, he wants them to speak only Venda. And when he's not, they speak Shangaan. And when they are out at play, they speak Zulu and Sisotho."

"Well," the principal, heaving a sigh of relief. "In that case, I think an exception can be made. The reason for such an exception is that there's currently no school for Vendas in Alexandra. And should the authorities come asking why we took in your son, we can tell them that. Anyway, your child is half-half."

Everyone broke into a nervous laugh, except me. I was bewildered by the whole thing. I looked at my mother, and she seemed greatly relieved as she watched the principal register me; a broad smile broke across her face. It was as if some enormously heavy burden had finally been lifted from her shoulders and her conscience.

"Bring him back two weeks from today," the principal said as he saw us to the door. "There're so many children registering today that classes won't begin until two weeks **hence**. Also, the school needs repair and cleaning up after the holidays. If he refuses to come, simply notify us, and we'll send a couple of big boys to come fetch him, and he'll be very sorry if it ever comes to that."

As we left the principal's office and headed home, my mind was still against going to school. I was thinking of running away from home and joining my friends in the junkyard.

I didn't want to go to school for three reasons: I was reluctant to surrender my freedom and independence over to what I heard every school-going child call "**tyrannous discipline**." I had heard

discipline punishment given as a correction	**hence** from this time	**tyrannous** unfair; severe; cruel

What are Mathabane's three reasons against going to school?

many bad things about life in tribal school—from daily beatings by teachers and mistresses who worked you like a mule to long school hours—and the sight of those canes in the principal's office gave **ample credence** to rumors that school was nothing but a torture chamber. And there was my allegiance to the gang.

But the thought of the strange woman's **lamentations** over her dead son presented a somewhat strong case for going to school: I didn't want to end up dead in the streets. A more **compelling** argument for going to school, however, was the vivid **recollection** of all that **humiliation** and pain my mother had gone through to get me the papers and the birth certificate so I could enroll in school. What should I do? I was torn between two worlds.

What are two reasons Mathabane lists for going to school?

But later that evening something happened to force me to go to school.

I was returning home from playing soccer when a neighbour **accosted** me by the gate and told me that there had been a bloody fight at my home.

"Your mother and father have been at it again," the neighbour, a woman, said.

"And your mother left."

I was stunned.

"Was she hurt badly?"

"A little bit," the woman said. "But she'll be all right. We took her to your grandma's place."

I became hot with anger.

"Is anyone in the house?" I stammered, trying to control my rage.

"Yes, your father is. But I don't think you should go near the house. He's raving mad. He's armed with a meat cleaver. He's

accost to approach and speak to in challenging way	**compelling** forceful	**lamentation** a cry of grief or sorrow
ample enough to satisfy	**credence** belief; proof	**recollection** something remembered
	humiliation the state of being disgraced or shamed	

chased out your brother and sisters, also. And some of the neighbours who tried to **intervene** he's threatened to carve them to pieces. I have never seen him this mad before."

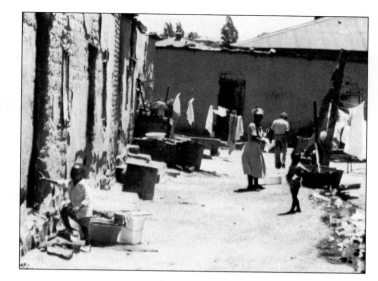

This is a typical ghetto yard.

I brushed aside the woman's warnings and went. Shattered windows convinced me that there had indeed been a **skirmish** of some sort. Several pieces of broken bricks, evidently broken after being thrown at the door, were lying about the door. I tried opening the door; it was locked from the inside. I knocked. No one answered. I knocked again. Still no one answered, until, as I turned to leave:

"Who's out there?" my father's voice came growling from inside.

"It's me, Johannes," I said...

I went to the broken window and screamed **obscenities** at my father, daring him to come out, hoping that if he as much as ever stuck his black face out, I would pelt him with the half-a-loaf brick in my hand. He didn't come out. He continued launching a **tirade** of obscenities at my mother and her mother... He was drunk, but I wondered where he had gotten the money to buy beer because it was still the middle of the week and he was dead broke. He had lost his entire wage for the past week in dice and had had to borrow bus fare.

"I'll kill you someday for all you're doing to my mother," I threatened him, overwhelmed with rage. Several nosey neighbours were beginning to **congregate** by open windows and doors. Not wanting to make a spectacle of myself, which was

There had been other disagreements in Mathabane's house. The neighbors had seen other spectacles.

congregate to collect or gather

intervene to come in between

obscenities curses

skirmish a conflict or dispute

tirade a long, violent, scolding speech

something many of our neighbors seemed to always expect from our family, I **backtracked** away from the door and vanished into the dark street. I ran, without stopping, all the way to the other end of the township where Granny lived. There I found my mother, her face swollen and bruised and her eyes puffed up to the point where she could scarcely see.

"What happened, Mama?" I asked, fighting to hold back the tears at the sight of her **disfigured** face.

"Nothing, child, nothing," she mumbled, almost apologetically, between swollen lips. "Your papa simply lost his temper, that's all."

"But why did he beat you up like this, Mama?" Tears came down my face. "He's never beaten you like this before."

My mother appeared reluctant to answer me. She looked searchingly at Granny, who was pounding **millet** with pestle and mortar and mixing it with **sorghum** and nuts for an African **delicacy**. Granny said, "Tell him, child, tell him. He's got a right to know. Anyway, he's the cause of it all."

"Your father and I fought because I took you to school this morning," my mother began. "He had told me not to, and when I told him that I had, he became very upset. He was drunk. We started arguing, and one thing led to another."

"Why doesn't he want me to go to school?"

"He says he doesn't have money to waste paying for you to get what he calls a useless white man's education," my mother replied. "But I told him that if he won't pay for your schooling, I would try and look for a job and pay, but he didn't want to hear that, also. 'There are better things for you to work for,' he said. 'Besides, I don't want you to work. How would I look to other men if you, a woman I owned, were to start working?' When I asked him why shouldn't I take you to school, seeing that you

---

backtrack to go back the way one came

delicacy a special, enjoyable food

disfigured marred or spoiled

millet a cereal grain whose small seeds are used for food

sorghum cereal grain ground into fine meal or made into a sweet syrup were now of age, he replied that he doesn't believe in schools. I told him that school would keep you off the streets and out of trouble, but still he was **belligerent**."

"Is that why he beat you up?"

"Yes, he said I disobeyed his orders."

"He's right, child," Granny **interjected**. "He paid *lobola* [bride price] for you. And your father ate it all up before he left me."

To which my mother replied, "But I desperately want to leave this beast of a man. But with his *lobola* gone I can't do it. That worthless thing you call your husband shouldn't have sold Jackson's scrawny cattle and left you penniless."

"Don't talk like that about your father, child," Granny said. "Despite all, he's still your father, you know. Anyway, he asked for *lobola* only because he had to get back what he spent raising you. And you know it would have been **taboo** for him to let you or any of your sisters go without asking for *lobola*."

"You and Papa seemed to forget that my sisters and I have minds of our own," my mother said. "We didn't need you to tell us whom to marry, and why, and how. If it hadn't been for your interference, I could have married that schoolteacher."

Granny did not reply; she knew well not to. When it came to the act of "selling" women as marriage partners, my mother was **vehemently** opposed to it. Not only was she opposed to this one aspect of tribal culture, but to others as well, particularly those involving relations between men and women and the upbringing of children. But my mother's sharply differing opinion was an exception rather than the rule among tribal women. Most times, many tribal women questioned her **sanity** in daring to question well-established **mores**. But my mother did not seem to care; she would always **scoff** at her opponents and call them fools in letting their husbands enslave them completely.

Mother wishes that they had enough money to return the *bride price* to her husband. She wants to buy her freedom back.

Why does Mathabane's mother hesitate to tell him why she was beaten? Why does she finally tell him?

belligerent marked by hostile or warlike behavior	**mores** traditional customs	**taboo** forbidden by social customs
interject to insert a remark	**sanity** soundness of mind	**vehemently** forcefully; violently
	scoff to show scorn	

Though I disliked school, largely because I knew nothing about what actually went on there, and the little I knew had painted a dreadful picture, the fact that a father would not want his son to go to school, especially a father who didn't go to school, seemed hard to understand.

"Why do you want me to go to school, Mama?" I asked, hoping that she might, somehow, clear up some of the confusion that was building in my mind.

"I want you to have a future, child," my mother said. "And, contrary to what your father says, school is the only means to a future. I don't want you growing up to be like your father."

The latter statement hit me like a bolt of lightning. It just about shattered every defense mechanism and every **pretext** I had against going to school.

Louis Trichardt is the name of the township where the author's father grew up.

"Your father didn't go to school," she continued, dabbing her puffed eyes to reduce the swelling with a piece of cloth dipped in warm water, "that's why he's doing some of the bad things he's doing. Things like drinking, gambling and neglecting his family. He didn't learn how to read and write; therefore, he can't find a decent job. Lack of any education has narrowly focused his life. He sees nothing beyond himself. He still thinks in the old, tribal way, and still believes that things should be as they were back in the old days when he was growing up as a tribal boy in Louis Trichardt. Though he's my husband, and your father, he doesn't see any of that."

"Why didn't he go to school, Mama?"

"He refused to go to school because his father led him to believe that an education was a tool through which white people were going to take things away from him, like they did black people in the old days. And that a white man's education was worthless insofar as black people were concerned because it prepared them for jobs they can't have. But I know it isn't totally so, child,

pretext an excuse for not doing something

because times have changed somewhat. Though our **lot** isn't any better today, an education will get you a decent job. If you can read or write you'll be better off than those of us who can't. Take my situation: I can't find a job because I don't have papers, and I can't get papers because white people mainly want to register people who can read and write. But I want things to be different for you, child. For you and your brother and sisters. I want you to go to school, because I believe that an education is the key you need to open up a new world and a new life for yourself, a world and life different from that of either your father's or mine. It is the only key that can do that, and only those who seek it earnestly and **perseveringly** will get anywhere in the white man's world. Education will open doors where none seem to exist. It'll make people talk to you, listen to you and help you; people who otherwise wouldn't bother. It will make you soar, like a bird lifting up into the endless blue sky, and leave poverty, hunger and suffering behind. It'll teach you to learn to **embrace** what's good and **shun** what's bad and evil. Above all, it'll make you a somebody in this world. It'll make you grow up to be a good and proud person. That's why I want you to go to school, child, so that education can do all that, and more, for you."

A long, awkward silence followed, during which I reflected upon the **significance** of my mother's lengthy speech. I looked at my mother; she looked at me.

Finally, I asked, "How come you know so much about school, Mama? You didn't go to school, did you?"

"No, child," my mother replied. "Just like your father, I never went to school." For the second time that evening, a mere statement of fact had a thunderous impact on me. All the confusion I had about school seemed to leave my mind, like darkness giving way to light. And what had previously been a dark, yawning **void** in my mind was suddenly transformed into a beacon of light that began to grow larger and larger, until it

embrace to adopt; to welcome	**perseveringly** keeping at something in spite of difficulties	**significance** meaning
lot fate; state in life		**void** a feeling of emptiness
	shun to avoid	

had swallowed up, blotted out, all the blackness. That beacon of light seemed to reveal things and facts, which, though they must have always existed in me, I hadn't been aware of up until now.

"But unlike your father," my mother went on, "I've always wanted to go to school, but couldn't because my father, under the **sway** of tribal traditions, thought it unnecessary to educate females. That's why I so much want you to go, child, for if you do, I know that someday I too would come to go, old as I would be then. Promise me, therefore, that no matter what, you'll go back to school. And I, in turn, promise that I'll do everything in my power to keep you there."

With tears streaming down my cheeks and falling upon my mother's **bosom**, I promised her that I would go to school "forever." That night, at seven and a half years of my life, the battlelines in the family were drawn. My mother on one side, **illiterate** but determined to have me drink, for better or worse, from the well of knowledge. On the other side, my father, he too illiterate, yet determined to have me drink from the well of ignorance. Scarcely aware of the **magnitude** of the decision I was making, or, rather, the decision which was being emotionally thrusted upon me, I chose to fight on my mother's side, and thus my **destiny** was forever altered.

bosom the breast of a human	**illiterate** not knowing how to read or write	**sway** influence
destiny a person's fate or future	**magnitude** greatness; importance	

Directions Write the answers to these questions using complete sentences.

Comprehension: Identifying Facts

1. Where did Mark Mathabane live as a child?

2. What does Mathabane want to do? Why? What does his mother want him to do?

3. Who comes to help Mathabane's mother take him to school?

4. What is wrong with the clothes his mother finds for him?

5. When he hears he is going to school, what does Mathabane do?

6. Whom did they meet on the way to school? What does she say?

7. What does the principal look like?

8. What makes Mathabane give up any idea of escaping from the principal's office?

9. What tribe is the school for? How does Mathabane qualify?

10. What happens to Mathabane's mother when his father returns home?

Comprehension: Understanding Main Ideas

11. What papers are needed to enroll in school? Why are they hard to get?

12. Why does Mathabane's father lose his temper? List two reasons.

13. What does Mathabane's father think of education?

14. Why doesn't Mathabane's mother leave her husband?

15. Why can't she borrow the money from her parents?

16. How is Mathabane's mother different from other women in her tribe?

17. Why does Mathabane's mother want him to go to school?

18. Why can't Mathabane's mother get a job?

19. How could Mathabane's mother finally get an education?

20. What does Mathabane finally decide to do?

Review Continued on Next Page

Understanding Literature: Turning Point

A turning point story is a story about an experience that changes a person's life. Mathabane's decision to attend school is a turning point in his life. That decision would change his life forever.

21. How would Mathabane's life in the neighborhood be different?

22. How would his life in his family be different?

23. Does his mother agree with his choice? Why or why not?

24. Does his father agree with his choice? Why or why not?

25. Do you agree that this is a turning point story? Explain your answer.

Critical Thinking

Reread the long speeches Mathabane's mother makes near the end of the story. She is explaining why education is important.

26. Why didn't his father attend school as a boy?

27. Why does his mother think it will be different for her sons?

28. She says, "It'll make people talk to you, listen to you and help you..." What does she mean?

29. She says education is "...like a bird lifting up into the endless blue sky..." What does she mean?

30. Do you think his mother will achieve her goal of going to school? Explain your answer.

Writing on Your Own Reread the quote at the beginning of the story. Find it again in Mathabane's mother's speech near the end of the story. Think about how it applies to your life, too. Write two or three paragraphs about what you hope education will do for you. How will it make your life different?

Biography

- "Biography is all about cutting people down to size. Getting an unruly quart into a pint pot." —Alan Bennett

- "A biography is considered complete if it merely accounts for six or seven selves, whereas a person may well have as many as a thousand." —Virginia Woolf

In some ways, a biography is like an autobiography. It tells all or part of someone's life. But biographies are not written by the subjects themselves. They are written by people who are interested in their subject. They can't know the subject's thoughts. These writers must rely on conversations with the subject or those who knew him or her. The author usually uses information from several places. The writer tries to judge how the subject's actions affect others. An authorized biography will probably be kind to its subject. That is because most of the information in it comes from the subject, or people speaking for the subject.

Until recently, most biographers wrote about their subject by choosing facts, quotations, and anecdotes that supported the biographer's opinion. Carl Sandburg wrote a three-part biography of Abraham Lincoln. In it, Sandburg makes Abraham Lincoln into an almost godlike figure. Sandburg obviously admired Lincoln.

He wanted his readers to admire him too. Modern Lincoln biographers write about Lincoln's mistakes and weaknesses as well as his greatness.

Biographers today have often been journalists. This background trained them to use many sources to present a balanced picture of the subject. Biographers often show their opinions of their subject by deciding which events and relationships are most important in that person's life.

Maxine Hong
Kingston
(1940–)
American

About the Author

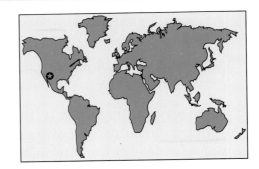

Maxine Hong Kingston was born in California. Her parents were Chinese immigrants. For a time she taught English in California and Hawaii. Kingston felt the conflict between her Asian heritage and the American culture around her. Her family had a strong tradition of storytelling. She also wanted to talk about her family's experiences. For those reasons, she began a writing career. Another of her books is *The Woman Warrior*. It focuses on Chinese American women.

About the Selection

China Men is the story of the men in Kingston's family. It tells how they came to America. It also tells how they tried to succeed in the "Land of the Gold Mountain." At the same time, they tried to keep their Chinese identity. They kept many old attitudes and ideas. Kingston describes how these ideas made it hard to fit in.

The following selection focuses on Kingston's father, Ed. With three other immigrants, he started a laundry in New York City. He then sent for his wife. The selection takes place in the 1930s. Dressed in their best clothes, Ed and his wife are exploring the city. Kingston was not born at the time of this story. Still, she uses **dialogue,** or conversations between characters. These help make her characters come alive. They seem like real people. The dialogue comes from the writer's imagination. As you read, think about the "American dream" and what it means.

China Men

Maxine Hong Kingston

They strolled in their **finery** along Fifth Avenue. "I washed all these windows," he told her. "When I first came here, I borrowed a **squeegee** and rags and a bucket, and walked up and down this street. I went inside each store and asked if they wanted the windows washed. The white foreigners aren't so hard to get along with; they nod to mean Yes and shake their heads to mean No, the same as anybody." New York glittered and shined with glass. He had liked pulling the water off the panes and leaving brief rainbows. While working, he had looked over the displays of all the wonderful clothes to own and wear. He had made the money to **pool** for starting the laundry. "In the spring," he promised her, "we'll buy you white cotton gloves."...

As you read, notice Ed's mixed feelings about his new country. For instance, he still calls white Americans *foreigners.*

"You ought to put your earrings in the safe deposit box at the bank. Pierced ears look a little **primitive** in this country." He also told her to buy makeup at a drugstore. "American people don't like oily faces. So you ought to use some powder. It's the custom. Also buy some **rouge**. These foreigners dislike yellow skin."

In the 1930s and 1940s, few American women had pierced ears.

finery elegant, dressy clothing	**primitive** too simple or crude	**squeegee** a tool used to scrape water from a flat surface
pool to combine one's money with others in a group project	**rouge** reddish powder used to add color to the face	

Some women's hair styles in the 1930s and early 1940s used false hairpieces, called *rats*. Another hair style, the *marcel*, had tight curls.

She also bought a long black rat of hair to roll her own hair over for an upswept hairdo. At a beauty parlor, she had her wavy hair cut and curled tighter with a marcel. She washed, ironed, and wrapped her silk pants and dresses and never wore them again.

He took her to see the Statue of Liberty. They climbed the ladder, she in high heels, up the arm to the torch, then the stairs to the crown. "Now we're inside her chin. This part must be the nose." From the windows of the crown, he showed her his city.

Why do you think Ed thinks of New York as *his city*?

In the 1930s, the *Empire State Building* was the tallest building in the world.

They also went to the top of the Empire State Building, took the second elevator to the very top, the top of the world. Ed loved the way he could look up at the **uncluttered** sky. They put money in the telescopes and looked for the laundry and their apartment. "So I have been on the tallest building in the world," she said. "I have seen everything. Wonderful. Wonderful. Amazing. Amazing."

Chinese immigrants called white Americans "ghosts" or "demons." A *demoness* is a female demon.

"Yes," he said. "Everything's possible on the **Gold Mountain**. I've danced with blondes." "No, really?" she said. "You didn't. You're making that up, aren't you? You danced with demonesses? I don't believe it."

Her favorite place to go was the free aquarium, "the fish house," where all **manner** of creatures swam. Walking between the lighted tanks, she asked, "When do you think we'll go back to China? Do you think we'll go back to China?" "Shh," he said. "Shh." The **electric eels** glowed in their dark tank, and the talking fish made noises. "There are bigger fish in China," she said.

electric eel a long, thin fish that can produce an electric current	**Gold Mountain** Chinese immigrants' name for the United States	**manner** kinds **uncluttered** empty; not filled with things

They went to the movies and saw *Young Tom Edison* with Mickey Rooney. They both liked the scene where the mother took Eh-Da-Son into the barn, but only pretended to **thrash** him; she faked the slaps and crying and scolding to fool the strict father, the father "the severe parent," according to Confucius, and the mother "the kind parent." ...After the movie, Ed explained to his wife that this cunning, **resourceful**, successful inventor, Edison, was who he had named himself after. "I see," she said. "Eh-Da-Son. Son as in *sage* or *immortal* or *saint*."

Mickey Rooney was a popular movie actor in the 1940s. He appeared in *Young Tom Edison* in 1940.

Confucius— (551?– 479 B.C.) was an important Chinese philosopher. His teachings are called Confucianism. They state that people's behavior should be based on duty and virtue.

New York City streets were filled with people and automobiles even in the early 1900s.

immortal one who lives forever

resourceful able to find ways to get things done

sage a wise person

thrash to beat or strike

Directions Write the answers to these questions using complete sentences.

Comprehension: Identifying Facts

1. How did Ed earn money to start the laundry?

2. List two things Ed and his wife see in New York.

3. What does his wife keep asking at the aquarium?

Comprehension: Understanding Main Ideas

4. Why does Ed want his wife to put her earrings away and wear makeup?

5. Why do they go up in the Statue of Liberty and the Empire State Building? What do they look for through the telescopes?

6. Why has Kingston's father chosen *Ed* as his American name?

Understanding Literature: Dialogue

Kingston can't know exactly what her parents said long ago. Still, she uses dialogue in this biography. Dialogue is the conversation between characters in a story. It gives the actual words they said. What a character says is often a clue to his or her personality. It can also reflect feelings and attitudes.

7. Point out several sentences in which Ed describes his feelings about white Americans.

8. Kingston uses dialogue to show the individual personalities of Ed and his wife. Give an example.

Critical Thinking

9. Why do you think that Chinese immigrants called America "the Gold Mountain"?

10. What do you think were the qualities about Thomas Edison that made the Chinese admire him?

Writing on Your Own In two or more sentences, explain how you know Ed feels successful in America. If possible, include quotations from his own words.

The Last Seven Months of Anne Frank
Willy Lindwer

Willy Lindwer
(1946–)
Dutch

About the Author

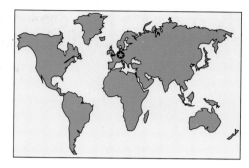

Willy Lindwer is a Dutch filmmaker. He was born in Amsterdam just after World War II. His Jewish parents survived the war by hiding. His grandmother, though, was killed by the Nazis in Poland. As an adult, Lindwer has concentrated on making documentary films. A documentary is a nonfiction movie. It tells the true stories of real people.

About the Selection

Earlier in this unit you read excerpts from Anne Frank's diary. *The Last Seven Months of Anne Frank* picks up Frank's story where her diaries end. In August 1944, four days after the last diary entry, the Nazis arrested the family. Lindwer made a documentary film about the last months of Frank's life. He found six women who had known Anne Frank and her family. Some were childhood friends. Others knew the Franks only in the Nazi concentration camps. Lindwer's interviews of these women went into his documentary. The film was first shown on television in 1988. But Lindwer found he could use only short pieces, or **excerpts,** in the film. So he published the full interviews in a book.

The women in Lindwer's book recount their memories of the Frank family. They also tell their own stories. And they tell how they feel today about that past suffering. All spent some time in the camps. The following selections are excerpts. An excerpt is a short passage take from a longer work. These are taken from longer interviews with several of the women.

The Last Seven Months of Anne Frank

Willy Lindwer

As you read, remember what you have already learned about Anne Frank and her family from reading her diary.

Hannah Elisabeth Pick-Goslar (Pick-Goslar was Frank's childhood friend. In Frank's published diary, she is called "Lies Goosens."):

Anne was given a diary on her thirteenth birthday. There was a party in the afternoon and we saw that she had gotten a very beautiful diary from her parents. I don't know if it was the first or second one that she had, because I remember that Anne was always writing in her diary, **shielding** it with her hand, even at school during the break. Everybody could see that she was writing. But no one was allowed to see what she had written. And I thought that she was writing entire books. I was always very curious to know what was in the diary, but she never showed it to anyone.

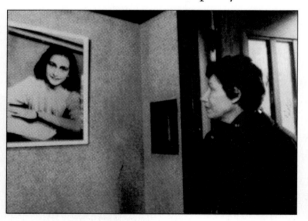

Hannah Elisabeth Pick-Goslar

I never could find out what was in it, but I have thought that there must have been much more than there was in the published diary. Maybe they never found all that she wrote

---

shielding hiding

before she went into hiding—she had already been writing for a couple of years—I remember that very well.

She did write in the diary that if she had a choice after the war, she wanted to become a writer in the Netherlands.

As I remember it, she was a bit spoiled, particularly by her father. Anne was her Daddy's girl; Margot was more like her mother. It's a good thing there were only two children. Mrs. Frank was a little religious, and Margot went in that direction too. Margot always said that after the war, if she could choose, she wanted to be a nurse in Israel.

> *Janny Brandes-Brilleslijper (Brandes-Brilleslijper met the Frank family in the Amsterdam central train station. They all were waiting to be sent away to Auschwitz.):*

In those days, I also went immediately to the Red Cross to look at the lists that showed who had **survived** and who had died. And I put a cross next to the names of those who I knew had actually died.

I also put a cross next to the names of Anne and Margot. Much later, in the summer of 1945, a tall, thin, **distinguished** man stood on the sidewalk. He looked through our window and Bob (my husband) opened the door, because he often protected me. In the beginning, I had to deal so much with family members whom I had to tell that their sons, daughters, and husbands would not be coming back. That was often **unbearable**. And it was especially difficult to deal with because I had survived and had come back.

And there stood Otto Frank. He asked if I knew what had happened to his two daughters. I knew, but it was hard to get the words out of my mouth. He had already heard from the Red Cross, but he wanted to have it **confirmed**....I had to tell him that...that his children were no more.

Many European Jews moved to *Israel* in the 1920s and 1930s. It was a place where Jews could live in safety. Israel became a nation in 1948.

Auschwitz was a Nazi concentration camp in Poland.

This woman has been in a concentration camp herself. Why would that make it harder for her to meet family members?

confirm to give proof	**distinguished** appearing important or famous	**survive** to go on living
		unbearable painful; hard to endure

He took it very hard. He was a man who didn't show his feelings **openly,** he had tremendous self-control. He was a tall, thin, **aristocratic** man. Later, we saw him frequently. By a remarkable chance, Anne's manuscript (her diary) was found at Annie Romijn's. And Annie Romijn was in our circle of friends. That's really amazing. And later he came often. He always stayed at the Hotel Suisse on Kalverstraat, where my relatives from Brussels always stayed. I always found that so nice.

Kalverstraat is a street in Amsterdam. *Brussels* is a city in Belgium, a country next to the Netherlands.

> *Rachel van Amerongen-Frankfoorder (van Amerongen-Frankfoorder first knew the Frank family while they were in a detention camp near Amsterdam.):*

Hebrew is one of the languages spoken in Israel.

In Israel, where we live, Anne Frank is a legend, and at the same time, a living girl. People are very interested in her. I believe that there is an Anne Frank Street in practically every town. Her diary has been translated into modern Hebrew.

The house where Anne and her family hid is a place that many tourists in Amsterdam visit.

People think that she is very special. Once, when my daughter was in the Netherlands with her twin daughters, one of the first things they wanted me to show them was the Anne Frank House. I didn't feel up to it; actually, I didn't want to go at all. For more than forty years, I had pushed that aside because I really wanted to live normally, and I didn't want to talk about it anymore.

Westerbork was a Nazi detention camp near Amsterdam. It was the first stop for people being taken to the concentration camps.

Nonetheless, I went to the Anne Frank House, and I had a very special feeling there. I had seen her, after all, from the time that she came to Westerbork. People took pictures there of every corner, every plank, everything; especially the Japanese, who you would suppose wouldn't be as **emotionally touched** as the Europeans. My daughter panicked, because she knew that I had known Anne. She

aristocratic noble or superior in appearance

emotionally with strong feelings

openly publicly; in front of others

touched affected

looked around and she said, "Mama, shouldn't you tell these people that you <u>knew</u> her? Shouldn't you do something? Tell them, tell them."

I couldn't do it; I absolutely couldn't. I wouldn't have known how to tell it.

Bloeme Evers-Emden (Evers-Emden got to know Anne and Margot Frank at a Jewish school in Amsterdam.):

I especially remember the last time I saw the Frank family [in Auschwitz]. Another selection had taken place. I spoke to Mrs. Frank, who was with Margot. Anne was somewhere else; she had *Krätze* (scabies). She had a rash of some kind or other. The Germans, **unhindered** by medical knowledge—at least the Germans who had the **say-so** over our lives—were terribly afraid because it might be **infectious** and she had to be **isolated**. As a result, Anne couldn't go with our group. Mrs. Frank, echoed by Margot, said, "We are, of course, going with her." I remember that I nodded, that I understood that.

Rachel van Amerongen-Frankfoorder

In the camps, a *selection* divided people into groups. Some were moved to other places; some were killed.

Scabies is an itchy skin disease.

That was the last time I saw them.

Before that, we naturally saw each other regularly, and I talked with them. They were always together—mother and daughters. Whatever **discord** you might **infer** from the diary was swept away now by **existential** need. They were always together. It is certain that they gave each other a great deal

discord arguments, disagreements	**infectious** capable of causing infection	**say-so** the right to decide
existential based on real experience	**infer** to conclude	**unhindered** not prevented or stopped
	isolated kept apart from others	

of support. All the things that a teenager might think of her mother were no longer of any **significance**.

What I mean is that there are people who talk about the war, whose bike was **requisitioned**, how terrible that was, and then they stop. For them, that was the very worst that happened. If you say, "Yes, but there are people who went into hiding, and, much worse, there were also people in the camps."

"Oh yes, that was too bad, but I had to give up my bike."

I think it was that way with Anne. When she was in hiding, which was a very **unhealthy** situation, her mother was someone against whom she **rebelled**. But in the camp, all of that actually completely fell away. By giving each other **mutual** support, they were able to keep each other alive— although no one can fight typhus.

Typhus is a serious illness, from which Anne Frank died. It is carried by fleas and other tiny insects. Typhus is common in places such as the camps, where living conditions are bad.

Bloeme Evers-Emden

mutual shared in common	**requisitioned** demanded, required	**unhealthy** dangerous, risky
rebel to go against rules or authority	**significance** importance	

Directions Write the answers to these questions using complete sentences.

Comprehension: Identifying Facts

1. Which of the women was a close childhood friend of Anne Frank?

2. Where do the other women meet the Frank family?

3. Which member of the Frank family survived the camps?

Comprehension: Understanding Main Ideas

4. These women and Anne Frank all share certain experiences. Describe them.

5. How do people in Israel today think about Anne Frank?

6. How did Anne's relationship with her mother change in the camps?

Understanding Literature: Excerpts

This selection is made up of excerpts. An excerpt is a short passage from a longer piece of writing. These excerpts are taken from much longer interviews with several women who knew Anne Frank. Each of them gives you an idea of how the speaker knew the Frank family. They also give you more information about her life and death.

7. How many different women are represented in these excerpts?

8. Which excerpt describes a visit from Anne Frank's father?

Critical Thinking

9. Why do you think visitors to Amsterdam go to the Anne Frank House?

10. One of these women at first did not want to talk about Anne Frank. Later she said, "It was much more difficult to remain silent." Why do you think that was true?

Writing on Your Own You have now seen Anne Frank from two different points of view. Earlier, you read parts of her diary. Now you have heard from others who knew her. Now it's your turn. Write one or two paragraphs explaining what you think about Anne Frank. Why is her story so important to so many people?

Journalism

- "You should always believe all you read in newspapers, as this makes them more interesting." —Rose Macaulay

- "In journalism there has always been a tension between getting it first and getting it right." —Ellen Goodman

Journalism is the gathering and communicating of news to the public. The Constitution guarantees freedom of the press to American journalists. This lets them keep the public well informed. Along with freedom comes the responsibility to report fairly and accurately. Imagine there is a fight between two public officials. A reporter covering the story should talk to both sides before writing the story. He or she might also need to talk to other witnesses. The story should use all these different points of view.

Some journalists report immediate news. Such "breaking news" is in newspapers and on TV as an event happens. Staff reporters often cover these stories. (They don't sign their articles or get public credit for putting the story together.) Feature articles and sidebars come later. They analyze the news. Sidebars are short articles running next to the main story. They may provide more background, or they may report related issues. This is called "in-depth" reporting.

One of the most immediate news sources is the Internet. It is a worldwide network of computers. Anyone connected to the Internet can get information from all over the world at any time. Many newspapers, big and small, have a Web site. A newspaper's Web site has material that the paper puts on the Internet for the public to read. Putting news on the Internet shortens the news cycle. The news cycle starts when a news item is printed. It ends when an update or reaction to it is printed.

The following articles represent news stories and editorials about a world event. As you read, notice how much of each article reports facts and how much is analysis. Several of the selections were taken from the Internet edition of a newspaper. You might not be able to find these newspapers at your local newsstand. But you might find them on the Internet.

Account Evened With India, Says PM

M. Ziauddin, From *Dawn* (Friday, 29 May 1998)

Dawn
(established 1947)
Pakistani

Literary Terms

news story the first reports of an event; mainly covers the basic facts

Web site a place on the Internet where information is published

About the Newspaper

Dawn is an English-language morning paper. It is one of the leading papers in Pakistan. Before independence, it was published in Delhi. Today it is published in Karachi

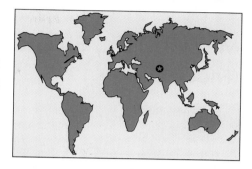

and Lahore, Pakistan. Those are Pakistan's largest cities. Karachi has more than five million people. Pakistan has many newspapers in English. Pakistanis also speak many other languages. Many papers are published in those languages, especially Urdu and Sindh.

You will find articles from *Dawn* on its **Web site.** *Dawn Online* (http://dawn.com/) is the Internet address of *Dawn.* Other foreign newspapers also have Web sites.

About the Selection

Early in May 1998, India held tests of nuclear weapons. They were the first in the region. A few weeks later, Pakistan held its own tests. The two countries have been rivals and enemies for more than fifty years. Until 1947, all of South Asia was the British colony of India. It then split into two independent countries. Most Pakistanis are Muslim. India's people are more varied and Hindus are the main religious group.

This selection is a **news story** from Pakistan. It reports that Pakistan has just made its first nuclear tests. The prime minister has announced them. He also predicted that other nations would punish Pakistan. Why? Most people in Pakistan were proud of their country's decision. At the same time, Pakistanis knew that the tests would bring trouble. Other nations with nuclear weapons have agreed to stop testing them. The Indian and Pakistani tests frightened many people.

ACCOUNT EVENED WITH INDIA, SAYS PM

M. Ziauddin, From *Dawn*
(Friday, 29 May 1998)

Pakistani citizens demonstrated in the streets to show their support of the nuclear tests.

ISLAMABAD: Pakistan on Thursday joined the exclusive club of nuclear nations by conducting five nuclear tests of varying **intensity** in Chagai hills, a remote region of Balochistan desert near the border with Iran and Afghanistan. Announcing the successful **completion** of a series of tests in response to those conducted by India on May 11–13, Prime Minister Nawaz Sharif told the nation on radio and television that he took the decision in the interest of national security and **integrity**.

Keep in mind that India and Pakistan have been rivals since the two nations were formed. *Islamabad* is Pakistan's capital.

Only a few countries have nuclear weapons. The writer calls them the *exclusive club of nuclear nations.*

He, however, warned the nation to be prepared to pay the price for taking this decision in the face of immense world pressure. The prime minister said in a few days time he would present to the nation a complete national **agenda** for meeting the **anticipated** hardships. He announced a number of official austerity measures to meet the challenges of the expected sanctions and asked the nation to reciprocate by trying to live within its means.

The prime minister also served final notice on the country's tax **evaders** and **corrupt** tax collectors, cautioning them to

agenda a list of things to be done

anticipated expected

completion ending

corrupt dishonest

evader a person who avoids doing something

integrity completeness

intensity strength

mend their ways; otherwise he warned that the government would not spare them. He assured the nation that the government would stop **forthwith** all of its demonstrative and wasteful **expenditures** and said all **palatial** official buildings would be pressed into the service of the nation. Some of these buildings would be turned into schools, some into hospitals and some others into women's universities. And some would be sold to retire debts. The prime minister announced that he would not use the Prime Minister's Secretariat and said the government has decided to observe complete austerity at the official level.

He said the president was in complete agreement with these decisions and all provincial governors, chief ministers, federal ministers, chiefs of navy, army, and air-force and high civil and military officials will join the nation in its sacrifices and austerity efforts. He asked those who had borrowed billions of rupees from the banks to return the national wealth and warned tax evaders to give up their anti-national habits. Describing the nuclear tests as a **defensive** step, the prime minister said these tests were conducted **solely** in the interest of national security and integrity.

Prime Minister Nawaz Sharif said every time Pakistan brought to the world attention India's **massive** arms build-up, New Delhi attributed it to Chinese threat to India's security. But he said despite its tremendous superiority in defensive **capability,** China was against expansionism while India had proven on more than one occasion that it harboured strong expansionist ambitions. Under the circumstances it was natural for Pakistan, Mr. Nawaz Sharif said, to feel concerned and in order to ward off the threat to national security, the country had even proposed that America, Russia and China should mediate and save Asia from arms race.

The prime minister expects other countries to impose *sanctions* because they oppose the nuclear tests. That is, they will stop or cut down trade and aid to Pakistan.

The *Secretariat* is a large government building in Islamabad.

Pakistan is divided into four provinces. Each has a *provincial governor.*

The *rupee* is the unit of money in both India and Pakistan.

capability the ability to do something	**expenditure** spending	**palatial** elaborate; like a palace
defensive done to defend oneself	**forthwith** immediatel	
	massive huge	**solely** only

He said if Pakistan had wanted it would have conducted nuclear tests 15–20 years ago but the **abject** poverty of the people of the region **dissuaded** Pakistan from doing so. But the world, he said, instead of putting pressure on India not to take the destructive road imposed all kinds of sanctions on Pakistan for no fault of her [own]. He said after the Indian tests, Pakistan had expected the world to impose a total economic **blockade** on India but unfortunately no such action was taken.

Near the end of World War II, the United States dropped atomic bombs on *Hiroshima* and *Nagasaki*, Japan. Japan today opposes nuclear weapons.

Prime Minister Nawaz Sharif praised China for its support during "this hour of crisis" and said Pakistan was proud of its great neighbour. Stating that Japan's position on the nuclear issue was based on the highest human principles, he, however, thought if Japan had had its own nuclear capability Hiroshima and Nagasaki would not have suffered destruction. He thanked President Clinton for his five telephone calls to express his sympathies following Indian explosions but said he expected the American president to appreciate Pakistan's **compulsions** for carrying out its own tests **despite** American advise against it.

The *big bomb* refers to a nuclear weapon. *Kashmir* is a disputed region on the Indian border.

The prime minister said Pakistan has taken the extreme step without bothering about the expected sanctions and spurning promises of all kinds of gifts and goodies. He said the world should not believe India when it says that it would use the 'big bomb' only if attacked because both in 1965 and 1971 India went to war against Pakistan accusing it of committing aggression and even today New Delhi was accusing Pakistan of keeping Azad Kashmir under its occupation. He asked the world to see Pakistan's nuclear tests in the context of India's aggressive and hegemonic designs but said if even then the world decided to impose sanctions on the country then Pakistan would accept these as the will of God.

abject miserable	**compulsion** the force or reason behind an action	**dissuade** to persuade someone not to take a certain action
blockade something that stops movement in and out of an area	**despite** in spite of	

Account Evened With India, Says PM

M. Ziauddin, From *Dawn* (Friday, 29 May 1998)

Directions Write the answers to these questions using complete sentences.

Comprehension: Identifying Facts

1. What is the name of the prime minister of Pakistan?

2. What are Pakistan's reasons for conducting nuclear tests?

3. What other country seems to have supported Pakistan's actions?

Comprehension: Understanding Main Ideas

4. How does the prime minister expect other countries to react to Pakistan's tests? How will that affect the country?

5. What does the prime minister want the people of Pakistan to do to help the country?

6. What specific actions will the Pakistani government take to cut down spending?

Understanding Literature: News Story

A news story presents the basic facts about an event. It answers the questions "who, what, when, why, how, and where." The first sentence of this story answers some of those questions. This is called the "lead." The rest of the news story reports on the prime minister's speech to the country. In it, he explains more of the "why" of the story.

7. Reread the first sentence of the news story. How does it answer the questions "when" and "where"?

8. Several paragraphs of the story are meant for a world audience, not just Pakistan. Which paragraphs are they?

Critical Thinking

9. What can you tell about Pakistan's relations with India from the tone of this article?

10. Do you think that Pakistan is a rich or a poor country?

Writing on Your Own Think of a recent event— in your city or in the world. Now write one or two sentences that would be the "lead" of a news story about that event. Your sentences should answer the basic questions: who, what, when, where, how, why?

Tests Are Nowhere Near India's

From *The Times of India* (Monday, 1 June 1998)

The Times of India
(established 1838)
Indian

Literary Term

journalism the gathering and communicating of news to the public

About the Newspaper

This newspaper first appeared in Bombay, India, in 1838. It was originally called *The Bombay Times and Journal of Commerce.* It was a paper mainly by and for the British residents

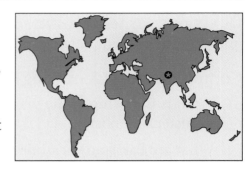

who ran India's colonial government. Today *The Times of India* is published in New Delhi. It is the most widely circulated English-language daily newspaper in India. It is part of a large Indian publishing group that also prints newspapers in Indian languages. Every day more than a million copies are sold from its printing plants in Mumbai, Delhi, Bangalore, Ahmedabad, Lucknow, and Patna. The *Times* is published every day including Sunday. It is a well-established newspaper with a good reputation for objective reporting.

The Times of India Online (http://www.timesofindia.com) is the Internet version of *The Times of India.*

About the Selection

People who work in **journalism** have the job of finding, collecting, and communicating news. The news reported in this story adds more information about India and Pakistan's nuclear tests. It is based mainly on a TV interview during which an Indian government official compared the two countries' tests. India had made the first tests. Pakistan had made tests a few weeks later. The official, George Fernandes, also discusses India's future nuclear plans. Besides reporting the speech, this journalist added other information. The article quotes scientists in the United States. Giving such "background information" is also part of a journalist's job.

TESTS ARE NOWHERE NEAR INDIA'S: FERNANDES

From *The Times of India*
(Monday, 1 June 1998)

NEW DELHI: Defence minister George Fernandes has asserted that Pakistan's nuclear blasts were "nowhere near" the Indian tests and said New Delhi exercised its nuclear **option** without holding **strategic** defence review because "scientists did feel that the tests were needed." In an interview to a private TV channel, Mr Fernandes said, "Everything that we have learnt about their [Pakistani] nuclear tests show that they are nowhere near where we are. In terms of our tests we [also] went in for low-intensity sub-kiloton tests. They are the most important tests in any kind of nuclear testing."

Asked if Islamabad's claim that it conducted tests similar to those by India was "mistaken and **deliberately** wrong," he said, "that's the general understanding that we have." Noting that New Delhi's concerns were much bigger and it had acted on those bigger concerns, he said there had been no testing since 1974 despite a lot of **development** in the nuclear science area and its **application** and "the scientists wanted to test it."

As you read this newspaper article, keep in mind that it gives India's point of view about the Pakistani tests.

New Delhi is India's capital city.

India was a British colony for many years. Indian newspapers use British spellings such as *defence* for *defense*.

Nuclear weapons are measured in *kilotons,* a force equal to the explosion of 1,000 tons of TNT. TNT is an explosive compound.

application a way to use something

deliberately on purpose

development growth; progress

option a choice

strategic related to military planning

These are different types and sizes of nuclear devices.

India had tested a 45 kiloton (KT) hydrogen bomb, a 15 KT fission bomb and a low-yield device on May 11 and two sub-kiloton devices on May 13. Pakistan conducted its tests on May 28 and 30.

The Central Intelligence Agency (CIA) is an American government agency. It gathers information about foreign governments.

Maintaining that Pakistan had carried out only one test on May 28, he said, "We got a bit of information that in fact there may not have [been] five tests. The US agency, the CIA, has put out a piece of information that the number five is only to match India's five. The general feeling is that there was only one."

Admitting that India carried out the Pokhran tests without holding a strategic defence review, he said, "There has been a lot of development in the nuclear science area. There has been **militarisation** of nuclear **weaponry**. We have to show not only to ourselves, but tell the world we [too] are there."

Asked whether India would conduct more tests, Mr Fernandes said, "We do not need to go for any more testing, whatever we needed to know we got it," but also added "in terms of a country's **security** concerns one does not say the last word at any point of time."

Fernandes is talking about whether India will now build nuclear weapons. To *weaponize* is to adapt something for use as a weapon.

Here *across the border* means Pakistan.

To a question if India would go in for weaponisation, the minister noted "What I have said is that any nuclear tests without weaponising do not make sense.

"Whether one needs to weaponise in the **context** of what has happened across the border is a matter on which in Parliament the Prime Minister had made a public offer to Pakistan that we should sit together, we should talk and we should not get into any kind of a nuclear weapon race. Therefore, it is going to be a two-way traffic and I hope Pakistan responds to the Prime Minister's appeal," he said.

context the setting or situation	**militarisation** (Amer. militarization) the process of being taken over or used by the military	**security** safety
maintaining declaring, insisting		**weaponry** different types of weapons seen as a group

Asked about control and command structure Mr Fernandes said "there will be the same kind of control which exist in those countries which have nuclear weaponry. They cannot be any different." Observing that the Prime Minister will be the only person to have his finger on the nuclear button, he said, "In India the Prime Minister is the **executive** head of government...And it shall be the Prime Minister."

On nuclear **deterrent,** he said, "The Army is happy that it has it and the Army believes that no one can push us around."

Mr Fernandes refused to give details on the size of deterrent that India required or the cost of creating it saying "these are matters which I do not believe can be **aired** in public." He said that the cost of developing a deterrent and an appropriate delivery system would not be "**backbreaking**" and added "a delivery system is something that we always had. Your aircraft are there. Your missiles are there. India is producing missiles."

Meanwhile, in Washington, the **global** network that tracks earthquakes and underground atomic blasts found only a faint echo from Saturday's Pakistan nuclear test that could mean the test was successful, but small or that the test was a failure and produced relatively few shock waves, says the *New York Times* quoting US experts. "It's a small event," said Terry Wallace, a seismologist at the University of Arizona, who works with the incorporated research institutions for **seismology,** a scientific group in Washington.

Mr Wallace said the blast had a preliminary magnitude of 4.3 equal to about 1,000 tons of high explosive; by contrast, the atomic bomb dropped on Hiroshima in 1945 had an explosive force of 15,000 tons.

Control and command structure means the government and military officials who are in charge of nuclear weapons.

In military language, a *delivery system* is the device, such as a missile, that carries a weapon to its target.

Here the New Delhi paper quotes an American newspaper and American scientists.

The shock waves from nuclear tests are measured with the Richter scale. This is the same scale used to measure earthquakes.

air to discuss in public

backbreaking very difficult

deterrent something that prevents or discourages an action

executive the branch of government that carries out the laws

global worldwide

seismology the study of earthquakes

The main Pakistani blast on Thursday was **monitored** as having magnitude of 4.8, equal to 8,000 to 15,000 tonnes. Such bombs are considered relatively small by the standards of world **arsenals,** where the explosive power of **warheads** can exceed millions of tonnes. Saturday's explosion was too small to show up on the government's main network for monitoring earthquakes around the world. "We've searched everything we have and we don't see anything." said Waverly Person, a spokesman at the national earthquake informations centre, in Golden, Colo. "We didn't record anything at all."

Nawaz Sharif is prime minister of Pakistan.

The daily quoted arms-control experts as saying that the truly **alarming** thing that prime minister Nawaz Sharif's government announced on Thursday was not that Pakistan had successfully conducted its own tests. Rather it was the declaration that Pakistan was already fitting nuclear warheads on top of a missile.

Michael Krepon, president of the Henry L. Stimson Centre, an independent research institute, said, "A crucial **threshold** has been crossed, if it's true and that means we have only two thresholds left. **Deployment** and use."

Indian Prime Minister Vajpayee (center) pays a visit to the site of the Indian blast.

The daily says India is said to have enough fissile material for perhaps 50 nuclear devices, maybe more. Pakistan has enough for perhaps 12. There is almost no evidence that either country has mastered the ability to make warheads small enough to fit on missiles, though not for lack of trying. It says senior administration officials cast doubt on Pakistan's claims to have already fitted its longest range missile with nuclear warheads. "That would be a fateful and foolish [decision]," one official said on condition of anonymity.

alarming frightening	**deployment** the spreading of troops or weapons in a larger area	**threshold** an entrance or beginning
arsenal a storehouse for weapons	**monitor** to measure with an instrument or device	**warhead** the front part of a missile or bomb that contains the explosive

Tests Are Nowhere Near India's

Directions Write the answers to these questions using complete sentences.

Comprehension: Identifying Facts

1. What is the main point of the Indian official's speech?

2. When did the Indian and Pakistani tests take place?

3. What expert is quoted late in the article? What is his specialty?

Comprehension: Understanding Main Ideas

4. What evidence does Fernandes offer about the actual number of Pakistani tests?

5. What does Fernandes say about India's plans to do more testing?

6. How did scientists monitor Pakistan's tests?

Understanding Literature: Journalism

The article from *The Times of India* illustrates some of the things a journalist does. This story reports on an interview with a government official. It then adds background material. It brings in facts and figures from experts. Another part of journalism is communicating with people. News may appear in a newspaper article. It may be on the Internet, as this one was. Radio and TV broadcasting are still another kind of journalism.

7. Where was Fernandes' interview originally given?

8. What are the other sources of information used in the article?

Critical Thinking

9. Why do you think this Indian newspaper quotes American scientists?

10. The official says that only the prime minister will "have his finger on the nuclear button." What does he mean?

Writing on Your Own Make a list of each journalistic source you use. (Remember that journalism includes radio, TV, newspapers, and magazines.) Then write a sentence about each type telling what kind of news or information you get from it. For example, where do you get sports news?

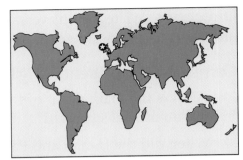

About the News Source

Radio listeners around the world know the voice of the *BBC*. Those letters stand for British Broadcasting Corporation. It was set up by the British government in 1927. It operates independently, though. In the 1930s the BBC began to send short-wave radio programs to all the countries in the British Empire. In 1967 it started the first regular color TV service in Europe. Today the BBC sends radio and TV programs to audiences all over the United Kingdom. Local programs include music, sports, plays, and news. BBC radio news and other programs are heard all over the world. The network has reporters in many foreign countries. It broadcasts in English and thirty-five other languages.

Like other world news sources, the BBC posts articles and information on its Web site. The Internet address is *BBC Online Network* (http://www.bbc.co.uk/home/today/index .html).You may be able to hear the BBC on your local public radio station.

Literary Term

news cycle the length of time between the publishing of a news item and an update or reaction to the item

About the Selection

The Indian and Pakistani tests were world news. Other countries then reacted. Some praised the tests, but others punished the two countries. They cut down trade and financial help. The **news cycle** is the timing of news stories that follow an event. You have already read Indian and Pakistani stories that react to the tests. This news story appeared on-line about two weeks after Pakistan's tests. It followed another new event in the on-going story.

Pakistan Nuclear Moratorium Welcomed

From the *BBC Online Network*

(Friday, June 12, 1998)

Pakistan's announcement of a **unilateral** moratorium on nuclear testing has been welcomed by the United States and the United Nations. UN Secretary General Kofi Annan hailed the move as an "important step in joining the international **norm** of nuclear testing and non-proliferation." A White House spokesman said the decision would help to limit **tensions** in the area.

A statement issued by Pakistan's foreign ministry said the country was ready to arrive at a "no-nuclear test agreement with India, as an important confidence-building measure at the regional level." "We are ready to engage **constructively** with India and other members of the international community to **formalise** this arrangement," the statement said. Pakistan hopes India will **reciprocate** and contribute towards a 'durable peace' in South Asia. Pakistan's Prime Minister, Nawaz Sharif, and his Indian counterpart, Atal Bihari Vajpayee, are due to meet at a regional summit in Sri Lanka.

India and Pakistan provoked world condemnation last month by carrying out nuclear tests, which triggered economic sanctions against them by the US, Japan and other states.

As you read, keep in mind the rivalry between India and Pakistan.

A *moratorium* is a temporary pause or delay in an action—in this case, more nuclear tests.

India and Pakistan are part of the larger area, or region, of Asia. A *regional summit* is a meeting between the heads of government of the countries in a region.

constructively helpfully	**norm** the usual pattern	**tension** an uneasy or angry relationship
formalise (Amer. formalize) to make official; to sign an agreement	**reciprocate** to respond to another's actions	**unilateral** involving only one side in an issue

Austerity measures

Sanctions are actions that a country takes to punish another country's actions. Economic sanctions include stopping trade or economic aid.

In response to the sanctions, Mr Sharif has unveiled a series of economic austerity measures. The measures, announced in a television address, include the transfer of more than one million acres of land from rich farmers to poorer farmers, and help for small businesses. Mr Sharif also said it was an honour for Pakistan to have joined the world's nuclear powers.

On May 21, India announced its own moratorium on nuclear testing, marking the end of its series of five nuclear test, and also invited world powers to hold talks on formalising new agreements on **arms** testing. Pakistan's nuclear **detonations**, set off to counteract the Indian explosions, were followed by statements of the country's **intention** to build nuclear missiles.

The *G8*, or Group of Eight, includes the world's major industrial countries. Officials from those countries often meet to discuss issues.

Arms race can be stabilised

Thursday's announcement came ahead of a meeting of foreign ministers from the G8 countries who will discuss Pakistan and India's nuclear tests when they gather in London on Friday. Mr Sharif is hoping that the G8 leaders will not impose further measures.

The prime ministers of India and Pakistan shake hands as they meet to discuss nuclear issues.

A BBC correspondent said that the announcement of the unilateral moratorium seemed to be designed to show that the arms race in South Asia could be **stabilised** and that Islamabad was now showing the **restraint** that the international community has been calling for.

arms weapons	**intention** a plan to do something	**stabilise** (Amer. stabilize) to stop change; to make steady
detonation an explosion	**restraint** control over actions or feelings	

Directions Write the answers to these questions using complete sentences.

Comprehension: Identifying Facts

1. What is a moratorium?

2. Which country's moratorium is announced in this report?

3. Which country tested nuclear weapons first—India or Pakistan?

Comprehension: Understanding Main Ideas

4. What was the main point of the announcement made by Pakistan's prime minister?

5. How did other countries and organizations react?

6. What other steps toward peace are India and Pakistan taking?

Understanding Literature: News Cycle

A major event such as a nuclear test sets off a cycle of news stories. This news cycle began with India's tests early in May. Newspapers around the world reacted. After the news story, they offered opinions in editorials. A few weeks later Pakistan also held nuclear tests. People reacted again. About two weeks later, Pakistan declared it would halt testing, This online report was on the BBC the next day.

7. Do the Internet and other electronic media make the news cycle shorter? How?

8. Read the section under the subhead "Arms race can be stabilised." How does this information explain the timing of the Pakistani announcement?

Critical Thinking

9. Reread the Pakistani prime minister's announcement on pages 210–212. Do you think Pakistan would have halted tests if India had not done so first? Why?

10. The information under the subhead "Austerity measures" is not news but happened weeks before. Why do you think the writer has included it in this article?

Writing on Your Own This story came from the Internet, but the BBC is known as a radio service. Rewrite the first section of this story as a radio announcement. Keep in mind that a radio news broadcast generally uses shorter sentences that are easy for listeners to understand.

The Frightening Joy
From *De Volkskrant* (Friday, 29 May 1998)

Building Atomic Security
Tomasz Wroblewski From *Zycie Warszawy* (Tuesday, 2 June 1998)

De Volkskrant
(established 1921)
Dutch

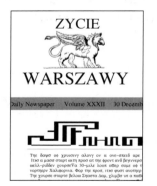

Zycie Warszawy
(established 1944)
Polish

Literary Term

editorial a news writer's personal opinion about an event or topic

About the Newspapers

De Volkskrant is published in Amsterdam, the capital of the Netherlands. (In Dutch, its name means "People's newspaper.") It is the second largest paper in the city. It comes out in the mornings every day except Sunday.

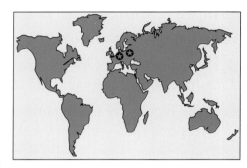

More than twenty newspapers are published in Warsaw, the capital of Poland. Many of them belong to various political parties. They give the opinions of those parties. *Zycie Warszawy,* however, is an independent newspaper. Its name means "Warsaw Life." In terms of readership, it is one of the city's larger papers. More than 200,000 people read it on weekdays. About 330,000 read the Saturday edition.

About the Selections

As you have read, India held nuclear tests early in May. Pakistan answered with its own tests later in the month. At home, many Indians and Pakistanis were happy. The tests gave an image of national strength and pride. Others thought that the money should be spent to help the poor.

World reactions differed greatly. Many countries were shocked and afraid. The United States asked both countries to be careful. It urged them to join in halting nuclear tests. Other countries were pleased. India and Pakistan were making their own decisions. These selections are from editorials in newspapers in Europe. An **editorial** gives the opinion of the writer or the paper. These editorials appeared soon after the tests.

The Frightening Joy

From *De Volkskrant*, Amsterdam
(Friday, 29 May 1998)

Despite the still-vivid memory of A-bombs falling on Japan, the world has been **perilously** close to the edge of nuclear war several times. Most frightening is the great joy in India and Pakistan over these shows of national power, because it clearly demonstrates that the people do not understand the **gravity** of the danger....This is cheering on the way to Armageddon.

As you read these two editorials, notice their different reactions to nuclear testing.

In the Bible, *Armageddon* is a great battle that is supposed to occur at the end of the world.

Indian Muslims shout slogans in favor of their prime minister's decision on nuclear testing.

gravity seriousness   **perilously** dangerously

Building Atomic Security

Tomasz Wroblewski
From *Zycie Warszawy*, Warsaw
(Friday, 29 May 1998)

There is a tired **slogan** that we all would be better off without nuclear warheads. The truth is that it is nuclear **potential,** not the lack of it, that is the **guarantor** of peace. It is the **escalation** of **armaments** and fear of atomic doom, not common sense or disarmament, that have **shielded** us from World War III....Indians and Pakistanis in reality are doing nothing less than what Americans and Russians did for the past half century—they are building an atomic **security** zone.

armaments weapons

escalation an increase or rapid growth

guarantor a person or thing that promises a certain result

potential the ability for action or growth in the future

security safety

shield to protect

slogan a saying or motto used by a group

The Frightening Joy and Building Atomic Security

Directions Write the answers to these questions using complete sentences.

Comprehension: Identifying Facts

1. How soon after Pakistan's tests did these editorials appear?

2. One paper says that having more weapons has actually prevented World War III. Which one?

3. Both editorials refer to historical events. What are they?

Comprehension: Understanding Main Ideas

4. What does the Dutch paper say that people in India do not understand?

5. What idea does the Polish paper call a "tired slogan"?

6. What is the Polish paper's opinion of disarmament?

Understanding Literature: Editorial

One feature of almost every newspaper is its editorial page. This page usually contains editorials and letters from readers. Often there is a political cartoon on the page, too. An editorial is a kind of essay. It deals with current issues and events—local or global. The opinions it gives are those of the writer or of the paper's owner. Like these two selections, an editorial is often about political views.

7. These newspapers are published far from India and Pakistan. Why was this event important enough for an editorial?

8. What does the title of the Dutch editorial mean?

Critical Thinking

9. Imagine a debate between the writers of these two pieces. What do you think they would say to each other?

10. Which of these opinions would be most welcome in India and Pakistan? Why?

Writing on Your Own These two European papers have completely different opinions about nuclear testing. Which point of view do you agree with? Imagine you are a resident of Amsterdam or Warsaw. Write a short letter to the editor of one of these newspapers. In your letter, explain why you agree or disagree with the point of view in the editorial.

Skills Lesson: Point of View

Did you ever tell friends about something you did? You described people and places the way *you* saw them. You told the story from *your* point of view. In this unit, many of the authors told their stories as they remembered and lived them. They used a first-person point of view: "I."

Journals, diaries, and letters are almost always written from a first-person point of view. So are autobiographies. A biography is more complicated. Biography is usually written from a third-person point of view. The writer speaks of everyone as "he" or "she." At the same time, a biography often tries to show the point of view of the person who is its subject. In addition, the writer has a point of view toward the person in the biography. Many biographies give a good picture of the subject. Some, though, attack or criticize that person.

Anne Frank's diary gives her point of view:

"Margot and I are getting a bit tired of our parents."

The reader sees Mark Mathabane's school and family through his eyes, too:

"I ran, without stopping, all the way to the other end of the township where Granny lived. There I found my mother, her face swollen and bruised."

In *The Last Seven Months of Anne Frank*, the reader learns more about Anne Frank. At the same time, the women tell their own stories. Those take a first-person point of view:

"He [Otto Frank] asked if I knew what had happened to his two daughters. I knew, but it was hard to get the words out of my mouth."

Review

1. What is point of view?

2. If a story refers to all the characters as "he" or "she," what is its point of view?

3. What is the usual point of view in a journal?

4. What is the point of view in Mark Mathabane's *Kaffir Boy?*

5. Is *The Last Seven Months of Anne Frank* a biography or autobiography?

Writing on Your Own Write a short paragraph about something you have done. Use the first-person point of view. Underline the words in the paragraph that show your point of view.

Unit 2 contains several types of nonfiction writing. All are about real life and real people. But they are also different. Journals and diaries are private and personal. People tell their journals their secret thoughts and feelings. Letters can be personal, too.

Other nonfiction is written to be read by others. Biographies and autobiographies are about a person's life. Journalism is an account of real events. People write their own autobiographies. Someone else writes a person's biography. It may be about someone the writer knows. Or the writer may research someone he or she has never met.

Selections

- *Anne Frank: The Diary of a Young Girl* by Anne Frank. A Dutch Jewish girl's diary shows her thoughts during World War II.

- "Letter to Indira Tagore" by Rabindranath Tagore. The Indian Nobel Prize winner writes a letter to his niece about a moonlit night.

- "Letter to the Reverend J. H. Twichell" by Mark Twain. Twain writes to a friend about looking for a lost sock in the dark.

- *When Heaven and Earth Changed Places* by Le Ly Hayslip. A Vietnamese villager explains the importance of growing rice.

- "By Any Other Name" by Santha Rama Rau. Two Indian girls do not fit in at the British colonial school.

- *Kaffir Boy* by Mark Mathabane. A young black South African describes his life in a Johannesburg slum.

- *China Men* by Maxine Hong Kingston. Kingston's father, a Chinese immigrant, shows his wife New York City.

- *The Last Seven Months of Anne Frank* by Willy Lindwer. A Dutch filmmaker interviews women who knew the Frank family.

The journalism selections report reactions to nuclear tests:

- "Account Evened With India, Says PM" From *Dawn* (Pakistan)

- "Tests Are Nowhere Near India's: Fernandes" From *The Times of India* (India)

- "Pakistan Nuclear Moratorium Welcomed" From the *BBC Online Network* (Britain)

- "The Frightening Joy" From *De Volkskrant* (Netherlands)

- "Building Atomic Security" From *Zycie Warszawy* (Poland)

Directions Write the answers to these questions using complete sentences.

Comprehension: Identifying Facts

1. Two selections in this unit are about the same person. Who is that person? What historical events affected that person's life?

2. In what country did Mark Mathabane grow up?

3. What is the term for a person's life story written by that person?

4. About whom did Maxine Hong Kingston write this biography?

5. The newspaper articles and editorials in this unit all focus on one subject. What is that subject?

Comprehension: Understanding Main Ideas

6. Why is Anne Frank's diary so important to her?

7. How is school a turning point in *Kaffir Boy* and "By Any Other Name"?

8. Why was rice growing important in a Vietnamese village?

9. Compare the tone of the letters from Twain and Tagore. What makes these letters personal?

10. Why did Pakistan test nuclear weapons in late May 1998?

Understanding Literature: Setting

The time and place where a story take place are its setting. The settings in Unit 2 range from steamy rice paddies in Vietnam to the skyscrapers of New York. Setting includes time, too. *When* events take place is sometimes as important as *where*. The setting of Anne Frank's diary, for instance, is the crowded "secret annexe" in 1944, when she wrote down her thoughts.

11. Why is setting important in Tagore's letter to his niece?

12. The couple in *China Men* visit sights in New York. What do they see? How do they react?

13. What is the setting of Mark Twain's letter?

14. What is the setting of *Kaffir Boy*? How does it affect the story?

15. In which of this unit's selections is setting most important? Explain your choice.

Critical Thinking

16. In "By Any Other Name," what did the English teacher think of Indians? Give two examples.

17. Why do you think people still care about Anne Frank's story?

18. In *China Men,* Ed and his wife are both newcomers. Which will be happier in the United States? Why?

19. How did India react to Pakistan's nuclear tests? What did it show about the relationship between the countries?

20. Which of the people in this unit would you like to meet? Explain your choice.

Speak and Listen

Many selections in this unit are written in the first person. Choose part of one of these selections. Then practice reading it aloud. As you practice, think about who wrote it. What kind of gestures or expressions would he or she use? Read your selection to the class.

Beyond Words

Think back to a setting from this unit that you remember well. Draw a picture to illustrate the story and its setting. Add details from what you read. If you need to, research other details. For example, you might want to find out what kind of hats and clothes Vietnamese villagers wore in the 1960s. Write a caption to tell where and when your picture takes place.

Writing on Your Own

Think of a "turning point" event in your life. Did an event change things for you? (Remember the fight in *Kaffir Boy.*) Have rituals been important in your life? (Remember the rice growing in Le Ly Hayslip's village.) Write a section of your own autobiography. In it, explain the importance of this event in your life.

Test-Taking Tip

If you have trouble with a question on a test, go on to the next question. Come back to any you skipped.

"Acting is not about dressing up...The whole essence of learning lines is to forget them so you can make them sound like you thought of them that instant."
—Glenda Jackson

"If it's a good script, I'll do it. And if it's a bad script, and they pay me enough, I'll do it."
—George Burns

UNIT 3 *Drama*

The writer of a play is called a playwright. Playwrights draw on many different sources for their inspirations. They may write a play based on a historical event. They may take a story from their own experience. Or they may totally invent the story. No matter where it comes from, a story told in play format is enjoyable because we can see it, hear it, smell it, and feel it. A play shows us how someone else interprets a story. Watching a play brings an added dimension to the experience of reading it.

A drama is a play that tells a story through dialogue and action performed by actors. Drama is an old form of literature. Dramatic plays started long ago as religious ceremonies in Greece. Gradually they became two distinct forms of drama: the tragedy and the comedy.

The protagonist is the main character in any drama. The antagonist is the opponent. In a tragedy, the antagonist destroys the protagonist. The antagonist could be the protagonist's own weaknesses. It could be another character's actions. The antagonist could also be a "bad guy," social injustice, or fate. A well-written tragedy offers its audience emotional release. It also reveals the workings of human nature. Shakespeare's Othello, for instance, is one of drama's greatest protagonists. The antagonist is an evil friend named Iago. Iago plays on Othello's jealousy and violent temper. Finally Othello destroys his wife, his career, and himself. The audience experiences Othello's grief as they identify with what he says and does.

A comedy is a play with a "happy ending." The conflict does not destroy the protagonist. The audience enjoys seeing the protagonist beat the antagonist. *Harvey,* for example, tells the story of Elwood P. Dowd. His best friend is Harvey, an invisible rabbit who is six feet tall. By the end of the play, Dowd has triumphed. He has avoided being sent to an institution for the insane. He has also convinced several other characters of Harvey's charms.

Tragic or comic, early drama followed a strict form. Greek dramas included a chorus. This was a group of actors who commented on and explained the action. Actors wore masks. Dialogue was spoken in verse. Verse is made up of word patterns that follow a definite, repeating rhythm and sometimes rhyme.

There are many forms of drama, from symbolist to naturalist to absurdist. This unit covers three forms of drama: classical, realistic, and expressionistic.

As you read, remember that you are not experiencing the complete play. Much of drama's power comes from the voices and movements of the cast. Scenery and costumes add to the effect. Reading the following selections aloud may help you get more of the feeling of a real play.

The following countries are represented in this unit: England, South Africa, and Sweden.

Classical Drama

- "I think that in the end...Shakespeare and all he inspired...will save the English-speaking world." —Laurens van der Post
- "My brain is hurting. I have just had two pages of *Macbeth* to translate into English." —Sue Townsend

Ancient dramas in the Western world were written in the Greek and Latin languages. These are called "classical languages." When Shakespeare wrote during the sixteenth century, English-language drama had become what is now called classical drama. These plays were usually stories about royalty or other wealthy, important people.

Classical drama has five acts and is written in blank verse. Classical drama is divided into acts and scenes. These are similar to chapters in a book. Acts are separate sections that often involve changes in setting. Time may pass between acts. Each act consists of one or more scenes. The first and second acts introduce and develop the action or conflict. The third act features the climax. This is an event that triggers the comic or tragic ending. Acts four and five tie together the loose plot strands to create a neat ending.

Dialogue, or the words the characters speak, is often in a form called blank verse. Blank verse is written in iambic pentameter and does not rhyme. Iambic pentameter describes the beat, or rhythm, of a line of verse. It has five two-beat sounds per line. The emphasis falls on the even-numbered beats.

Shakespeare's plays are considered some of the best examples of classical drama ever written. Many playwrights of his time also wrote in this style. Plays of later times that follow the classical form are called neoclassical. (*Neo-* means "new.")

Macbeth
William Shakespeare

William Shakespeare
(1564–1616)
English

Literary Terms

blank verse unrhymed iambic pentameter

drama a play

playwright the author of a play

sonnet a fourteen-line poem divided into four sections, in iambic pentameter

About the Author

William Shakespeare was born in the small English town of Stratford-upon-Avon. He was well known as an actor and **playwright**. Shakespeare also wrote many **sonnets**. A sonnet is a fourteen-line poem, separated into three sections of four lines. The last two lines also rhyme.

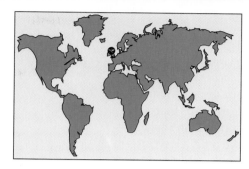

Shakespeare used the classical five-act structure of a **drama**, or play. He used **blank verse**, a form of unrhymed poetry. Shakespeare based his plays on well-known stories. This is why most of them are set in far-off places or ancient times.

About the Selection

Macbeth is a Scottish lord who wants to be king. At his wife's urging, he kills the rightful king. Macbeth then has his best friend, Banquo, killed. Banquo's son, Fleance, escapes. Having killed his friend, Macbeth is overcome by guilt. In the following scene, Macbeth and Lady Macbeth host a dinner party. During the party, Macbeth sees Banquo's ghost. He feels himself accused of murder. The guests see Macbeth speaking, but they do not see the ghost. They wonder if he has gone mad. It is the beginning of the end for Macbeth. *Macbeth* is a five-act play.

Some people find Shakespeare hard to understand. If you read the play aloud, the words come alive. A paraphrase has also been provided. This is a version of the scene that has been put in modern English. It will help you if you get stuck.

Macbeth

William Shakespeare

This version of scene four from Act III of *Macbeth* appears as Shakespeare wrote it. It uses words that were common in England at the time. It is written in blank verse. As you read, compare it with the modern English version on the facing page.

Notes called *stage directions* describe where each scene is set. They tell the actors where and how to move.

The words following each character's name tell the character what to say. These speeches are called dialogue.

Act III, Scene 4: The hall of the palace.
A banquet prepared. Enter Macbeth, Lady Macbeth, Ross, Lennox, Lords, and Attendant.

MACBETH.   You know your own degrees, sit down at first
And last, the hearty welcome.

LORDS.   Thanks to your majesty.

MACBETH.   Ourself will mingle with society,
And play the humble host:
Our hostess keeps her state, but in best time
We will require her welcome.

LADY MACBETH.   Pronounce it for me, sir, to all our friends,
For my heart speaks they are welcome.

First Murderer appears at the door

MACBETH.   See, they encounter thee with their hearts' thanks.
Both sides are even: here I'll sit i'th' midst.
Be large in mirth, anon we'll drink a measure
The table round. *[turns to the door]*
There's blood upon thy face.

MURDERER.   'Tis Banquo's then.

MACBETH.   'Tis better thee without than he within.
Is he dispatched?

MURDERER.   My lord, his throat is cut, that I did for him.

MACBETH.   Thou art the best o'th' cut-throats! Yet he's good
That did the like for Fleance: if thou didst it,
thou art the nonpareil.

MURDERER.   Most royal sir,
Fleance is 'scaped.

MACBETH.   Then comes my fit again: I had else been perfect;
Whole as the marble, founded as the rock,
As broad and general as the casing air:
But now I am cabined, cribbed, confined, bound in
To saucy doubts and fears. But Banquo's safe?

Macbeth
William Shakespeare

Act 3, Scene 4. The hall of the palace.
A banquet has been prepared. Macbeth, Lady Macbeth, Ross, Lennox,
Lords, and Attendants enter.

MACBETH	You know your **ranks**. Sit down accordingly. From the top table downward, I give you **hearty** welcome!
LORDS	Thanks to Your Majesty!
MACBETH	I'll **mingle** with the guests and play the humble host. Our hostess will stay seated. She'll welcome you at the proper time.
LADY MACBETH	Do so on my **behalf**, sir, to all our friends, for they are welcome with all my heart.

The Lords rise and bow. The First Murderer enters

MACBETH	[*To Lady Macbeth*] See—their heartfelt thanks are yours. [*He looks for a vacant seat*] Both sides are even. I'll sit here in the middle. [*He spots the Murderer*] Enjoy yourselves! We'll pass around the drinking cup just now! [*To the Murderer*] There's blood on your face.
FIRST MURDERER	It's Banquo's then.
MACBETH	It's better outside you than inside him. Is he killed?
FIRST MURDERER	My lord, his throat is cut. That I did for him.
MACBETH	You are the best of cutthroats! Yet he's as good who did the same for Fleance. If you did it, you have no equal!
FIRST MURDERER	Most royal sir— Fleance escaped.
MACBETH	My illness comes back. I'd otherwise be **sound**. **Flawless** as marble. Solid as rock. As free and **liberated** as the air around us. Now I'm closed in, cramped, confined—the prisoner of nagging doubts and fears. But Banquo's fixed?

This version of *Macbeth* is written in modern English, the language we use today. Read it aloud to follow the action more easily. As you read, compare this version with the original. Find words and phrases that you know.

As Macbeth is walking among his seated guests, he sees the *First Murderer* at the doorway. The stage direction [*To the Murderer*] means they are speaking to each other in private. The audience, but not the guests, can hear their conversation.

Macbeth has ordered the murders of *Banquo* and his son, *Fleance*. He is pleased to know Banquo has been killed. He is upset that Fleance has escaped unhurt.

Macbeth wants to be sure that Banquo is dead. He asks the question again.

behalf interest	**hearty** sincere	**mingle** to mix
flawless perfect; without any marks	**liberated** free from outside control	**rank** official position
		sound healthy

What does the
dialogue between
Macbeth and the
Murderer reveal?

MURDERER. Ay, my good lord: safe in a ditch he bides,
With twenty trenchéd gashes on his head;
The least a death to nature.

MACBETH. Thanks for that:
There the grown serpent lies; the worm that's fled
Hath nature that in time will venom breed,
No teeth for th' present. Get thee gone; to-morrow
We'll hear ourselves again.

Murderer goes

LADY MACBETH. My royal lord,
You do not give the cheer. The feast is sold
That is not often vouched, while 'tis a-making,
'Tis given with welcome: to feed were best at home;
From thence the sauce to meat is ceremony;
Meeting were bare without it.

The Ghost of Banquo appears, and sits in Macbeth's place

MACBETH. Sweet remembrancer!
Now good digestion wait on appetite,
And health on both!

LENNOX. May't please your highness sit?

MACBETH. Here had we now our country's honour roofed,
Were the graced person of our Banquo present;
Who may I rather challenge for unkindness
Then pity for mischance!

ROSS. His absence, sir,
Lays blame upon his promise. Please't your highness
To grace us with your royal company?

MACBETH. The table's full.

LENNOX. Here is a place reserved, sir.

MACBETH. Where?

LENNOX. Here, my good lord...What is't that moves your highness?

MACBETH. Which of you have done this?

LORDS. What, my good lord?

MACBETH. Thou canst not say I did it: never shake
Thy gory locks at me.

FIRST MURDERER	Yes, my good lord. Safe in a ditch he dwells, with twenty trench-like **gashes** in his head, the least of them fatal.
MACBETH	Thanks for that. The adult serpent's dead. The youngster that escaped has the makings of trouble, but he's harmless now. Go. Tomorrow we'll talk together again.

The First Murderer leaves

LADY MACBETH	My royal lord, you do not play the host! A tavern meal lacks welcoming **toasts**. Mere food alone is best consumed at home. What gives a feast its flavor is the ceremony. It's a poor feast without it.

The ghost of Banquo enters and sits in Macbeth's place

MACBETH	[*affectionately*] I'm glad you reminded me! [*To the company*] To appetites and good digestion! And health to both!
LENNOX	Do please sit, sir.
MACBETH	We'd have here under one roof the noblest in the land if our friend Banquo were present. I hope it's a case of thoughtlessness, not **mischance**.
ROSS	His absence, sir, is a **breach** of his promise. [*Indicating a seat*] Would Your Highness grace us with your royal company?
MACBETH	The table's full.
LENNOX	Here's a place reserved, sir.
MACBETH	Where?
LENNOX	Here, my good lord. What is upsetting Your Highness?
MACBETH	[*pointing to the Ghost*] Which of you has done this?
LORDS	What, my good lord? [*The Ghost makes signals*]
MACBETH	You cannot say I did it! Don't shake your **gory locks** at me!

Lady Macbeth gently scolds Macbeth for deserting the banquet guests. She asks him to make a toast to start the banquet.

Why do you think Macbeth calls attention to Banquo's absence from the banquet?

Lennox offers an empty chair to Macbeth. Only Macbeth can see the *Ghost* sitting in the chair. Macbeth's outburst upsets his guests.

---

affectionately with love and tenderness

breach a failure to live up to a promise

gash a long, deep cut

gory stained with blood

locks the hair of the head

mischance bad luck

toast a speech made along with a drink to honor someone

Ross.	Gentlemen, rise, his highness is not well.
Lady Macbeth.	Sit, worthy friends: my lord is often thus,
	And hath been from his youth: pray you, keep seat,
	The fit is momentary, upon a thought
	He will again be well: if much you note him,
	You shall offend him and extend his passion:
	Feed, and regard him not. *[aside]* Are you a man?
Macbeth.	Ay, and a bold one, that dare look on that
	Which might appal the devil.
Lady Macbeth.	O proper stuff!
	This is the very painting of your fear:
	This is the air-drawn dagger which, you said,
	Led you to Duncan. O, these flaws and starts
	(Imposter to true fear) would well become
	A woman's story at a winter's fire,
	Authorized by her grandam. Shame itself!
	Why do you make such faces? When all's done,
	You look but on a stool.
Macbeth.	Prithee, see there! behold! look! lo! how say you?
	Why what care I? If thou canst nod, speak too.
	If charnel-houses and our graves must send
	Those that we bury back, our monuments
	Shall be the maws of kites.

The Ghost vanishes

Lady Macbeth.	What! quite unmanned in folly?
Macbeth.	If I stand here, I saw him.
Lady Macbeth.	Fie, for shame!
Macbeth.	Blood hath been shed ere now, i'th' olden time,
	Ere humane statute purged the gentle weal;
	Ay, and since too, murders have been performed
	Too terrible for the ear: the time has been,
	That, when the brains were out, the man would die,
	And there an end: but now they rise again,
	With twenty mortal murders on their crowns,
	And push us from our stools. This is more strange
	Than such a murder is.
Lady Macbeth.	My worthy lord,
	Your noble friends do lack you.

ROSS	Gentlemen, rise. His Highness is not well.
LADY MACBETH	Sit, good friends. My lord is often like this and has been since his youth. Please, stay in your seats. The **fit** will soon pass. He'll be well again in a moment. If you take too much notice, you'll offend him and extend his fit. Eat up, and ignore him. [*To Macbeth, angrily*] Are you a man?
MACBETH	Yes, and a bold one, that dares to look at what might scare the devil.
LADY MACBETH	Oh, really! This is a fear of your imagination. This is that air-borne dagger which you said led you to Duncan! Oh, these fits and **starts**— these fake fears—would better suit an old wife's tale told at a winter fireside. Shame on you! Why are you making such faces? When all is said and done, you are only looking at a stool!
MACBETH	See there—look! There! Now what do you say? [*To the Ghost*] Why, what do I care? If you can nod, speak too! If graves and tombs will send back those we bury, we'd better feed our corpses to the vultures!

The Ghost disappears

LADY MACBETH	Is your foolishness taking away your **manhood**?
MACBETH	As sure as I stand here, I saw him!
LADY MACBETH	What nonsense!
MACBETH	[*To himself*] Blood has been shed before now, in the old days before just laws reformed society. Yes, and since then, too, murders have been **committed**, too terrible to hear about. There was a time when smashed brains meant the man would die, and that was that. But now men rise again, with twenty fatal gashes in their heads, and steal our seats. This is stranger than murder.
LADY MACBETH	My worthy lord. Your noble friends are missing you.

Lady Macbeth tries to turn attention away from Macbeth. She says that he often has this kind of *fit*. In fact, she knows what he has done. She is afraid others may guess his crimes by watching his behavior.

Earlier in the play, Macbeth describes a vision in which he see a *dagger* covered in blood. It is hanging in midair and pointing toward Duncan's room. He says it was a sign telling him to kill the king.

Remember, only Macbeth (and the audience) can see the Ghost.

commit to do or perform

fit a sudden, violent outburst

manhood courage

start a quick, jerking movement

MACBETH.   I do forget.
Do not muse at me, my most worthy friends;
I have a strange infirmity, which is nothing
To those that know me. Come, love and health to all;
Then I'll sit down. Give me some wine, fill full.

The Ghost reappears

I drink to th' general joy o'th' whole table,
And to our dear friend Banquo, whom we miss;
Would he were here! to all, and him we thirst,
And all to all!

LORDS.   Our duties, and the pledge.

MACBETH.   Avaunt! and quit my sight! let the earth hide thee!
Thy bones are marrowless, thy blood is cold;
Thou hast no speculation in those eyes
Which thou dost glare with!

LADY MACBETH.   Think of this, good peers,
But as a thing of custom: 'tis no other;
Only it spoils the pleasure of the time.

MACBETH.   What man dare, I dare:
Approach thou like the ruggéd Russian bear,
The armed rhinoceros, or th'Hyrcan tiger,
Take any shape but that, and my firm nerves
Shall never tremble: or be alive again,
And dare me to the desert with thy sword;
If trembling I inhabit then, protest me
The baby of a girl. Hence, horrible shadow!
Unreal mock'ry, hence! *[The Ghost vanishes]*
    Why, so; being gone,
I am a man again. Pray you, sit still.

LADY MACBETH.   You have displaced the mirth, broke the good meeting,
With most admired disorder.

MACBETH.   Can such things be,
And overcome us like a summer's cloud,
Without our special wonder? You make me strange
Even to the disposition that I owe,
When now I think you can behold such sights,
And keep the natural ruby of your cheeks,
When mine is blanched with fear.

| MACBETH | [*Recovering*] I'm forgetting. [*To the guests*] Don't **brood** over me, my most worthy friends. I have a strange **disability**, which is nothing to those who know me. Come! [*Raising his glass*] Love and health to all! Then I'll sit down. Give me some wine. Fill it up! |

The Ghost returns

	I drink to the general joy of the whole table, and to our dear friend Banquo, who is not present. Would he were here! [*Proposing a toast*] To all, and to him we lack, and health to everyone!
LORDS	Our duties, and the toast!
MACBETH	[*Seeing the* Ghost] Go away! **Quit** my sight! Back to your grave! Your bones are marrowless, your blood is cold. You have no power of seeing in those glaring eyes!
LADY MACBETH	Think of this, good noblemen, as a **chronic ailment**. That's what it is. Unfortunately, it upsets things.
MACBETH	[*To the Ghost*] Whatever man dares, I dare! Approach me like a rugged Russian bear, an armor-plated rhinoceros, or a wild tiger! Take any shape but your own, and my firm nerves will never tremble. Or come alive again, and dare me to the desert with your sword! If I fall to trembling then, call me a baby girl! **Begone**, horrible shadow! Unreal mockery, begone! [*The Ghost goes*] Why, then. Once it is gone, I am a man again. [*To the guests*] Please—keep your seats.
LADY MACBETH	[*Reproaching him*] You've spoiled the enjoyment— destroyed the atmosphere—with your ridiculous behavior!
MACBETH	Can such things happen— like a cloud spoiling a summer's day—without astonishing us? You make me doubt myself. You can behold such sights and keep the natural color of your cheeks. Mine turn white with fear.

Lady Macbeth finally succeeds in getting Macbeth's attention. He realizes he needs to explain his odd behavior.

Why does Macbeth *propose a toast* to Banquo?

When Macbeth begins to rave again, Lady Macbeth makes an excuse for it.

---

ailment a sickness

begone a command meaning "go away"

brood to think moodily about something

chronic continuing for a long time

disability a weakened physical or mental condition

quit to leave

reproach to scold; to blame

Ross.	What sights, my lord?
Lady Macbeth.	I pray you, speak not; he grows worse and worse; Question enrages him: at once, good night. Stand not upon the order of your going, But go at once.
Lennox.	Good night, and better health Attend his majesty!
Lady Macbeth.	A kind good night to all! *[They leave]*
Macbeth.	It will have blood; they say, blood will have blood: Stones have been known to move and trees to speak; Augures and understood relations have By maggot-pies and choughs and rooks brought forth The secret'st man of blood. ... What is the night?
Lady Macbeth.	Almost at odds with morning, which is which.
Macbeth.	How say'st thou, that Macduff denies his person At our great bidding?
Lady Macbeth.	Did you send to him, sir?
Macbeth.	I hear it by the way; but I will send: There's not a one of them but in his house I keep a servant fee'd. I will to-morrow (And betimes I will) to the Weïrd Sisters: More shall they speak; for now I am bent to know, By the worst means, and worst. For mine own good All causes shall give way: I am in blood Stepped in so far that, should I wade no more, Returning were as tedious as go o'er: Strange things I have in head that will to hand, Which must be acted ere they may be scanned.
Lady Macbeth.	You lack the season of all natures, sleep.
Macbeth.	Come, we'll to sleep. My strange and self-abuse Is the initiate fear that wants hard use: We are yet but young in deed.

They go

ROSS	What sights, my lord?
LADY MACBETH	Please don't say anything. He gets worse and worse. Questions enrage him. Now, goodnight! No ceremonial leave-taking. Go at once.
LENNOX	Good night, and may His Majesty enjoy better health.
LADY MACBETH	A kind goodnight to all! [She hustles them out]
MACBETH	It will have blood. They say, "Blood will have blood." Gravestones have been known to move, and trees to speak. Magpies, crows and ravens have spotted the most secretive of murderers. What time of night is it?
LADY MACBETH	Almost morning. It's hard to tell the difference.
MACBETH	What do you make of Macduff ignoring our invitation?
LADY MACBETH	Did you **summon** him, sir?
MACBETH	I hear rumors. But I'll summon him all right. I keep a spy in all their houses. Early tomorrow, I'll go to the Weird Sisters. They must tell me more. I must know the worst, by whatever means. Nothing shall stand in the way of my interests. My path has been so bloody, stopping now and going back would be no easier than going forward. I have some projects in my head that need action first and thought later. They must be done before they are thought of.
LADY MACBETH	You lack what all creatures need—sleep.
MACBETH	Come, we'll go to sleep. My **delusions** are beginner's fear. I need experience. We've only just started.

They go

Ross asks Macbeth what he saw. Why does Lady Macbeth interrupt?

Macduff is a nobleman who opposed Macbeth's choice as king. He also discovered the body of murdered King Duncan. He is suspicious about who really murdered him.

The *Weird Sisters* are witches who appeared at the beginning of the play. They predicted that Macbeth would be king. Macbeth wants to see them now to learn what will happen in his future.

Macbeth believes that he is afraid because he's new to crime and violence. He says that, as he carries out more bloody deeds, he'll become used to it.

delusion a false or imaginary belief

summon to call; to tell to come

Directions Write the answers to these questions using complete sentences.

Comprehension: Identifying Facts

1. What is the setting for the scene?

2. Who is attending the banquet?

3. Who interrupts Macbeth as he is greeting his guests?

4. Who has the Murderer killed? How do you know?

5. Who is Fleance? What has happened to him?

6. Who reminds Macbeth to pay attention to his guests? What does she ask him to do?

7. Who sees a ghost?

8. Whose ghost is it? How do you know?

9. How does Lady Macbeth explain Macbeth's odd behavior?

10. Whom does Macbeth want to ask for advice? Why?

Comprehension: Understanding Main Ideas

11. Why does Lady Macbeth call Macbeth away from his conversation with the Murderer?

12. Macbeth knows that Banquo is dead. Still, he talks about him as if he were alive. Why?

13. Macbeth is the only character who sees the ghost. Why?

14. Macbeth says, "Which of you has done this?" What does he mean? Why does this upset the guests?

15. Why does Lady Macbeth ask, "Are you a man?"

16. Why does Macbeth call the ghost a mockery?

17. Macbeth says to Lady Macbeth, "You can behold such sights and keep the natural color of your cheeks. Mine turn white with fear." What does he mean?

18. Macduff is not at the banquet. Why does this worry Macbeth?

19. We know that Macbeth is seeing things—a dagger in midair and a ghost at the table. What else does he do that might mean he is mentally unstable?

20. Macbeth says he has projects in mind that "need action first and thought later." What does he mean?

Understanding Literature: Drama

A drama is a play. In a drama the story is told by actors performing for an audience. The author of a drama is called a playwright. He or she writes dialogue to tell the actors what to say. The playwright also writes stage directions that describe the setting. They tell the actors what to do and how to do it. Stage directions tell actors when to enter and exit. They may describe movements or tone of voice, too.

21. Look at the stage directions in the modern English version of the scene from *Macbeth*. Which one tells us that only the Murderer can hear Macbeth?

22. Which stage direction tells Lady Macbeth to speak as if she is annoyed with Macbeth?

23. Which stage direction shows that Macbeth is about to propose a toast?

24. Look at the dialogue near the end of the scene. Lennox says, "Good night, and may His Majesty enjoy better health." To whom is he speaking?

25. Lady Macbeth says, "A kind goodnight to all!" Who does she mean?

Critical Thinking

During the course of this scene, Lady Macbeth seems uneasy. She criticizes Macbeth's behavior. She tries to get him to act normally. Finally, she ends the banquet early.

26. Do you think her first line in the scene is fitting for a queen? Why or why not?

27. Look at her next lines. Are they fitting? Why or why not?

28. How does she try to reassure the guests?

29. Later she says, "Shame on you! Why are you making such faces?" Why has her tone changed?

30. Look at her last line. How do you think she feels about Macbeth?

Writing on Your Own The Ghost in this scene from *Macbeth* does not have any lines. If he did, what do you think he would say? Write two lines of dialogue for his first appearance. Write another two lines of dialogue for his second appearance.

Realistic Drama

- "The most difficult performance in the world is acting naturally, isn't it?" —Angela Carter
- "We [actors] are born at the rise of the curtain and we die with its fall...." —Micheál MacLiammóir

As drama developed, many rules changed or disappeared. Students and audiences still study and enjoy classical drama. But other kinds of plays speak just as strongly to audiences. A pioneer of realistic drama in the late 1800s was Henrik Ibsen of Norway. Realistic drama was a strong force in the theater in the 1950s. A realistic drama tells a story just as it might happen in real life. The characters speak in everyday language, not in verse. They are ordinary people rather than royalty or millionaires. Their problems center on job and family. The play is set in an average home and neighborhood. Many television dramas would be considered realistic. Modern American writers in the realistic style include Arthur Miller and William Inge.

Even Shakespeare's dramas have moments that might be called realistic. These moments usually concern the poor or minor characters. They do not speak in verse but in normal language. They face everyday problems and events.

"Master Harold" ... and the Boys
Athol Fugard

Athol Fugard
(1932–)
South African

Literary Term

realistic drama a play that tells a story just as it might happen in real life

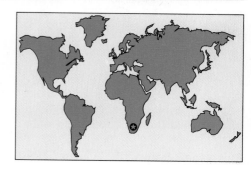

About the Author

Athol Fugard was born in Middleburg, South Africa. His plays focus on the politics of South Africa. Often their subject is *apartheid.* Apartheid was a government policy in South Africa for many years. It kept blacks and whites strictly separated. It denied black South Africans many rights. Fugard's works show the destruction apartheid caused. But they also show how the human spirit can win over hatred. Fugard has acted in, written, and directed many plays. Some of his other works are *A Lesson from Aloes, Boesman and Lena, Sizwe Banzi Is Dead,* and *The Blood Knot.*

About the Selection

Fugard wrote *"Master Harold" ... and the Boys* in 1982. This drama shows people affected by apartheid. It is a **realistic drama** about South Africans. It tells a story about everyday life. Hally (short for Harold) is the teenage son of a white, middle-class family. They own a restaurant. He goes to a private school where he is an average student. Sam and Willie are black waiters in the restaurant. They have known Hally since he was a child. Sam has become a sort of foster father to Hally. Hally's own father is an alcoholic and an embarrassment to him.

The following selection is in two parts. In the first part Hally and Sam remember an extraordinary day together when Hally was a child. The second part shows how apartheid could ruin even the best relationships between blacks and whites. Despite their problems, Sam and Hally may be able to learn from each other. Maybe their relationship will be stronger. There is hope for the future.

"MASTER HAROLD" ... AND THE BOYS

ATHOL FUGARD

This scene is from a one-act play. All the action takes place in one act. There are no breaks or scene changes. As you read, look for the events and speeches that makes this play realistic.

Hally is a seventeen-year-old white boy dressed in a school uniform. Sam and Willie are black men in their thirties. They are wearing white waiters' coats.

Time: 1950

Place: The St. George's Park Tea Room on a wet and windy afternoon in Port Elizabeth, South Africa.

HALLY   Come on, guess. If your memory is so good, you must remember it as well.

SAM   We got up to a lot of tricks in there, Hally.

HALLY   This one was special, Sam.

SAM   I'm listening.

HALLY   It started off looking like another of those useless nothing-to-do afternoons. I'd already been down to Main Street looking for adventure, but nothing had happened. I didn't feel like climbing trees in the Donkin Park or pretending I was a private eye and following a stranger ... so as usual: See what's cooking in Sam's room. This time it was you on the floor. You had two thin pieces of wood and you were smoothing them down with a knife. It didn't look particularly interesting, but when I asked you what you were doing, you just said, "Wait and see, Hally. Wait ... and see" ... in that secret sort of way of yours, so I knew there was a surprise coming. You teased me, you **bugger**, by being **deliberately** slow and not answering my questions!

(*Sam laughs*)

And whistling while you worked away! God, it was **infuriating**! I could have brained you! It was only when you tied them together in a cross and put that down on the brown paper that I realized what you were doing. "Sam is making a kite?" And when I asked you and you said "Yes" ...! (*Shaking his head with* **disbelief**) The **sheer audacity** of it took my breath away. I mean, seriously, what ... does a black man know about flying a kite? I'll be honest with you, Sam, I had no hopes for it. If you think I was excited and happy, you got another guess coming. In fact, I was ... scared that we were going to make fools of ourselves. When we left the **boarding house** to go up onto the hill, I was praying quietly that there wouldn't be any other kids around to laugh at us.

SAM   (*Enjoying the memory as much as Hally*) Ja, I could see that.

HALLY   I made it obvious, did I?

SAM   Ja. You refused to carry it.

HALLY   Do you blame me? Can you remember what the poor thing looked like? Tomato-box wood and brown paper! Flour and water for glue! Two of my mother's old stockings for a tail, and then all those bits and pieces of string you made me tie together so that we could fly it! ... No, that was now only asking for a miracle to happen.

SAM   Then the big argument when I told you to hold the string and run with it when I let go.

Earlier, we learned that, as a young boy, Hally often visited Sam and Willie at home in the Jubilee Boardinghouse. During these visits, Sam and Hally talked about his schoolwork. They learned a lot from each other.

What does this remark show you about South Africa at this time?

Ja means "yes."

Why did Sam have to use old, used materials to build the kite?

---

audacity boldness; daring

boarding house a place to live where one pays for a room and meals

bugger a slang word meaning companion or chap

deliberately carefully considered; on purpose

disbelief a refusal to believe

infuriating causing great anger

sheer pure; not mixed with anything

HALLY	I was prepared to run, all right, but straight back to the boarding house.
SAM	(*Knowing what's coming*) So what happened?
HALLY	Come on, Sam, you remember it as well as I do.
SAM	I want to hear it from you.

(*Hally pauses. He wants to be as accurate as possible*)

HALLY	You went up a little distance from me down the hill, you held it up ready to let it go. ... "This is it," I thought. "Like everything else in my life, here comes another **fiasco**." Then you shouted, "Go, Hally!" and I started to run. (*Another pause*) I don't know how to describe it, Sam. Ja! The miracle happened! I was running, waiting for it to crash to the ground, but instead suddenly there was something alive behind me at the end of the string, tugging at it as if it wanted to be free. I looked back ... (*Shakes his head*) ... I still can't believe my eyes. It was flying! Looping around and trying to climb even higher into the sky. You shouted to me to let it have more string. I did, until there was none left and I was just holding that piece of wood we had tied it to. You came up and joined me. You were laughing.
SAM	So were you. And shouting, "It works, Sam! We've done it!"
HALLY	And we had! I was so proud of us! It was the most **splendid** thing I had ever seen. I wished there were hundreds of kids around to watch us. The part that scared me, though, was when you showed me how to make it dive down to the ground and then just when it was on the point of crashing, swoop up again!
SAM	You didn't want to try it yourself.

fiasco a complete failure	**splendid** glorious; excellent

HALLY Of course not! I would have been **suicidal** if anything had happened to it. Watching you do it made me nervous enough. I was quite happy just to see it up there with its tail fluttering behind it. You left me after that, didn't you? You explained how to get it down, we tied it to the bench so that I could sit and watch it, and you went away. I wanted you to stay, you know. I was a little scared of having to look after it by myself.

SAM (*Quietly*) I had work to do, Hally.

HALLY It was sort of sad bringing it down, Sam. And it looked sad again when it was lying there on the ground. Like something that had lost its soul. Just tomato-box wood, brown paper and two of my mother's old stockings! But, ... I'll never forget that first moment when I saw it up there. I had a stiff neck the next day from looking up so much.

Notice the stage directions in this play. They often tell the actors exactly how to look or move.

(*Sam laughs. Hally turns to him with a question he never thought of asking before*)

Why did you make that kite, Sam?

SAM (*Evenly*) I can't remember.

HALLY Truly?

SAM Too long ago, Hally.

HALLY Ja, I suppose it was. It's time for another one, you know.

SAM Why do you say that?

HALLY Because it feels like that. Wouldn't be a good day to fly it, though.

evenly without a change in tone

suicidal deeply unhappy; self-destructive

The brackets, [ ], indicate that something has been added to let you know what has happened in the part of the play that has been omitted in this excerpt.

SAM   No. You can't fly kites on rainy days.

[*Later, Sam and Hally are arguing about Hally's father. Hally seems both to hate and love his father, who is **addicted** to alcohol.*]

SAM   (*Almost shouting*) Stop now!

HALLY   (*Suddenly **appalled** by how far he has gone*) Why?

SAM   Hally? It's your father you're talking about.

HALLY   So?

SAM   Do you know what you've been saying?

(*Hally can't answer. He is **rigid** with **shame**. Sam speaks to him sternly*)

           No, Hally, you mustn't do it. Take back those words and ask for forgiveness! It's a terrible sin for a son to **mock** his father with jokes like that. You'll be punished if you carry on. Your father is your father, even if he is a … cripple man.

Why is Willie's manner of speaking different from Sam's and Hally's?

WILLIE   Yes, Master Hally. Is true what Sam say.

SAM   I understand how you are feeling, Hally, but even so …

HALLY   No, you don't!

SAM   I think I do.

HALLY   And I'm telling you you don't. Nobody does.

(*Speaking carefully as his shame turns to rage at Sam*)

           It's your turn to be careful, Sam. Very careful! You're treading on dangerous ground. Leave me and my father alone.

SAM   I'm not the one who's been saying things about him.

HALLY   What goes on between me and my Dad is none of your business!

SAM   Then don't tell me about it. If that's all you've got to say about him, I don't want to hear.

addicted controlled by a bad habit	**mock** to make fun of	**shame** a painful feeling caused by having done something wrong
appalled filled with horror or dismay	**rigid** stiff	

(For a moment Hally is at a loss for a response)

HALLY   Just get on with your bloody work and shut up.

SAM   Swearing at me won't help you.

HALLY   Yes, it does! Mind your own ... business and shut up!

SAM   Okay. If that's the way you want it, I'll stop trying.

(He turns away. This infuriates Hally even more)

HALLY   Good. Because what you've been trying to do is **meddle** in something you know nothing about. All that concerns you in here, Sam, is to try and do what you get paid for—keep the place clean and serve the customers. In plain words, just get on with your job. My mother is right. She's always warning me about allowing you to get too familiar. Well, this time you've gone too far. It's going to stop right now.

(No response from Sam)

   You're only a servant in here, and don't forget it.

(Still no response. Hally is trying hard to get one)

   And as far as my father is concerned, all you need to remember is that he is your boss.

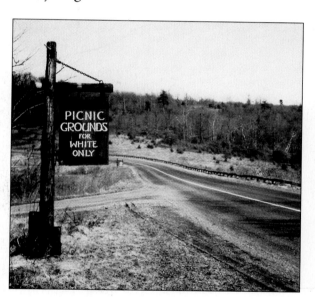

SAM   (*Needled* at last) No, he isn't. I get paid by your mother.

HALL   Don't argue with me, Sam!

SAM   Then don't say he's my boss.

Bloody is a British swear word used to give the next word strong emphasis.

meddle to interfere   **needled** made angry

HALLY	He's a white man and that's good enough for you.
SAM	I'll try to forget you said that.
HALLY	Don't! Because you won't be doing me a favor if you do. I'm telling you to remember it.

(*A pause. Sam pulls himself together and makes one last effort*)

Remember that Sam is older than Hally. Why is Sam warning Hally? What is he afraid will happen?

SAM	Hally, Hally ... ! Come on now. Let's stop before it's too late. You're right. We *are* on dangerous ground. If we're not careful, somebody is going to get hurt.
HALLY	It won't be me.
SAM	Don't be so sure.
HALLY	I don't know what you're talking about, Sam.
SAM	Yes, you do.
HALLY	(*Furious*) ... I wish you would stop trying to tell me what I do and what I don't know.

(*Sam gives up. He turns to Willie*)

| SAM | Let's finish up. |
| HALLY | Don't turn your back on me! I haven't finished talking. |

(*He grabs Sam by the arm and tries to make him turn around. Sam **reacts** with a flash of anger*)

This stage direction tells Sam to act very angry when Hally grabs him.

SAM	Don't do that, Hally! (*Facing the boy*) All right, I'm listening. Well? What do you want to say to me?
HALLY	(*Pause as Hally looks for something to say*) To begin with, why don't you also start calling me Master Harold, like Willie.
SAM	Do you mean that?
HALLY	Why ... do you think I said it?
SAM	And if I don't?
HALLY	You might just lose your job.
SAM	(*Quietly and very carefully*) If you make me say it once, I'll never call you anything else again.

react act as in response to something

HALLY	So? (*The boy confronts the man*) Is that meant to be a threat?
SAM	Just telling you what will happen if you make me do that. You must decide what it means to you.
HALLY	Well, I have. It's good news. Because that is exactly what Master Harold wants from now on. Think of it as a little lesson in respect, Sam, that's long **overdue**, and I hope you remember it as well as you do your geography. I can tell you now that somebody who will be glad to hear I've finally given it to you will be my Dad. Yes! He agrees with my Mom. He's always going on about it as well. "You must teach the boys to show you more respect, my son."
SAM	So now you can stop complaining about going home. Everybody is going to be happy tonight.
HALLY	That's perfectly correct. You see, you mustn't get the wrong idea about me and my Dad, Sam. We also have our good times together. ...
SAM	... Come, Willie, let's finish up and go.

Why does Hally's father refer to Sam and Willie as *the boys*?

(*Sam and Willie start to tidy up the tea room. Hally doesn't move. He waits for a moment when Sam passes him*)

HALLY	(*Quietly*) Sam ...

(*Sam stops and looks **expectantly** at the boy. Hally spits in his face. A long and **heartfelt** groan from Willie. For a few seconds Sam doesn't move*)

SAM	(*Taking out a handkerchief and wiping his face*) It's all right, Willie.

(*To Hally*)

Ja, well, you've done it ... Master Harold. Yes, I'll start calling you that from now on. It won't be difficult anymore. You've hurt yourself, Master Harold. I saw it coming, I warned you, but you wouldn't listen. You've just hurt yourself *bad*. And you're a coward, Master

---

expectantly eagerly waiting to hear or see something

heartfelt deeply felt; sincere

overdue past due

What just happened here? What does Sam mean? How does Hally's white skin protect him?

Harold. The face you should be spitting in is your father's ... but you used mine, because you think you're safe inside your fair skin ...

(*Pause, then moving **violently** toward Hally*) Should I hit him, Willie?

WILLIE	(*Stopping Sam*) No, Boet Sam.
SAM	(*Violently*) Why not?
WILLIE	It won't help, Boet Sam.
SAM	I don't want to help! I want to hurt him.
WILLIE	You also hurt yourself.
SAM	And if he had done it to you, Willie?
WILLIE	Me? Spit at me like I was a dog? (*A thought that had not occurred to him before. He looks at Hally*) Ja. Then I want to hit him. I want to hit him hard!

Boet is an expression meaning "brother" or a close friend.

(*A dangerous few seconds as the men stand staring at the boy. Willie turns away, shaking his head*)

But maybe all I do is go cry at the back. He's little boy, Boet Sam. Little *white* boy. Long trousers now, but he's still little boy.

SAM	(*His violence **ebbing** away into defeat as quickly as it flooded*) You're right. So go on, then: groan again, Willie. You do it better than me. (*To Hally*) You don't know all of what you've just done ... Master Harold. It's not just that you've made me feel dirtier than I've ever been in my life ... I mean, how do I wash off yours and your father's **filth**? ... I've also failed. A long time ago I promised myself I was going to try and do something, but you've just shown me ... Master Harold ... that I've failed. ...
HALLY	(*Great pain*) I love him, Sam.

---

ebbing fading away; becoming less	**filth** foul matter; dirt	**violently** with strong physical force or rough action

SAM   I know you do. That's why I tried to stop you from saying these things about him. It would have been so simple if you could have just **despised** him for being a weak man. But he's your father. You love him and you're ashamed of him. You're ashamed of so much! ... And now that's going to include yourself. That was the promise I made to myself: to try and stop that happening. (*Pause*) After we got him to bed you came back with me to my room and sat in a corner and carried on just looking down at the ground. And for days after that! You hadn't done anything wrong, but you went around as if you owed the world an **apology** for being alive. I didn't like seeing that! That's not the way a boy grows up to be a man! ... But the one person who should have been teaching you what that means was the cause of your shame. If you really want to know, that's why I made you that kite. I wanted you to look up, be proud of something, of yourself ... (*Bitter smile at the memory*) ... And you certainly were that when I left you with it up there on the hill. Oh, ja ... something else! ... If you ever do write it as a short story, there *was* a twist in our ending. I couldn't sit down there and stay with you. It was a "Whites Only" bench. You were too young, too excited to notice then. But not anymore. If you're not careful ... Master Harold ... you're going to be sitting up there by yourself for a long time to come, and there won't be a kite in the sky. (*Sam has got nothing more to say. He exits into the kitchen, taking off his waiter's jacket*)

(*Hally goes behind the counter and collects the few coins in the cash register. As he starts to leave ...*)

SAM   Don't forget the comic books.

Now we know why Sam built the kite for Hally. He wanted to give him a reason to look up. He didn't want Hally to feel that he had to look down because he was ashamed of his father.

apology an expression of regret for something one has done	**despise** to look down on

(Hally returns to the counter and puts them in his case. He starts to leave again)

SAM   *(To the retreating back of the boy)* Stop ... Hally...

(Hally stops, but doesn't turn to face him)

Hally... I've got no right to tell you what being a man means if I don't behave like one myself, and I'm not doing so well at that this afternoon. Should we try again, Hally?

HALLY   Try what?

SAM   Fly another kite, I suppose. It worked once, and this time I need it as much as you do.

HALLY   It's still raining, Sam. You can't fly kites on rainy days, remember.

SAM   So what do we do? Hope for better weather tomorrow?

HALLY   *(Hopeless gesture)* I don't know. I don't know anything anymore.

SAM   You sure of that, Hally? Because it would be pretty hopeless if that was true. It would mean nothing has been learnt in here this afternoon, and there was a ... a lot of teaching going on ... one way or the other. But anyway, I don't believe you. I reckon there's one thing you know. You don't *have* to sit up there by yourself. You know what that bench means now, and you can leave it any time you choose. All you've got to do is stand up and walk away from it.

Why is Sam willing to take the first step to heal the damage done to their relationship?

Sam says he's hoping for *better weather tomorrow.* What else is he hoping tomorrow will bring?

Directions Write the answers to these questions using complete sentences.

Comprehension: Identifying Facts

1. Sam made a surprise for Hally. What was it?

2. Hally says a miracle happened. What was it?

3. What reason does Sam give for leaving Hally and the kite?

4. What did Sam use to make the kite?

5. How does Hally feel about his father?

6. Why does Hally get mad at Sam?

7. Hally tells Sam to "just get on with your job." What is Sam's job?

8. According to Hally, who is Sam's boss? According to Sam, who is his boss?

9. Hally tells Sam to call him by a different name. What is it?

10. Who else will be glad that Hally is asking respect from Sam?

Comprehension: Understanding Main Ideas

11. Why was Hally surprised that Sam knew how to fly a kite?

12. Why did Hally refuse to carry the kite?

13. Hally says that Sam was being "too familiar." What does this mean?

14. Hally tells Sam to call him Master Harold. What is the significance of this?

15. Why does Sam start to move violently toward Hally?

16. Willie describes Hally by saying, "Long trousers now, but he's still little boy." What does he mean?

17. Sam says that he's failed. How did he fail?

18. Why is Hally ashamed of his father?

19. What was the real reason why Sam left Hally alone with the kite?

20. What does Sam apologize for?

Review Continued on Next Page

Understanding Literature: Realistic Drama

"Master Harold"...and the Boys is a realistic drama. It's a play that tells a story as it might have happened in real life. A realistic drama must have a believable setting. It must have realistic characters who must say and do realistic things. The audience watching a realistic drama should believe that they are watching a slice of life.

21. What is the setting of this play? Is it realistic?

22. Read the description of how the three characters are dressed. Do they look like real people? Why or why not?

23. Look at the action in the play. Is it realistic? Why or why not?

24. Is Hally troubled by real problems? What are they?

25. *"Master Harold"...and the Boys* is a play in one act. How might that make it seem more realistic?

Critical Thinking

26. What was Sam's real reason for making the kite for Hally?

27. What role does Sam play in Hally's life?

28. How do you think Sam has learned to speak English well?

29. How has apartheid affected the relationship between Sam and Hally?

30. Do you think there's hope for the future of Sam and Hally's friendship?

Writing on Your Own This play is set in 1950. South Africa has undergone many changes since then. Ask your librarian or teacher for recent articles about South Africa. Look for information about apartheid and a man named Nelson Mandela. What has happened to the apartheid system? Write a paragraph describing the changes.

Expressionistic Drama

- "We reason deeply when we forcibly feel." —Mary Wollstonecraft
- "He who is sorrowful can force himself to smile, but he who is glad cannot weep."
  —Selma Lagerlöf

Expressionistic drama began in Europe and became most popular after 1900. Writers exaggerated a character's inner feelings. Expressionistic playwrights did not want to present events realistically. They tried to increase the audience's emotional participation in other ways. These writers used lighting, staging, design, and directing in new ways. In Eugene O'Neill's *Strange Interlude,* for example, the protagonist is split into two characters. The split shows the conflict between the character's public and private nature. Thornton Wilder's *Our Town* uses a narrator, as a realistic play might. But only very little scenery is used to move the action. Samuel Beckett's *Waiting for Godot* emphasizes the frustration of human existence. The characters wait and wait, but Godot never appears.

The Stronger
August Strindberg (translated by Ants Oras)

August Strindberg
(1849–1912)
Swedish

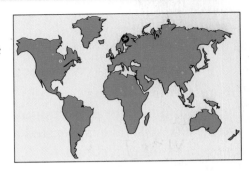

Literary Terms

expressionistic drama a play that seems realistic but changes some elements for dramatic effect

prop a piece of equipment used on stage during a play

About the Author

August Strindberg was one of eleven children in a poor family. After an unpleasant childhood, he went to college in Uppsala and then Stockholm. He tried teaching and acting. Then he went back to his studies. He received a cash award from the King of Sweden and began writing. One of his plays earned him a job at the Royal Library. He wrote many short stories, novels, and plays. Strindberg's plays often show conflicts between men and women. One of his most famous plays is *Miss Julie*. Strindberg's late plays inspired other expressionistic playwrights.

About the Selection

Strindberg's works range from naturalistic to expressionistic. **Expressionistic drama** is not meant to be realistic. It may seem realistic but changes some elements for dramatic effect. As Strindberg grew older, his works depended more and more on dialogue. He used fewer **props** and stage directions. A prop (short for "property") is a piece of equipment used on stage to help the story. *The Stronger* is one result of this trend. The play breaks away from many of the usual forms of drama. One of the main characters never speaks. She seems to be present only so the other woman is not speaking to herself. This play presents psychological conflict only by the words spoken

THE STRONGER

August Strindberg

PERSONS
MME. X, *actress, married*
MLLE. Y, *actress, single*
A Waitress

A corner in a ladies' café; two small iron tables, a red velvet sofa and some chairs. Mme. X enters in winter clothing, wearing a hat and a cloak and carrying a fine Japanese basket on her arm. Mlle. Y sits with a half-empty beer bottle in front of her, reading an illustrated paper, then changing it for another.

MME. X: How are you, little Amelie?—You're sitting alone here on Christmas Eve like a **disconsolate** old bachelor.

(Mlle. Y looks up from the paper, nods, goes on reading.)

MME. X: You know, I am **heartily** sorry to see you like this, alone, all alone in a café on Christmas Eve. I feel quite as sorry as that evening in a Paris restaurant when I saw a bridal party, with the bride sitting and reading a comic paper and the groom playing **billiards** with the witnesses. Goodness, I thought, with such a beginning how is this to continue and to end!

He played billiards on his wedding evening!—Yes, and she read a comic paper! Well, but that is hardly the same situation as here.

Mme. X is the abbreviation for Madame X. *Mlle. Y* is the abbreviation for Mademoiselle Y. These are French titles of address. The first is for a married woman and the second for an unmarried one.

As you read, think about why the author did not give specific names to his characters.

The *witnesses* were the wedding guests. They sign, or witness, a paper that makes the wedding legal.

---

billiards a game similar to pool, played with a cue and solid balls on a large oblong table with raised edges

disconsolate very sad

heartily with enthusiasm

(*The Waitress enters, places a cup of hot chocolate before Mme. X and goes out.*)

M<small>ME</small>. X: I tell you what, Amelie! Now I really believe you would have done better to have kept him. Remember, I was the first to urge you "Forgive him!" Don't you recall it?—You could have been married to him, with a home of your own. Don't you remember last Christmas, how happy you felt out in the country with your **fiancé**'s parents; How you praised the happiness of a home and how you **longed** to get away from the theater?—Yes, darling Amelie, a home is the best of all things—next to the theater—a home and some brats too—but that you wouldn't understand.

What seems to have happened in Mlle. Y's personal life?

(*Mlle. Y looks **contemptuous**.*)

M<small>ME</small>. X: (*drinks a few spoonfuls from her cup, opens her basket and shows her Christmas presents*): Now you'll see what I've bought for my piglets. (*Shows a doll*) Look at this. This is for Lisa. Look how it rolls its eyes and turns its neck. There! And here is Maja's pop gun. (*Loads it and shoots at Mlle. Y.*)

Who is Mme. X referring to as her *piglets*?

(*Mlle. Y makes a scared gesture.*)

M<small>ME</small>. X: Did this startle you? Did you fear I'd shoot you? What?—Good heavens, I don't believe you could possibly have thought that. I'd be less surprised if you were shooting me, since I got in your way—I know you can't forget that—although I was completely innocent. You still believe I eased you out of the theater with my **intrigues**, but I didn't! I didn't, even though you think I did!—But what is the use of telling you, for you still believe I did it. (*Takes out a pair of embroidered slippers*) And these are for my old man. With tulips embroidered, by myself—I **abhor** tulips, you understand, but he wants tulips on everything.

abhor to dislike intensely; to find disgusting	**fiancé** a French term meaning a man engaged to be married	**longed** greatly wished for
contemptuous showing scorn	**intrigue** a secret or underhanded scheme	

(*Mlle. Y looks up from her paper ironically and with some curiosity.*)

MME. X: (*puts a hand in each slipper*) Look how small Bob's feet are. Well? And you ought to see how daintily he walks. You've never seen him in his slippers.

(*Mme. Y laughs aloud.*)

MME. X: Look, I'll show you. (*Makes the slippers walk along the table.*)

(*Mlle. Y laughs aloud.*)

MME. X: Now look, and when he is out of sorts he stamps with his foot like this. "What!...Those servants, they'll never learn how to make coffee! Goodness! Now those **morons** haven't clipped the lamp wick properly." And then there's a **draught** from the floor and his feet freeze: "Blast it, how cold it is, and these **unspeakable** idiots can't keep the fire going." (*Rubs one slipper's sole against the other's upper.*)

(*Mlle. Y bursts out laughing.*)

MME. X: And then he comes home and has to search for his slippers, which Marie has put under the **chiffonier** ...Oh, but it is sinful to sit thus and make a fool of one's old man. Whatever he is, he is nice, a decent little fellow—you ought to've had such a husband, Amelie.—Why are you laughing! Why? Why?—And look here, I know he is faithful to me; yes, I do know that, for he told me himself . . . What are you grinning at?...When I was on my Norway tour, that nasty Frédérique came and tried to seduce him—Could you imagine such an infamy? (*Pause.*) But I'd have

Irony is the use of words or expressions that say one thing but mean another. Is Mlle. Y really interested in what Mme. X is saying?

This play was written before electricity was used for lights. A daily duty for a house servant was to trim the *wicks* in the oil-burning lamps. The wicks were tightly woven fibers that drew the fuel to the flame. A neatly trimmed wick ensured a steady light

chiffonier a high chest of drawers, often with a mirror	**moron** a remarkably stupid person	**unspeakable** too bad to be described
draught (Amer. draft) a current of air		

scratched out her eyes if she'd come near me after my return! (*Pause.*) What a good thing Bob told me about it himself rather than let me hear it through gossip! (*Pause.*) But Frédérique was not the only one, believe me! I don't know why, but the women are positively crazy about my husband—perhaps they think he has some say about theater engagements because he is in the government department!—Who knows but you yourself may have been chasing him!—I never trusted you more than just so much—but now I do know he doesn't care for you, and I always thought you were bearing him some grudge.

(*Pause. They view each other, both embarrassed.*)

Rallentando is an Italian musical term meaning a gradually decreasing tempo or speed. It is used here as a stage direction. It tells the character to speak the rest of the line more slowly. Why does the author give this direction?

MME. X: Come to see us in the evening, Amelie, and show you aren't cross with us, at least not with me! I don't know why, but it is so uncomfortable to be **at loggerheads** with you, of all people. Possibly because I got in your way that time—(*rallentando*) or—I just don't know why in particular!

(*Pause. Mlle. Y gazes curiously at Mme. X.*)

MME. X: (*pensively*) Our acquaintance was such an odd one—when I first saw you I was afraid of you, so afraid that I couldn't risk letting you out of my sight; whenever I came or went I was always near you—I couldn't afford to have you for an enemy, so I became your friend. But there was always something **discordant** in the air when you came to our home, for I saw my husband couldn't stand you—it all felt somehow awkward, like ill-fitting clothes—and I did what I could to make him take to you but to no purpose—until you got yourself engaged to be married! Then a **violent** friendship flared up so that for a moment it looked as though the two of you had only now ventured to show your real

---

at loggerheads an expression meaning "quarreling"

discordant unpleasant; disturbing

pensively in a sadly thoughtful way

violent intense

feelings because you were safe—and so what?—What happened?—I wasn't jealous—how queer!—And I recall the **christening** when you stood godmother to our baby—I made Bob kiss you—and he did, but you were so confused—that is to say, I didn't notice at the time—haven't thought about it since—not once until—this moment. (*Gets up furiously.*)

Why are you silent? You haven't said a word all this time, you've only let me sit and talk. You've been sitting and staring and making me unwind all these thoughts which lay like raw silk in their cocoon—thoughts—maybe suspicious ones—let me see.—Why did you break off your engagement? Why haven't you been to our house since that happened? Why aren't you coming to see us tonight?

Silkworms spin raw silk threads into a *cocoon* about their bodies. Unraveling a cocoon is a difficult, time-consuming task. Mme. X is finding it difficult to unravel her thoughts.

(*Mlle. Y seems on the point of speaking.*)

Mme. X: Be quiet! You needn't say a word, for now I grasp it all myself. It was because—because—because!—Yes indeed!—Every bit of it falls into its place! That's it!—Shame! Shame! I won't sit at the same table with you. (*Moves her things to the other table.*)

So that was why I had to embroider tulips on his slippers although I hate tulips—because you like them! That was why—(*throws the slippers on the floor*)—that was why we had to spend the summer on Lake Mälar—because you couldn't bear the sea at Saltsiö; that was why my son had to be christened Eskil—because such was the name of your father; that was why I had to wear your colors, read your authors, eat your favorite dishes, drink your drinks—your chocolate, for example; that was why—Oh, my God—this is frightful to think of, frightful!—Everything came from you to me, even your **passions** and

Lake Mälar is near Stockholm, Sweden. It is a popular resort area.

---

christening a ceremony for naming and baptizing a child

passion a strong feeling for or about something

addictions!—Your soul **slithered** into mine like a worm into an apple, eating and eating, digging and digging, until all that was left was a **rind** with some black, messy substance inside! I wanted to escape from you but couldn't; you lay like a snake **bewitching** me with your black eyes—I felt how my wings rose only to drag me down; I lay with tied feet in the water, and the harder my hands struck out, the more I worked myself down, down right to the bottom where you lay like an enormous crab in order to grip me with your claws—and this is where I now am.

Shame, shame! How I hate you, how I hate you, how I hate you! Yet you only sit, silent, calm, uncaring; not caring whether the moon is waxing or waning, whether it is Christmas or New Year's, whether people are happy or unhappy; incapable of love or hatred; rigid like a stork over a mousehole—unable to grab your quarry, unable to chase it, yet well able to wait until it comes into your clutches. Here you sit in your corner—do you know that it is because of you that it's called the Rat-trap?—Here you scan your paper to find out whether anybody has got into trouble or is **wretched** or must give up the theater; here you sit, watching out for victims, calculating your chances like a **pilot** planning a shipwreck, and collecting your tribute!

Poor Amelie, do you know that I pity you because you are unhappy, unhappy like a hurt beast and full of **malice** because you are hurt?—I can't feel angry with you although I would like to—you are the cornered one after all—well yes, that affair with Bob, why

When the moon is *waxing,* it is growing gradually larger. When the moon is *waning,* it is becoming gradually smaller.

When Mme. X says Mlle. Y is like a *stork,* she's using a *simile.* A simile is a figure of speech that makes a comparison using *like* or *as.*

bewitch to fascinate

malice ill will

pilot a person who steers a ship

rind the outer skin or coating of a thing

slither to move along by gliding, as a snake

wretched miserable; very unhappy

should I bother about it?—In what way does it harm me?—And whether it was you or somebody else who taught me to drink chocolate, what of it? (*Drinks a spoonful from her cup; knowingly*) After all, chocolate is good for one's health. And if I learned from you how to dress—*tant mieux*—that only strengthened my husband's affection for me—and so you lost what I won—Yes, there are indications that you really have lost him. Yet of course, you intended me to fade out of the picture—as you have done, sitting here as you do and regretting what you did—but look here, I just won't do it!—We **shan't** be **petty**, don't you agree? And why should I take only what no one else wants!

Tant mieux is a French expression meaning "so much the better."

Perhaps, all things considered, I may indeed be the stronger—for you never got anything out of me, you only gave—and now I am like that thief—as you woke up you found I had all the things you missed.

How else could it come about that everything turned worthless and barren in your hand? With all your tulips and fine **affections** you never managed to keep a man's love—as I have done; you never learned the art of living from your writers, as I did; nor did you ever get any little Eskil of your own, even though Eskil is the name of your father!

And why are you always silent, silent, silent? Yes, I mistook this for strength; but perhaps all it meant was that you hadn't anything to say—that you never were able to think a thought. (*Gets up and takes the slippers from the floor*) Now I'm going home—with the tulips—*your* tulips! You were unable to learn anything from people—unable to bend—and so you snapped like a dry stalk—but I won't snap.

Thanks ever so much, Amelie, for all your kind lessons; thanks for teaching my husband how to love! Now I'm going home to love him. (*Goes.*)

---

affections emotions or feelings

petty mean; small

shan't a short form of shall not

Directions Write the answers to these questions using complete sentences.

Comprehension: Identifying Facts

1. What is the setting of the play? Remember that setting includes both time and place.

2. Who are the three characters?

3. Which two of the actors never speak?

4. What is Mme. X drinking?

5. Where did Mlle. Y spend last Christmas?

6. What gifts does Mme. X have in her basket? Who are they for?

7. What has Mme. X embroidered on her husband's slippers? Why?

8. What has happened to Mlle. Y's plans to marry?

9. Who is the godmother for Mme. X's son?

10. A stage direction near the middle of the play tells Mme. X to move. Why does she move? Where does she move to?

Comprehension: Understanding Main Ideas

11. Why are other actresses attracted to Mme. X's husband?

12. Why was Mme. X once uneasy when Mlle. Y visited her home? How did she explain it at the time?

13. How did the behavior of Mme. X's husband change when Mlle. Y got engaged?

14. Mme. X has done a number of things to please her husband. List them.

15. Why did these actions please him?

16. Mme. X compares Mlle. Y to several living creatures. List them.

17. Do these comparisons help you understand how Mme. X feels about Mlle. Y? How?

18. How does Mlle. Y react to Mme. X's accusations?

19. Mme. X says the café is called the Rat-trap because of Mlle. Y. What does she mean?

20. What does Mme. X decide to do?

Understanding Literature: Expressionistic Drama

The Stronger is an example of expressionistic drama. An expressionistic drama is a play that seems realistic but that changes some elements for dramatic effect. Strindberg, the author of this play, was one of the first playwrights to write in this style. In this play, he uses characters in a new way.

21. What is unusual about the characters' names?

22. Why does Strindberg use these names?

23. What is unusual about the dialogue in the play?

24. Why do you think Strindberg has only one character speak?

25. Think about the title. Who is, finally, the stronger? Explain.

Critical Thinking

26. What do you know about Mme. X's husband?

27. What do you know about Mme. X's marriage?

28. What do you think happened between Mlle. Y and Mme. X's husband?

29. Do you think Mme. X's imagination has run wild? Why or why not?

30. How do you think Mme. X will act when she gets home? Why?

Writing on Your Own Imagine that you are Mlle. Y. Reread the part of the play just before the stage direction, "Mlle. Y seems on the point of speaking." Why does she decide not to speak? What thoughts are in her mind? Write your response.

Characterization

Characterization is the way a writer develops characters by revealing their personality traits. In a play, physical descriptions help reveal characters. What characters say and do shows still more about them. What others say about them adds to the characterization. And how others react to them reveals still more.

When we first see a character, we develop an idea about who he or she is. This is based simply on how the actor looks and moves. We learn more about the character as we listen to dialogue. We begin to form an opinion about the person based on what we hear. These are external clues. They are things we can see and hear. Playwrights use such external clues to reveal what the internal person is really like.

For example, in *Macbeth,* Shakespeare shows little by little that Macbeth is going mad. As Macbeth is planning how to murder King Duncan, he sees a vision of a blood-stained dagger hanging in midair. It points toward Duncan's sleeping chamber. After the murder of Banquo, Macbeth sees and talks to his ghost. At the end of that same scene, Macbeth tells us he has spies in the homes of noblemen. He's now afraid to trust anyone. He wants the advice of the Weird Sisters. He believes they can foretell the future. Shakespeare shows us through Macbeth's words and actions that he is gradually losing his mind.

Review

1. Why do you think most plays begin with a physical description of the characters?

2. In *"Master Harold"...and the Boys,* what does Willie's manner of speech reveal about him?

3. In *"The Stronger,"* what does Mlle. Y's behavior reveal about her?

4. What does Mme. X's dialogue reveal about her?

5. Who is the least likable character in the plays in this unit? Why?

> **Writing on Your Own** Choose one of the characters from the plays in this unit. Write one paragraph describing the character. Be sure to answer these questions. How does the person look, move, and speak? How does the person behave toward others? How do others react to this person?

UNIT 3 SUMMARY

In Unit 3 you read three types of plays. Shakespeare's *Macbeth* is called a classical drama. Fugard's *"Master Harold"...and the Boys* is a realistic play. Strindberg's *The Stronger* is an expressionistic drama.

These different types of plays have much in common with each other. For instance, each of the playwrights describes a setting. They tell us when and where a play takes place. All plays have stage directions. Actors follow these directions to know when and how to speak and move. Characters, the people in a story, are essential in a play. So is dialogue, the conversations between the characters. Playwrights use more than just words to tell a story. They skillfully bring together setting, stage directions, characters, and dialogue.

Playwrights use these elements differently depending on the type of play they're writing. For example, the dialogue in classical drama is written in blank verse. The dialogue in a realistic play or expressionistic drama is written in everyday language. The settings of classical dramas are sometimes places where you'd find royalty and nobility. Or they may be imaginary places from myths and legends. In contrast, the settings for realistic plays are ordinary, real life places. In expressionistic drama, one of these elements may be changed or exaggerated for a special effect. In realistic drama, each element is carefully used to create a story just as it might have happened in real life.

Selections

- *Macbeth* by William Shakespeare. In one of Shakespeare's best-known plays, Macbeth commits murder to become king but must struggle against guilt and his opponents.

- *"Master Harold"...and the Boys* by Athol Fugard. The attitudes of apartheid threaten the friendship between a white boy and the black man who is like a father to him.

- *The Stronger* by August Strindberg. In a play in which only one character speaks, Strindberg explores the inner thoughts of Mme. X as she realizes something about her marriage.

UNIT 3 REVIEW

Directions Write the answers to these questions using complete sentences.

Comprehension Identifying Facts

1. Who is murdered in one of the plays? In which play?

2. What country is the setting for *"Master Harold"...and the Boys*? What year is it set in?

3. What is the term for the words the characters in a play say?

4. Which play has a ghost as a character?

5. How long ago did Shakespeare write *Macbeth*?

Comprehension: Understanding Main Ideas

6. What is a classical drama? List at least three elements.

7. What play focuses on apartheid and its effects?

8. Macbeth sees two visions. What are they? What do they mean?

9. Why is Sam so fond of Hally?

10. When Mme. X. says "a home is the best of all things," Mlle. Y looks contemptuous? Why?

Understanding Literature: Setting

The setting—the time and place—in a play is very different from the setting in a story. In a story, the setting can be anything a writer can imagine and describe with words. The setting in a play, though, is limited to what can be shown or represented on a stage. The stage sets in Shakespeare's day were small and quite simple. The audience had to imagine things such as battles. Stage sets now can be much more elaborate and creative. Still, a playwright must tell the story within the limits of a stage.

11. The objects on stage in a play are called "properties," or "props." What props are needed for the stage setting in the scene from *Macbeth*? Remember to include costumes, too.

12. Two of the plays have similar settings—a café or a restaurant. Why does a café make a good setting?

13. Two of the plays must be set in a certain period of time. Which ones? Why?

14. Strindberg sets his play on Christmas Eve. However, he doesn't name a year. Is the play timeless? Why?

15. Which playwright provides the most details about the setting? How does this contribute to your understanding and enjoyment of the play?

Critical Thinking

16. Do you think Fugard used *"Master Harold"...and the Boys* to show his attitude toward apartheid? How?

17. Although you read these plays, they were written to be performed. How would your experience be different if you were in a theater audience?

18. Why do you think Shakespeare continues to be popular with audiences?

19. What do realistic drama and expressionistic drama have in common?

20. Identify the play in the unit you liked best. Explain the reasons for your choice.

Speak and Listen

Choose a short segment of dialogue between two characters from Shakespeare's original of *Macbeth*. Work with a partner. Read the dialogue aloud. Practice putting the emphasis on certain words to convey meaning. Refer to the paraphrase. It will help you understand the passage. Present the scene to the class.

Beyond Words

Plays are often advertised on playbills or small posters. Design and produce a playbill for one of the plays that includes the name of the play and the playwright. Suppose that the play is being done by your school's drama club. Use a drawing or graphic to draw attention to the poster.

Writing on Your Own Newspapers and magazines publish reviews of play performances. These reviews are written by theater critics who have seen the play. The reviews are their opinions about the play's dialogue, the actors' work, and the stage sets. Imagine that you've just seen a production of one of the plays in this unit. Choose one of the above topics and write a review about it. Tell your opinion.

Test-Taking Tip

Studying together in small groups and asking questions of one another is one way to review material for tests.

"As honey sweetens/the mouth readily/a poem should make sense/right away."
—Atakuri Molla

"To read a poem is to hear it with our eyes; to hear it is to see it with our ears."
—Octavio Paz

"There is the view that poetry should improve your life. I think people confuse it with the Salvation Army."
—John Ashbery

UNIT 4 *Poetry*

People who love poetry find it exciting and vivid. They like the images and emotions that are packed into a few lines. Others may find it hard to pull out the meaning of the poem. They may never read it aloud to hear the rhyme and rhythm. They may not realize that songs they love are also poetry. This unit has a variety of poems. Some will be easy to understand, others will not. It's okay for people to disagree about what a poem means. To enjoy a poem, relax. Slow down. Don't try to get all the ideas at once. Read it aloud more than once. Think about the images. Enjoy.

Poetry packs the most feeling into the least space. The writer of a poem is called a poet. A poet usually expresses ideas within the limits of a specific poetic form. Classical poets developed many different combinations of rhyme, rhythm, and length. Rhyme is the use of words with the same vowel and end sounds. Rhythm is the beat. It is a regular pattern of stress on certain syllables.

Good poetry proves the saying that a picture is worth a thousand words. Poets often use a carefully chosen symbol. A symbol can be a person, place, thing, or event. It stands for something else. By using a familiar symbol, the poet communicates the emotions and facts connected with it. A flying bird, for instance, may stand for freedom. In another poem, a bird may stand for fate, or doom. For years, the wall that divided Berlin was a strong symbol. It stood for cruel separation. The 1989 fall of the Berlin Wall, though, brought people back together. It meant harmony.

Word choice is important in poetry. This is because the words must fit a certain rhythm or rhyme. At the same time, it must create an image. For example, a poet might write about people walking or moving along the Berlin Wall. But the poet would be more likely to choose other words that strengthen that symbol. Look at the connotations—the images or emotion connected to words—of *boiling, bubbling,* or *surging*. They suggest moving water—many people stood in the rain and made toasts to freedom. They also suggest the disorder that large numbers of people can cause.

Poems can be divided into many different genres, or types. Early poems were usually songs to a deity. Others were epics, long stories written in verse. They were sung or chanted aloud. Gradually, other forms developed. A popular genre in English was the sonnet. It is a fourteen-line poem in iambic pentameter. It has any one of several rhyme schemes (patterns of rhyming words). Haiku is a traditional Japanese poetic form. A haiku has seventeen unrhymed syllables. Humorous subjects appear in limericks. Free verse often doesn't rhyme. Serious poets may attempt a villanelle.

Poems can also be grouped by purpose. Elegies, for example, are poems that mourn someone's death. Poems may be grouped by a literary technique. Robert Browning wrote dramatic monologues. In those poems, a character reveals personality by talking to the reader. Today's poets use simpler forms. Some poets may combine several genres in new ways.

All poems use some kind of rhythmic pattern. They express an idea, impression, or emotion. In this unit, notice the wide range of forms. Look at their relationship to the idea of the poem. Also, remember that enjoying a good poem may take time and effort. Sometimes reading a poem out loud adds to your appreciation. The more you think about a good poem, the better it becomes.

The following countries are represented in this unit: Israel, China, Vietnam, the Philippines, Chile, Japan, and Wales.

The Diameter of the Bomb

Yehuda Amichai (translated by Chana Bloch)

Yehuda Amichai
(1924–)
Israeli

Literary Terms

free verse poetry that uses actual speech patterns for the rhythms of sound and does not have a strict rhyming pattern or regular line length

symbol a person, place, or thing that represents an idea or thought

About the Author

Yehuda Amichai is one of modern Israel's most important writers. He was born in Würzburg, Germany, to a Jewish family. After Hitler came to power in 1936, they

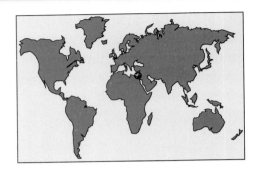

moved to Jerusalem. Amichai served in the British army during World War II. He later fought for independence with the Israeli army. He began to publish poetry in magazines in the 1940s. He also has written novels, short stories, and plays. Many of these works have won awards. His works have been translated into more than twenty languages. The focus of Amichai's poetry is often on modern living. He writes in the Hebrew language used by the Israeli people in everyday life.

About the Selection

"The Diameter of the Bomb" shows how one event connects to many others. The explosion of a bomb reaches only a certain distance Yet its effects may be felt far beyond that circle. Like many modern poets, Amichai uses free verse. **Free verse** is poetry that doesn't rhyme. Notice how the poem begins with phrases that could be taken from the newspaper. It quickly becomes more personal. Amichai uses many **symbols** to help the reader connect emotionally with the subject. Symbols are persons or objects that stand for an idea. They speak to a reader's emotions. What emotions do you feel when you read words like *graveyard* or *howl of orphans?* Look for other symbols as you read.

The Diameter of the Bomb

Yehuda Amichai

The diameter of the bomb was thirty centimeters
and the diameter of its **effective** range about seven meters,
with four dead and eleven wounded.

And around these, in a larger circle
5 of pain and time, two hospitals are scattered
and one **graveyard**. But the young woman
who was buried in the city she came from,
at a distance of more than a hundred
    kilometers,
    enlarges the circle considerably,
10 and the **solitary** man mourning her death

at the distant shores of a country far across the sea
includes the entire world in the circle.
And I won't even mention the howl of orphans
that reaches up to the throne of God and
15 beyond, making
a circle with no end and no God.

As you read, look for symbols used by the poet.

The poet measures distances using the metric system. One hundred *centimeters* equals one *meter*. A meter is equal to about 39 inches, slightly longer than a yard. Later he refers to *kilometers*, a distance of 1,000 meters.

Why is the man now alone?

effective having the desired result

enlarge to make larger

graveyard a place where people are buried

kilometer a distance of 1000 meters, equal to about .62 miles.

solitary alone

Directions Write the answers to these questions using complete sentences.

Comprehension: Identifying Facts

1. What is the diameter of the bomb? What is its real range?

2. Where is one woman buried? Why is she buried there?

3. How many people are killed and wounded?

Comprehension: Understanding Main Ideas

4. How do the two hospitals create a larger circle around the bomb?

5. Who brings the entire world into the circle?

6. How do you know that some of those killed were parents? Explain.

Understanding Literature: Free Verse

"The Diameter of the Bomb" is written in free verse. It does not have a strict rhyme pattern. It does not have regular line lengths. It is written as though the poet were talking.

7. Do you like free verse? Why or why not?

8. Do you think that the last part of the poem is more "poetic" than the first part? Why or why not?

Critical Thinking

9. Explain what "The Diameter of the Bomb" is about.

10. Do you think the poet is thinking of one event? Or could this bombing occur anywhere?

Writing on Your Own Think of an event that happened at your school or in the world. Write a paragraph telling how one event leads to another.

Taking Leave of a Friend
Li Po (translated by Ezra Pound)

Li Po
(701–762)
Chinese

Literary Term

simile a figure of speech that makes a comparison using the words *like* or *as*

About the Author

Li Po lived more than 1,200 years ago, but is considered one of China's greatest poets. He was a popular poet in his lifetime, too. (His name is sometimes spelled Li Bo.)

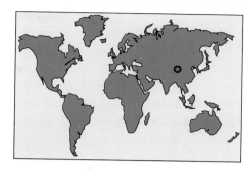

He was born in what is now Szechwan, in western China. Li Po spent much of his life traveling across China. In about 742, he worked as a poet at the court of the Chinese emperor, then he went traveling again. He became a poet for one of the emperor's sons, Prince Lin. Later this caused him political trouble. Li Po spent some time in prison but was pardoned.

Ezra Pound was a well-known American poet. He had a strong influence on English and American poetry in the early 1900s. While living in Paris in the 1920s, Pound translated from Italian, Chinese, and Japanese literature. *Personae,* from which "Taking Leave of a Friend" comes, was published in 1909.

About the Selection

Li Po probably wrote about a thousand poems. He followed traditional Chinese forms. As in this poem, he often wrote about nature, friendship, and the passing of time. He also speaks of traveling and living in the mountains. You can see these themes in "Taking Leave of a Friend." This poem uses **similes**. A simile is a figure of speech that makes a comparison using the words *like* or *as*. Look for similes as you read the selection. Think about how Li Po feels as he and his friend say good-bye.

Taking Leave of a Friend — Li Po

As you read, notice how the poet pictures nature.

Blue mountains to the north of the walls,
White river winding about them:
Here we must make **separation**
And go out through a thousand miles
    of dead grass.

What does the writer say his mind is like?

5 Mind like a floating wide cloud,
Sunset like the parting of old acquaintances
Who bow over their clasped hands at a distance.
Our horses **neigh** to each other
    as we are **departing**.

depart to leave; to go away   **neigh** the cry of a horse   **separation** the act of leaving one another

Chang

Taking Leave of a Friend
Li Po

Directions Write the answers to these questions using complete sentences.

Comprehension: Identifying Facts

1. What color do the mountains seem to be?

2. Describe the rest of the scene where this occurs.

3. What do the horses do?

Comprehension: Understanding Main Ideas

4. Does the title of the poem give the main idea? Explain.

5. How far apart will the friends be? What words show this?

6. What action shows that the friends want to be in touch as long as they can?

Understanding Literature: Similes

A simile is a figure of speech that compares two things. For example, you might say, "A smile is *like* a sunny day." That is a clue to help you find a simile. A simile uses the words *like* or *as*.

7. What does the poet compare to a cloud?

8. What does he say is like a sunset?

Critical Thinking

9. Is this a truly sad poem? Why or why not?

10. Is the place where the friends part a pleasant one? Explain.

Writing on Your Own Imagine you are one of the two friends in this poem. Write a paragraph or a short poem about how you feel at this time. Tell how you feel about leaving your friend. You might also tell where you are going and what your trip will be like.

Thoughts of Hanoi

Nguyen Thi Vinh (translated by Nguyen Ngoc Bich with Burton Raffel and W. S. Merwin)

About the Author

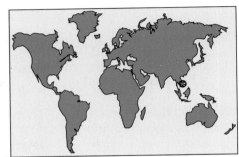

Nguyen Thi Vinh was born in 1924. She was one of a group of writers in South Vietnam who became known in the early 1960s. She has written a novel and short stories as well as poetry. These works reflect her experiences of the many years of war in Vietnam.

About the Selection

After the end of World War II, Vietnam suffered years of civil war. In 1954 the country was split in two. Communists ruled the north. A republic governed the south. In "Thoughts of Hanoi" Nguyen Thi Vinh looks back to a time before the country was divided. (Hanoi was then the capital city.) The poem is a sort of **elegy**, a sad poem about someone's death. The poem does not mourn a specific person's death. But the author asks whether some familiar things still exist in the city. The poem speaks to a childhood friend, now on the other side in the war. The author uses **personification** for Hanoi. The city is given human characteristics. It almost becomes a character in itself. It seems that Nguyen fears that the Hanoi of the past is dead.

Thoughts of Hanoi
Nguyen Thi Vinh

The night is deep and chill
as in early autumn. **Pitchblack**,
it **thickens** after each lightning flash.
I dream of Hanoi:
5 Co-ngu Road
ten years of **separation**
the way back sliced by a frontier of **hatred**.

I want to bury the past
to burn the future
10 still I **yearn**
still I fear
those endless nights
waiting for dawn.

Brother,
15 how is Hang Dao now?
How is Ngoc Son temple?
Do the trains still run
each day from Hanoi
to the neighboring towns?

20 To Bac-ninh, Cam-giang, Yen-bai,
the small villages, islands
of brown thatch in a **lush** green sea?

The girls
   bright eyes
25   **ruddy** cheeks
four-piece dresses
     raven-bill scarves
sowing harvesting
     spinning weaving
30 all year round,

As you read, notice what the poet is remembering.

Hanoi was the French colonial capital of Vietnam before the country was divided. It then became the capital of Communist North Vietnam.

Ngoc Son ("Jade Mountain") temple is on an island in a lake in the center of Hanoi.

The poet names some of the towns near Hanoi.

hatred strong dislike or hate	**pitchblack** very dark; as dark as tar	**separation** the state of being apart
lush having lots of plants	**ruddy** having a healthy, reddish color	**thicken** to become deeper or denser
		yearn to wish for deeply

Ploughing is another
spelling of the word
plowing.

            the boys
                ploughing
                        transplanting
            in the fields
35   in their shops
            running across
                    the meadow at evening
            to fly kites
                    and sing alternating songs.
40   Stainless blue sky,
          jubilant voices of children
      stumbling through the alphabet,
          village **graybeards** strolling to the temple,
      grandmothers basking in twilight sun,
45   chewing **betel** leaves
      while the children run—

      Brother,
      how is all that now?
      Or is it **obsolete**?
50   Are you like me,
          reliving the past,
      imagining the future?
      Do you count me as a friend
      or am I the enemy in your eyes?
55   Brother, I am afraid
      that one day I'll be with the March-North Army
      meeting you on your way to the South.
      I might be the one to shoot you then
      or you me
60   but please
      not with hatred.

      For don't you remember how it was,
      you and I in school together,
      plotting our lives together?
65   Those roots go deep!

      Brother, we are men,
      conscious of more
      than material needs.
      How can this happen to us
70   my friend
      my foe?

Why does the speaker
in the poem call the
person both his *friend*
and his *foe*?

betel an Asian plant whose leaves are chewed

graybeards old men

jubilant happily excited

obsolete out of date

reliving living over again; remembering

Mindoro
Ramón Sunico

About the Author

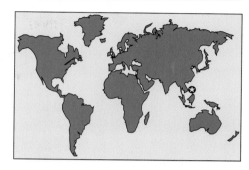

Ramón Sunico was born in 1955 in the Philippines. He was a teacher and is now a publisher. (He is also called "RayVi.") Sunico manages Cacho Publishing House in Manila, Philippines. His company has published fiction and books on medicine and law. He is now especially interested in books for children. He has translated stories from English, German, and Filipino. Sunico wants books to tackle present-day issues. His company publishes stories with themes such as relationships, the environment, and dealing with handicaps.

About the Selection

The **imagery** in this poem contrasts with that in "Thoughts of Hanoi." Imagery is pictures created by words. Sunico uses quiet images to show a scene of beauty from the Philippine island of Mindoro. Nguyen remembered a city that was gone. "Mindoro" celebrates a living island. It uses images of nature, such as mayflies. Look for images that tell you about the life of people here. Is that life hard or easy?

Literary Term

imagery pictures created by words; the use of words that appeal to the senses

Mindoro
Ramón C. Sunico

Notice how the poet describes the setting. Think about what the images mean.

The sun dissolves:
some pieces float
on the green sea
which hurries to darkness.

5 The blood light flickers
while **sporadically**
a wave
slaps against the side of our slippery boat.

sporadically
happening now and
then

The red threads

10 of last-light

dance

on the shoulders of our **oarsman**.

No one notices

the stars

15 begin

to cluster like **mayflies**.

The call

of land

to us

20 is sharper than a fishhook:

the rented

home

and dinner steaming.

We are

25 all **mutes**

riding along on this boat.

To the left

the sea

slices the afternoon in two.

30 To the right

the mountains of Mindoro ripen.

Last-light is a poetic term for the last rays of the sun. What color is the light?

Why do you think everyone in the boat is quiet?

| **mayfly** an insect that hatches in the water and only lives a few days | **mute** a person who can't talk | **oarsman** the man rowing a boat |

Thoughts of Hanoi | Mindoro
Nguyen Thi Vinh | Ramón Sunico

Directions Write the answers to these questions using complete sentences.

Comprehension: Identifying Facts

1. Name two specific things the poet remembers about the city of Hanoi.

2. What time of day is it in the poem "Mindoro"?

3. In "Mindoro," how are the poet and his friends traveling?

Comprehension: Understanding Main Ideas

4. "Thoughts of Hanoi" is about the conflict between North and South Vietnam. Which side is the poet on?

5. How does the poet know the other person in "Thoughts of Hanoi"?

6. In "Mindoro," what are the people thinking about?

Understanding Literature: Imagery

Poets use imagery to create a picture with words. Images usually appeal to the senses—sight, smell, hearing, or touch. Imagery can touch the reader's feelings. It can also help the reader share what the poet is imagining.

7. Look at "Thoughts of Hanoi." What image does the poet use for the small villages?

8. Look at "Mindoro." Name one of the images of the sunset. What sense does this image appeal to?

Critical Thinking

9. What would be another good title for "Mindoro"? Why?

10. How does "Thoughts of Hanoi" make you feel?

Writing on Your Own Think about a place that means a lot to you. Write one or two sentences about that place. Use imagery to compare it to something else. You might think about a place you enjoyed going when you were a child. Can you remember a sight, or sound, or smell? Try to make others share that feeling.

Ode to a Pair of Socks
Pablo Neruda (translated by Ken Krabbenhoft)

Pablo Neruda
(1904–1973)
Chilean

Literary Terms

figurative language language that makes a comparison and is not meant to be taken literally

surrealism a writing style that has a dreamlike quality

About the Author

Pablo Neruda was born in Parral, in the rainy southern part of Chile. (His real name was Neftalí Ricardo Reyes y Basoalto.) During his career he became Latin America's best-known poet.

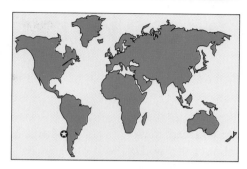

A book of poems, published in 1924, made him famous. It was called *Twenty Love Poems and a Song of Despair*. At the same time, Neruda worked as a diplomat. This work took him all over the world. Over the years, he wrote many books of poetry. One major work is *Canto General*, published in 1950. In 1971 he received the Nobel Prize for Literature. Neruda was active in Chilean politics and the government of Salvador Allende. He was ambassador to France from 1970 to 1972. He died in 1973 in Santiago, Chile.

About the Selection

One critic calls Neruda "many poets in one." His poetry changed during his lifetime. He began as a symbolist poet. He moved from there to surrealism. **Surrealism** is a writing style with a dreamlike quality. Surrealist writers use whatever words come into their mind. They do not change what they write. They believe that their readers will follow these free-flowing thoughts.

In the 1950s, Neruda began to write more realistically. He looked at everyday objects and saw wonder in them. He wrote several books of odes to ordinary things. An ode is a poem in praise of something. Some of Neruda's odes were to laziness, to an onion, and to a storm. The following poem is one of those odes. As you will see, Neruda looks at objects in a unique way. He describes them with **figurative language**. He makes comparisons that are not meant to be taken literally. This ode comes from *Odes to Common Things* (a translation published in 1994).

Ode to a Pair of Socks

Pablo Neruda

As you read, think about the mood of the poem. Is the poet serious or teasing?

Maru Mori brought me
a pair
of socks
that she knit with her
5 shepherd's hands.
Two socks as soft
as rabbit fur.
I thrust my feet
inside them
10 as if they were
two
little boxes
knit
from threads
15 of sunset
and sheepskin.

My feet were
two woolen
fish
20 in those **outrageous** socks,
two **gangly**,
navy-blue sharks

impaled
on a golden thread,
25 two giant blackbirds,
two cannons:
thus
were my feet
honored
30 by
those
heavenly
socks.
They were
35 so beautiful
I found my feet
unlovable
for the very first time,
like two **crusty** old
40 firemen, firemen
unworthy
of that embroidered
fire,
those **incandescent**
45 socks.

crusty gruff; stern in manner	**impaled** speared; stuck on a sharp stick	**unlovable** difficult to love
gangly tall, thin, and ungraceful	**incandescent** glowing; very bright	**unworthy** not deserving
	outrageous extreme	

298 *Unit 4 Poetry*

Nevertheless
I fought
the sharp temptation
to put them away
50 the way schoolboys
put
fireflies in a bottle,
the way scholars
hoard
55 **holy writ.**
I fought
the mad urge
to lock them
in a golden
60 cage
and feed them birdseed
and **morsels** of pink melon
every day.
Like jungle
65 explorers
who deliver a young deer
of the rarest species
to the roasting **spit**
then **wolf** it down
70 in shame,
I stretched
my feet forward
and pulled on
those
75 gorgeous
socks,
and over them
my shoes.

So this is
80 the moral of my **ode:**
beauty is beauty
twice over
and good things are doubly
good
85 when you're talking about a
pair of wool
socks
in the dead of winter.

What does the poet first think about doing with the new socks? What does he do instead?

Why might socks be *doubly good* in winter?

hoard to save for the future

holy writ a piece of religious writing; the Bible

morsel a bit of food

nevertheless however

ode a poem that praises something or someone

spit a narrow rod that holds meat to be cooked over a fire

wolf to eat hungrily, like an animal

Directions Write the answers to these questions using complete sentences.

Comprehension: Identifying Facts

1. How does Neruda get the socks?

2. What are the socks made of?

3. What does the poet finally do with the socks?

Comprehension: Main Idea

4. Why do the poet's feet suddenly seem "unlovable"?

5. Why does the poet think about putting the socks away?

6. What does the poet say about beauty in his moral?

Understanding Literature: Figurative Language

Figurative language is language that makes a comparison but is not meant to be taken literally. It is also called a "figure of speech." Two kinds of figurative language are *similes* and *metaphors.* Both make comparisons. A simile uses *like* or *as.* A metaphor says one thing *is* another. For example, Neruda says, "My feet were two woolen fish." Clearly, this isn't a literal comparison. His feet aren't fish. But the words make a picture so that you see the object differently. Poets often use figurative language.

7. Besides fish, Neruda compares his feet to other things. Name two of them.

8. When the poet first gets the socks, he compares them to something. Write the words he uses about the socks themselves.

Critical Thinking

9. How do you think the knitter felt about this poem? Explain.

10. From this poem, do you think you would like to know Pablo Neruda? Why or why not?

> **Writing on Your Own** Think of something ordinary that you like. Think about how it makes you feel. Write a short poem or paragraph about it. Tell what it is and how it makes you feel.

Three Haiku

Basho (translated by Olivia Gray)

Kikaku (translated by Harry Behn)

Anonymous (translated by Harry Behn)

About the Authors

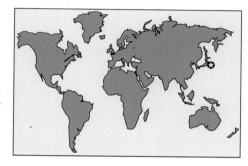

Basho made **haiku** a respected poetry form in Japan. He was born in 1644 into a samurai family. Until his early twenties he served as a samurai warrior. Among samurai, writing poetry was an admired skill. Later, Basho turned entirely to writing and teaching. He used different pen names. His pen name *Basho* comes from a kind of banana tree that grew near where he lived.

Takarai Kikaku was born in 1661. He became one of Basho's students. Some of Kikaku's works have been put to music. Writing poetry was so important in Japanese society that poets competed. Basho and Kikaku often wrote verses on the same themes. Often they answered each other's verses. One story says that they were sitting in a garden together when Basho wrote the first haiku that follows.

Literary Terms

connotation images or emotions connected to a word

haiku a Japanese poetry form, made of seventeen unrhymed syllables

About the Selections

These poems are traditional Japanese haiku. In Japanese, a haiku has seventeen unrhymed syllables. (Translations may not follow this rule.) Still, of all poems, haiku use the most symbols. That is because they are so short. They use words and symbols to call up feelings in the reader. They also depend on **connotations**. Those are the feelings and images connected with a word.

Three Haiku
Basho, Kikaku, Anonymous

As you read, note the form of the poems.

Ancient pool. Sound
of a frog's leap—
Splisssssshhhhh. . . .

　　　　　　—Basho

What is the mood of this poem?

A **bantam** rooster
spreading his **ruff** of feathers
thinks he's a lion!

　　　　　　—Kikaku

Small bird, forgive me.
I'll hear the end of your song
in some other world.

　　　　　　—Anonymous

bantam a small barnyard fowl

ruff a collar that stands out from the neck

Directions Write the answers to these questions using complete sentences.

Comprehension: Identifying Facts

1. Name the three animals in the three poems.

2. What does the rooster think he is?

3. What is the setting of the haiku by Basho?

Comprehension: Understanding Main Ideas

4. What makes the "Splish" sound in the first poem?

5. How does the rooster try to look impressive?

6. What does the poet ask the small bird to do?

Understanding Literature: Haiku

Haiku is a Japanese poetry form. It has a strict style. Usually, a haiku is three lines long. The first line has five syllables. The middle line has seven syllables. The last line has five syllables. (When a haiku is translated from Japanese, the syllable count may not be the same.) A haiku uses images and the power of suggestion to create emotion. Usually it draws images from nature. It may give a "snapshot" of a single image.

7. All three of these haiku draw from nature. Explain.

8. The haiku by Basho uses images that contrast. Explain what kind of mood this creates.

Critical Thinking

9. How does the poet make the rooster seem funny?

10. Which haiku do you like best? Why?

Writing on Your Own Think of an image from nature. Write a haiku to show that image. Try to create a certain mood in your poem.

Do Not Go Gentle Into That Good Night
Dylan Thomas

Dylan Thomas
(1914–1953)
Welsh

Literary Terms

iambic pentameter
five two-beat sounds
in a line of poetry

rhyme scheme a
pattern of end rhymes
in a poem

stanza a group of
lines that forms a unit
and often has the
same rhythm and
rhyme pattern

villanelle a nineteen-
line poem with several
repeating rhymes

About the Author

Dylan Thomas was born in 1914 in Swansea, in southwest Wales. He left school when he was sixteen and worked as a newspaper reporter. Thomas began writing poetry early. His first book of poems was published when he was twenty. His poetry shows an intense energy and love of life. He used language and rhythm musically. Thomas' short stories and plays also show a love of words. The radio play *Under Milk Wood* describes a day in a Welsh village. Audiences loved to hear Thomas read his own works aloud. He made several tours in the United States in the 1950s.

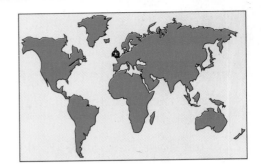

About the Selection

"Do Not Go Gentle Into That Good Night" is a fine example of a villanelle. A **villanelle** is a form used in France in the 1500s. It has nineteen rhymed lines. They follow a pattern of repeating rhymes. The poem is split into five **stanzas** of three lines and one stanza of four lines. (A stanza is a group of lines that form a unit in a poem.) Look at the **rhyme scheme**, or pattern of end rhymes. Notice how many rhymes there are. "Do Not Go Gentle" also uses **iambic pentameter**. Iambic pentameter describes the beat, or rhythm, of a line of verse. Each line has five two-beat sounds. The emphasis falls on the even-numbered beats.

Do Not Go Gentle Into That Good Night Dylan Thomas

Do not go gentle into that good night,
Old age should burn and **rave** at close of day;
Rage, rage against the dying of the light.

Though wise men at their end know dark is right,
5 Because their words had forked no lightning they
Do not go gentle into that good night.

Good men, the last wave by, crying how bright
Their frail deeds might have danced in a green bay,
Rage, rage against the dying of the light.

10 Wild men who caught and sang the sun in flight,
And learn, too late, they **grieved** it on its way,
Do not go gentle into that good night.

As you read, notice the rhyme scheme.

Thomas is using *gentle* as an adverb instead of *gently.*

Forked no lightning means that their words had not lit up the world, like a lightning flash.

---

grieve to cause harm or sadness   **rage** to speak furiously   **rave** to speak wildly

Grave means "serious" here.

Grave men, near death, who see with blinding sight

Blind eyes could blaze like meteors and be gay,

15 Rage, rage against the dying of the light.

How does the poet want his father to feel about dying?

And you, my father, there on the sad height,

Curse, bless, me now with your fierce tears, I pray.

Do not go gentle into that good night.

Rage, rage against the dying of the light.

Do Not Go Gentle Into That Good Night
Dylan Thomas

Directions Write the answers to these questions using complete sentences.

Comprehension: Identifying Facts

1. How does the poet say that people should behave when death is near?

2. What four kinds of men does the poet name?

3. To whom is Thomas writing this poem?

Comprehension: Understanding Main Ideas

4. What do wise men know at their end?

5. What is the main idea of the poem as a whole?

6. What does the poet think that serious people will regret?

Understanding Literature: Rhyme Scheme

The term *rhyme scheme* means the pattern of rhymes. This poem is a villanelle. In this form of poetry, the first five stanzas have three lines. The first and third lines rhyme. This rhyme scheme, or pattern, is *aba*. The letter *a* stands for the lines whose last words rhyme with *night*. In the last stanza, the first, third and fourth lines rhyme. The last stanza is *abaa*.

7. Look at the third stanza. What two words rhyme?

8. Look at the second line of each stanza. What rhyming words do you find at the ends of the lines?

Critical Thinking

9. What regrets keep both wise men and good men from dying quietly?

10. How do you think the poet feels about his father? Explain.

Writing on Your Own Do you agree with the poet about what a dying person should do? Why or why not? Write a paragraph telling your own outlook.

Style is an author's way of writing. It includes not only what the writer says but also the way he or she says it. These examples show two different styles:

> The thief lied.
>
> That rascal was never on friendly terms with the truth.

The first sentence is serious and factual. The second is in a humorous style. The author seems amused but not bothered by the other person's lies.

The poems in this unit have many styles. In "The Diameter of the Bomb," Yehuda Amichai begins on a low key. His words could almost come from a police report:

> The diameter of the bomb was
>   thirty centimeters
> and the diameter of its effective
>   range about seven meters,
> with four dead and eleven wounded.

By the ending, though, his deep outrage at this tragedy shows:

> And I won't even mention the howl
>   of orphans
> that reaches up to the throne of
>   God and
> beyond, making
> a circle with no end and no God.

Pablo Neruda writes about a pair of socks. His style is not ordinary, though. His style is to have fun with them.

> I fought
> the mad urge
> to lock them in a golden
> cage
> and feed them birdseed
> and morsels of pink melon
> every day.

Review

1. What is style?

2. Does style give you a sense of who the writer is? Why or why not?

3. How are the styles of "Do Not Go Gentle Into That Good Night" and "Mindoro" different?

4. Describe how "Taking Leave of a Friend" and the three haiku are alike in style.

5. Which do you prefer, free verse, haiku, or rhymed verses? Explain.

Writing on Your Own Think about the poems you read. Write your own poem. You can use free verse, haiku, or rhymed lines. You might choose something serious or something funny on any subject.

UNIT 4 SUMMARY

A poem packs a lot of meaning into few words. The words must fit certain rhythms or rhyme schemes. They must create images. In this you read poetry from seven countries. The poems cover a time span from the eighth century to the twentieth century.

Poems belong to many forms. These depend on length and meter, or rhythm. For instance, a sonnet has fourteen lines and a certain meter. A haiku has three lines and seventeen syllables. Free verse doesn't rhyme. Blank verse is unrhymed verse with five beats in a line. (Shakespeare's plays are in blank verse.) Some poets combine traditional forms to create new forms.

Poems can also be grouped by their purpose. An *ode* is a poem of praise. Some odes praise beautiful landscapes. Others salute great athletes. An *elegy* mourns a death.

You may think that poetry is not as easy to read as prose. Keep in mind that a poem is like the words of a song. It can help to read a poem aloud.

Selections

- "The Diameter of the Bomb" by Yehuda Amichai. An Israeli poet shows how one tragic event has a widespread effect.

- "Taking Leave of a Friend" by Li Po. A Chinese poet of the eighth century looks at two friends parting.

- "Thoughts of Hanoi" by Nguyen Thi Vinh. A poet from Vietnam looks back at the city before war split the country.

- "Mindoro" by Ram n Sunico. A modern Filipino poet describes sunset near an island.

- "Ode to a Pair of Socks" by Pablo Neruda. A Nobel prize-winner describes the joy of getting a pair of hand-knit socks.

- "Three Haiku" by Basho, Kikaku, and an unknown poet. Three very short poems are in a traditional Japanese form. They give three quick "snapshots:" a frog by a pool, a cocky rooster, and a small singing bird.

- "Do Not Go Gentle Into That Good Night" by Dylan Thomas. A Welsh poet talks about fighting against death.

UNIT 4 REVIEW

Directions Write the answers to these questions using complete sentences.

Comprehension: Identifying Facts

1. What poetry form is used in "The Diameter of the Bomb"?

2. What is the name of the Japanese poetry form in this unit?

3. One of these selections has a traditional rhyming form. Which is it? Who wrote it?

4. Name a poet who wrote odes to everyday things.

5. What country does Ramón Sunico write about?

Comprehension: Understanding Main Ideas

6. Name two poems in this unit that are about serious things.

7. Name two poems that are happy or funny.

8. Compare and contrast "Thoughts of Hanoi" and "The Diameter of the Bomb." How are they alike and different?

9. What gift does Pablo Neruda receive? How does he feel about that gift?

10. What is the setting of "Taking Leave of a Friend"?

Understanding Literature: Mood

Mood is the feeling that a piece of writing causes. Even within a short piece, the mood may change. That gives a change of pace. Still, the work has an overall feeling. Images are one thing that set a mood. The image of feet as gangly navy-blue sharks adds to a playful mood in Neruda's "Ode." Word choices are another way to create mood. Words such as burn and rage help create the mood of "Do Not Go Gentle Into That Good Night."

11. What is mood?

12. Think about "The Diameter of the Bomb." How does the mood change from the beginning to the end of the poem?

13. Choose one of the three haiku. Explain how an image creates the mood.

14. What are some of the images in "Mindoro"? What mood do they create?

15. What is the mood of "Thoughts of Hanoi"? Name three words or phrases that help create this mood.

Critical Thinking

16. Think of the images used in the poems in this unit. Name the image you like best. Tell why you like it.

17. The poem "Taking Leave of a Friend" was written over 1,200 years ago. Tell why people might like it so much that we still read it.

18. Dylan Thomas's poem has a pattern of rhyme and meter. Do you think this makes the poem more powerful? Why or why not?

19. What is your favorite poem from this unit? Explain your choice.

20. If you could meet one of these poets, which one would it be? Explain your choice.

Speak and Listen

Think of a poem you like. It could be one from this unit. It could be one you find in the library. Read the poem to yourself several times, then practice reading the poem aloud. Read the poem to the class when you can read it well. Explain to the class what the poem means to you.

Beyond Words

Images are very important in poetry. Choose one image you like from the poems in this unit. Draw a picture to show what that image suggests to you. Your drawing can be realistic. It can also just suggest an image. For example, you might just use color to show the image. Your drawing might barely suggest a tree or boat.

Writing on Your Own Think about how a poem is like and not like a short story. Write an essay comparing poems with short stories. Tell how they are alike and different. You might want to name a poem from this unit that tells a story. Compare it with a short story on the same theme. Or you might name a poem that does not tell a story. Write about how it is like or different from a short story.

Test-Taking Tip

Before you begin a test, look it over quickly. Try to set aside enough time to complete each section.

"There is nothing that you may not get people to believe if you will only tell it them loud enough and often enough."

—Ouida

"Folks don't like to have somebody around knowin' more than they do ... You're not gonna change any of them by talkin' right ... and when they don't want to learn there's nothing you can do but keep your mouth shut or talk their language."

—Harper Lee

UNIT 5 *Persuasive Literature*

You see or hear persuasive writing every day. Think about ads, speeches, and editorials. Their purpose is to persuade. Ads are all around. Many people do not like this. They think that people are being led to buy, buy, buy. They feel the ads persuade us all too well. Some people think ads are fine. They show us choices. They say all media help us share ideas. Some people think this is good.

In this unit, you will read two forms of persuasive writing. They are speeches and essays. You will also see that persuasive writing has long been a part of literature.

Literary works written mainly to influence opinion are persuasive. The purpose of persuasive writing is more important than its form. Because of that, persuasive writing is found in all genres, or types of writing. In the 1500s, Edmund Spenser wrote a poem, "The Faerie Queene." Its purpose was to flatter Elizabeth I of England as both a ruler and a woman. In the 1850s, Harriet Beecher Stowe wrote the novel *Uncle Tom's Cabin.* (A novel is a longer work of fiction.) With her book, Stowe tried to turn the American public against slavery. During the 1950s Arthur Miller wrote the play "The Crucible." It tried to expose the American anti–Communist hysteria. The play showed McCarthyism as a destructive force like the Salem witch hunts three hundred years earlier. The Russian writer Alexander Solzhenitsyn wrote a series of novels, *The Gulag Archipelago.* He meant to expose the evils and inhumanity of the Soviet prison system.

Poems, novels, and plays written to persuade are not always great literature. Besides, you have read those genres elsewhere in *World Literature.* For those reasons the selections in this unit are nonfiction, as is most persuasive writing. The authors of these selections criticize, reassure, threaten, praise, argue with, and inspire their audiences. Nonetheless, they do use literary techniques. For example, the speeches by Lincoln and Kennedy use metaphors. A metaphor is a figure of speech that says one thing *is* something else. For example, "My love *is* a rose." Jamaica Kincaid uses irony. This form uses words that seem to say one thing but mean the opposite.

As you read, notice the language, imagery, and organization of these selections. Though some were written long ago, they are models that present-day authors still imitate.

The following countries are represented in this unit: France, Russia, the United States, and Antigua.

Speeches

- "A speech reminds us that words ... have the power to make dance the dullest beanbag of a heart." —Peggy Noonan
- "Audiences are always better pleased with a smart retort, some joke or epigram, than with any amount of reasoning." —Charlotte Perkins Gilman

Speeches are usually written. But they are meant to be spoken to an audience. They respond to an event or occasion. One kind of speech is a proclamation, a letter about important events meant to be read out loud. Trials and other events are also good times for a speech. Speeches work best when they are read out loud. Hearing a good speech, an audience can enjoy its sound as well as its ideas and images.

The occasions for these speeches have passed. Their audiences are gone. Yet the form and content of each still "speaks" to similar events today. Speakers all around the world often still quote from these selections.

Letter to the English
Joan of Arc (translated by Willard Trask)

Joan of Arc
(1412–1431)
French

Literary Term

proclamation a letter about important events meant to be read aloud

About the Speaker

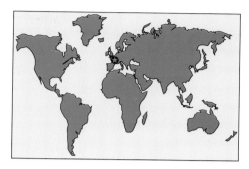

Joan of Arc was the uneducated daughter of a farmer. France and England had been at war, on and off, for many years. Now the English held most of France, including Paris. At age thirteen, Joan began to hear voices. She believed they were saints with a message from God. The voices told her to support the young French king, Charles VII, and help him drive the English out. Joan eventually convinced the king to let her lead an army to Orléans. The city was under attack by the English. Joan inspired the French troops to drive the English away. After that victory, Charles VII was officially crowned.

Soon after, French enemies turned Joan over to the English. A church court convicted her as a heretic, a questioner of the faith. Joan was burned at the stake in Rouen in May 1431. Joan is a national heroine in France today.

About the Selection

The following selection is a **proclamation**. A proclamation is a letter that is read aloud. It may then posted where it can be studied. Most people in the 1400s could not read. So they got the news by hearing it read out loud. A proclamation is the old version of a news broadcast.

This letter was addressed to the English, but Joan knew that the French would also hear it. It was delivered just before the planned attack.

Letter to the English

Joan of Arc

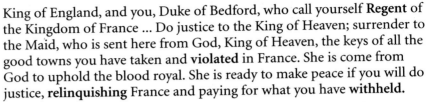

As you read, note to whom Joan addresses her speech.

The English *king*, Henry VI, was only a child. The *Duke of Bedford* was his uncle.

Blood royal refers to the claim that Charles was the true heir to the French throne.

Nill is an old word meaning "will not."

King of England, and you, Duke of Bedford, who call yourself **Regent** of the Kingdom of France ... Do justice to the King of Heaven; surrender to the Maid, who is sent here from God, King of Heaven, the keys of all the good towns you have taken and **violated** in France. She is come from God to uphold the blood royal. She is ready to make peace if you will do justice, **relinquishing** France and paying for what you have **withheld**.

As to you, you archers and men-at-arms, gentle and others, who are before the town of Orléans, go **hence** into your own country in God's name; and if you do not so, expect to hear news of the Maid, who will shortly come to see you, to your very great damage.

King of England, if you do not do so, I am a commander, and in whatever place in France I come upon your men, I will make them leave it, will they or nill they; and if they will not yield obedience, I will have them all slain. I am sent here from God, King of Heaven, to put you, hand to hand, out of all France. Yet if they will yield obedience, I will grant them mercy.

And think not otherwise: for you shall not hold the Kingdom of France from God, King of Heaven, Saint Mary's son, but King Charles shall hold it, the true heir. For so God, King of Heaven, wills it; and so it has been **revealed** to him by the Maid, and he shall enter Paris with a fair company.

If you will not believe this news from God and the Maid, wherever we find you, there we shall strike; and we shall raise such a battle-cry as there has not been in France in a thousand years, if you will not do justice. And know surely that the King of Heaven will send more strength to the Maid than you can bring against her and her good soldiers in any assault. And when the blows begin, it shall be seen whose right is the better before the God of Heaven.

You, Duke of Bedford: The Maid prays and beseeches you not to bring on your own destruction. If you will do her justice, you may yet come in her company there where the French shall do the fairest deed that ever was done for **Christendom**. So answer if you will make peace in the city of Orléans. And if you do not so, consider your great danger speedily.

Christendom all Christians	**regent** one who rules in place of a king	**reveal** to show
hence from here	**relinquish** to release or let go	**violate** to ruin by force
		withhold to keep back

Letter to the English
Joan of Arc

Directions Write the answers to these questions using complete sentences.

Comprehension: Identifying Facts

1. What two people does Joan address at the beginning of her letter?

2. Who does Joan say has sent her to lead this battle?

3. What is Joan's main goal for France?

Comprehension: Understanding Main Ideas

4. What does Joan demand that the English do if they want peace?

5. What reason does Joan give for stating that Charles should be king?

6. Why does Joan believe she and her troops will win this battle?

Understanding Literature: Proclamation

A proclamation is a letter that is read aloud. It is then published or posted where it can be read. Joan wrote her proclamation over five hundred years ago, when most people could not read. The proclamation was read aloud to them. Today, most people can read. News is spread by television and radio. Yet proclamations are still used. They may be used to celebrate events. The mayor of a town may issue a proclamation to honor a good citizen or the opening of a new school.

7. Joan threatens the English. How does her proclamation show that she would rather they left on their own?

8. Why do you think Joan addresses one part of her letter to the English soldiers?

Critical Thinking

9. How do you think the English leaders reacted to this letter? What about ordinary soldiers?

10. Joan died for her beliefs. Do you think from this letter that she perhaps expected to?

Writing on Your Own Think of someone you would like to honor. Write a proclamation to declare a certain day that person's day. You might have a day to honor a teacher or a sports hero. Open by directing the letter to a person or group. (For instance: "Students of the Blank School.") Then state why the person is being honored. Also tell when the day is.

Nobel Lecture
Alexander Solzhenitsyn

Alexander
Solzhenitsyn
(1918–)
Russian

Literary Term

persuasive meant to
influence

About the Speaker

Alexander Solzhenitsyn
was born in Kislovodsk,
Russia. In World War II he
fought in the Soviet army.
After the war, Solzhenitsyn
was arrested for writing
critical remarks about

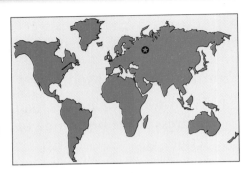

Josef Stalin. (Stalin was the leader of the Soviet Union.)
Solzhenitsyn spent eight years in prisons. This was the
background for his first novel, *One Day in the Life of Ivan
Denisovich*. A few years later, though, the government no
longer let him publish. In 1969 Solzhenitsyn was kicked out
of the Soviet Writers Union. The next year he won the Nobel
Prize for Literature.

In 1973 the first part of *The Gulag Archipelago* was published
in France. It exposed the Soviet prison system. Solzhenitsyn
was arrested and then exiled. He lived in the United States
for some years. In 1994, after the Soviet Union collapsed,
Solzhenitsyn returned to live in Russia.

About the Selection

This is Solzhenitsyn's Nobel Prize speech, but he never gave
it. In 1970, he was afraid to go to Sweden, where the prizes
are given. He thought Russian officials would not let him
return home. The speech was read in his absence.
Solzhenitsyn tries to persuade others to stand up for truth.
But he knows what the cost of standing up can be. This
makes his speech doubly **persuasive**. It is meant to influence
others. He not only speaks persuasively, but his own life is
persuasive. We know he has lived by his words.

Nobel Lecture
Alexander Solzhenitsyn

From time **immemorial** man has been made in such a way
that his vision of the world, so long as it has not been instilled
under hypnosis, his motivations and scale of values, his
actions and intentions are determined by his personal and
group experience of life. As the Russian saying goes, "Do not
believe your brother, believe your own crooked eye." And that
is the most sound basis for an understanding of the world
around us and of human conduct in it. And during the long
epochs when our world lay spread out in mystery and
wilderness, before it became **encroached** by common lines of
communication, before it was transformed into a single,
convulsively pulsating lump—men, relying on experience,
ruled without mishap within their limited areas, within their
communities, within their societies, and finally on their
national territories. At that time it was possible for individual
human beings to perceive and accept a general scale of values,
to distinguish between what is considered normal, what
incredible; what is cruel and what lies beyond the boundaries
of wickedness; what is honesty, what **deceit**. And although the
scattered peoples led extremely different lives and their social
values were often strikingly at odds, just as their systems of
weights and measures did not agree, still these **discrepancies**
surprised only occasional travellers, were reported in journals
under the name of wonders, and bore no danger to mankind
which was not yet one.

But now during the past few decades, imperceptibly,
suddenly, mankind has become one—hopefully one and

Solzhenitsyn begins by
talking about culture.
As you read, watch for
where he begins to talk
about writing.

Solzhenitsyn uses *man*
and *mankind* to mean
all people, men and
women.

convulsively shaking violently	**encroached** gradually entered or occupied	**immemorial** beyond the limits of memory
deceit a trick	**epoch** a long period of history	**pulsating** moving in a regular rhythm
discrepancy a difference; a conflict		

dangerously one—so that the **concussions** and inflammations of one of its parts are almost instantaneously passed on to others, sometimes lacking in any kind of necessary immunity. Mankind has become one, but not steadfastly one as communities or even nations used to be; not united through years of **mutual** experience, neither through possession of a single eye, affectionately called crooked, nor yet through a common native language, but, surpassing all barriers, through international broadcasting and print. An avalanche of events descends upon us—in one minute half the world hears of their splash. But the yardstick by which to measure those events and to **evaluate** them in **accordance** with the laws of unfamiliar parts of the world— this is not and cannot be conveyed via soundwaves and in

Solzhenitsyn refers back to the Russian saying in the first paragraph.

How does the world hear about international events so fast? Do you think he really means one minute?

newspaper columns. For these yardsticks were matured and **assimilated** over too many years of too specific conditions in individual countries and societies; they cannot be exchanged in midair. In the various parts of the world men apply their own hard-earned values to events, and they judge stubbornly, confidently, only according to their own scales of values and never according to any others.

And if there are not many such different scales of values in the world, there are at least several; one for evaluating events near at hand, another for events far away; aging societies possess one, young societies another; unsuccessful people one, successful people another. The **divergent** scales of values scream in **discordance**, they dazzle and daze us, and in order that it might not be painful we steer clear of all other values, as though from insanity, as though from

accordance agreement	**discordance** a harsh, confused sound	**evaluate** to judge the worth of
assimilate to take in	**divergent** drawing apart; differing	**mutual** shared
concussion a shock; an injury		

illusion, and we confidently judge the whole world according to our own home values. Which is why we take for the greater, more painful and less bearable disaster not that which is in fact greater, more painful and less bearable, but that which lies closest to us. Everything which is further away, which does not threaten this very day to invade our threshold—with all its groans, its stifled cries, its destroyed lives, even if it involves millions of victims—this we consider on the whole to be perfectly bearable and of **tolerable** proportions.

Which events and disasters attract people's attention most?

In one part of the world, not so long ago, under persecutions not inferior to those of the ancient Romans', hundreds of thousands of silent Christians gave up their lives for their belief in God. In the other hemisphere a certain madman, (and no doubt he is not alone), speeds across the ocean to DELIVER us from religion—with a thrust of steel into the high priest! He has calculated for each and every one of us according to his personal scale of values!

Words in capital letters are emphasized more than others.

That which from a distance, according to one scale of values, appears as enviable and flourishing freedom, at close quarters, and according to other values, is felt to be infuriating **constraint** calling for buses to be overthrown. That which in one part of the world might represent a dream of incredible prosperity, in another has the **exasperating** effect of wild **exploitation** demanding immediate strike. There are different scales of values for natural catastrophes: a flood craving two hundred thousand lives seems less significant than our local accident. There are different scales of values for personal insults: sometimes even an **ironic** smile or a **dismissive** gesture is **humiliating**, while for others cruel beatings are forgiven as an unfortunate joke. There are different scales of values for punishment and wickedness: according to one, a month's arrest, banishment to the country, or an isolation-cell where one is fed on white rolls

---

constraint force that limits freedom of thought or action

dismissive in a manner that discards or sends away

exasperating annoying

exploitation the unfair use of something for selfish reasons

humiliating causing shame or loss of dignity

ironic mocking

tolerable able to be endured

White rolls and milk are used as symbols for "soft" prison treatment.

and milk, shatters the imagination and fills the newspaper columns with rage. While according to another, prison sentences of twenty-five years, isolation-cells where the walls are covered with ice and the prisoners stripped to their underclothes, lunatic asylums for the sane, and countless unreasonable people who for some reason will keep running away, shot on the frontiers—all this is common and accepted. While the mind is especially at peace concerning that exotic part of the world about which we know virtually nothing, from which we do not even receive news of events, but only the trivial, out-of-date guesses of a few correspondents.

What different sets of values does the writer contrast? Notice the results he discusses in the next paragraph.

Yet we cannot reproach human vision for this duality, for this **dumbfounded** incomprehension of another man's distant grief, man is just made that way. But for the whole of mankind, compressed into a single lump, such mutual **incomprehension** presents the threat of **imminent** and violent destruction. One world, one mankind cannot exist in the face of six, four or even two scales of values: we shall be torn apart by this **disparity** of rhythm, this disparity of vibrations.

A man with two hearts is not for this world, neither shall we be able to live side by side on one Earth.

Notice that the writer restates the question in several ways. He is leading up to an answer.

But who will co-ordinate these value scales, and how? Who will create for mankind one system of interpretation, **valid** for good and evil deeds, for the unbearable and the bearable, as they are **differentiated** today? Who will make clear to mankind what is really heavy and intolerable and what only grazes the skin locally? Who will direct the anger to that which is most terrible and not to that which is nearer? Who might succeed in transferring such an understanding beyond the limits of his own human experience? Who might succeed in impressing upon a **bigoted**, stubborn human creature the distant joy and grief of others, an understanding of dimensions and deceptions which he himself has never

bigoted stubbornly holding a belief and disliking those who disagree	**differentiate** to show a difference between	**imminent** about to happen
	disparity difference	**incomprehension** lack of understanding
	dumbfounded stunned into silence	**valid** reliable

experienced? Propaganda, constraint, scientific proof—all are useless. But fortunately there does exist such a means in our world! That means is art. That means is literature.

They can perform a miracle: they can overcome man's **detrimental** peculiarity of learning only from personal experience so that the experience of other people passes him by in vain. From man to man, as he completes his brief spell on Earth, art transfers the whole weight of an unfamiliar, lifelong experience with all its burdens, its colours, its sap of life; it recreates in the flesh an unknown experience and allows us to possess it as our own.

How do art and literature help people understand others' values?

And even more, much more than that; both countries and whole continents repeat each other's mistakes with time lapses which can amount to centuries. Then, one would think, it would all be so obvious! But no; that which some nations have already experienced, considered and rejected, is suddenly discovered by others to be the latest word. And here again, the only substitute for an experience we ourselves have never lived through is art, literature. They possess a wonderful ability: beyond distinctions of language, custom, social structure, they can convey the life experience of one whole nation to another. To an inexperienced nation they can convey a harsh national trial lasting many decades, at best sparing an entire nation from a superfluous, or mistaken, or even **disastrous** course, thereby **curtailing** the **meanderings** of human history. It is this great and noble property of art that I urgently recall to you today from the Nobel **tribune**.

And literature conveys **irrefutable** condensed experience in yet another **invaluable** direction; namely, from generation to generation. Thus it becomes the living memory of the nation. Thus it preserves and kindles within itself the flame of her spent history, in a form which is safe from deformation and

curtail to cut short	**invaluable** beyond price	**meandering** going along a winding course
detrimental harmful		
disastrous causing disaster	**irrefutable** impossible to prove wrong	**tribune** a platform from which to speak to a group

Solzhenitsyn says that the lessons of art and literature can be passed from country to country. They can also be passed down through history.

slander. In this way literature, together with language, protects the soul of the nation.

(In recent times it has been fashionable to talk of the levelling of nations, of the disappearance of different races in the melting-pot of **contemporary** civilization. I do not agree with this opinion, but its discussion remains another question. Here it is merely fitting to say that the disappearance of nations would have **impoverished** us no less than if all men had become alike, with one personality and one face. Nations are the wealth of mankind, its **collective** personalities; the very least of them wears its own special colours and bears within itself a special **facet** of divine intention.)

But woe to that nation whose literature is disturbed by the **intervention** of power. Because that is not just a violation against "freedom of print," it is the closing down of the heart of the nation, a slashing to pieces of its memory. The nation ceases to be mindful of itself, it is deprived of its spiritual unity, and despite a supposedly common language, **compatriots** suddenly cease to understand one another. Silent generations grow old and die without ever having talked about themselves, either to each other or to their descendants. When writers such as Achmatova and Zamjatin—**interred** alive throughout their lives—are condemned to create in silence until they die, never hearing the echo of their written words, then that is not only their personal tragedy, but a sorrow to the whole nation, a danger to the whole nation.

What does Solzhenitsyn say are the effects of censorship? Anna *Achmatova* was a Russian poet whose works were attacked by authorities. Yevgeny *Zamjatin* was another writer whose books were banned.

In some cases moreover—when as a result of such a silence the whole of history ceases to be understood in its entirety— it is a danger to the whole of mankind.

At various times and in various countries there have arisen heated, angry and exquisite debates as to whether art and the

collective grouped together	**contemporary** living at the same time	**interred** buried
compatriot a person from one's own country	**facet** one part or angle	**intervention** an act of interfering
	impoverish to make poor	

artist should be free to live for themselves, or whether they should be for ever mindful of their duty towards society and serve it albeit in an unprejudiced way. For me there is no **dilemma**, but I shall refrain from raising once again the train of arguments. One of the most brilliant addresses on this subject was actually Albert Camus' Nobel speech, and I would happily subscribe to his conclusions. Indeed, Russian literature has for several decades **manifested** an **inclination** not to become too lost in contemplation of itself, not to flutter about too **frivolously**. I am not ashamed to continue this tradition to the best of my ability. Russian literature has long been familiar with the notions that a writer can do much within his society, and that it is his duty to do so.

Camus, a French writer, won the 1957 Nobel Prize.

Let us not violate the RIGHT of the artist to express exclusively his own experiences and **introspections**, disregarding everything that happens in the world beyond. Let us not DEMAND of the artist, but— reproach, beg, urge and **entice** him— that we may be allowed to do. After all, only in part does he himself develop his talent; the greater part of it is blown into him at birth as a finished product, and the gift of talent imposes responsibility on his free will. Let us assume that the artist does not OWE anybody anything: nevertheless, it is painful to see how, by retiring into his self-made worlds or the spaces of his subjective whims, he CAN surrender the real world into the hands of men who are **mercenary**, if not worthless, if not insane. ...

dilemma a situation that requires a difficult choice

entice to tempt

frivolously not seriously; playfully

inclination a leaning toward something

introspection examining one's own thoughts

manifest to show

mercenary concerned only with making money

What then is the place and role of the writer in this cruel, **dynamic**, split world on the brink of its ten destructions? After all we have nothing to do with letting off rockets, we do not even push the lowliest of hand-carts, we are quite scorned by those who respect only material power. Is it not natural for us too to step back, to lose faith in the steadfastness of goodness, in the **indivisibility** of truth, and to just impart to the world our bitter, **detached** observations: how mankind has become hopelessly corrupt, how men have **degenerated**, and how difficult it is for the few beautiful and refined souls to live amongst them?

But we have not even **recourse** to this flight. Anyone who has once taken up the WORD can never again evade it; a writer is not the detached judge of his compatriots and contemporaries, he is an accomplice to all the evil committed in his native land or by his countrymen. And if the tanks of his fatherland have flooded the asphalt of a foreign capital with blood, then the brown spots have slapped against the face of the writer forever. And if one fatal night they suffocated his sleeping, trusting Friend, then the palms of the writer bear the bruises from that rope. And if his young fellow citizens breezily declare the superiority of **depravity** over honest work, if they give themselves over to drugs or seize hostages, then their stink mingles with the breath of the writer.

Shall we have the **temerity** to declare that we are not responsible for the sores of the present-day world?

However, I am cheered by a vital awareness of WORLD LITERATURE as of a single huge heart, beating out the cares

How is a writer affected by terrible events?

degenerate to become much worse	**dynamic** full of energy; changing	**recourse** something to turn to for help
depravity a wicked act	**indivisibility** state of not being able to be divided	**temerity** foolish boldness
detached not connected		

and troubles of our world, albeit presented and **perceived** differently in each of its corners.

What symbol does Solzhenitsyn choose for world literature?

Apart from age-old national literatures there existed, even in past ages, the **conception** of world literature as an **anthology** skirting the heights of the national literatures, and as the sum total of mutual literary influences. But there occurred a lapse in time: readers and writers became acquainted with writers of other tongues only after a time lapse, sometimes lasting centuries, so that mutual influences were also delayed and the anthology of national literary heights was revealed only in the eyes of descendants, not of contemporaries.

But today, between the writers of one country and the writers and readers of another, there is a **reciprocity** if not instantaneous then almost so. I experience this with myself. Those of my books which, alas, have not been printed in my own country have soon found a responsive, worldwide audience, despite hurried and often bad translations. Such distinguished western writers as Heinrich Böll have undertaken critical **analysis** of them. All these last years, when my work and freedom have not come crashing down, when contrary to the laws of gravity they have hung suspended as though on air, as though on NOTHING—on the invisible dumb **tension** of a sympathetic public **membrane**; then it was with grateful warmth, and quite unexpectedly for myself, that I learnt of the further support of the international brotherhood of writers. On my fiftieth birthday I was astonished to receive congratulations from well-known western writers. No pressure on me came to pass by unnoticed. During my dangerous weeks of exclusion from the Writers' Union the WALL OF DEFENCE advanced by the world's prominent writers protected me from worse persecutions; and Norwegian writers and artists hospitably prepared a roof for me, in the event of my threatened exile being put into effect. Finally even the advancement of my name for the Nobel Prize was raised not in

analysis a study of how parts fit together	**membrane** a thin layer of material	**reciprocity** an equal exchange
anthology a collection of writings	**perceived** seen; known through the senses	**tension** the condition of being stretched
conception an idea; a mental picture		

Mauriac was a French writer who won the Nobel Prize in 1952. How does this kind of support help prove the writer's point about world literature?

the country where I live and write, but by François Mauriac and his colleagues. And later still entire national writers' unions have expressed their support for me.

Thus I have understood and felt that world literature is no longer an abstract anthology, nor a generalization invented by literary historians; it is rather a certain common body and a common spirit, a living heartfelt unity reflecting the growing unity of mankind. State frontiers still turn crimson, heated by electric wire and bursts of machine fire; and various ministries of internal affairs still think that literature too is an "internal affair" falling under their **jurisdiction**; newspaper headlines still display: "No right to interfere in our internal affairs!" Whereas there are no INTERNAL AFFAIRS left on our crowded Earth! And mankind's sole **salvation** lies in everyone making everything his business; in the people of the East being vitally concerned with what is thought in the West, the people of the West vitally concerned with what goes on in the East. And literature, as one of the most sensitive, responsive instruments possessed by the human creature, has been one of the first to adopt, to assimilate, to catch hold of this feeling of a growing unity of mankind. And so I turn with confidence to the world literature of today—to hundreds of friends whom I have never met in the flesh and whom I may never see.

Friends! Let us try to help if we are worth anything at all! Who from time immemorial has **constituted** the uniting, not the dividing, strength in your countries, **lacerated** by discordant parties, movements, **castes** and groups? There in its **essence** is the position of writers: expressers of their native language—the chief binding force of the nation, of the very earth its people occupy, and at best of its national spirit.

I believe that world literature has it in its power to help mankind, in these its troubled hours, to see itself as it really is, notwithstanding the **indoctrinations** of prejudiced people and

caste a social class

constitute to make up

essence the basic quality of something

indoctrination the teaching of a certain point of view

jurisdiction the area where one has authority

lacerated torn

salvation rescue from evil or problems

parties. World literature has it in its power to convey condensed experience from one land to another so that we might cease to be split and dazzled, that the different scales of values might be made to agree, and one nation learn correctly and **concisely** the true history of another with such strength of recognition and painful awareness as it had itself experienced the same, and thus might it be spared from repeating the same cruel mistakes. And perhaps under such conditions we artists will be able to cultivate within ourselves a field of vision to embrace the WHOLE WORLD: in the centre observing like any other human being that which lies nearby, at the edges we shall begin to draw in that which is happening in the rest of the world. And we shall **correlate**, and we shall observe world proportions.

Centre is the British spelling of *center*.

And who, if not writers, are to pass judgment—not only on their unsuccessful governments, (in some states this is the easiest way to earn one's bread, the occupation of any man who is not lazy), but also on the people them-selves, in their cowardly humiliation or self-satisfied weakness? Who is to pass judgment on the light-weight sprints of youth, and on the young pirates **brandishing** their knives?

We shall be told: what can literature possibly do against the ruthless **onslaught** of open violence? But let us not forget that violence does not live alone and is not capable of living alone: it is necessarily interwoven with falsehood. Between them lies the most **intimate**, the deepest of natural bonds. Violence finds its only refuge in falsehood, falsehood its only support in violence. Any man who has once **acclaimed** violence as his METHOD must **inexorably** choose falsehood as

How are violence and lies connected?

acclaim to praise	**correlate** to show a relationship	**intimate** very close
brandish to wave in a threatening way		**onslaught** an attack
concisely briefly	**inexorably** in a way that will not be stopped	

his PRINCIPLE. At its birth violence acts openly and even with pride. But no sooner does it become strong, firmly established, than it senses the **rarefaction** of the air around it and it cannot continue to exist without descending into a fog of lies, clothing them in sweet talk. It does not always, not necessarily, openly throttle the throat, more often it demands from its subjects only an oath of allegiance to falsehood, only **complicity** in falsehood.

And the simple step of a simple courageous man is not to **partake** in falsehood, not to support false actions! Let THAT enter the world, let it even reign in the world—but not with my help. But writers and artists can achieve more: they can CONQUER FALSEHOOD! In the struggle with falsehood art always did win and it always does win! Openly, irrefutably for everyone! Falsehood can hold out against much in this world, but not against art.

And no sooner will falsehood be **dispersed** than the nakedness of violence will be revealed in all its ugliness—and violence, **decrepit**, will fall.

That is why, my friends, I believe that we are able to help the world in its white-hot hour. Not by making the excuse of possessing no weapons, and not by giving ourselves over to a frivolous life—but by going to war!

Proverbs about truth are well-loved in Russian. They give steady and sometimes striking expression to the **not inconsiderable** harsh national experience:

ONE WORD OF TRUTH SHALL OUTWEIGH THE WHOLE WORLD.

And it is here, on an imaginary fantasy, a **breach** of the principle of the conservation of mass and energy, that I base both my own activity and my appeal to the writers of the whole world.

He refers to the scientific principle that matter and energy can neither be created nor destroyed. How does his statement break that law?

breach a break	**disperse** to scatter in different directions	**partake** to share; to take part
complicity state of being involved in a wrong action	**not inconsiderable** important enough to demand attention	**rarefaction** the state of being thin or less dense
decrepit worn out		

Directions Write the answers to these questions using complete sentences.

Comprehension: Identifying Facts

1. What, according to Solzhenitsyn, has decided people's view of the world in the past?

2. What change has quickly made people become one?

3. How do different scales of value affect how people see a disaster?

4. What does he say can make one person feel another's joy or grief?

5. How do art and literature affect nations?

6. How does censorship affect a country?

7. In what ways did the world's writers help Solzhenitsyn?

8. Who suggested Solzhenitsyn for a Nobel Prize?

9. What power does world literature have?

10. What is the relationship between violence and lying?

Comprehension: Understanding Main Ideas

11. In earlier times, why didn't it matter that groups had different values?

12. Why do different sets of values matter more today?

13. How does literature extend people's experience?

14. What is the debate over the role of the artist?

15. What happens if artists do not speak out?

16. Why is a single heart a good symbol for world literature?

17. How did the actions of other writers help protect Solzhenitsyn?

18. Why can a country no longer have "internal affairs"?

19. What has world literature become?

20. How do writers and artists fight falsehood?

Review Continued on Next Page

Understanding Literature: Persuasive Writing

Persuasive writing is writing that tries to change another's mind. This kind of writing can take many forms. Sometimes drama, poetry, short stories, or novels are persuasive. Usually persuasive writing is some form of nonfiction. Solzhenitsyn's speech is a form of persuasive writing.

21. Why was the "Nobel Lecture" written?

22. What does Solzhenitsyn expect of other writers and artists?

23. Would you say this speech is hopeful? Why or why not?

24. Whom do you think the writer is trying to persuade?

25. Do you think the writer influenced others? Explain.

Critical Thinking

26. Imagine you are a writer in a country that suppresses or censors writers. How would you feel about this speech?

27. Solzhenitsyn could not attend the Nobel ceremonies. Why do you think he sent this speech?

28. If you had been Solzhenitsyn, would you have gone back to Russia? Explain.

29. Do you agree that writers can change the world? Why or why not?

30. Did you like this speech? Why or why not?

Writing on Your Own An outline can help you understand a subject. Make an outline of the Nobel lecture. Your outline can list the main idea of each paragraph or section.

The Gettysburg Address
Abraham Lincoln

Abraham Lincoln
(1809–1865)
American

About the Speaker

Abraham Lincoln was born in Kentucky and grew up in Indiana. As a young man, he moved to a small town in Illinois. Lincoln educated himself by reading a lot.

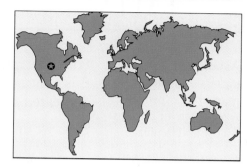

Lincoln tried many jobs. Then his speaking skills led him into politics. His campaign debates put Lincoln in the national spotlight as a spokesman against slavery. In 1860 the new Republican party named him its candidate for President. He won the election.

Literary Term

speech a written work meant to be read aloud

Soon after the election, the Civil War began. The struggle to save the Union claimed most of Lincoln's attention. Many moving words about democracy and freedom come from his **speeches** during this time. Speeches are works meant to be spoken out loud. In 1865 Lincoln was shot and killed while watching a play.

About the Selection

During the first two years of the Civil War, the Union army lost several major battles. In July 1863 they won their first big victory against the Confederate army. The battle was near Gettysburg, Pennsylvania. More than eleven thousand soldiers died there. In November 1863, the Union decided to keep part of the Gettysburg battlefield as a cemetery. Lincoln was asked to speak. His three-minute address disappointed some who heard it. Today it is considered one of the world's great speeches.

THE GETTYSBURG ADDRESS
ABRAHAM LINCOLN

As you read, watch for patterns that add interest to a speech. Also watch for phrases that sound familiar.

A *score* is twenty years. *Four score and seven* would equal eighty-seven years.

Four score and seven years ago our fathers brought forth on this continent, a new nation, **conceived** in liberty, and dedicated to the **proposition** that all men are created equal.

Now we are engaged in a great civil war, testing whether that nation, or any nation so conceived and so dedicated, can long endure. We are met on a great battlefield of that war. We have come to dedicate a portion of that field, as a final resting place for those who here gave their lives that that nation might live. It is altogether fitting and proper that we should do this.

Was Lincoln right that the world would not notice or remember this talk?

But in a larger sense, we cannot dedicate—we cannot **consecrate**—we cannot **hallow**—this ground. The brave men, living and dead, who struggled here, have consecrated it, far above our poor power to add or **detract**. The world will little note, nor long remember, what we say here, but it can never forget what they did here. It is for us the living, rather, to be dedicated here to the unfinished work which they who fought here have thus far so nobly advanced.

It is rather for us to be here dedicated to the great task remaining before us—that from these honored dead we may take increased devotion to that cause for which they gave the last full **measure** of devotion—that we here highly resolve that these dead shall not have died in vain—that this nation, under God, shall have a new birth of freedom—and that government of the people, by the people, for the people, shall not perish from the earth.

conceive to form in the mind

consecrate to dedicate to a serious purpose

detract to take away

hallow to set apart as holy

measure an amount

proposition an idea or statement

Inaugural Address
John F. Kennedy

John Fitzgerald
Kennedy
(1917–1963)
American

Literary Term

metaphor a figure of
speech that says one
thing *is* another

About the Speaker

Born in Massachusetts,
John F. Kennedy was the
second son of a wealthy
Irish Catholic family.
Kennedy was educated in
private schools and
graduated from Harvard.

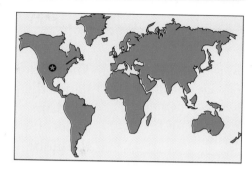

He served in the navy during World War II. He then went into
politics. In 1952 he won a seat in the Senate. Kennedy's work in
the Senate and his quick-witted speaking style drew the
attention of Democratic leaders. So did his book *Profiles in
Courage*. He was named to run for president in 1960. Kennedy
appeared confident during presidential debates on national TV.
He convinced the American public that his religion and
inexperience with foreign policy were not serious problems. He
narrowly defeated Richard Nixon to become the thirty-fifth
U.S. president. Kennedy was shot and killed in November 1963.

About the Selection

Kennedy won the 1960 election for several reasons. People
thought he would bring the energy of youth to the
presidency. Nixon was only a few years older. But he had
been Dwight Eisenhower's vice president. People associated
him with the Korean War, McCarthyism, and other bad
memories. Kennedy campaigned as a new kind of politician.
He wanted to represent the poor and young as well as the
rich and established. An inaugural address is the speech
given when a President is inaugurated, or sworn in. This
speech was given in Washington on January 20, 1961. Note
that Kennedy also uses **metaphor** in his address.

INAUGURAL ADDRESS
JOHN F. KENNEDY

As you read, watch for passages that show Kennedy means his words for the entire world.

Kennedy uses the word *man* to mean all humans, men and women.

What does he mean by *the power to abolish all forms of human life*?

Tempered means strengthened.

The world is very different now. For man holds in his mortal hands the power to **abolish** all forms of human poverty and all forms of human life. And yet the same revolutionary beliefs for which our **forebears** fought are still at issue around the globe—the belief that the rights of man come not from the generosity of the state but from the hand of God.

We dare not forget today that we are the **heirs** of that first revolution. Let the word go forth from this time and place, to friend and foe alike, that the torch has been passed to a new generation of Americans—born in this century, tempered by war, **disciplined** by a hard and bitter peace, proud of our ancient **heritage**—and unwilling to witness or permit the slow **undoing** of those human rights to which this nation has always been committed, and to which we are committed today at home and around the world.

Let every nation know, whether it wishes us well or ill, that we shall pay any price, bear any burden, meet any hardship, support any friend, oppose any foe to assure the **survival** and the success of liberty.

This much we pledge—and more.

To those old allies whose cultural and spiritual origins we share, we pledge the loyalty of faithful friends. United, there is little we cannot do in a host of new cooperative ventures.

abolish to put an end to

disciplined trained to act according to certain rules

forebear an ancestor

heir person who inherits a thing from the person who once had it

heritage what is handed down from earlier generations

survival the act of staying in existence

undoing the destruction of something already accomplished

Divided, there is little we can do—for we dare not meet a powerful challenge at odds and split **asunder**.

To those new states whom we welcome to the ranks of the free, we pledge our word that one form of colonial control shall not have passed away merely to be replaced by a far more iron **tyranny**. We shall not always expect to find them supporting our view. But we shall always hope to find them strongly supporting their own freedom—and to remember that, in the past, those who foolishly sought power by riding the back of the tiger ended up inside.

A number of countries in Africa and Asia had recently become independent of *colonial* rule.

To those peoples in the huts and villages of half the globe struggling to break the bonds of mass misery, we pledge our best efforts to help them help themselves, for whatever period is required—not because the Communists may be doing it, not because we seek their votes, but because it is right. If a free society cannot help the many who are poor, it cannot save the few who are rich. ...

Finally, to those nations who would make themselves our **adversary**, we offer not a pledge but a request: that both sides begin **anew** the quest for peace, before the dark powers of destruction **unleashed** by science **engulf** all humanity in planned or accidental self-destruction.

John Kennedy delivers his inaugural speech.

We dare not tempt them with weakness. For only when our arms are sufficient beyond doubt can we be certain beyond doubt that they will never be employed.

What *dark powers of destruction* had science let loose in this period?

adversary an enemy

anew again

asunder into separate parts

engulf to swallow up; to surround completely

tyranny rule by a harsh, powerful government

unleashed let loose; released

But neither can two great and powerful groups of nations take comfort from our present course—both sides **overburdened** by the cost of modern weapons, both rightly alarmed by the steady spread of the deadly atom, yet both racing to alter that uncertain balance of terror that stays the hand of mankind's final war.

Kennedy takes the oath of office.

So let us begin anew—remembering on both sides that **civility** is not a sign of weakness, and sincerity is always subject to proof. Let us never **negotiate** out of fear. But let us never fear to negotiate.

Let both sides explore what problems unite us instead of **belaboring** those problems which divide us.

Let both sides, for the first time, **formulate** serious and precise proposals for the inspection and control of arms—and bring the absolute power to destroy other nations under the absolute control of all nations.

Let both sides seek to **invoke** the wonders of science instead of its terrors. Together let us explore the stars, conquer the deserts, **eradicate** disease, tap the ocean depths and encourage the arts and commerce.

All this will not be finished in the first 100 days. Nor will it be finished in the first 1,000 days, nor in the life of this Administration, nor even perhaps in our lifetime on this planet. But let us begin.

belaboring going over again and again	**formulate** to plan	**negotiate** to work to reach agreement
civility courtesy	**invoke** to call upon for help	**overburdened** having too heavy a burden
eradicate to get rid of		

In your hands, my fellow citizens, more than mine, will rest the final success or failure of our course. Since this country was founded, each generation of Americans has been summoned to give testimony to its national loyalty. The graves of young Americans who answered the call to service surround the globe.

Now the trumpet summons us again—not as a call to bear arms, though arms we need—not as a call to battle, though **embattled** we are—but a call to bear the burden of a long twilight struggle year in and year out, "rejoicing in hope, patient in **tribulation**"—a struggle against the common enemies of man: tyranny, poverty, disease and war itself.

Can we forge against these enemies a grand and **global alliance**, north and south, east and west, that can assure a more fruitful life for all mankind? Will you join in that historic effort?

In the long history of the world, only a few generations have been granted the role of defending freedom in its hour of **maximum** danger. I do not shrink from this responsibility— I welcome it. I do not believe that any of us would exchange places with any other people or any other generation. The energy, the faith, the devotion which we bring to this **endeavor** will light our country and all who serve it—and the glow from that fire can truly light the world.

And so, my fellow Americans: ask not what your country can do for you—ask what you can do for your country.

My fellow citizens of the world: ask not what America will do for you, but what together we can do for the freedom of man.

How does this statement make the speech especially effective? What was Kennedy asking people to do?

---

embattled ready for battle

endeavor a sincere attempt

global alliance an agreement among world nations

maximum the greatest possible

tribulation suffering

The Gettysburg Address
Abraham Lincoln
Inaugural Address
John F. Kennedy

Directions Write the answers to these questions using complete sentences.

Comprehension: Identifying Facts

1. How long after the United States became a nation did Lincoln speak at Gettysburg?

2. Why does Lincoln say that the existence of the United States is being tested?

3. What is the occasion for Kennedy's speech?

Comprehension: Understanding Main Ideas

Lincoln and Kennedy make requests of the audience.

4. What does Lincoln ask of his audience?

5. What things does Kennedy name as the real enemies of all the world?

6. What does Kennedy ask of the American people?

Understanding Literature: Metaphor

A metaphor is a figure of speech that says one thing is another. For example,

"love is a thunderstorm" is a metaphor. It compares a thunderstorm to being in love. (The writer seems to be in a stormy romance.) Both speeches contain metaphors, although Kennedy's address uses more.

7. In the first paragraph of the Gettysburg Address, Lincoln uses metaphors about birth. What is he describing? Name one metaphor he uses.

8. Explain a metaphor about sound or light in the Kennedy speech.

Critical Thinking

9. What message did Kennedy send to America's enemies? Have any of his goals been reached in the time that has passed?

10. Choose one of the speeches. Tell why you think it is persuasive.

Writing on Your Own Both speeches discuss serious events. Yet they do not seem negative or depressing. Write a paragraph to explain how the speakers avoid negative emotions.

Essays

- "An essay ... has a minimum of one anecdote and one universal idea." —Carol Bly
- "The more opinions you have, the less you see." —Wim Wenders

A writer explaining a personal point of view is writing an essay. An essay may be about a basic issue or current event. In either case, the writer will present facts as he or she understands them. The writer's talents and limitations affect what is written.

Essays have existed from the beginning of literature. Plato, a Greek philosopher of long ago, wrote dialogues. These imaginary conversations showed his ideas about truth, beauty, and government. Around 1450, the printing press was introduced into Europe. It then became easier to publish essays. This helped many thinkers of the 1500s to the 1800s become famous interpreters of their societies. They include Michel de Montaigne, Thomas Paine, and Ralph Waldo Emerson.

By the 1700s and 1800s many people could afford to buy books and newspapers. Also, more people could read. This meant many new readers. Essayists began to write opinion articles. They wrote their ideas about many things, from gossip to literary criticism. This trend continues today. Newspaper editorials and advice columns are kinds of essays. The essay also still exists in the form of regular columns in newspapers and magazines.

What makes modern essayists popular? It may be their point of view, writing style, or both. They are not the final authority on any subject. But their ideas are useful. They can help readers form their own opinions.

Of Repentance
Michel de Montaigne (translated by J. M. Cohen)

Michel de Montaigne (1533–1592) French

Literary Terms

essay a written work that shows a writer's opinions on some basic or current issue

style an author's way of writing

About the Author

Michel de Montaigne was the son of a rich French nobleman. Books and ideas were important to his family. They also became his main interest. Until he was six years old,

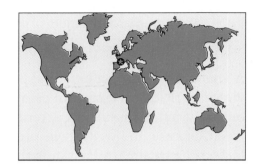

Montaigne heard and was taught to speak only Latin. He came to know that language well. Montaigne practiced law for several years. Then in 1571 his father died. He left Montaigne his share of the family money. Montaigne retired. He spent the rest of his life happily pursuing things that interested him, especially writing. His **essays,** or comments on society, show that he was a thoughtful man and a keen observer. An essay is a piece of writing that show's a writer's opinions on some basic or current issue.

About the Selection

Montaigne filled three books with his essays. They are detached, amused, lively observations on life. His early works tend to imitate the thoughts of the classic writers he must have studied. As he matured, he developed his own literary **style,** or way of writing. His writing is graceful and personal. His essays about friendship, education, and religion reflect his own experiences—his travels, the unrest of the French religious wars, the loss of a close friend. He gradually developed the habit of watching and learning from the world around him. "I stand back" was his official motto. "Of Repentance" is part of his third book of essays. It was published in 1588.

Of Repentance

Michel de Montaigne

The other day, when I was on the estate of a kinsman of mine in Armagnac, I saw a peasant whom everybody called *The Thief.* He told us his story, which was like this: Born a beggar, and realizing that if he were to earn his living by the work of his hands, he would never succeed in securing himself against want, he decided to become a thief; and thanks to his physical strength, he practised his trade quite safely throughout his youth. He gathered his harvest and his **vintage** from other men's lands, but at such great distances and in such great stacks that no one could conceive how one man could carry away so much on his shoulders in a single night. And he took care, besides, to **equalize** and distribute the damage that he caused, so as to **minimize** the loss to each individual. Now, in his old age, he is rich for a man of his condition, thanks to his trade, which he openly confesses. And to **reconcile** God to his winnings, he has made it, he said, his daily task to **compensate** the heirs of the men he robbed by voluntary gifts. If he does not complete his task—for to do it all at once is beyond him—he will, he says, leave it as a charge to his heirs, to repay them according to the wrong he did to each, which is known to him alone. From his account, whether true or false, it seems that this man regards theft as a dishonest action, and hates it, though less than he hates poverty. He **repents** of it quite simply, but in so far as it was thus **counterbalanced** and compensated, he does not repent of it.

As you read, think about what the thief has to repent. What is Montaigne's attitude toward him?

Armagnac is a region in southwestern France.

Do you think the man repents or not?

---

compensate to repay

counterbalance to use one act to make up for another

equalize to make equal

minimize to make as small as possible

reconcile to bring into agreement

repent to feel sorry for an action

vintage a crop of grapes grown for wine

Of Repentance
Michel de Montaigne

Directions Write the answers to these questions using complete sentences.

Comprehension: Identifying Facts

1. How did the Thief decide to make his living as a young man?

2. Why didn't anyone believe that the Thief had stolen their crops?

3. How has the Thief tried to make up for stealing?

Comprehension: Understanding Main Ideas

4. Explain why the Thief decided that stealing would be a good career for him.

5. What will the Thief do if he still hasn't paid everyone back by the time he dies?

6. Does the Thief regret his actions as a young man?

Understanding Literature: Essays

An essay is a comment on some part of society. It may be about a basic issue or something in the news. It gives the writer's point of view on the subject.

7. What is Montaigne's personal connection with the Thief?

8. Explain what you think is Montaigne's attitude toward the Thief.

Critical Thinking

9. Montaigne seems to say that people may feel one way about a general principle. But they may act differently in a specific case. Match each general principle with its specific example.

   A. being on time
   B. honesty
   C. minimum drinking age of twenty-one

   a. cheating on a test
   b. drinking champagne on prom night
   c. choosing to catch a late bus to school

10. Do you like or dislike the person called "the Thief"? Why or why not?

Writing on Your Own Pick one of the pairs in question 9. Write a paragraph to explain why people can believe in a general principle but act in a different way.

Jamaica Kincaid
(1949–)
Antiguan

Literary Terms

irony using words that seem to say one thing but mean the opposite

tone the attitude an author takes toward a subject

About the Author

Jamaica Kincaid was born in St. John's, Antigua, an island in the West Indies. She grew up on this "small place" but left for New York City when she was sixteen. Her original name

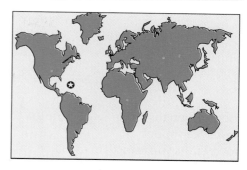

was Elaine Potter Richardson. She changed it when she became a writer. She wanted her name to reflect her Caribbean heritage. Kincaid's first novel, *Annie John,* was published in 1985. It is based on her own childhood. She has also written short stories. She has been a staff writer for *The New Yorker* magazine. Many of Kincaid's works are concerned with colonial control and corruption. Her opinions may sting, but they certainly get her readers' attention.

About the Selection

A Small Place is a nonfiction book about Antigua. It was published in 1988. In this chapter, the writer tries to persuade tourists to think about their effect on the island. She argues that they carry on the tradition of foreign control. They help to destroy the local culture. She points out many ways that the islanders have been forced to change. The **tone** of her writing, or the attitude she takes toward her topic, is often angry and biting. She also uses **irony** to help make her point. Irony is the use of words that say one thing but really mean the opposite. Kincaid makes a powerful argument. She makes her readers think about what they are doing when they travel.

A Small Place
Jamaica Kincaid

How do you think the writer feels about tourists? As you read, look for clues.

The island of *Antigua* is in the Caribbean Sea, east of Puerto Rico.

Aeroplane is the British spelling of *airplane*. Other British spellings, such as *favour* and *colour,* are used later.

If you go to Antigua as a tourist, this is what you will see. If you come by aeroplane, you will land at the V. C. Bird International Airport. Vere Cornwall (V. C.) Bird is the Prime Minister of Antigua. You may be the sort of tourist who would wonder why a Prime Minister would want an airport named after him—why not a school, why not a hospital, why not some great public monument? You are a tourist and you have not yet seen a school in Antigua, you have not yet seen the hospital in Antigua, you have not yet seen a public monument in Antigua. As your plane descends to land, you might say, What a beautiful island Antigua is— more beautiful than any of the other islands you have seen, and they were very beautiful, in their way, but they were much too green, much too **lush** with vegetation, which indicated to you, the tourist, that they got quite a bit of rainfall, and rain is the very thing that you, just now, do not want, for you are thinking of the hard and cold and dark and long days you spent working in North America (or, worse, Europe), earning some money so that you could stay in this place (Antigua) where the sun always shines and where the climate is deliciously hot and dry for the four to ten days you are going to be staying there; and since you are on your

lush growing thick with plants

This is Nelson Dockyard in Antigua.

holiday, since you are a tourist, the thought of what it might be like for someone who had to live day in, day out in a place that suffers constantly from drought, and so has to watch carefully every drop of fresh water used (while at the same time surrounded by a sea and an ocean—the Caribbean Sea on one side, the Atlantic Ocean on the other), must never cross your mind.

You **disembark** from your plane. You go through customs. Since you are a tourist, a North American or European—to be **frank,** white—and not an Antiguan black returning to Antigua from Europe or North America with cardboard boxes of much needed cheap clothes and food for relatives, you move through customs swiftly, you move through customs with ease. Your bags are not searched. You emerge from customs into the hot, clean air: immediately you feel **cleansed,** immediately you feel blessed (which is to say special); you feel free. You see a man, a taxi driver; you ask him to take you to your destination; he **quotes** you a price. You immediately think that the price is in the local **currency,** for you are a tourist and you are familiar with these things (rates of exchange) and you feel even more free, for things seem so cheap, but then your driver ends by saying, "In U.S. currency." You may say, "Hmmmm, do you have a formal sheet that lists official prices and destinations?" Your driver obeys the law and shows you the sheet, and he apologises for the **incredible** mistake he has made in quoting you a price off the top of his head which is so vastly different (favouring him) from the one listed. You are driven to your hotel by this taxi driver in his taxi, a brand-new Japanese-made vehicle. The road on which you are travelling is a very bad road, very much in need of repair. You are feeling wonderful, so you say, "Oh, what a marvellous change these bad roads are from the splendid

Customs is the official process for inspecting what people bring into a country.

Why would the tourist say bad roads are *a marvellous change*? What does this remark show about the tourist?

cleansed clean; free of dirt	**disembark** to get out of a craft, such as a boat or plane	**incredible** too unlikely to be believed
currency the form of money a country uses	**frank** bluntly honest	**quote** to state or offer a price

highways I am used to in North America." (Or, worse, Europe.) Your driver is reckless; he is a dangerous man who drives in the middle of the road when he thinks no other cars are coming in the opposite direction, passes other cars on blind curves that run uphill, drives at sixty miles an hour on narrow, curving roads when the road sign, a rusting, beat-up thing left over from colonial days, says 40 MPH. This might frighten you (you are on your holiday; you are a tourist); this might excite you (you are on your holiday; you are a tourist), though if you are from New York and take taxis you are used to this style of driving; most of the taxi drivers in New York are from places in the world like this. You are looking out the window (because you want to get your money's worth); you notice that all the cars you see are brand-new, or almost brand-new, and that they are all Japanese-made. There are no American cars in Antigua—no new ones, at any rate; none that were manufactured in the last ten years. You continue to look at the cars and you say to yourself, Why, they look brand-new, but they have an awful sound, like an old car—a very old, **dilapidated** car. How to account for that? Well, possibly it's because they use leaded gasoline in these brand-new cars whose engines were built to use non-leaded gasoline, but you mustn't ask the person driving the car if this is so, because he or she has never heard of unleaded gasoline. You look closely at the car; you see that it's a model of a Japanese car that you might hesitate to buy; it's a model that's very expensive; it's a model that's quite impractical for a person who has to work as hard as you do and who watches every penny you earn so that you can afford this holiday you are on. How do they afford such a car? And do they live in a **luxurious** house to match such a car? Well, no. You will be surprised, then, to see that most likely the person driving this brand-new car filled with the

dilapidated shabby from neglect	**luxurious** quite splendid and comfortable

wrong gas lives in a house that, in comparison, is far beneath the **status** of the car; and if you were to ask why you would be told that the banks are encouraged by the government to make loans available for cars, but loans for houses not so easily available; and if you ask again why, you will be told that the two main car dealerships in Antigua are owned in part or outright by **ministers** in government. Oh, but you are on holiday and the sight of these brand-new cars driven by people who may or may not have really passed their driving test (there was once a **scandal** about

Have you changed your mind about the writer's opinion of the tourist? Why or why not?

driving licences for sale) would not really stir up these thoughts in you. You pass a building sitting in a sea of dust and you think, It's some **latrines** for people just passing by, but when you look again you see the building has written on it PIGOTT'S SCHOOL. You pass the hospital, the Holberton Hospital, and how wrong you are not to

think about this, for though you are a tourist on your holiday, what if your heart should miss a few beats? What if a blood vessel in your neck should break? What if one of those people driving those brand-new cars filled with the wrong gas fails to pass safely while going uphill on a curve and you are in the car going in the opposite direction? Will you be comforted to know that the hospital is staffed with doctors that no actual Antiguan trusts; that Antiguans

latrine a small building used for a public bathroom

minister a high government official

scandal talk about a public disgrace or action

status social position relative to others

always say about the doctors, "I don't want them near me"; that Antiguans refer to them not as doctors but as "the three men" (there are three of them); that when the Minister of Health himself doesn't feel well he takes the first plane to New York to see a real doctor; that if any one of the ministers in government needs medical care he flies to New York to get it?

What is the difference between medical care for officials and for ordinary people?

It's a good thing that you brought your own books with you, for you couldn't just go to the library and borrow some. Antigua used to have a splendid library, but in The Earthquake (everyone talks about it that way—The Earthquake; we Antiguans, for I am one, have a great sense of things, and the more meaningful the thing, the more meaningless we make it) the library building was damaged. This was in 1974, and soon after that a sign was placed on the front of the building saying, THIS BUILDING WAS DAMAGED IN THE EARTHQUAKE OF 1974. REPAIRS ARE **PENDING**. The sign hangs there, and hangs there more than a **decade** later, with its **unfulfilled** promise of repair, and you might see this as a sort of quaintness on the part of these islanders, these people descended from slaves—what a strange, unusual **perception** of time they have. REPAIRS ARE PENDING, and here it is many years later, but perhaps in a world that is twelve miles long and nine miles wide (the size of Antigua) twelve years and twelve minutes and twelve days are all the same. The library is one of those splendid old buildings from colonial times, and the sign telling of the repairs is a splendid old sign from colonial times. Not very long after The Earthquake Antigua got its independence from Britain, making Antigua a state in its own right, and Antiguans are so proud of this that each year,

decade a period of ten years	**pending** not yet decided; waiting for action	**unfulfilled** not finished; not completed
	perception a way of seeing or observing	

to mark the day, they go to church and thank God, a British God, for this. But you should not think of the confusion that must lie in all that and you must not think of the damaged library. You have brought your own books with you, and among them is one of those new books about economic history, one of those books explaining how the West (meaning Europe and North America after its conquest and settlement by Europeans) got rich: the West got rich not from the free (free—in this case meaning got-for-nothing) and then undervalued labour, for generations, of the people like me you see walking around you in Antigua but from the **ingenuity** of small shopkeepers in Sheffield and Yorkshire and Lancashire, or wherever; and what a great part the invention of the wristwatch played in it, for there was nothing noble-minded men could not do when they discovered they could slap time on their wrists just like that (isn't that the last straw; for not only did we have to suffer the **unspeakableness** of slavery, but the satisfaction to be had from "We made you bastards rich" is taken away, too), and so you needn't let that slightly funny feeling you have from time to time about **exploitation**, **oppression**, **domination** develop into full-fledged unease, **discomfort**; you could ruin your holiday. They are not responsible for what you have; you owe them nothing; in fact, you did them a big favour, and you can provide one hundred examples. For here you are now, passing by Government House. And here you are now, passing by the Prime Minister's Office and the Parliament Building, and overlooking these, with a splendid view of St. John's Harbour, the American **Embassy**. If it were not for you, they would not have Government House, and Prime Minister's Office, and Parliament Building and embassy of powerful country. Now you are

Sheffield, Yorkshire, and *Lancashire* are in England. English settlers used slave labor to grow sugar on Antigua.

discomfort the feeling of being uneasy or not comfortable	**exploitation** the use of a person or resource for selfish purposes	**oppression** strict rule or control through the use of force
domination control or rule of one person or group by another	**ingenuity** cleverness; inventive skill	**unspeakableness** a condition too bad to be described

passing a mansion, an **extraordinary** house painted the colour of old cow dung, with more **aerials** and antennas attached to it than you will see even at the American Embassy. The people who live in this house are a merchant family who came to Antigua from the Middle East less than twenty years ago. When this family first came to Antigua, they sold dry goods door to door from suitcases they carried on their backs. Now they own a lot of Antigua; they regularly lend money to the government, they build enormous (for Antigua), ugly (for Antigua), concrete buildings in Antigua's capital, St. John's, which the government then rents for huge sums of money; a member of their family is the Antiguan Ambassador to Syria; Antiguans hate them. Not far from this mansion is another mansion, the home of a drug smuggler. Everybody knows he's a drug smuggler, and if just as you were driving by he stepped out of his door your driver might point him out to you as the **notorious** person that he is, for this drug smuggler is so rich people say he buys cars in tens—ten of this one, ten of that one—and that he bought a house (another mansion) near Five Islands, contents included, with cash he carried in a suitcase: three hundred and fifty thousand American dollars, and, to the surprise of the seller of the house, lots of American dollars were left over. Overlooking the drug smuggler's mansion is yet another mansion, and leading up to it is the best paved road in all of Antigua—even better than the road that was paved for the Queen's visit in 1985 (when the Queen came, all the roads that she would travel on were paved anew, so that the Queen might have been left with the impression that riding in a car in Antigua was a pleasant experience). In this mansion lives a woman **sophisticated** people in Antigua call Evita. She is a notorious woman. She's young and beautiful and the

Antigua is a member of the British Commonwealth, whose head is the *Queen* of England.

aerial an antenna for receiving radio or TV	**extraordinary** very unusual	**sophisticated** having a broad knowledge of the world
	notorious famous for bad activities	

girlfriend of somebody very high up in the government. Evita is notorious because her relationship with this high government official has made her the owner of **boutiques** and property and given her a say in cabinet meetings, and all sorts of other privileges such a relationship would bring a beautiful young woman.

What do you think Kincaid is saying about wealthy people in Antigua?

Oh, but by now you are tired of all this looking, and you want to reach your destination—your hotel, your room. You long to **refresh** yourself; you long to eat some nice **lobster**, some nice local food. You take a bath, you brush your teeth. You get dressed again; as you get dressed, you look out the window. That water—have you ever seen anything like it? Far out, to the horizon, the colour of the water is navy-blue; nearer, the water is the colour of the North American sky. From there to the shore, the water is pale, silvery, clear, so clear that you can see its pinkish-white sand bottom. Oh, what beauty! Oh, what beauty! You have never seen anything like this. You are so excited. You breathe shallow. You breathe deep. You see a beautiful boy skimming the water, godlike, on a Windsurfer. You see an incredibly unattractive, fat, **pastrylike**-fleshed woman enjoying a walk on the beautiful sand, with a man, an incredibly unattractive, fat, pastrylike-fleshed man; you see the pleasure they're taking in their surroundings. Still standing, looking out the window, you see yourself lying on the beach, enjoying the amazing sun (a sun so powerful and yet so beautiful, the way it is always overhead as if on permanent guard, ready to stamp out any cloud that dares to darken and so empty rain on you and ruin your holiday; a sun that is your personal friend). You see yourself taking a walk on that beach. You see yourself meeting new people (only they are new in a very limited way, for they are people just like you). You see yourself

Of the people just described, which are probably Antiguan and which probably tourists? How does the writer feel about them?

boutique a small shop that sells special, often expensive, goods

lobster a sea animal that is used for food

pastrylike looking like baked goods made of dough

refresh to make less tired, as if by resting or eating

eating some delicious, locally grown food. You see yourself, you see yourself ... You must not wonder what exactly happened to the contents of your **lavatory** when you flushed it. You must not wonder where your bathwater went when you pulled out the stopper. You must not wonder what happened when you brushed your teeth. Oh, it might all end up in the water you are thinking of taking a swim in; the contents of your lavatory might, just might, graze gently against your ankle as you wade carefree in the water, for you see, in Antigua, there is no proper sewage-disposal system. But the Caribbean Sea is very big and the Atlantic Ocean is even bigger; it would amaze even you to know the number of black slaves this ocean has swallowed up. When you sit down to eat your delicious meal, it's better that you don't know that most of what you are eating came off a plane from Miami. And before it got on a plane in Miami, who knows where it came from? A good guess is that it came from a place like Antigua first, where it was grown dirt-cheap, went to Miami, and came back. There is a world of something in this, but I can't go into it right now.

She means that waste water is piped into the ocean.

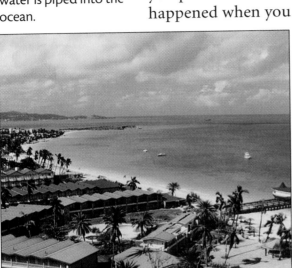

This is Dickinson Bay, Antigua, after Hurricane Georges, 1998.

How does the writer prove her claim that tourists are ugly? Does she mean ugly to look at?

The thing you have always suspected about yourself the minute you become a tourist is true: A tourist is an ugly human being. You are not an ugly person all the time; you are not an ugly person ordinarily; you are not an ugly person day to day. From day to day, you are a nice person. From day to

lavatory a bathroom

day, all the people who are supposed to love you on the whole do. From day to day, as you walk down a busy street in the large and modern and **prosperous** city in which you work and live, dismayed, puzzled (a **cliché**, but only a cliché can explain you) at how alone you feel in this crowd, how awful it is to go unnoticed, how awful it is to go unloved, even as you are surrounded by more people than you could possibly get to know in a lifetime that lasted for **millennia**, and then out of the corner of your eye you see someone looking at you and absolute pleasure is written all over that person's face, and then you realise that you are not as revolting a presence as you think you are (for that look just told you so). And so, ordinarily, you are a nice person, an attractive person, a person capable of drawing to yourself the affection of other people (people just like you), a person at home in your own skin (sort of; I mean, in a way; I mean, your dismay and puzzlement are natural to you, because people like you just seem to be like that, and so many of the things people like you find **admirable** about yourselves—the things you think about, the things you think really define you—seem rooted in these feelings): a person at home in your own house (and all its nice house things), with its nice back yard (and its nice back-yard things), at home on your street, your church, in community activities, your job, at home with your family, your relatives, your friends—you are a whole person. But one day, when you are sitting somewhere, alone in that crowd, and that awful feeling of **displacedness** comes over you, and really, as an ordinary person you are not well equipped to look too far inward and set yourself aright, because being ordinary is already so **taxing,** and being ordinary takes all you have out of you, and though the words "I must get away" do not actually pass across your lips, you make a leap from being that nice blob just sitting like a boob in your **amniotic sac** of the

admirable worth admiration	**cliché** an expression or idea that has been used over and over	**millennium** a period of one thousand years
amniotic sac a pouch that holds a developing baby before it is born	**displacedness** a state of being out of place or in the wrong place	**prosperous** successful; wealthy
		taxing tiring; difficult

modern experience to being a person visiting heaps of death and ruin and feeling alive and inspired at the sight of it; to being a person lying on some faraway beach, your stilled body stinking and glistening in the sand, looking like something first forgotten, then remembered, then not important enough to go back for; to being a person marvelling at the **harmony** (ordinarily, what you would say is the backwardness) and the union these other people (and they are other people) have with nature. And you look at the things they can do with a piece of ordinary cloth, the things they fashion out of cheap, **vulgarly** colored (to you) twine, the way they squat down over a hole they have made in the ground, the hole itself is something to marvel at, and since you are being an ugly person this ugly but joyful thought will swell inside you: their ancestors were not clever in the way yours were and not **ruthless** in the way yours were, for then would it not be you who would be in harmony with nature and backwards in that charming way? An ugly thing, that is what you are when you become a tourist, an ugly, empty thing, a stupid thing, a piece of rubbish pausing here and there to gaze at this and taste that, and it will never occur to you that the people who inhabit the place in which you have just paused cannot stand you, that behind their closed doors they laugh at your strangeness (you do not look the way they look); the physical sight of you does not please them; you have bad manners (it is their custom to eat their food with their hands; you try eating their way, you look silly; you try eating the way you always eat, you look silly); they do not like the way you speak (you have an accent); they collapse helpless from laughter, **mimicking** the way they imagine you must look as you carry out some everyday bodily **function**. They do not like you. *They do not like me!* That thought never actually occurs to you. Still, you feel a little uneasy. Still, you feel a little foolish.

| **function** a normal use or activity | **harmony** a pleasant agreement in feeling or actions | **ruthless** cruel; without mercy |
| | **mimic** to copy closely | **vulgarly** in bad taste; crudely |

Still, you feel a little out of place. But the **banality** of your own life is very real to you; it drove you to this extreme, spending your days and your nights in the company of people who despise you, people you do not like really, people you would not want to have as your actual neighbour. And so you must devote yourself to puzzling out how much of what you are told is really, really true (Is ground-up bottle glass in peanut sauce really a delicacy around here, or will it do just what you think ground-up bottle glass will do? Is this rare, **multicoloured**, snout-mouthed fish really an **aphrodisiac**, or will it cause you to fall asleep permanently?). Oh, the hard work all of this is, and is it any wonder, then, that on your return home you feel the need of a long rest, so that you can recover from your life as a tourist?

That the native does not like the tourist is not hard to explain. For every native of every place is a potential tourist, and every tourist is a native of somewhere. Every native everywhere lives a life of **overwhelming** and crushing banality and boredom and desperation and **depression**, and every deed, good and bad, is an attempt to forget this. Every native would like to find a way out, every native would like a rest, every native would like a tour. But some natives—most natives in the world—cannot go anywhere. They are too poor. They are too poor to go anywhere. They are too poor to escape the **reality** of their lives; and they are too poor to live properly in the place where they live, which is the very place you, the tourist, want to go—so when the natives see you, the tourist, they envy you, they envy your ability to leave your own banality and boredom, they envy your ability to turn their own banality and boredom into a source of pleasure for yourself.

Do you think the writer is sometimes a tourist herself? How does she feel about that?

aphrodisiac a food or drug that brings about sexual desire	**depression** a state of sadness	**overwhelming** crushing; destructive
banality the quality of having little meaning	**multicoloured** (Amer. multicolored) having many colors	**reality** things as they actually exist

Directions Write the answers to these questions using complete sentences.

Comprehension: Identifying Facts

1. What kind of weather is usual in Antigua?

2. Why do many cars in Antigua have an awful sound?

3. Why do Antiguans have better cars than houses?

4. What is the subject of one of the books the tourist brings?

5. Where does the Minister of Health go to see a doctor?

6. What does Pigott's School look like?

7. When did the library close for repairs? Why did it close?

8. What is one sign that the drug smuggler is rich?

9. How were Antiguans treated by the British long ago?

10. How do most native Antiguans feel about tourists?

Comprehension: Understanding Main Ideas

11. What are the problems with taking a taxi in Antigua?

12. Why is Antigua's lack of rainfall a joy for tourists and a problem for the native Antiguans?

13. How is going through customs different for tourists than for the native Antiguans?

14. Why should a tourist worry about the condition of the hospital in Antigua?

15. What sorts of people have gotten rich in Antigua?

16. What is wrong with the beautiful ocean water around the island?

17. How does the writer show that the government is corrupt? Give an example.

18. Why are the new people a tourist meets not really new?

19. How does the writer suggest that the tourist get rid of guilt feelings about the way the native Antiguans were treated?

20. Why can't most native Antiguans be tourists at some time?

Understanding Literature: Tone

Tone is the attitude the author takes toward a subject. The tone may be humorous, affectionate, or optimistic. It might be bitter, angry, or depressed. The tone may shift at certain points in the writing. One thing that affects the tone of *A Small Place* is that the author's use of irony. Irony is using words that seem to say one thing but mean something else.

21. What is the tone of *A Small Place*?

22. What is ironic about tourists being pleased the island is not too lush?

23. Name another contrast between what the tourist sees and what the reality is.

24. How does Kincaid explain why people want to be tourists?

25. What do you think is the harshest thing the author says?

Critical Thinking

26. How does reading this selection make you feel? Explain.

27. Why do you think that only the airport is named for the Prime Minister?

28. How do you think the writer wants readers to respond to this piece?

29. Kincaid is from Antigua. She now lives in New York City. Is she a good spokesperson for Antigua? Why or why not?

30. Is the writer suggesting that people never travel? Explain.

Writing on Your Own Think of a place that you know well. Think of how it would look to a tourist. Think of what you know of that a tourist wouldn't see. Write a paragraph about the place. Tell what the tourist sees and what more there is to the picture.

Skills Lesson Setting

The setting of a piece of writing includes time and place. Writers of scary stories can create a setting that sets your heart beating. You turn the page fast to see what will happen next. Writers of history stories try to take you back to other times. They use touches such as these:

> "The airplane circled the wheat field like a great moth. Its canvas wings shone white. The engine whined with insect sharpness."

Setting can be important in speeches and essays, too. For example, Lincoln says:

> "Now we are engaged in a great civil war. ..." "We are met on a great battlefield of that war. ..." "... a final resting place for those who here gave their lives. ..."

The setting has a serious meaning. Without this place, there would have been no speech.

Setting is at the heart of Jamaica Kinkaid's writing on Antigua. She draws a savage comparison. It is between the beauty tourists see and the natives' poverty.

> "From there to the shore, the water is pale, silvery clear, so clear that you can see its pinkish-white sand bottom. Oh, what beauty!"

Compare that with:

> "You must not wonder what exactly happened to the contents of your lavatory when you flushed it. ... Oh, it might all end up in the water you are thinking of taking a swim in ... in Antigua there is no proper sewage-disposal system."

Review

1. What is setting?

2. Why do time and place matter in Joan of Arc's letter?

3. Name a selection in this unit in which you think time is more important than place.

4. How does the setting in long-ago rural France make the Thief's story possible?

5. Which setting did you find most interesting? Explain.

Writing on Your Own Think of an event at which you might make a speech. (You might choose a school event, a sports dinner, or a family occasion.) Write a few sentences to start a speech for that audience. First explain the time and place of the event. Then begin to give your own thoughts about it.

UNIT 5 SUMMARY

In this unit you read examples of persuasive writing. Persuasive writing is meant to influence opinion. The selections in this unit are all nonfiction. Most persuasive writing is in that form. Examples of persuasive writing in fiction can be found in other parts of this book.

This unit includes speeches and essays. Speeches are given for many reasons. They are meant for a special audience. They are in response to some event or occasion. Even when written, a speech is meant to be heard. You will find it helpful to read the speeches out loud. You may find recordings of some.

Essays give a writer's personal point of view. They may be written about a basic issue or a current event. The writer presents the facts as she or he sees them. The writer's way of thinking shapes the essay. So does the writer's style, or way of writing.

Selections

- "Letter to the English" by Joan of Arc. The French heroine sends a proclamation that warns the English to leave France.

- "Nobel Lecture" by Alexander Solzhenitsyn. On winning the Nobel Prize, the Russian writer gives his view of the importance of world literature.

- "The Gettysburg Address" by Abraham Lincoln. The President speaks to dedicate a cemetery at the site of the Battle of Gettysburg.

- "Inaugural Address" by John F. Kennedy. After being sworn in as President of the United States, the new President addresses the country and the world.

- "Of Repentance" by Michel de Montaigne. The French essayist tells the story of a man known as the Thief.

- A *Small Place* by Jamaica Kincaid. A chapter from her book takes an ironic look at tourists who come to the island of Antigua.

UNIT 5 REVIEW

Directions Write the answers to these questions using complete sentences.

Comprehension Identifying Facts

1. Which two selections are from France?

2. Two selections were written during the Cold War. Identify them and tell what countries their authors are from.

3. Two forms of persuasive writing are used in this unit. What are they?

4. What literary form does Montaigne use in "Of Repentance"?

5. What was the occasion for Solzhenitsyn's speech?

Comprehension: Understanding Main Ideas

6. What is the main thing Solzhenitsyn asks for in "Nobel Lecture"?

7. What principle is discussed in "Of Repentance"?

8. What does Joan of Arc want to accomplish with her speech?

9. How are Lincoln's and Kennedy's speeches alike? Name one way.

10. A Small Place at first seems to be about travel. What is it really about?

Understanding Literature: Essays, Letters, Speeches

Essays, letters, and speeches are nonfiction. (Sometimes a fiction writer uses a series of letters. This is a literary device. They are not real letters.) An essay is a written work that shows a writer's opinions on some issue. A letter contains thoughts and feelings written to a certain person. Most letters are personal. Some letters are meant for the public. A speech is usually written. But it is meant to be read aloud. It is meant for a special event. Some essays and speeches are meant to persuade. Their writers try to influence the opinion of the reader. Writers of essays and speeches use the same devices that are used in fiction. Such devices in this unit include metaphor and irony.

11. What do essays, letters, and speeches have in common?

12. How is a speech different from a letter or essay?

13. "Letter to the English" is called both a speech and a letter. Explain why both labels can be right.

14. In which essay in the unit does the writer seem more personally involved?

15. All of the selections in this unit are called persuasive writing. Which selection do you think is the most persuasive?

Critical Thinking

16. Do you think the speeches have the same effect being read as they would being spoken?

17. Choose one of the selections. Explain why it is still being read.

18. Choose two of the writers in this unit. Compare their styles of writing.

19. Which selection in this unit do you like least? Why?

20. Which selection do you think asks the most of its audience? Explain.

Speak and Listen

Choose a speech from this unit or find one in the library. You can also search the Internet. If you don't find one you like, write your own. After you choose a speech, practice reading it. Then read it out loud in class.

Beyond Words

Find pictures of some of the speakers or places from this unit. You might find them in textbooks. You might use magazines or the Internet. Copy the pictures, then cut them out. Put them on a flat surface to make a collage. (A collage is a piece of art made by pasting objects on a surface.) You do not have to find exactly the places or people that are in the unit. But they should be things that suggest the ideas of the speeches or essays.

Writing on Your Own Think about the beliefs or wishes expressed in this unit. Each writer had strong ideas about something that was important to him or her.

Do you think their writing would have been as good if they had not had strong ideas? Write an essay about one of the writers. Tell what belief the writer had. Do you think that belief made the writing stronger? Explain why you feel the way you do.

Test-Taking Tip

Read the test directions twice. Sometimes they will give you a hint. For example, the directions may remind you to look for the best answer.

"Humor is by far the most significant activity of the human brain."

　—Edward De Bono

"We are not amused!"

　—Queen Victoria

UNIT 6 Humorous Literature

We all like to laugh. Some writers write in ways that make us laugh. Still, not all those writers are just having fun with human nature. Some use wit as a way to get readers to read about serious problems. Beneath the wit of their work is a bite. They hope their readers will see that something in the world needs to be changed.

The works you will read are told in several ways. Some quickly make it clear that they are just for fun. Others are told with a straight face. At first you might not be sure that you are reading humor. You may want to read some selections more than once. The next reading may show you a funny spot that you missed the first time.

Humorous literature is created to be funny. Some humor comes from feeling better than someone who makes a mistake. We laugh at the stuffy banker who slips on a banana peel. She is lying on the sidewalk and we aren't. Other humor comes from the unexpected—a sudden reversal of events. We laugh because we expect the banker to sit on a leather chair, not the sidewalk. Whatever our reasons, laughter is the reaction a humorist wants. A humorist is someone who writes funny works. The humorist may write a light piece to pass the time. Or the humorist may poke fun at human behavior with the idea of changing it. In either case, the desire to be funny is more important than the form of expression the writer chooses.

The tone of humor depends on how angry human behavior has made the humorist. Some writers may let the reader sit back and enjoy someone (even the writer) slipping on a banana peel. Or the writer may inspire us to rush out and pick up the banana peel before someone else slips.

Humor can take almost any literary form. Neil Simon's early plays were comedies poking fun at the stress-filled lives of New Yorkers. The French writer Molière wrote many humorous plays with a serious point. Ogden Nash and Edward Lear wrote funny poems. The Unit 6 selections are grouped into three forms of humorous writing: satire, columns, and stories.

The following countries are represented in this unit: Ireland, Argentina, the United States, Austria, and Ukraine.

Satire

- "A fondness for satire indicates a mind pleased with irritating others; for myself, I never could find amusement in killing flies." —Mme. Marie-Jeanne Roland
- "If you describe things exactly as they are, you will be thought of as a satirist." —Quentin Crisp

One of the oldest forms of literary humor is satire. Satire is humor that makes fun of foolishness or evil. Writers who decide to challenge others' behavior can become angry. They can try to make people laugh at those actions. Or they can do both. Satire is a way for a writer to be angry while making people laugh at evil or foolish acts.

The talents of certain writers are well suited to satire. Geoffrey Chaucer's *Canterbury Tales* are one example. These stories and character portraits from the 1300s use satire throughout. Other well-known satirists include Mark Twain, François Rabelais, and Charles Dickens.

Satire requires an ability to describe human behavior accurately and vividly. A satirist sees tiny traits and behaviors. Careful word choice goes into using irony, puns, and other literary techniques. Above all, a writer using satire must have a strong sense of right and wrong. The writer must understand the difference between what society says is okay and what it knows is right. Satirists try to remind their readers of basic truths that are often ignored. Many satirists are very angry at what they see. One of the following selections is a reaction to social injustice. The other shows anger at foolish behavior.

A Modest Proposal
Jonathan Swift

Jonathan Swift
(1667–1745)
Irish

Literary Terms

pamphlet a short printed essay about a specific problem

satire humorous writing that makes fun of foolishness or evil

tone the attitude an author takes toward a subject

About the Author

Though his parents were English, Jonathan Swift was born in Dublin, Ireland. Swift became an Anglican priest in 1695. For the rest of his life he served in churches in England or Ireland. Swift was named dean of the cathedral in Dublin in 1713. He settled there and wrote some of his greatest works.

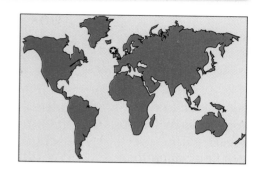

His religious training gave Swift a perfect background for **satire**. Satire is humor that makes fun of foolishness or evil. Swift's literary career began with a satire about religion. His interest in English politics led him to write **pamphlets** about current public problems. A pamphlet is a short printed essay about a specific problem. Swift's most famous work, *Gulliver's Travels* (1726), combines Swift's political and moral views. This work is considered a model of satire.

About the Selection

Swift wrote "A Modest Proposal" in 1729. In it he reveals the terrible poverty of the Irish people. He also satirizes the English attitude toward them. The innocent **tone** of "A Modest Proposal" fooled many people. Tone is the attitude an author takes toward a subject. Thinking he was serious, many readers of Swift's time were angry at him. He does not seriously suggest that the English want to cook and eat Irish babies for lunch. But he does want to show that their indifference and contempt toward the Irish are just as evil. Beneath Swift's seeming sincerity lies the deep anger of a morally outraged man.

A Modest Proposal

Jonathan Swift

As you read, look for ways the writer sets up the satire. Remember that he is writing from an Irish point of view.

A Modest Proposal FOR PREVENTING THE CHILDREN OF POOR PEOPLE IN IRELAND FROM BEING A BURDEN TO THEIR PARENTS OR COUNTRY, AND FOR MAKING THEM BENEFICIAL TO THE PUBLIC

It is a melancholy object to those who walk through this great town or travel in the country, when they see the streets, the roads, and cabin doors, crowded with beggars of the female-sex, followed by three, four, or six children, all in rags and **importuning** every passenger for an **alms**. These mothers, instead of being able to work for their honest livelihood, are forced to employ all their time in strolling to beg **sustenance** for their helpless infants, who, as they grow up, either turn thieves for want of work, or leave their dear native country to fight for the Pretender in Spain, or sell themselves to the Barbadoes.

Some poor people became soldiers for pay. Others went as servants to Caribbean islands.

Does Swift seem to appeal to common sense at this point? Might this tempt you to take him seriously?

I think it is agreed by all parties that this **prodigious** number of children in the arms or on the backs, or at the heels of their mothers, and frequently of their fathers, is in the present **deplorable** state of the kingdom a very great additional **grievance**; and therefore whoever could find out a fair, cheap, and easy method of making these children sound, useful members of the **commonwealth** would deserve so well of the public as to have his statue set up for a preserver of the nation.

alms charity; a hand-out

commonwealth the community as a whole; the nation

deplorable terrible

grievance something to complain about

importuning begging

prodigious enormous

sustenance something that supports life, especially food

But my intention is very far from being confined to provide only for the children of **professed** beggars; it is of a much greater extent, and shall take in the whole number of infants at a certain age who are born of parents in effect as little able to support them as those who demand our charity in the streets.

As to my own part, having turned my thoughts for many years upon this important subject and maturely weighed the several schemes of other projectors, I have always found them grossly mistaken in their computation. It is true, a child just dropped from its dam may be supported by her milk for a solar year, with little other nourishment; at most not above the value of two shillings, which the mother may certainly get, or the value in scraps, by her lawful occupation of begging; and it is exactly at one year old that I propose to provide for them in such a manner as instead of being a charge upon their parents or the parish, or wanting food and **raiment** for the rest of their lives, they shall on the contrary contribute to the feeding, and partly to the clothing, of many thousands....

The writer refers to the Irish as if they were animals. *Dam* is a word usually used for mother animals such as sheep. A *shilling* is an old English coin, worth only a small amount.

I am assured by our merchants that a boy or a girl before twelve years old is no salable commodity; and even when they come to this age they will not yield above three pounds, or three pounds and half a crown at most on the Exchange; which cannot turn to account either to the parents or the kingdom, the charge of **nutriment** and rags having been at least four times that value.

How could a child be a *salable commodity*? Is Swift suggesting that people don't see children as real human beings? A *pound* and *half a crown* are units of money.

I shall now humbly propose my own thoughts, which I hope will not be liable to the least objection.

I have been assured by a very knowing American of my acquaintance in London, that a young healthy child well nursed is at a year old a most delicious, nourishing, and **wholesome** food, whether stewed, roasted, baked, or boiled; and I make no doubt that it will equally serve in a **fricassee** or a **ragout**.

The writer uses the word *humbly* the same way he offers a "modest proposal." He is actually about to propose something shocking—in a satiric way.

I do therefore humbly offer it to public consideration that of the hundred and twenty thousand children, already **computed**, twenty thousand may be reserved for breed, whereof only one-

compute to count	**nutriment** food	**ragout** a stew of meat and vegetables
fricassee a dish made with cut-up pieces of meat in gravy	**professed** announced publicly	**raiment** clothing
		wholesome healthful

fourth part be males, which is more than we allow sheep, black cattle, or swine; and my reason is that these children are seldom the fruits of marriage, a **circumstance** not much regarded by our savages, therefore one male will be sufficient to serve four females. That the remaining hundred thousand may at a year old be offered in sale to the persons of quality and fortune through the kingdom, always advising the mother to let them suck plentifully in the last month, so as to render them plump and fat for a good table. A child will make two dishes at an entertainment for friends; and when the family dines alone, the **fore** or hind quarter will make a reasonable dish, and seasoned with a little pepper or salt will be very good boiled on the fourth day, especially in winter.

Persons of quality means those in the upper classes.

I have reckoned upon a medium that a child just born will weigh twelve pounds, and in a solar year if **tolerably** nursed increaseth to twenty-eight pounds.

I grant this food will be somewhat dear, and therefore very proper for landlords, who, as they have already devoured most of the parents, seem to have the best title to the children....

In what way have the landlords already *devoured* the parents? What is Swift's attitude toward the English landlords?

Butchers we may be assured will not be wanting; although I rather recommend buying the children alive, and dressing them hot from the knife as we do roasting pigs.

A very worthy person, a true lover of his country, and whose virtues I highly **esteem**, was lately pleased in **discoursing** on this matter to offer a **refinement** upon my scheme. He said that many gentlemen of this kingdom, having of late destroyed their deer, he conceived that the want of venison might be well supplied by the bodies of young lads and maidens, not exceeding fourteen years of age nor under twelve, so great a number of both sexes in every county being now ready to starve for want of work and service; and these to be disposed of by their parents, if alive, or otherwise by their nearest relations. But with due **deference** to so excellent a friend and so deserving a patriot, I cannot be altogether in his sentiments; for as to the males, my American acquaintance assured me from frequent experience that their flesh was

This is Swift's real point, that people are starving because of lack of work.

circumstance an event; a situation	**discourse** to discuss	**refinement** a small change that will improve
deference courteous respect for another's wishes	**esteem** to think highly of	**tolerably** sufficiently; enough
	fore the front part	

generally tough and lean, like that of our schoolboys, by continual exercise, and their taste disagreeable; and to fatten them would not answer the charge....

But as to myself, having been wearied out for many years with offering vain, idle, **visionary** thoughts, and at length utterly despairing of success, I fortunately fell upon this proposal, which, as it is wholly new, so it hath something solid and real, of no expense and little trouble, full in our own power, and whereby we can **incur** no danger in *disobliging* England. For this kind of commodity will not bear **exportation,** the flesh being of too tender a consistence to admit a long continuance in salt, *although perhaps I could name a country which would be glad to eat up our whole nation without it....*

Swift shows special bitterness here. What is he saying about England's "appetite"?

I desire those politicians who dislike my overture, and may perhaps be so bold to attempt an answer, that they will first ask the parents of these mortals whether they would not at this day think it a great happiness to have been sold for food at a year old in the manner I prescribe, and thereby have avoided such a perpetual scene of misfortunes as they have since gone through by the oppression of landlords, the impossibility of paying rent without money or trade, the want of common sustenance, with neither house nor clothes to cover them from the **inclemencies** of the weather, and the most **inevitable** prospect of **entailing** the like or greater miseries upon their breed for ever.

I profess, in the sincerity of my heart, that I have not the least personal interest in endeavoring to promote this necessary work, having no other motive than the *public good of my country, by advancing our trade, providing for infants, relieving the poor, and giving some pleasure to the rich.* I have no children by which I can propose to get a single penny; the youngest being nine years old, and my wife past child-bearing.

How does it help the satire to include the real facts here?

How does the final paragraph contribute to the satire?

disoblige to go against the wishes of	**exportation** being sent to another country for sale	**incur** to bring upon oneself
entailing resulting in	**inclemency** storms; discomforts	**inevitable** sure to happen
		visionary imaginary; not practical

Directions Write the answers to these questions using complete sentences.

Comprehension: Identifying Facts

1. How do the parents of most of the children in this satire make a living?

2. At what age does the satire suggest that children be sold for eating?

3. Why are older children not suitable for this use?

Comprehension: Understanding Main Ideas

4. What problems in Ireland is Swift actually writing about?

5. Why does Swift say that this meat would be suitable for English landlords?

6. Why does Swift say that his proposal won't bother the English?

Understanding Literature: Satire

Satire is humor that pokes fun at foolishness or evil. Although it is a kind of humor, satire seldom makes the reader laugh. The writer is often angry about the topic. It is clear in this piece that Swift is angry and bitter.

7. Satire usually uses heavy irony. Find an ironic statement in this satire.

8. Swift tosses out a few specific insults in this work. What does he suggest about Americans?

Critical Thinking

9. Quote one statement in which Swift reveals his strong feelings about the tragedy of Ireland's poor.

10. At the end, Swift again pretends to be a well-meaning observer. What does he say to show he will not make money from his scheme?

Writing on Your Own Reread the paragraph in the introduction about Swift's background. Write one paragraph to explain how it might have made him angry about the problems of the Irish.

Cup Inanity and Patriotic Profanity

Andrew Graham-Yooll, From the *Buenos Aires Herald* (July 2, 1998)

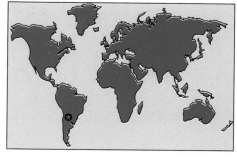

Buenos Aires Herald
(established 1876)
Argentinian

Literary Terms

editorial a news writer's personal opinion about an event or topic

sarcasm a heavy, sometimes mean-spirited kind of irony

About the Newspaper

The *Buenos Aires Herald* is Argentina's only English-language daily newspaper. William Cathcart, from Scotland, founded the *Herald* in 1876. The *Herald* has survived wars, government repression, terrorism, and economic crises. Over the years, it has become known for independent, biting **editorials.** Most news stories simply state and analyze the facts. An editorial, though, gives a news writer's opinion about an event. Today the *Herald* can be found on the Internet. Its address is http://www.buenosairesherald.com.

About the Selection

Argentina and Great Britain have had a love-hate relationship for years. Argentina was a Spanish colony but also had many settlers from Britain. Britain and Argentina fought a short war in 1982. Argentina lost. This made relations worse. In 1998, Argentina beat Great Britain during the World Cup soccer matches. Many Argentinians saw the victory as revenge for the war. (However, France was the winner of the World Cup.)

Both English and Argentinians are known for "soccer hooligans"—sometimes called "yobs." These fans often start fights over games. They justify their bad behavior by calling it "patriotism." In this editorial, the writer uses **sarcasm**, a heavy kind of irony, to show his dislike of their behavior.

Cup Inanity and Patriotic Profanity

Andrew Graham-Yooll,

From the *Buenos Aires Herald* (Thursday, July 2, 1998)

• •

As you read, note the author's tone and point of view.

What *vindication* might the Argentine team want?

Maradoña, an Argentine soccer star, scored a goal in 1986 in a game against England. He used his hands illegally.

The Dutch team did beat Argentina later.

Argentina won the World Cup in 1978. That year the government arrested, tortured, and killed thousands of Argentinians.

What a wonderful victory for Argentina's soccer squad. **Self-congratulatory commentary** yesterday was also packed full of **plaudits** for the dozen or so **millionaires** who had taken such an outstanding step for the well-being of a nation.

Celebration was everywhere and the **significance** of beating England referred to patriotic **vindication** and other such inanities which filled every inch of air and available screen space. In truth, it helped Argentina to **definitively** overcome the "hand of God" incident in the 1986 World Cup involving Diego Armando Maradoña's paw, but victory was a squeak, and secured against a ten-man team. For a sense of sporting balance, it was OK. Balance requires, of course, that the Dutch thrash Argentina on Saturday.

Even if the national team wins, please, not another 1978, when people were being tortured in Sierra Chica prison while the patriotic mob were screaming their support for the tormentors in Government House. A few people may still be able to remember that: 1978 was also described as a sporting event.

commentary an explanation; a series of remarks	**millionaire** a person with at least one million dollars	**significance** the meaning; the importance
definitively finally; completely	**plaudits** strong praise	**vindication** proof that clears away blame or guilt
	self-congratulatory giving praise to oneself	

However, Tuesday must have been really good for Argentina. The MERVAL Stock Exchange index rose four percent yesterday. And it had risen just under half a point just before the match started, against an average six months of decline.

For the **duration** of the match, three hours all told, the country froze, with a loss of GDP of 230 million pesos, according to Perfil newspaper.

That hardly matters. As a result of Tuesday's score we are all going to be so patriotic that we can assume that the foreign debt will be paid off shortly, there will be no more poor in Argentina, unemployment will be something entirely unknown (and easily forgotten), **pensioners** will have a decent retirement, cheques with the relief for the small-holders who have lost everything outside Goya will be in the post tomorrow. And the Wizard of Oz will be made President on July 31....

The *peso* is the unit of money in Argentina. *GDP* stands for *Gross Domestic Product,* a measure of a country's economy.

Cheque is another spelling of *check.* Other British-style spellings, such as *centre,* are used later in the article.

On Tuesday patriotism meant filling the streets with litter from waste bins emptied out of office windows. The patriotic rubbish blocked drains and spread a carpet of filth over the city centre's streets. Patriotism was to wear the national **ensign** as a silly hat, scarf, Superman cape, screwed up ball of cloth....Patriotism was to trail this **makeshift** dress along the street, turning it **grubby** not in triumph but in neglect. Patriotism was to wave bottles of beer until they had been drunk dry and then fling the empty so as to smash a store window. Patriotism involves yelling **racist** insults presented as patriotic slogans, and using the most **debased** language to describe people who are different.

French police arrest an English hooligan before the World Cup match between England and Argentina in 1998.

debased lowered in worth	**ensign** a flag	**pensioner** a person who receives pay after retiring
duration the period of time that something lasts	**grubby** dirty	
	makeshift a temporary substitute	**racist** referring to another race in an insulting way

No soccer horde has a monopoly on this behaviour and none is exempted.

Winston Churchill, or some other English worthy, once said that the British were **ungovernable**, except in war. And after the battle they were unspeakable.

This was much the case in many pubs throughout the English section of the United Kingdom yesterday.

French, Spanish, Germans and other visitors in England, who wanted to join in what they thought was sporting revelry (they obviously did not understand the natives), met with barrage after **onslaught** of drunken abuse and racist **epithets** which illustrated the many applications of a limited language education.

Yob is a slang expression for a hooligan or street criminal.

The factors that have helped develop the yob culture, in Britain, Argentina, and wherever, are not the relaxation of rules, as some **disciplinarians** wish to have it, but the championing of **banality** in most societies that are described as advanced capitalist states—which is where the enterprising sell banality for mass **consumption**. (The so-called less-advanced societies are irrelevant here as they are mostly repressed by **dictatorial** rule of varying degrees of severity. However, there is always room to praise the good administration of places such as Turkey or Saudi Arabia, for example.)

This sentence shows irony. Governments in *Turkey* and *Saudi Arabia* exert strict control.

Cricket, rugby, and soccer are all games that were taken to British colonies such as the *West Indies*.

Anyway, the magnificent Argentine victory on Tuesday provided the confirmation that the English inventors of many sports get thrashed by their pupils (by West Indians in cricket, South Africans in rugby, Argentines in soccer, and so on) with great regularity. And that confirms nothing more than that teachers and pupils descend to the pits of disgrace whether celebrating or mourning the incidents of wargames.

banality the quality of having little meaning	**dictatorial** having the powers of a strong, single ruler	**epithet** an insulting word or phrase
consumption buying	**disciplinarian** a person who strictly carries out rules	**onslaught** a violent attack or charge
		ungovernable not possible to control

Cup Inanity and Patriotic Profanity

Andrew Graham-Yooll, From the *Buenos Aires Herald* (July 2, 1998)

Directions Write the answers to these questions using complete sentences.

Comprehension: Identifying Facts

1. What victory is being celebrated?

2. What happened in the Argentine economy after the match?

3. What were some of the actions of "patriotic" Argentinian soccer fans?

Comprehension: Understanding Main Ideas

4. What does the writer think causes the "yob culture"?

5. Where is the "yob culture" found?

6. When the writer speaks of "wargames," what does he mean?

Understanding Literature: Sarcasm

Sarcasm is a heavy, sometimes mean-spirited kind of irony. It can be personal and meant to hurt. Even the title of this editorial shows the author's harsh opinion.

7. The author pokes fun at the importance of the win by exaggerating its wonderful effects. What are some of the things he says will happen?

8. The writer describes foreigners in England trying to join in the *sporting revelry*. How is this phrase sarcastic?

Critical Thinking

9. In what ways did the losers and winners act the same after the match?

10. Explain the writer's comparison of two events in 1978. What is his point?

Writing on Your Own Think of some way you have seen people behave in public. Have you seen behavior that is mean or stupid? Write an editorial making fun of this type of behavior. Talk about groups only. Do not write about individuals.

Columns

- "Many true words are spoken in jest." —Dinah Maria Mulock Craik
- "There are few things, apparently, more helpful to a writer than having once been a weird little kid." —Katherine Paterson

Columns are articles that appear regularly in periodicals. Their authors receive a by-line. A by-line tells who wrote an article. Columns are a popular form of humor. Hundreds of men and women write on the local level or for wider readership. They write about a range of topics. Columnists like Dave Barry began as local writers. But they became so popular that their articles now appear all over the world. Yet their columns still retain a local flavor. This appeals to many readers.

Following are selections by two columnists who write from the viewpoint of the average person. They struggle with parenting, work, and home repair. Readers recognize and share the stress of these activities. They enjoy relieving their tensions with a good laugh. This wide appeal has made these columns extremely popular, in America and abroad.

Staying at a Japanese Inn: Peace, Tranquillity, Insects

Dave Barry

Dave Barry
(1948–)
American

Literary Terms

column a regularly appearing article in a periodical

exaggeration a use of words to make something seem worse than it is; stretching the truth to a great extent

stereotype a simplified idea about another person

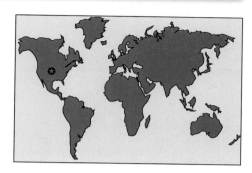

About the Author

Dave Barry began his career writing for a small Pennsylvania newspaper. He later took a job with the Associated Press in Philadelphia and taught classes on writing. Soon, he began writing a weekly humor **column**. Impressed, the *Miami Herald* newspaper offered him a staff position. Subjects for Barry's column have included hopeless attempts at home repair, battles with the hardy plants and animals of the tropics, and more. Barry won the Pulitzer Prize for journalism in 1988. He now lives and writes in Miami.

About the Selection

Dave Barry's column is syndicated by the Knight-Ridder News Service. This means it appears weekly in newspapers all over America. Many of his columns concentrate on his own family's experiences. Barry traveled to Japan with his wife, Beth, and their son, Robby. *Dave Barry Does Japan* is about his experiences. The book uses cultural differences between the United States and Japan as the basis for humor. In this selection from the book, Barry uses many techniques to make us laugh. He uses **exaggeration** to make things seem worse or more extreme than they are. But he doesn't poke fun only at the Japanese. Barry uses American **stereotypes** about Japanese culture as a mirror to show us our own faults. A stereotype is a simplified idea about another person. At the same time, he shows stereotypes about Americans. Barry also uses sarcasm, but only lightly, to entertain.

Staying at a Japanese Inn: Peace, Tranquillity, Insects

Dave Barry

As you read, note how the author uses exaggeration.

Kyoto is a city in Japan known for its beautiful sites.

When we arrived in Kyoto, we took a cab to our inn, which was a **traditional** type of Japanese inn called a *ryokan*.[1] When we pulled up in front, three women in **kimonos** came out and began bowing and saying things in Japanese and picking up our luggage. Using our Japanese skills, we said "thank you" or possibly "good night," and we bowed, and they bowed some more, which was not easy for them to do while holding our luggage, and then we started to go into the inn, at which point the women started speaking excitedly and pointing at our shoes.

Japan has a thing about shoes. You can wear them into stores and **westernized** hotels and restaurants, but you're not supposed to wear them into homes or traditional inns. You're supposed to take your shoes off at the door and put on slippers. And then if you go to the bathroom, you're supposed to take off *those* slippers and put on *another* pair of slippers, which are just for the bathroom. This custom may seem silly, but there's a sound reason for it: It keeps foreigners confused. At least that's what it did for us. I was always forgetting to change **footwear**, plus the slippers were always too small for me, so to keep my feet in them, I had to kind of **mince** around.

Following the baggage-carrying *ryokan* ladies, I minced with Beth and Robby to our room, which was in the very simple, very

---

[1] Literally, "type of inn."

footwear anything worn on the feet

kimono a long, loose robe with wide sleeves and tied with a sash

mince to walk with very short steps

traditional referring to customs followed for many years

westernized influenced by European or American ways

beautiful Japanese style, everything in light-colored wood. There was a sliding paper screen that opened up into a little **cicada**-infested rock garden with a brook **babbling** through it. The room had no beds or bureaus or chairs, only straw floor mats and a low table. In a *ryokan,* when you want to sleep, a maid comes in and puts down some **futons** for you. In fact, the maid comes in a lot; you got the feeling she was always just outside the door, day and night, ready to come in and do something for you. Our maid, who was wearing a kimono and a beeper, came in about thirty seconds after we arrived....

She said "*Hai domo!*" to us a lot. As far as I was able to determine, "*Hai domo!*" means "Yes, very!" We came to think of her as the Very Lady.

Do you think *hai domo* really means, *Yes, very!*?

She gestured to indicate that we should kneel with her around the low table, then she welcomed us to the *ryokan* **via** a nice little traditional ceremony wherein she poured us some tea and served us some kind of mysterious green substance. We smiled and bowed and drank the tea, and we each ate about one **molecule** of the green substance, and we smiled some more to indicate that it was the best darned mysterious green substance we had ever eaten and we would almost surely be wolfing it down later on.

The traditional Japanese tea ceremony is called Chado.

Then the Very Lady showed us, via ancient traditional *ryokan* hand gestures, how to operate the TV remote control. She also showed us the bathroom, which was, like the rest of the inn, done in the beautiful, simple Japanese style, with lots of light-colored wood, accented by a Woody Woodpecker hand mirror.[2] The maid also showed us our *yukata*, which are lightweight **bathrobelike** garments that you're supposed to wear while you stroll (or, in my case, mince) around

---

[2] Here is another interesting ryokan bathroom fact: There was never any shampoo, but every day there were three new toothbrushes.

babble to make a low, quiet sound like water	**cicada** a type of large insect; the males make a loud, humming noise	**molecule** a tiny bit
bathrobelike like a robe worn after a bath	**futon** a thin mattress usually used on the floor or on a frame	**via** by way of

How does Barry poke fun at ancient cultures meeting modern times in this paragraph?

the *ryokan*. The idea is that you become extremely relaxed and contemplate the rock garden and listen to the brook babble and the cicadas chatter until you achieve total inner peace. Or, if you are a typical **hyperactive** American suburban mall-oriented family like us, you go stark raving mad.

Maybe the problem was that the cicadas went off at about 4:30 a.m. and apparently had gotten hold of small but powerful amplifiers. So between them and the sudden unexpected appearances of the Very Lady, we never got quite enough sleep in the *ryokan*....

What kind of humor is Barry using here?

Another interesting thing to do in the Kyoto area is go see the **cormorant** fishing. This is a unique and traditional and weird method of catching fish using cormorants, which are a type of musical instrument similar to the trumpet.

No, just kidding. Cormorants are a type of **aquatic** bird sort of like **pelicans**. They're used in a centuries-old nighttime fishing technique still practiced in a few places, including a town near Kyoto called Uji. We took a train out there one evening, and found it to be a pleasant little river village, nice and peaceful except for a man at the train station shouting angrily over a huge truck-mounted public-address system. That's what **political activists** do in Japan: They shout angrily at you over powerful amplifiers turned up loud enough to **pulverize** concrete. As a persuasive technique, this leaves much to be desired. We saw quite a few of these trucks in Tokyo, and nobody paid any attention; everybody just walked briskly past.

This is smart. If you stood still and listened, you'd be deaf as a tire iron within minutes. So if the activists ever *did* attract any followers, they'd have a...time carrying out whatever political actions they had in mind:

"WE MUST STRENGTHEN OUR MILITARY!"

"WHAT DID HE SAY?"

"HE SAYS HE WANTS TO LENGTHEN OUR **CAPILLARIES**."

"NO, THANKS, I ALREADY ATE."

aquatic living in or one water	**hyperactive** very active	**political activist** a person who takes action to bring about political change
capillary a tiny blood vessel	**pelican** a large bird whose bill has a pouch that holds fish	
cormorant a water bird		**pulverize** to pound into a powder

Anyway, we walked briskly away from the angry shouting man at the Uji station, and I asked a **pedestrian** for directions, using the international symbol for cormorant fishing, which is when you have one hand pretend to be a cormorant and swoop down on the other hand, which is pretending to be a fish.

Could the scene at the *Uji station* happen in the United States?

He aimed us toward the river, where we found fishermen preparing some long, narrow wooden boats. At the end of each boat was a pole sticking out over the water; suspended from this was a wire basket in which the fishermen had built a log fire. The purpose of the fire is to attract the fish, although why a creature who lives under water would be attracted to fire is beyond me. Perhaps these are unusually stupid fish.

When night had fallen and the fires were burning brightly, the fishermen brought out some baskets, three per boat, each one containing two cormorants. The men put leashes around each bird's neck, looped so that the bird could get a fish into its mouth but not swallow it. Then the men pushed off from shore and started drifting down the river, two men controlling each boat and a third man in front, near the burning basket, holding leashes attached to the six cormorants, who swam around and **squabbled** with each other.

At first this approach didn't look terribly practical; my impression was that it would be a lot less trouble to try to scoop up the fish with trumpets. But it turned out that cormorants, once they stopped squabbling, did a pretty good job. They'd disappear under water, and every third or fourth time they'd come up with a fish. Whenever this happened, the leash man would haul the cormorant in, snatch the fish away, and shove the cormorant back out. You'd think eventually the cormorants would get **ticked off** about this, maybe start plotting acts of revenge....But I guess the cormorants aren't a whole lot smarter than the fish.

Still, it made for a pleasant evening's **diversion**, a uniquely Japanese experience, and we were in a good mood as we headed back to our little Kyoto *ryokan,* with its peaceful babbling brook and its cheerfully chattering cicadas. Someday I will go back and kill them with a **flamethrower**.

diversion something that entertains	**pedestrian** a person who travels on foot	**ticked off** a slang term meaning to be annoyed or angry
flamethrower a military weapon that sends out a stream of burning fuel	**squabble** to quarrel; to argue about something small	

Staying at a Japanese Inn: Peace, Tranquillity, Insects

Dave Barry

Directions Write the answers to these questions using complete sentences.

Comprehension: Identifying Facts

1. What are the features of a typical Japanese inn?

2. What do you sleep on in a traditional inn?

3. What are cormorants, and how are they used in Japan?

Comprehension: Understanding Main Ideas

4. Describe the Japanese custom about shoes.

5. How well does the Japanese method of relaxing work for the Barrys? Why or why not?

6. Give an example of old meeting new in this story.

Understanding Literature: Exaggeration

Exaggeration is a special use of words. It makes something seem far better or worse than it really is. It stretches the truth to a great extent. Exaggeration is common in everyday speech. Here are some examples: "He eats everything in sight." "You've grown as tall as a tree."

7. How does Barry exaggerate the noise the cicadas make?

8. Give one more example of exaggeration in this column.

Critical Thinking

9. Several conflicts are shown in this story. Describe one.

10. Did you think this story was funny? Why or why not?

Writing on Your Own Think of a typical American custom. Choose something small, like the Japanese custom with shoes. Imagine how this custom might look to someone from another country. Write a description of it from that point of view. Use exaggeration.

Why Can't We Have Our Own Apartment?

Erma Bombeck

Erma Bombeck
(1927–1996)
American

Literary Term

theme the main idea
of a literary work

(handwritten notes: 1986 '6, 1927, 69)

About the Author

Erma Bombeck grew up, went to college, married a teacher, and started a family. She found family concerns amusing, boring, and frustrating. As her family grew, she began

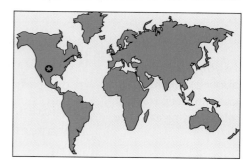

sharing her feelings in newspapers. In 1964 she began to write a humor column for a weekly paper in suburban Dayton, Ohio. The next year her column moved to a larger newspaper. Soon it was syndicated, or distributed to newspapers all over the country. Bombeck's column, "At Wit's End," appeared several times a week. Some six hundred papers carried it.

Bombeck survived the Great Depression. That may have helped her develop her sense of humor. Her humor has amused millions of readers. Bombeck collected her impressions in several best-selling books. The titles of them are jokes themselves. Some of her most popular books are *Just Wait Until You Have Children* and *The Grass Is Always Greener Over the Septic Tank.*

About the Selection

The following selection is from *If Life Is a Bowl of Cherries— What Am I Doing in the Pits?* It was published in 1978. Bombeck writes as a middle-aged parent and homemaker. She deals with the challenges and irritations of grown children. Her basic **themes,** or topics, are the small questions of daily family life. A theme is the main idea of a literary work.

Why Can't We Have Our Own Apartment? <u>Erma Bombeck</u>

As you read, think about the theme of the column. Keep track of who is saying each line.

We knew the kids would take it the wrong way, but we had to do it anyway.

"Children," we said, "your father and I want to get our own apartment."

One looked up from his homework and the other two even turned down the volume on the TV set. "What are you saying?"

"We are saying we'd like to move out and be on our own for a while."

"But why?" asked our daughter. "Aren't you happy here? You have your own room and the run of the house."

"I know, but a lot of parents our age are striking out on their own."

"It'll be expensive," said our son. "Have you thought about **utilities** and phone bills and newspapers and a hundred little things you take for granted around here?"

"We've thought it all through."

"Spit it out," said our daughter. "What's bothering you about living with us? Did we ask too much? What did we ask you to do? Only cook, make beds, do laundry, take care of the

> **utility** a household service, such as electricity, telephone, or water

yard, keep the cars in running order and bring in the money. Was that so hard?"

"It's not that," I said gently. "It's just that we want to fix up our own apartment and come and go as we please."

"If it's your car you wanted, why didn't you say so? We could make arrangements."

"It's not just the car. We want to be able to play our **stereos** when we want to and come in late without someone saying, 'Where have you been?' and invite people over without other people hanging around eating our chip dip."

"What will you do for furniture?"

"We don't need all that much. We'll just take a few small **appliances**, some **linens**, our bedroom **suite**, the typewriter, the luggage, the card table and chairs, the old TV you never use, and some pots and pans and a few tables and chairs."

"You'll call everyday?"

We nodded.

As we headed for the car I heard one son whisper sadly, "Wait till they get their first utility bill. They'll be back."

What family member would you expect to say what the daughter is saying?

appliance a piece of household equipment, such as a toaster, stove, or microwave

linens household goods made of cloth, such as sheets and towels

stereo sound equipment, often used to play music

suite a matched set of furniture

Why Can't We Have Our Own Apartment?
Erma Bombeck

Directions Write the answers to these questions using complete sentences.

Comprehension: Identifying Facts

1. Who are the family members featured in this column?

2. What do the parents want to do?

3. What problems does the son raise?

Comprehension: Understanding Main Ideas

4. How are roles reversed in this story?

5. What are some of the things the children must have complained about?

6. What kinds of things do the parents plan to take with them?

Understanding Literature: Theme

Theme is the main idea of a literary work. The theme may be a large question, such as what is the meaning of life. It may be an idea or motive such as love, greed, or ambition. A theme can also be simpler ideas, such as the quirks of everyday living.

7. What is the theme of this piece?

8. How does the writer make her treatment of the theme funny?

Critical Thinking

9. What can you conclude about the use of the car in this family?

10. What part of this piece did you find funniest? Explain.

Writing on Your Own In this piece, Bombeck describes a scene that may be like something she actually thought about doing in her family. Think of something you might like to do about your family life but never have done. Write a few sentences telling what you want to do. Tell why you want to do it and whether you think you might really do it.

Stories

- "My function as a writer is not story-telling but truth-telling: to make things plain."
  —Laura Riding Jackson

- "There have been great societies that did not use the wheel, but there have been no societies that did not tell stories." —Ursula K. Le Guin

Humorous stories can be either fiction or nonfiction. In either case, their main purpose is to amuse. Many anecdotes, or short stories, are meant to be humorous. If a funny story is fairly short and ends with a punchline, it is called a joke. If someone tells a longer story in person, it is usually called a monologue or a routine. Performers on television, radio, and recordings often deliver monologues as part of their act. Humorous stories are long enough not to depend on a big finish. Their details and plot are often funnier than their punchlines or points. They often make us laugh at ourselves as well as their characters and situations.

The following selections find humor in different situations. One pokes fun at "high culture." The other makes us chuckle at everyday human behavior.

Lohengrin
Leo Slezak (translated by Charles E. Pederson)

Leo Slezak
(1873–1946)
Austrian

About the Author

Leo Slezak was born in Moravia, then part of Austria (now the Czech Republic). Having a beautiful voice, he soon began to sing opera. In 1896 he sang his first leading role—as Lohengrin. He sang for many years with the Vienna Royal Opera (Hofoperntheater) and the famous conductor Gustav Mahler. In 1900 he sang *Lohengrin* at Covent Garden in London. His first American performance was as Otello at the Metropolitan Opera in New York in 1909. His singing career lasted until 1933. Slezak was also a gifted and witty writer. He wrote several comic **autobiographies,** or books about his own life. He also acted in films.

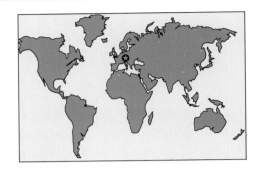

About the Selection

Leo Slezak sang many operatic roles in his long career. Still, he could see that many people find opera hard to understand. He uses this knowledge in his writing. He is supposed to have said about the opera *Il Trovatore:* "Even I don't get what's going on in this one!" He wrote a popular book that is a **parody** of opera guidebooks.

The opera *Lohengrin* was written by German composer Richard Wagner. Its first performance was in 1850. Wagner based the story of the "Swan Knight" on several legends from the Middle Ages. In the following selection, Slezak quickly outlines the action of the opera. (Remember that the part of Lohengrin was his own most famous role.) This parody exaggerates the funny aspects of both plot and character.

Lohengrin

Leo Slezak

It's a **complicated** matter, so pay careful attention, or you may never figure out what is going on.

As background you must know that long ago, magic was all the rage. In those days, people—mostly princes—were changed into all kinds of animals. It often happened that you might think you had a genuine canary from the Harz mountains, and then one day it would **reveal** itself to be a charmed **archduke**, whom some miserable, jealous fairy had changed into a bird....

As the curtain rises, the stage is spotted with men. (I can hear you correcting me now. "You should say people," you say, but truly it is a bunch of men.) They are **randomly** beating their swords on their shields and singing.

King Heinrich, wearing a long false beard, sits beneath a large oak, holding court.

Telramund, an upper-class noble, has brought a **lawsuit** against Elsa von Brabant, maintaining that she killed her brother, little Gottfried.

The king does not believe Telramund, and it's not true anyway.

Elsa is called forward and questioned. She denies having done it.

Who is telling the truth? Telramund or Elsa?

I almost forgot to mention that Telramund is married. His wife is named Mrs. Ortrud. She's a truly gloomy woman, and actually she forced Telramund to bring the suit.

As you read, notice how Slezak uses parody. He exaggerates the action and the story of the opera.

The *Hartz* (spelled *Harz* in German) *mountains* are a region of Germany famous for legends. "Hartz Mountain" is also a breed of canary.

Think about the time and place of this opera. Is there something silly about the name *Mrs. Ortrud*?

archduke a royal rank equal to that of a prince

complicated not easy to understand

lawsuit a complaint brought before a court of law

randomly without a definite pattern or plan

reveal to make known

Days of yore is a phrase like "once upon a time." It means a time long past.

In days of yore, "trial by battle" was also all the rage. If it could not be proved who was guilty or innocent, two men were allowed to fight it out. The loser was guilty. Seems like a **dubious** way to go about it.

Still, Telramund challenges anyone to strike for Elsa's honor.

Even though none of the knights thinks Elsa capable of such mean behavior, no one leaps to her defense, **despite** repeated blasts on the announcement trumpet. The king orders the trumpet to be blasted once more.

Suddenly a shining knight is seen in the distance, standing in a boat pulled by a snow-white swan.

The chorus of men shouts in confusion, pointing at the knight and looking in a sick way at the orchestra conductor. That apparently does not help, since everyone has different ideas about what's going on—what the Latin scholar calls "tohu vabohu."

Tohu vabohu is actually a Hebrew term meaning "chaos."

What is the author suggesting about why the swan leaves?

Lohengrin enters, spotlights hit him from all sides, and he sings the Swan Song a quarter note flat. The swan, hearing this, swims away.

Now comes the interesting part.

You can actually hear Telramund trembling, but he doesn't give up. He can't, since giving up is not written into the script.

First, Lohengrin goes to Elsa and asks would she like him to fight for her and would she consider marrying him, though only on condition that she never ask who he is and where he comes from.

What? Not to know with whom one has the pleasure? The nerve!

She vows never to ask, he goes over and defeats Telramund but spares his life, Mrs. Ortrud flies into a rage, Elsa flings herself on the neck of the Nameless One, the men beat their swords on their shields with joy, the king strokes his false beard, blesses the couple's **union**, and the curtain falls.

Does this seem like a good spot for a happy ending?

That's Act I.

---

despite in spite of	**dubious** causing doubt as to worth or truth	**union** a marriage

Act II opens in the dark.

From a corner come **unnaturally** long **criticisms** and **mutual** accusations. Mrs. Ortrud and Telramund are arguing. He calls her "companion of his disgrace." She is also unfriendly to him.

After much back and forth, they decide to make Elsa curious and turn her against Lohengrin.

On the night before a wedding in the middle ages, the bride-to-be apparently always appeared on a balcony to talk to the moon, or if no moon was available, to the breeze.

Today such exaggerated gestures are simply not done, plus people would think you're cracked if you acted that way.

Cracked is a slang word for "crazy."

While the bride-to-be **gabs** with the breeze, Mrs. Ortrud—below the balcony—sighs so loudly that Elsa can't help but hear her. She goes down, scoops up Mrs. Ortrud from the doorway, and brings her back inside the palace.

If that isn't the dumbest thing she could do, I don't know what is.

The most experienced women in the chorus have the part of maidens in the bridal train. They scatter flowers. The men occupy themselves with marching and singing in **syncopation**. Everyone strides majestically to the church. Suddenly Mrs. Ortrud shoves her way to stand before Elsa, claiming that she should be first in line.

The author uses *experienced* to refer to both their acting experience and, ironically, their age.

This causes great excitement. In the midst of it come the king and Lohengrin. Lohengrin immediately sizes up the situation, lightning bolts shooting from his eyes. Going to Elsa, he takes her aside and tells her not to get all excited and go asking him any questions, otherwise he would have to leave at once. Elsa says that of course she has no such thoughts and is so happy even to be marrying him at all. He presses her to his chest and they stride on to the church.

At the last moment, Telramund leaps from behind a pillar and scolds Lohengrin. He accuses Lohengrin of being a **sorcerer** and

criticism a judgment that finds fault	**mutual** shared in common	**syncopation** a musical accent not on the usual beat
gab a slang word meaning to talk; to chatter	**sorcerer** a wizard	**unnaturally** unusually; in an unexpected way

notes that the whole situation stinks—a lot. He goes on to question any person who rides around on swans, who sends swans away, whom no one can ask who one is, and where are his ID, his papers, his **visa**! Telramund declares the whole business of the trial by battle to be nonsense and wants a new hearing.

To be brief, Telramund is upset—with good reason, he feels.

But once a judgment has been made in someone's favor, that person can legally do anything. Telramund gets a stab in the stomach and is tossed aside.

Does this seem like a good spot for a happy ending?

Lohengrin and Elsa resume their interrupted striding to the church, the men beat their swords on their shields with joy, and under the approving nods of the king, the curtain falls.

Act III—The Bridal Chamber

Lohengrin and Elsa are **ushered** in by the king, who—with some winks and a few practical words of advice—leaves again.

What do you picture as the room's furnishings?

The room's furnishings alone tell the audience it's not going to be a pleasant wedding night.

Lohengrin sings for such a long time that, to get him to stop, Elsa finally asks him who he is. The fatal bomb explodes. On top of that, Telramund enters to kill Lohengrin. He misses his thrust and falls to the floor, struck dead by lightning bolts from Lohengrin's eyes.

He is cleared away.

Boric acid is a salty solution used in medicine. What is the effect of comparing Elsa's tears to boric acid?

Lohengrin says nothing to Elsa. He has to speak to the king first. Another of Lohengrin's mean tricks. As Elsa's tears fall like boric acid, the curtain falls.

Change of scenery. Same scene as Act I.

The king appears on horseback. The horse expresses its inner feelings, while the men beat their swords on their shields with eagerness, shouting for victory. It's off to war for them, each one panting for a hero's death.

Lohengrin is to lead a **battalion**. He enters and says he can't go with them. To his good luck, Elsa has asked him the forbidden question and he has to go home now.

The men beat their swords on their shields with despair.

battalion a large group of soldiers	**usher** to show people the way	**visa** a paper that permits a person to enter a country

Elsa is brought in. She **swoons**. In this opera, she seems only to stride or swoon.

Lohengrin strikes a **pose** and sings the tale of the Holy Grail. He has no evidence for what he's singing, only a lot of **unprovable** stuff for which no review board in the world would let him out of the army. But everyone present believes him. Maybe they do only because it's late and no one wants to **prolong** the performance by **pressing** him for details or getting into a debate.

As Elsa gasps for breath, Lohengrin says good-bye, giving her a horn, a ring, and a sword. She is supposed to learn to play the horn, she should save the ring, and give the sword to her brother.

Talk about confusing!

Lohengrin leaves.

The men beat their swords on their shields with sadness.

Suddenly, Mrs. Ortrud appears again. She just won't go away. She cries that it was she who turned Elsa's brother into a swan, that she was guilty the entire time.

Lohengrin blasts a hole in her with the lightning from his eyes. She dies.

The swan dives, and from the water leaps an exaggeratedly attractive boy—a prince. He hugs Elsa. It's little brother Gottfried!

With no animal to pull his boat, Lohengrin can't leave. Then a handy dove comes and carries him off—although that seems just a little **unrealistic**.

Elsa swoons and screams, and the curtain falls—thank heavens, because it is late indeed. The opera is over!

The *Holy Grail* is said by legend to be the cup used by Jesus at the Last Supper. Many knights of old went in search of it.

What is funny about saying the dove is *unrealistic*?

---

pose a position taken on purpose, as to have a picture taken

press to ask in an urgent way

prolong to make last longer

swoon to faint

unprovable not possible to prove

unrealistic not likely to happen in real life

Directions Write the answers to these questions using complete sentences.

Comprehension: Identifying Facts

1. What does the lawsuit against Elsa accuse her of doing?

2. How does Lohengrin arrive?

3. What does the swan turn into at the end?

Comprehension: Understanding Main Ideas

4. Why do Lohengrin and Telramund fight? Who wins?

5. What does Lohengrin tell Elsa she must never do? What will happen if she does?

6. Who has actually caused most of the trouble in the opera? How?

Understanding Literature: Parody

Parody is an exaggerated look at a situation. It may be a tongue-in-cheek imitation of a person, event, or serious work of literature. A parody picks out certain features of the work. Then it exaggerates them. You also may have heard a parody of a well-known song or poem.

7. How does Slezak use parody to make fun of the chorus?

8. How does Slezak make fun of the hero, Lohengrin?

Critical Thinking

9. The author opens by saying the opera is complicated. Name a part of the story where he makes it sound as complicated as possible.

10. Did you enjoy this parody? Why or why not?

> **Writing on Your Own** Think about staging the opera *Lohengrin.* Choose one part that would be hard to stage. Use your imagination to tell how you might stage it.

A Wedding Without Musicians
Sholom Aleichem

Sholom Aleichem
(1859–1916)
Ukrainian

Literary Terms

anecdote a short, funny story

humorist someone who writes funny works

irony the use of words that seem to say one thing but mean the opposite

About the Author

Sholom Aleichem was born Sholem (or Solomon) Rabinowitz in Pereyaslav, Ukraine. (Ukraine was then part of the Russian Empire.) He was a short-story writer, dramatist, and **humorist,** or someone who writes funny works. At first he taught and wrote in Russian and Hebrew. Then he began to write in Yiddish. That is the traditional language of Eastern European Jews. His pen name comes from a traditional Hebrew greeting for old friends. By 1894 he used that name all the time. He left Russia in 1905 and later moved to the United States.

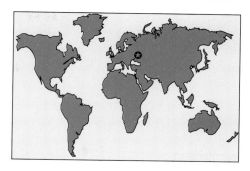

Sholom Aleichem's works often describe the simple life of small-town Jews. He wrote more than forty books of novels and stories. Many have been translated into English. They include *Stempenyu, Inside Kasrilevke,* and *The Old Country.* The play and movie of *Fiddler on the Roof* are based on Aleichem's stories in *Tevye the Dairyman.*

About the Selection

Jews faced serious hardships in Russia and the Ukraine in the 1800s. They could live only in certain places. They were kept out of schools and jobs. In spite of this, Aleichem looks at his characters and situations with humor and **irony.** Irony is using words to mean the opposite of what they seem to say. "A Wedding Without Musicians" comes from a collection called *The Railroad Stories* (1911). It is typical of Aleichem's tales. It is written like a story someone is telling aloud. It is almost like a long **anecdote,** a short, funny story.

A Wedding Without Musicians

Sholom Aleichem

As you read, note the details in this anecdote.

The *Straggler Special* is a local train. The writer is referring to an earlier story about the same train.

Pogroms—mob attacks against Jews—happened fairly often in Russia under the tsars. They were especially serious from the 1880s to the early 1900s. The government did little to stop pogroms.

The last time I told you about our **Straggler** Special, I described the miracle of *Hashono Rabo*. This time I shall tell you about another miracle in which the Straggler Special figured, how thanks to the Straggler Special the town of Heissin was saved from a terrible fate.

This took place during the days of the Constitution when **reprisals** against the Jews were going on everywhere. Though I must tell you that we Jews of Heissin have never been afraid of **pogroms**. Why? Simply because there is no one in our town who can carry out a pogrom. Of course you can imagine that if we looked very hard we could find one or two volunteers who wouldn't deny themselves the pleasure of **ventilating** us a little, that is, breaking our bones or burning down our houses. For example, when reports of pogroms began drifting in, the few squires, who are enemies of our people, wrote **confidential** letters to the proper authorities, saying it might be a good idea if "something were done" in Heissin also; but since there was no one here to do it, would they be so kind as to send help, in other words, would they **dispatch** some "people" as quickly as possible.

confidential meant to be secret

dispatch to send off quickly to a place

pogrom an organized attack on a group (Russian for "riot")

reprisal an act of force in revenge for an assumed wrong

straggler something that lags behind the others

ventilate to put in motion; to blow away

And before another twenty-four hours had passed a reply came, also confidentially, that "people" were being sent. From where? From Zhmerinko, from Kazatin, Razdilno, Popelno and other such places that had distinguished themselves in beating up Jews. Do you want to know how we learned of this deep secret? We found it out through our regular source of news, Noah Tonkonoy. Noah Tonkonoy is a man whom God has **endowed** with a pair of extra-long legs and he uses them to good purpose. He never rests and he is seldom to be found at home. He is always busy with a thousand things and most of these things have to do with other people's business rather than his own. By trade he is a printer, and because he is the only printer in Heissin he knows all the squires and the police and has dealings with **officialdom** and is in on all their secrets.

Noah Tonkonoy spread the good news all over town. He told the secret to one person at a time, in strictest confidence, of course, saying, "I am telling this only to you. I wouldn't tell it to anyone else." And that was how the whole town became aware of the fact that a mob of **hooligans** was on the way, and that a plan for beating up Jews had been worked out. The plan told exactly when they would start, on which day, at which hour, and from which point, and by what means— everything to the last detail.

You can imagine what terror this struck in our hearts. Panic spread quickly. And among whom do you think it spread first? Among the poor, of course. It's a peculiar thing about poor people. When a rich man is afraid of a pogrom, you can understand why. He is afraid, poor fellow, that he will be turned into a **pauper**. But those of you who are already paupers, what are you afraid of? What have you got to lose? But you should have seen how they bundled up their

endow to provide with a talent or quality	**hooligan** a troublemaker; a young man who does vicious or violent acts	**officialdom** an entire group of officials **pauper** a very poor person

Running hither and yon is an expression using old words for "here and there."

children and packed up their **belongings** and began running hither and yon, looking for a place to hide. Where can a person hide? This one hides in a friendly peasant's cellar, another in the **Notary's** attic, a third in the **Director's** office at the factory. Everyone finds a spot for himself.

I was the only one in town who wasn't anxious to hide. I am not boasting about my bravery. But this is the way I see it: what's the sense of being afraid of a pogrom? I don't say that I am a hero. I might have been willing to hide too, when the hour of **reckoning** came. But I asked myself first, "How can I be sure that during the slaughter the friendly peasant in whose cellar I was hiding, or the Notary, or the Director of the factory himself, wouldn't...." You understand. And all that aside, how can you leave a town wide open like that? It's no trick to run away. You have to see about doing something. But, alas, what can a Jew do? He appeals to a friendly official. And that is just what we did.

He is wondering if a Jew can trust a non-Jew in this circumstance.

In every town there is at least one friendly official you can appeal to. We had one too, the Inspector of Police, a jewel of a fellow, willing to listen to us and willing to accept a gift on occasion. We went to the Inspector with the proper gifts and asked for his protection. He reassured us at once. He told us to go home and sleep in peace. Nothing would happen. Sounds good, doesn't it? But we still had our walking newspaper, Noah, who was broadcasting another secret through the length and **breadth** of the town. The secret was that a telegram had just arrived. He swore by everything holy that he had seen it himself. What was in that telegram? Only one word—*Yediem.* An ugly word. It means simply, "We are coming." We ran back to the Inspector. "Your honor," we told him, "it looks bad." "What looks bad?" he asked, and we told him, "A telegram has just arrived." "From

What do you think it means that the Inspector would accept a gift?

belongings personal possessions

breadth the width

director a person who directs or manages a business

notary a notary public; a person who signs or witnesses signing documents

reckoning paying or settling what is owed

where?" We told him. "And what does it say?" We told him, "Yediem." At this he burst out laughing. "You are big fools," he said. "Only yesterday I ordered a regiment of Cossacks from Tolchin."

When we heard this we breathed more easily. When a Jew hears that a Cossack is coming, he takes courage, he can face the world again. The question remained: who would arrive first, the Cossacks from Tolchin, or the hooligans from Zhmerinko? Common sense told us that the hooligans would arrive first, because they were coming by train, while the Cossacks were coming on horseback. But we pinned all our hopes on the Straggler Special. God is merciful. He would surely perform a miracle and the Straggler would be at least a few hours late. This wasn't too much to hope for, since it happened nearly every day. But this one time it looked as though the miracle wouldn't take place. The Straggler kept going from station to station as regular as a clock. You can imagine how we felt when we learned, confidentially, of course, through Noah Tonkonoy, that a telegram had arrived from the last station, from Krishtopovka. *Yediem*, it said, and not just *yediem*—but *yediem* with a *hurrah!* in front of it.

Naturally we took this last bit of news straight to the Inspector. We begged him not to rely on the Cossacks who might or might not arrive from Tolchin sometime, but to send police to the station, at least for the sake of appearances, so that our enemies wouldn't think that we were completely at their mercy. The Inspector listened to our pleas. He did what we asked, and more. He got himself up in full uniform, with all his orders and medals, and took the whole police force, that is the **gendarme** and his assistant, to the station with him to meet the train.

gendarme a police officer

Cossacks made up special military units in the Russian army.

How big is the town's police force?

But our enemies weren't asleep either. They also put on their full dress uniforms, complete with ribbons and medals, took a couple of priests along, and also came to meet the train. The Inspector asked them sternly, "What are you doing here?" And they asked him the same question, "What are you doing here?" They **bandied** words back and forth, and the Inspector let them know in no uncertain terms that their trouble was for nothing. As long as he was in charge, there would be no pogrom in Heissin. They listened, smiled knowingly, and answered with **insolence**, "We shall see."

Just then a train whistle was heard from the distance. The sound struck terror to our hearts. We waited for another whistle to blow and after that for the shouts of "Hurrah!" What would happen after the Hurrah! we knew only too well from **hearsay**. We waited, but heard nothing more. What had happened? The sort of thing that could only happen to our Straggler Special.

When the Straggler Special drew into the station, the engineer stopped the locomotive, stepped out calmly and made his way toward the **buffet**. We met him halfway. "Well, my good fellow, and where are the cars?" "Which cars?" "Can't you see that you are here with the locomotive and without cars?"

bandy to talk back and forth

buffet a restaurant in which people serve themselves from a counter

hearsay gossip

insolence a rude or insulting attitude

He stared at us. "What do I care about the cars? They are the business of the crew." "Where is the crew?" "How should I know where the crew is? The conductor blows the whistle when he is ready and I whistle back to let him know that I am starting, and off we go. I don't have an extra pair of eyes in back of my head to see what's going on behind me." That was his story and according to that he was right. But right or wrong, there stood the Straggler Special without cars and without passengers. In other words, it was a wedding without musicians.

What do you think of the engineer's attitude?

Later we learned that a band of hooligans had been on the way to Heissin, all of them **handpicked** youths, armed to the teeth with clubs and knives and other weapons. Their spirits were high and **liquor** flowed freely. At the last station, Krishtopovka, they invited the crew to join them and treated everybody to drinks—the conductor, the fireman, the gendarmes. But in the midst of this **revelry** they forgot one little detail, to **couple** the cars back to the locomotive. And so the locomotive went off at the usual time to Heissin and the rest of the Straggler Special remained standing in Krishtopovka.

Neither the hooligans nor the other passengers nor the crew noticed that they were standing still. They continued to empty bottle after bottle and to make merry, until the **station master** suddenly noticed that the locomotive had

couple to attach; to link together

handpicked chosen carefully

liquor a strong alcoholic drink

revelry a loud celebration

station master the person in charge of a railroad station

Raising a *hue and cry* means to make a great protest or a great noise.

gone off and left the cars behind. He spread the alarm, the crew came tumbling out. A hue and cry was raised. The hooligans blamed the crew, the crew blamed the hooligans, but what good did it do? At last they decided that the only thing to do was to set out for Heissin on foot. They took heart and began marching toward Heissin, singing and shouting as they went.

And so they arrived in their usual good form, singing and yelling and **brandishing** their clubs. But it was already too late. In the streets of Heissin the Cossacks from Tolchin were riding up and down on horseback with whips in their hands. Within half an hour not one of the hooligans remained in town. They ran off like rats in a **famine**, they melted like ice in summer.

What is ironic about the Straggler Special as a hero? How does this add to the anecdote?

Now, I ask you, didn't the Straggler Special deserve to be showered with gold, or at least written up?

brandish to wave about in a threatening way

famine a severe lack of food

Directions Write the answers to these questions using complete sentences.

Comprehension: Identifying Facts

1. How do the townspeople first hear about the planned pogrom?

2. What does the telegram say? What do people think it means?

3. What public official is a friend to the Jews in the town?

Comprehension: Understanding Main Ideas

4. Why are the hooligans coming to town?

5. Why are people relieved to know the hooligans are coming by train?

6. How do the Cossacks manage to arrive before the hooligans?

Understanding Literature: Anecdote

An anecdote is a short, funny story. An anecdote has a single point. It may touch on some part of a person's personality. It may focus on a single idea. It can give us a fuller picture of a person. It can make an abstract concept more solid. This story includes more details and is a bit longer than a typical anecdote. It is still a short, funny story.

7. How does the story begin?

8. Why is the Straggler Special a strange hero?

Critical Thinking

9. Cruel treatment was a serious problem for Jews in Russia. Why do you think anyone would tell funny stories about it?

10. Did you like this story? Why or why not?

Writing on Your Own Write a brief outline of the story. Tell what happens at the beginning of the story. Then write the events in the middle. Finally, tell how it ends.

Dialogue

Dialogue is the conversation between characters in a story. It gives their exact words. It lets readers know what characters are thinking. Dialogue also shows how characters relate to one another.

There are two ways in which dialogue is special. Quotation marks go around the speaker's words. Usually, another phrase tells who is speaking. Here is an example.

> "Stop right there!" the police officer yelled.
>
> "Not on your life," Lance whispered.

"Stop right there!" is what the officer said. "Not on your life," is what Lance said. The phrase *the police officer yelled* shows the officer is speaking. *Lance whispered* shows Lance is speaking.

Almost all of "Why Can't We Have Our Own Apartment?" is in dialogue. It's easy to tell who is speaking. The exact words of the parents and children play a large part in the humor. Each seems to say what you would expect the other to say. Here is an example.

> "But why?" asked our daughter. "Aren't you happy here? You have your own room and the run of the house."

> "I know, but a lot of parents our age are striking out on their own."

This example is from "A Wedding Without Musicians." The short sentences make the characters sound out of breath.

> "Your honor," we told him, "it looks bad." "What looks bad?" he asked, and we told him, "A telegram has just arrived." "From where?" We told him. "And what does it say?" We told him, "*Yediem*."

Review

1. What does dialogue show?

2. Why does a writer use dialogue?

3. How can you recognize dialogue?

4. How does Bombeck's dialogue add to the humor?

5. What is the effect of the dialogue in the Aleichem story?

Writing on Your Own Write a dialogue between two characters. Include words to show who is speaking. Put quotation marks around the speaker's exact words.

UNIT 6 SUMMARY

In Unit 6 you read examples of different kinds of humorous writing. Some are funny because the writers describe funny situations. Not all the pieces are just for fun, though. Some authors use humor to make a serious point. Satire and irony are ways of using humor. Satire can be very serious while it is humorous.

Jonathan Swift and Andrew Graham-Yooll use humor in a serious way. They write about something that made them angry. Their words may make us laugh. They can also make us uncomfortable. They let us see how ridiculous or awful a situation is. Sholom Aleichem makes fun of those who were mistreating the Jews. The other three writers intend for us to laugh in a different way. Dave Barry makes fun of himself. Leo Slezak makes fun of an opera story. Erma Bombeck turns a family story upside down.

Humor in writing can serve several purposes. You probably did not laugh out loud at the satires by Swift and Graham-Yooll. The story by Sholom Aleichem is set in a serious situation. But it might have made you smile. The Barry, Bombeck, and Slezak stories probably made you laugh. They were written to entertain.

Selections

- "A Modest Proposal" by Jonathan Swift. Swift makes an outrageous suggestion for dealing with poverty in Ireland.

- "Cup Inanity and Patriotic Profanity" by Andrew Graham-Yooll. The writer views the behavior of soccer fans celebrating a victory.

- "Staying at a Japanese Inn: Peace, Tranquillity, Insects" by Dave Barry. Barry tells about trying to fit into a different culture.

- "Why Can't We Have Our Own Apartment?" by Erma Bombeck. Parents switch roles with children and ask to move out.

- "Lohengrin" by Leo Slezak. Slezak makes the story of an opera sound absurd.

- "A Wedding Without Musicians" by Sholom Aleichem. Part of a train doesn't arrive, and it is a good thing for Jews in a small village.

UNIT 6 REVIEW

Directions Write the answers to these questions using complete sentences.

Comprehension Identifying Facts

1. What is the term for a work that makes fun of evil or foolishness? Name one from this unit.

2. What country did Dave Barry and his family visit?

3. Which author writes about Jewish life in the early 1900s?

4. What is a humorist?

5. Which selection is a parody? What does it parody?

Comprehension: Understanding Main Ideas

6. What is the serious social situation discussed in "A Modest Proposal"?

7. What danger threatens the Jews of Heissin in "A Wedding Without Musicians"?

8. Name a selection that is meant just to amuse. Explain your choice.

9. Name a selection that is meant to affect the reader's opinion. Explain your choice.

10. What is the tone of Graham-Yooll's editorial?

Understanding Literature: Irony and Exaggeration

Irony is the use of words that seem to say one thing but mean the opposite. Exaggeration is the use of words to make something seem worse than it is. It stretches the truth. In this unit, the authors use irony and exaggeration to be funny. Several of them also turn this type of humor to a serious purpose.

11. How does the writer of "Cup Inanity and Patriotic Profanity" exaggerate the effects of a soccer victory on Argentina?

12. What is ironic about the way the printer tells secrets in "A Wedding Without Musicians"?

13. How does Dave Barry use exaggeration in describing the political activist?

14. What is ironic about the title "Why Can't We Have Our Own Apartment?"

15. Give another example of exaggeration from one of the selections.

Critical Thinking

16. Do you think you would enjoy the opera *Lohengrin*? Does reading the parody make a difference? Explain.

17. Which author do you think has the gloomiest view of life? Explain.

18. What is ironic about a humorist having a gloomy view of life?

19. Erma Bombeck and Johnathan Swift have very different writing styles. Describe the differences.

20. Which selection did you like most? Why?

Speak and Listen

Go to the library. Find a short humorous work of literature. You may want to look for humorous poems or anecdotes. You might want to choose a monologue like those used by stand-up comics. Read the piece to yourself until you feel comfortable reading it. Then read it to the class. Or you might learn it well enough to tell it rather than reading it.

Beyond Words

Work with classmates. Look for cartoons that tell a funny story without using words. Make copies of the cartoons. Then make a bulletin board display of them.

Writing on Your Own Think of a funny TV show that you like. What is in the show that makes it funny to you? What kind of humor does it use? Write a paragraph explaining why you like the show.

Test-Taking Tip

When taking a short-answer test, first answer the questions you know. Then go back to spend time on the questions you are less sure of.

Correcting Common Writing Mistakes

1. Make subjects and verbs agree
- Singular subject must have a singular verb.
- Plural subjects must have plural verbs.
- Compound subjects must have plural verbs.

2. Make pronouns agree with antecedents
- In gender:
  - Replace the name of a male person with a masculine pronoun.
  - Replace the name of a female person with a feminine pronoun.
  - Replace singular names with *it* or *its*.
  - Replace plural names with *they, them,* or *their.*
- In number:
  - Make the pronoun singular if its antecedent is singular.
  - Make the pronoun plural if its antecedent is plural.

3. Capitalize proper nouns and proper adjectives
- Capitalize proper nouns.
- Capitalize the first word of any sentence or title.
- Capitalize the names of languages.
- Capitalize the pronoun *I.*
- Capitalize all proper adjectives.

4. Use correct verb tenses
- Action verbs tell what someone did.
- State-of-being verbs express the condition of the subject.
- Helping verbs help the main verb express tense, or time.
  - Use one main verb in a verb phrase.
  - Use helping verbs in a verb phrase.
  - Use the main verb last in a verb phrase.

- Make sure the verb tenses are logical.
- Use the same verb tenses if the actions occurred at the same time.
- Use different verb tenses if the actions occurred at different times.

5. Use and spell verb forms correctly
- Form the past tense of a regular verb by adding *-ed* or *-d.*
- Use the past participle to form the past perfect tenses.

6. Use and spell possessives and plurals correctly
- Use a possessive noun to show ownership or a relationship between two things.
- Make a singular noun possessive by adding an apostrophe (') and the letter *s.*
- Make a plural noun possessive by adding only an apostrophe.
- Add both an apostrophe and the letter *s* if the plural noun does not end in an *s.*

7. Avoid run-on sentences
- Begin sentences with a capital letter.
- End each sentence with a period, question mark, or exclamation point.
- Do not end a sentence or separate two sentences with a comma.
- Use a comma plus a conjunction to connect two complete ideas.

8. Avoid sentence fragments
- Make sure each sentence has a subject and a verb that express a complete idea.
- Use a subject and a predicate.
- Do not capitalize the first word of a phrase that does not begin a new idea.

Paragraphs

The Three Parts of a Paragraph

1. The topic sentence

The topic sentence states the main idea in a paragraph. It is usually the first sentence of a paragraph. It lets the reader know what your paragraph is going to be about. The topic sentence should get the reader's attention. It should make the reader want to read the rest of your paragraph.

Ask yourself these questions to help you write your topic sentence:
- What is the purpose of my paragraph?
- What is the main point I want to make?
- Why am I writing this paragraph?
- What will this paragraph be about?

2. The body

The body of a paragraph is the group of sentences that tell more about your main idea. It supports the point of view of your topic sentence. The body can include:
- Facts
- Details
- Explanations
- Reasons
- Examples
- Illustrations

3. The conclusion or summary

The last sentence of a paragraph is a conclusion or a summary. A conclusion is a judgment. It is based on the facts that you presented in your paragraph. Your conclusion must make sense.

A summary is a statement that briefly repeats the main ideas of your paragraph. It repeats your idea or ideas in slightly different words. It does not add new information.

The Purposes of a Paragraph

Every paragraph has one of five purposes. The five purposes are:

1. To give information or facts

Facts are included in all three parts of a paragraph. You may gather facts by reading, listening, or observing.

2. To explain your ideas

You may use this kind of paragraph to:
- Make something clear
- Help someone understand an idea
- Give the meaning of something
- Give reasons for something

3. To ask for information

In this kind of paragraph, make your questions clear and specific. That way, you get specific answers.

4. To persuade

This kind of paragraph helps you to convince someone to act or believe a certain way. You must be sure of what you are saying, then you can persuade someone.

5. To tell a story

You can tell an imaginary or true story in this kind of paragraph. A true story should follow the order in which things happened.

Checklist for Proofreading and Revising

✔ **Use this checklist to proofread and revise your papers.**

Check your paper
❑ Do I have a meaningful title?
❑ Do I have a conclusion or a summary at the end?

Check your paragraphs
❑ Do I start every paragraph on a new line?
❑ Is the first line of every paragraph indented?
❑ Does my first sentence (topic sentence) in every paragraph explain the main idea of my paragraph? Does it attract my reader's attention well?
❑ Do sentences in the middle of my paragraphs support the main idea?
❑ Do I include facts, details, explanations, reasons, examples, or illustrations to support my main idea?
❑ Do I need to take out any sentences that do not relate to my main idea?

Check your sentences
❑ Do I capitalize the first word of every sentence?
❑ Do I end every sentence with the correct punctuation mark?
❑ Do I express a complete idea in every sentence?
❑ Do my pronouns all have clear antecedents?
❑ Do I have any run-on sentences that I need to correct?
❑ Can I improve my sentences?

❑ Can I add adjectives, adverbs, or prepositional phrases?
❑ Can I combine short, related ideas into longer, more varied sentences?

Check your verbs
❑ Do I have a subject and a verb in every sentence?
❑ Do my subject and verb agree in every sentence?
❑ Is my verb tense logical in every sentence?
❑ Is my verb tense consistent in every sentence?
❑ Are my irregular verbs correct?

Check your punctuation and capitalization
❑ Did I capitalize all my proper nouns and proper adjectives?
❑ Did I capitalize and punctuate all my direct quotations correctly?
❑ Did I use a comma to separate words in a series?

Check your spelling
❑ Did I choose the correct spelling for each homonym?
❑ Did I use an apostrophe only in contractions and possessive nouns?
❑ Did I spell every plural noun correctly?
❑ Did I spell all words with *ie* or *ei* correctly?
❑ Did I drop the silent *e* before adding an ending beginning with a vowel?
❑ Did I double the final consonant before adding an ending?

Planning and Writing Reports

Plan the report
- Choose a broad subject you would like to explore.
- Select a topic in that subject area.
- Find out how much information is in the library about your topic.
- Limit your topic so that you have enough information to write a complete report.
- Write a title for your report.
- List your subtopics, or the parts of your larger topic.

Find information
- Go to the library to find information on your topic.
- Look in the library catalog for books that have useful information.
- Check almanacs, encyclopedias, atlases, or other sources in the library reference section.
- Check *The Reader's Guide to Periodical Literature* for magazines with information you could use.
- Take notes on the information you find.
- Use index cards.
- Start each card with this information about the source you find facts in:
  - authors' names
  - book or article and magazine title
  - page numbers
  - volume numbers
  - date of publication
- Copy all the information that you may need.
- Copy any quotations exactly as they are printed.
- Use a different card for each source.

Get organized
- Put your note cards in order by topic and subtopic.
- Choose an order that seems suitable for your topics.
- Do not use notes that seem not to fit anywhere.
- List your main topics.
- Write a final topic outline.

Write your report
- Write your report using note cards and an outline.
- Begin your report with a topic paragraph stating the main idea.
- Use your own words to write the ideas you found in your sources (paraphrase).
- Write an author's exact words if you use direct quotations.
- Name the author or source of any direct quotations you use.
- Repeat your main ideas in a summary paragraph at the end.
- Proofread your report.
- Revise and rewrite it as needed.
- Include a title page at the front of your report.

Prepare a bibliography
- Use the bibliographic information on your note cards.
- Put your cards in alphabetical order.
- Include a blank page after your bibliography.

ARCTIC OCEAN
Beaufort Sea
Baffin Bay
GREENLAND
ICELAND
Bering Sea
Gulf of Alaska
Hudson Bay
Labrador Sea
CANADA
IREL
NORTH AMERICA
of
UNITED STATES OF AMERICA
NORTH ATLANTIC OCEAN
PORTO
NORTH PACIFIC OCEAN
CANARY ISLANDS
WESTERN SAHARA
MC
HAWAII
Gulf of Mexico
MEXICO
THE BAHAMAS
CUBA
DOMINICAN REPUBLIC
MAURITANI.
BELIZE
PUERTO RICO (U.S.)
HONDURAS
HAITI
SENEGAL
GUATEMALA
Caribbean Sea
THE GAMBIA
EL SALVADOR
PANAMA
GUINEA-BISSAU
NICARAGUA
VENEZUELA
GUYANA
GUINEA
COSTA RICA
SURINAME
SIERRA LEONE
FRENCH GUIANA
LIBERIA
COLOMBIA
ECUADOR
SOUTH AMERICA
PERU
SOUTH PACIFIC OCEAN
BRAZIL
BOLIVIA
PARAGUAY
CHILE
SOUT ATLAN OCEA
ARGENTINA
URUGUAY
N
W E
S
FALKLAND ISLANDS (U.K.)
SOUTH GEORGIA ISLAND (U.K.)
160°W 140°W 120°W 100°W 80°W 60°W 40°W 20°W

ARCTIC OCEAN

80°N

SWEDEN
NORWAY FINLAND
ESTONIA
LATVIA
LITHUANIA
POLAND BELARUS
GERMANY
CZECH EUROPE
AUSTRIA
HUNGARY MOLDOVA
ITALY ROMANIA
BOSNIA
ALBANIA BULGARIA ARMENIA
GREECE TURKEY
AZERBAIJAN
TUNISIA
Mediterranean
Sea
ISRAEL SYRIA IRAQ
JORDAN
KUWAIT
LIBYA EGYPT UNITED
ARAB EMIRATES
SAUDI ARABIA

ASIA

RUSSIA

KAZAKHSTAN

GEORGIA
Caspian
Sea
UZBEKISTAN
KYRGYZSTAN
TURKMENISTAN TAJIKISTAN
IRAN AFGHANISTAN
PAKISTAN

MONGOLIA

CHINA

BHUTAN
NEPAL INDIA

Sea of
Okhotsk

NORTH
KOREA
SOUTH
KOREA
JAPAN

Sea of
Japan

East
China
Sea

TAIWAN

NORTH
PACIFIC
OCEAN

60°N

40°N

AFRICA
NIGER
CHAD
SUDAN ERITREA
YEMEN
GERIA
OMAN
Arabian Sea
CENTRAL AFRICAN
REPUBLIC ETHIOPIA
CAMEROON DEM. REP.
OF CONGO UGANDA
GABON (ZAIRE)
KENYA
NGO RWANDA
BURUNDI
TANZANIA

INDIA
BANGLADESH MYANMAR
LAOS
Bay
of Bengal THAILAND
CAMBODIA
VIETNAM
SRI LANKA
BRUNEI
MALAYSIA
SINGAPORE

South
China
Sea

Philippine
Sea

PHILIPPINES

20°N

0° Equator

ANGOLA
ZAMBIA MALAWI
NAMIBIA ZIMBABWE
BOTSWANA MADAGASCAR
MOZAMBIQUE
SWAZILAND
SOUTH LESOTHO
AFRICA

INDIAN
OCEAN

Java Sea
INDONESIA
Arafura Sea
Timor Sea

PAPUA
NEW GUINEA

Coral Sea

FIJI

NEW CALEDONIA

20°S

AUSTRALIA

Great Australian
Bight

Tasman Sea

NEW ZEALAND

40°S

60°S

ANTARCTICA

80°S

20°E 40°E 60°E 80°E 100°E 120°E 140°E 160°E

North America

Caribbean Sea

ST. LUCIA

Managua ★

GRENADA

Barranquilla

Caracas

10°N

San José

Valencia

Panama

VENEZUELA

Cúcuta

Georgetown

Medellín

GUYANA

Paramaribo

Bogotá

Puerto Ayacucho

SURINAME

Cayenne

COLOMBIA

FRENCH
GUIANA

Mitú

Macapá

0°

Quito

ECUADOR

Santarém

Belém

Guayaquil

Galápagos
Islands

Talara

Fortaleza

PERU

Teresina

Trujillo

Porto Velho

Recife

10°S

Maceió

Huánuco

BRAZIL

Aracaju

Lima

Barreiras

Ica

Cuzco

Salvador

BOLIVIA

La Paz

Brásilia

Santa Cruz

Goiânia

20°S

Sucre

Iquique

PACIFIC OCEAN

Antofagasta

PARAGUAY

Rio de Janeiro

São Paulo

CHILE

Asunción

30°S

Córdoba

Rosario

Santiago

URUGUAY

Buenos Aires

Concepción

Montevideo

ATLANTIC OCEAN

ARGENTINA

Valdivia

40°S

Puerto Montt

N

W   E

S

Comodoro Rivadavia

50°S

FALKLAND ISLANDS
(U.K.)

SOUTH GEORGIA ISLAND
(U.K.)

90°W   80°W   70°W   60°W   50°W   40°W

South America

Europe

Reykjavik ★ **ICELAND**

NORTH
ATLANTIC
OCEAN

Norwegian Sea

**Faroe
Islands**

SWEDEN

FINLAND

RUSSIA

NORWAY

*Gulf
of
Bothnia* Helsinki ★

Oslo
★

Stockholm
★ ★Tallinn

ESTONIA

Moscow ★

Baltic Sea

LATVIA

Riga ★

SCOTLAND

North Sea

Belfast
★

IRELAND Dublin
★

Copenhagen

DENMARK ★

LITHUANIA

Vilnius
★

★ Minsk

WALES **U. K.**

NETHERLANDS

Amsterdam
★

Berlin
★

Warsaw ★

BELARUS

London ★

GERMANY

POLAND

★ Kiev

Brussels
★

UKRAINE

BELGIUM
LUX.

Prague
CZECH
REP. ★ Ostrava

★ Paris

SLOVAKIA

Vienna ★ ★Bratislava

MOLDOVA

FRANCE

Bern
★

AUSTRIA ★ Budapest

Chisinau
★

HUNGARY

ROMANIA

SWITZERLAND

SLOVENIA

★Zagreb

Belgrade ★

Bucharest
★

Black Sea

Bay of Biscay

Monte Carlo
★

BOSNIA AND
HERZEGOVINA

CROATIA

★Sarajevo

BULGARIA ★Varna

PORTUGAL

MONACO

ITALY *Adriatic
Sea*

SERBIA

★Sofia

*Caspian
Sea*

ANDORRA

★ Madrid

Corsica

MACEDONIA ★Skopje

Ankara
★

Lisbon

SPAIN

Sardinia

★ Rome

Tiranë
★

ALBANIA

*Balearic
Islands*

Tyrrhenian Sea

*Aegean
Sea*

★ Gibraltar

Algiers

GREECE

Rabat

Ionian Sea

★Athens

Tunis

N

W E

S

★ Valletta
MALTA

Mediterranean Sea

Tripoli

Alexandria

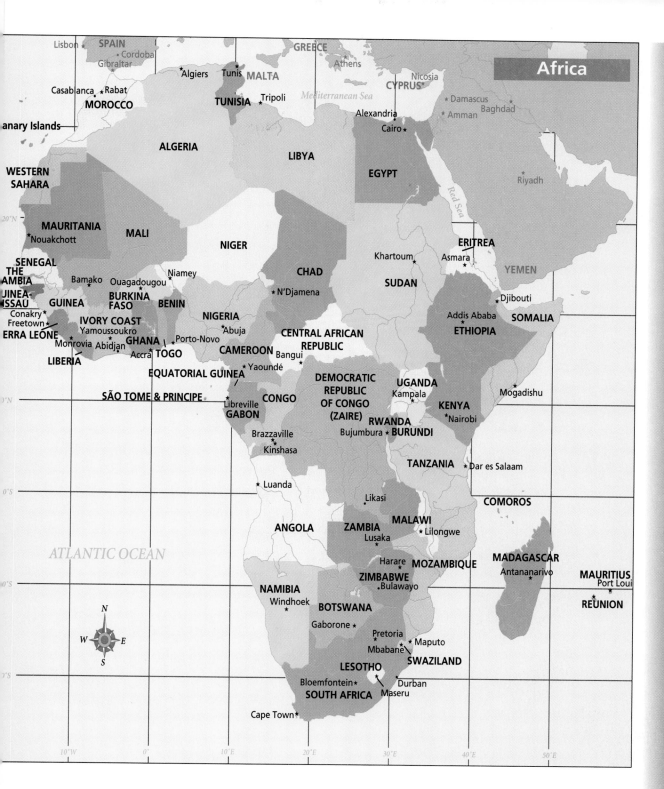

Lisbon ★ SPAIN
• Cordoba
Gibraltar

GREECE

Athens ★

Africa

★ Algiers Tunis ★ MALTA
★ TUNISIA ★ Tripoli

Casablanca ★ ★ Rabat
MOROCCO

Nicosia
★
CYPRUS
★

★ Damascus Baghdad ★
Amman ★

anary Islands

Alexandria ★
Cairo ★

ALGERIA

LIBYA

EGYPT

Mediterranean Sea

Red Sea

Riyadh ★

**WESTERN
SAHARA**

20°N

MAURITANIA
★ Nouakchott

MALI

NIGER

Khartoum ★

ERITREA
★ Asmara

YEMEN

SENEGAL
**THE
AMBIA**

Niamey ★
Bamako ★ Ouagadougou ★
**BURKINA
FASO**

CHAD

★ N'Djamena

SUDAN

★ Djibouti

Addis Ababa ★

SOMALIA

UINEA-
ISSAU
Conakry ★
Freetown ★
ERRA LEONE
Monrovia ★

GUINEA

BENIN

NIGERIA
★ Abuja

**CENTRAL AFRICAN
REPUBLIC**

ETHIOPIA

IVORY COAST
Yamoussoukro ★
Abidjan ★ **GHANA** ★ Porto-Novo
Accra ★ **TOGO**

CAMEROON
Bangui ★

LIBERIA

EQUATORIAL GUINEA ★ Yaoundé

0°N

SÃO TOME & PRINCIPE

**DEMOCRATIC
REPUBLIC
OF CONGO
(ZAIRE)**

UGANDA
Kampala ★

Mogadishu ★

Libreville ★
GABON

CONGO

KENYA
★ Nairobi

RWANDA
Bujumbura ★ **BURUNDI**

Brazzaville ★
★ Kinshasa

0°S

★ Luanda

Likasi •

TANZANIA
★ Dar es Salaam

COMOROS

ANGOLA

ZAMBIA
Lusaka •

MALAWI
★ Lilongwe

ATLANTIC OCEAN

Harare •
ZIMBABWE
• Bulawayo

MOZAMBIQUE

MADAGASCAR
Antananarivo
★

MAURITIUS
Port Loui

0°S

NAMIBIA
Windhoek
★

BOTSWANA

Gaborone ★

RÉUNION
★

N

W E

S

Pretoria ★
Mbabane ★ ★ Maputo
SWAZILAND

LESOTHO
Bloemfontein ★
SOUTH AFRICA Maseru ★ Durban

Cape Town ★

10°W   0°   10°E   20°E   30°E   40°E   50°E

Asia and Australia

RUSSIA

RUSSIA

•Moscow

•Novosibirsk

East Siberian Sea

75°N

60°N

Sea of Okhotsk

Bering Sea

Karaganda

KAZAKHSTAN

Ulaanbaatar •

MONGOLIA

45°N

AZERBAIJAN

GEORGIA

TURKMENISTAN

UZBEKISTAN

Tashkent•

KYRGYZSTAN

NORTH KOREA

Pyongyang•

Seoul•

JAPAN

ARMENIA

Black Sea

TAJIKISTAN

Beijing •

SOUTH KOREA

•Tokyo

TURKEY

CHINA

SYRIA

•Tehran

AFGHANISTAN

East China Sea

PACIFIC OCEAN

30°N

Baghdad

ISRAEL

IRAQ

IRAN

NEPAL

BHUTAN

JORDAN

KUWAIT

PAKISTAN

New Delhi

Chengdu

QATAR

INDIA

Dhaka

TAIWAN

U.A.E.

Calcutta•

MYANMAR

SAUDI ARABIA

BANGLADESH

Hanoi•

Hong Kong

OMAN

Bombay•

Rangoon

LAOS

•Manila

15°N

Red Sea

YEMEN

Vientiane•

Bangkok•

•Mindoro

•Sanaa

THAILAND

VIETNAM

PHILIPPINES

KAMPUCHEA

Phnom Penh•

•Davao

Colombo•

BRUNEI

SRI LANKA

MALAYSIA

0°

Kuala Lumpur•

Jakarta•

Java Sea

INDONESIA

PAPUA NEW GUINEA

Arafura Sea

Port Moresby•

Timor Sea

Coral Sea

FIJI

NEW CALEDONIA

AUSTRALIA

30°S

Perth•

Great Australian Bight

Adelaide•

•Canberra

Auckland•

Tasman Sea

Wellington•

NEW ZEALAND

N

W E

S

30°E

60°E

90°E

120°E

150°E

180°E

INDIAN OCEAN

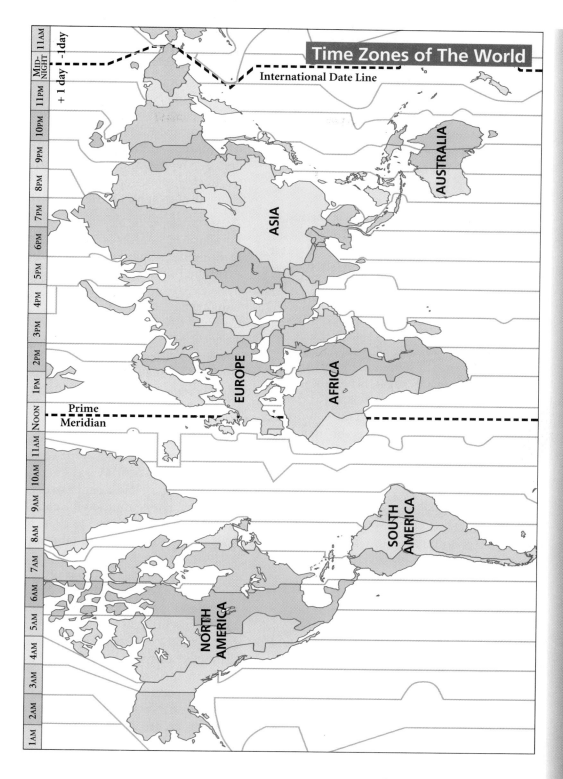

Time Zones of The World

International Date Line

+ 1 day | -1 day

Prime
Meridian

Adapted from *Information Please Almanac, New York Times 1998 Almanac,* and *AGS Survey of World Cultures.* Information on Wales adapted from Robert Evans (e-mail: Robert.Evans@cs.cf. ac.uk). Information on Sweden ©1994-98 by Antti Lahelma and Johan Olofsson, used by permission. (http://www.lysator.liu.se/nordic/scnfaq73.html)

Antigua and Barbuda

Population: 65,647 (1996 estimated).
Nationality: noun: Antiguan(s); adjective: Antiguan. **Ethnic groups:** mostly black African origin; British, Portuguese, Lebanese, Syrian. **Languages:** English (official), local dialects. **Religions:** Anglican, other Protestants, some Roman Catholic. **Area:** 170 sq. mi. (440 sq km); about 2.5 times larger than Washington, DC.
Profile: Columbus claimed Antigua for Spain in 1493. The British settled there in 1632, growing tobacco and sugar. Slavery was outlawed in 1834. Natural disasters and the closing of industries hindered the economy in the 1800s. Today, tourism is the main industry. Barbuda has recently tried to break away because of political and cultural differences.

Argentina (Argentine Republic)

Population: 34,672,997 (1996 estimated).
Nationality: noun: Argentine(s); adjective: Argentine. **Ethnic groups:** White, mestizo, Indian, and other nonwhite groups.
Languages: Spanish, English, Italian, German, French. **Religions:** 90% nominally Roman Catholic (less than 20% practicing), 2% Protestant, 2% Jewish, 6% other. **Area:** 1,068,298 sq. mi. (2,766,890 sq km); about three-tenths the size of the United States.
Profile: Argentina is the second largest and the southernmost country in South America. While generally temperate, the varying altitudes create different climates. Among its many natural resources are petroleum products, uranium, timber, beef, pork, fish, cotton, fruits, wool and cereals. Because Argentina ships so much grain worldwide, it has been called "the granary of the world." Argentina is also known for its musical and dance style, the tango, and for its frequent world championships in polo. Its literacy rate is one of the highest in the world.

Austria (Republic of Austria)

Population: 8,023,244 (1996 estimated)
Nationality: noun: Austrian(s); adjective: Austrian. **Ethnic groups:** 99.4% German, 0.3% Croatian, 0.2% Slovene, 0.1% other.
Languages: German. **Religions:** 85% Roman Catholic, 6% Protestant, 9% none or other.
Area: 32,377 sq. mi. (83,855 sq km); its size is between South Carolina and Maine.
Profile: Originally conquered by the Romans Austria was united under Charlemagne and later became part of the Habsburg empire. Part of the country was overrun by the Turks several times, the last being in the late 1600s. The killing of Archduke Franz Ferdinand in 1914 triggered World War I. After the war, the Austrian empire had disappeared, replaced by a republic. Hitler annexed the country before World War II. From 1945 to 1955, the United States, the USSR, Great Britain, and France occupied the country. Then it became a neutral democracy. Austria is proud of its mountains and natural beauty. Its people enjoy outdoor sports such as skiing. Its rich history has brought together many cultures of Eastern and Western Europe. The result is a distinctive culture unlike those of other German-speaking countries. Today, Austria is a neutral country, allowing it to act as an international center of government and politics. Yet, despite its international flavor, Austria holds its rural heritage dear.

Chile (Republic of Chile)

Population: 14,508,158 (1997 estimated).
Nationality: noun: Chilean(s); adjective: Chilean. **Ethnic groups:** European and European-Indian, Indian, other. **Language:** Spanish. **Religions:** 89% Roman Catholic, 11% Protestant, small Jewish population. **Area:** 292,259 sq. mi. (756,950 sq km); slightly larger than Texas.
Profile: Chile is sometimes called the "Shoestring Nation" because it is ten times as long as it is wide. In the north, it is warm; in the south, cold. The Andes mountains are a tourist attraction for fishers, skiers, and others. Although Chile's farmlands are fertile due to mountain runoff, it cannot produce enough food to feed its people. Mineral deposits are the country's main source of income.

China (People's Republic of China)

Population: 1,221,591,778 (1997 estimated).
Nationality: noun: Chinese (singular and plural); adjective: Chinese. **Ethnic groups:** Han Chinese; Zhuang, Uygur, Hui, Yi, Tibetan, Miao, Manchu, Mongol, Buyi, Korean, and numerous others. **Languages:** Standard Chinese or Mandarin (Putonghua based on the Beijing dialect); Yue (Cantonese), Wu (Shanghainese), Minbei (Fuzho), Minnan (Hokkien-Taiwanese), Xiang, Gan, Hakka dialects, and minority languages (see "Ethnic groups"). **Religions:** officially atheist, but traditionally pragmatic and eclectic; Taoism, Buddhism, 2-3% Muslim, 1% Christian. **Area:** 3,705,392 sq. mi. (9,596,960 sq km); its size is between the United States and Canada.
Profile: China has one of the world's oldest civilizations. With more than a billion citizens, it has the largest population in the world. Until the early 1900s, China was ruled by dynasties. During this time, the Chinese people made many important contributions to civilization. When the last dynasty failed, China became a republic. However, since 1949, the government has been ruled by the Communist Party. The arts have always been important in China. Evidence appears in beautiful porcelain and landscape painting, for example, as well as in the writings of Confucius.

Colombia (Republic of Colombia)

Population: 37,418,290 (1997 estimated).
Nationality: noun: Colombian(s), adjective: Colombian. **Ethnic groups:** mestizo, white, mulatto, black, other. **Language:** Spanish. **Religions:** 95% Roman Catholic. **Area:** 439,734 sq. mi. (1,138,910 sq km); between Texas and Alaska.
Profile: In the early 1800s, Colombia originally was part of Gran Colombia, which included the modern-day countries of Ecuador, Panama, Venezuela, and Colombia. Its climate varies from the swampy Pacific coast—the rainiest in South America—to the cold, high mountain ranges in the west. Colombia holds first place for the production of mild coffee. Although the government has remained fairly stable, illegal trafficking in drugs has caused many problems.

England. *See* United Kingdom.

France (French Republic)

Population: 58,609,285 (1997 estimated).
Nationality: noun: Frenchman (men), Frenchwoman (women), French (collective plural); adjective: French. **Ethnic groups:** Celtic and Latin with Teutonic, Slavic, North African, Indochinese, and Basque minorities. **Languages:** French (100% of population); rapidly declining regional dialects (Provençal, Breton, Alsatian, Corsican,

Catalan, Basque, Flemish). **Religions:** 90% Roman Catholic, 2% Protestant, 1% Jewish, 1% Muslim (North African workers), 6% unaffiliated. **Area:** 176,460 sq. mi. (457,030 sq km); its size is between California and Texas. **Profile:** France, the largest country in Western Europe, has a varied geography and climate. Its culture stretches back thousands of years. Contributors include the Celts, Romans, and Germanic peoples who once invaded this land. Strong leaders such as Charlemagne, Louis XIV, and Napoleon brought France to a position of world importance. The French today have maintained their appreciation of the arts. They delight in preparing and cooking food. A high standard of living gives them time to enjoy family life, another important part of their culture. Sports, such as soccer and bicycling, are popular.

Germany (Federal Republic of Germany)
Population: 82,071,765 (1997 estimated). **Nationality:** noun: German(s); adjective: German. **Ethnic groups:** German, Turkish, other. **Languages:** German. **Religions:** 45% Protestant, 37% Roman Catholic, 18% unaffiliated or other. **Area:** 137,803 sq. mi. (356,910 sq km); about the size of Virginia and North and South Carolina combined. **Profile:** Germany, a central European nation, has historically been a strong military power in Europe. As part of the Holy Roman Empire and Prussia, it controlled the cultures of the lands it invaded. Germany and Adolf Hitler's Third Reich were defeated in World War II, and the country was divided into East and West Germany. Even divided, the people spoke the same language and many practiced the same Christian faith. They formally agreed to reunite in 1990. Since then, Germany has had to deal with many

problems brought on by the complex process of reunifying, including finding ways to finance industrial improvements in the former East Germany. A reunified Germany draws from the country's past. It includes a love of outdoor sports, regional costumes worn on special occasions, and foods that were first prepared before modern-day refrigeration.

Great Britain. *See* United Kingdom.

India (Republic of India)
Population: 966,783,171 (1997 estimated). **Nationality:** noun: Indian(s); adjective: Indian. **Ethnic groups:** Indo-Aryan, Dravidian, Mongoloid and others. **Languages:** Hindi, English, and fourteen other official languages; twenty-four languages spoken by a million or more persons each; numerous other languages and dialects; Hindi is the national language and primary tongue of 30% of the people; English enjoys associate status but is the most important language for national, political, and commercial communication; Hindustani, a variant of Hindi/Urdu, is spoken throughout northern India. **Religions:** 80% Hindu, 14% Muslim, 2.4% Christian, 2% Sikh. **Area:** 1,269,340 sq. mi. (3,287,590 sq km); slightly more than one-third the size of the United States. **Profile:** The Indus River valley was home to the first Indians. They had a well-developed civilization; it was one of the oldest in the world. As invaders conquered India, the civilization weakened. Europeans came to India around 1600. Among them were the British, who formed the British East India Trading Company. The company grew until it gave the British almost complete control of India for centuries. After many years of

struggle, India finally became an independent nation in 1947. Today, India is a democratic republic. Most of its people are Hindus. This means that its customs and traditions are based on the Hindu religion. The most famous of India's beautiful temples and mosques is the Taj Mahal.

Ireland

Population: 3,606,952 (1996 estimated). **Nationality:** noun: Irishman (men), Irishwoman (women), Irish (collective plural); adjective: Irish. **Ethnic groups:** Celtic with English minority. **Languages:** Irish (Gaelic) and English (official); English widely spoken. **Religions:** 93% Roman Catholic, 3% Anglican, 4% other. **Area:** 27,135 sq. mi. (70,280 sq km); slightly larger than West Virginia.
Profile: In the 400s St. Patrick converted Ireland, at first a collection of warring Celtic chieftainships, to Christianity. It was first invaded by the Vikings in the 800s. Although joined with England in 1800 by the Act of Union, Ireland was not well represented in the British parliament. In 1949 Ireland severed all ties to the British crown and became a fully independent republic. Since then its history has been dominated by economic problems and "The Troubles." In this anti-British violence, the Irish Republican Army, a guerrilla group, has attempted to drive the British troops from Northern Ireland. Ireland's cultural contributions are strongest in literature. Consider the writings of Jonathan Swift, George Bernard Shaw, William Butler Yeats and James Joyce. The most important national holiday in Ireland is Saint Patrick's Day, March 17.

Israel (State of Israel)

Population: 5,534,672 (1997 estimated). **Nationality:** noun: Israeli(s); adjective: Israeli. **Ethnic groups:** Jewish, non-Jewish (mostly Arab). **Languages:** Hebrew (official), Arab (official for Arab minority); English most widely used foreign language. **Religions:** 82% Judaism, 14% Islam (mostly Sunni Muslim), 2% Christian, 2% Druze or other. **Area:** 8,019 sq. mi. (20,770 sq km); slightly larger than Massachusetts.
Profile: The Jewish people, led by Moses, escaped slavery in Egypt and set up a kingdom along the Mediterranean Sea. Through the years, the numbers of Jews living in Palestine (as the area was called) decreased as the Arab population increased. After World War I, the Jews began resettling in Palestine. During World War II, millions of Jews fled to Palestine to avoid the Holocaust. In 1948 the United Nations divided Palestine into two states, one for the Jews and one for the Arabs. The Israeli people, who come from all parts of the world, are bound together by the Jewish religion. They are set apart from their neighbors by language, religion, and customs. They tend to be literate, skilled, and hardworking. Border fights continue between Israel and its Arab neighbors. Many people on both sides have been killed. Israel is short of water and fertile land. Its farms are typically on the coast, where the climate is pleasant and there is enough rainfall for farming. The main crops are olives, grapes, and citrus fruits, especially lemons and oranges.

Japan

Population: 125,732,794 (1997 estimated). **Nationality:** noun: Japanese (singular, plural); adjective: Japanese. **Ethnic groups:**

Japanese, other (mostly Korean). **Language:** Japanese. **Religions:** most Japanese observe both Shinto and Buddhist rites; about 16% belong to other faiths, including 0.8% Christian. **Area:** 145,882 sq. mi. (377,835 sq km); slightly larger than Montana. **Profile:** Japan is a mountainous country made up of four main islands. In its early years, powerful families or military leaders ruled. Under the leadership of Emperor Mutsuhitos, many advancements were made. A constitution was written and a two-house Parliament established. Japan was destroyed during World War II. But with the help of the United States and others, it rebuilt its industries and government. Today, Japan is a high-technology, industrial country. Though Western influence is strong, the Japanese maintain their own culture. Education is especially important to them.

Netherlands (Kingdom of the Netherlands)
Population: 15,649,729 (1997 estimated). **Nationality:** noun: Dutchman (men), Dutchwoman (women); adjective: Dutch. **Ethnic groups:** Dutch, Moroccans, Turks, and other. **Languages:** Dutch (official). **Religions:** 34% Roman Catholic, 25% Protestant, 36% unaffiliated, 3% Muslim. **Area:** 14,413 sq. mi. (37,330 sq km); 1.3 times size of Maryland.
Profile: During the Holy Roman Empire, the Netherlands was originally the low-lying area near the mouths of the Rhine, Meuse, and Scheldt rivers in northwestern Europe. Despite its small size, the Netherlands became a world power in the 1600s. It maintained extraordinary influence and prestige in European affairs into the 1900s. While devastated by World War II, political stability allowed a dramatic postwar recovery. Today, its main crops are grains, potatoes, sugar

beets, livestock; its natural resources include natural gas, crude oil, and fertile soil. The Netherlands are famous for flower farming, especially tulips.

Nigeria (Federal Republic of Nigeria)
Population: 107,129,469 (1997 estimated). **Nationality:** noun: Nigerian(s), adjective: Nigerian. **Ethnic groups:** 250 tribal groups; Hausa and Fulani in north, Yoruba in southwest, and Ibos in southeast make up 65% of population. **Languages:** English (official); Hausa, Yoruba, Ibo, Fulani, and several other languages also widely used. **Religions:** 50% Muslim, 40% Christian, 10% indigenous beliefs. **Area:** 356,668 sq. mi. (923,770 sq km); about 1.3 times the size of Texas.
Profile: Nigeria's history goes back around 2,000 years. It is the most populated country in Africa. It is also one of the richest countries in Africa, with mineral resources and large oil deposits on the Niger River. There is also coal in the river's delta. But most Nigerians are farmers. Since Nigerians tend to speak English and love movies, most movies are in English. Its four ethnic groups distrust one another. In 1967 a civil war broke out when one group tried to set up an independent country, Biafra. The war ended in 1970 with the Biafrans' defeat.

Pakistan (Islamic Republic of Pakistan)
Population: 132,185,299 (1997 estimated). **Nationality:** noun: Pakistani(s), adjective: Pakistani. **Ethnic groups:** Punjabi, Sindhi, Pashtun (Pathun), Baloch, Juhajir (immigrants from India and their descendants). **Languages:** Urdu and English (official); total spoken languages: 48% Punjabi, 12% Sindhi, 10% Siraiki, 8% Pashtu, 8% Urdu, 3% Balochi. **Religions:** 97% Muslim

(77% Sunni, 20% Shi'a); 3% Christian, Hindu, and other. **Area:** 310,401 sq. mi. (803,940 sq km); about twice the size of California.

Profile: Around 350 B.C. Alexander the Great made the middle of the Indus River valley—what is now Pakistan—part of his empire. Arab invaders brought the religion of Islam at the start of the 700s. Ever since, the region has been deeply committed to Islam. Pakistan remains a strong Islamic country. Wheat, rice, cotton and tobacco—its main crops—are grown in the Indus River valley; livestock is farmed in the drier areas of the north and west. Pakistan's natural resources include land, extensive natural gas reserves, some crude oil, coal, and iron ore. Its industry is limited to textiles and food processing. Seeking a balance of power with India, Pakistan tested nuclear weapons in 1998.

Philippines (Republic of the Philippines)
Population: 76,103,564 (1997 estimated). **Nationality:** noun: Filipino(s); adjective: Philippine. **Ethnic groups:** Christian Malay, Muslim Malay, Chinese, other. **Languages:** Filipino (based on Tagalog) and English (both official). **Religions:** 83% Roman Catholic, 9% Protestant, 5% Muslim, 3% Buddhist and other. **Area:** 115,830 sq. mi. (300,000 sq km); slightly larger than Arizona.

Profile: The Philippine islands were controlled by the Spanish from around 1500 to 1898. As a result, Christianity became the main religion, in particular, Roman Catholicism. Control passed to the United States after the Spanish-American War in 1898. Of the 7,000 islands in the Philippines, only about 700 are inhabited. Many have rich soil and natural resources. The islands' tropical climate is good for farming and lumbering. The people are mostly Filipinos, a mixture of Malaysian, Spanish, Chinese, Indian, and Arabian heritage. Many Filipinos work for the wealthy farmers who own most of the land.

Poland (Republic of Poland)
Population: 38,615,239 (1997 estimated). **Nationality:** noun: Pole(s), adjective: Polish. **Ethnic groups:** Polish, German, Ukranian, Byelorussian. **Language:** Polish. **Religions:** 95% Roman Catholic (about 75% practicing), 5% Eastern Orthodox, Protestant, and other. **Area:** 120,726 sq. mi. (312,680 sq km); about the size of Virginia and North and South Carolina combined.

Profile: Poland and its strong culture have developed over many centuries. One influence is its early Slavic culture. Another is its varied geography and climate, and a long history of conflict. Both still color Polish life today. Early on, Poland had much power. Then it ceased to exist as a nation. But culture has kept the Poles unified over the years. Today, this cultural unity is bringing Poland a renewed sense of independence. Once a Communist nation, today it is a democratic republic. Poles enjoy a common language and a rich history of contributions to the arts and sciences.

Russia (Russian Federation)
Population: 147,305,569 (1997). **Nationality:** noun: Russian(s), adjective: Russian. **Ethnic groups:** Russian, Tartar, Ukranian, Chuvash. **Languages:** Russian (official), ethnic languages. **Religions:** Russian Orthodox, Muslim. **Area:** 6,592,745 sq. mi. (17,075,200 sq km); almost twice the size of the United States.

Profile: In the 800s, the Russian state began in the city of Kiev. In the 1200s Mongol invaders destroyed Kiev. The tsars ruled Russia from Moscow until 1917 when the Communists took over. Mikhail Gorbachev tried to reform

Communist society in 1985. But the democratic movement took control with Boris Yeltsin as its leader. In December 1991 the Soviet Union broke into separate republics, and the Commonwealth of Independent States came into being. They comprise fifteen separate, independent countries. The largest is Russia, or "Great Russia." It has more than half the population and about three-quarters of the land of the old Soviet Union. The Commonwealth's chief crops are grain, potatoes, sugar beets, vegetables, and sunflowers; its natural resources include coal, petroleum, natural gas, gold, and iron; its major industries are the extraction and processing of raw materials, and machine-building, from rolling mills to high-performance aircraft. Russia measures about 6,000 miles from western to eastern border. Within these borders is a great variety of climate, from frozen Siberia to the arid southwest. Much of the country is in the northern latitudes. More than half the Commonwealth is flat with rolling hills. Russia also has a great diversity of people. More than 100 distinct languages are spoken and many religious faiths are followed. The culture of Russia is old and deep. It has excelled in classical music, literature, ballet, and art. Russia has also produced many great scientists.

South Africa (Republic of South Africa)
Population: 42,327,458 (1997 estimated).
Nationality: noun: South African(s), adjective: South African. **Ethnic groups:** black, white, Indian, other. **Languages:** Afrikaans, English, Zulu, Xhosa, Sotho, Ndebele, Pedi, Swazi, Tsonga, Venda, Tswana (all official).
Religions: most whites and about 60% of blacks are Christian; roughly 60% of Indians are Hindu, 2% Muslim, 28.5% traditional

beliefs. **Area:** 471,444 sq. mi. (1,221,040 sq km); its size is between Texas and Alaska.
Profile: The Dutch settled the republic of South Africa, at the southern end of Africa, in the 1600s. It consists of four provinces: the Cape, Natal, Orange Free State, and the Transvaal. Except for a narrow coastal plain, the country is mostly a great plateau, including grasslands, savanna, and desert. South Africa's well-developed economy produces 40% of the manufactured goods of Africa, 50% of its minerals, and 20% of its farm products. It is the wealthiest nation in Africa. In 1948 apartheid (or "separate development") became official government policy. However, in May 1996, South Africa did away with apartheid and became a democracy. It is now under the leadership of Nelson Mandela.

South Korea (Republic of Korea)
Population: 45,948,811 (1997 estimated).
Nationality: noun: Korean (s); adjective: Korean. **Ethnic groups:** homogenous; small Chinese minority (about 20,000). **Languages:** Korean; English widely taught in high school.
Religions: 48.6% Christian, 47.4% Buddhism, 3% Confucianism; pervasive folk religion.
Area: 38,023 sq. mi. (98,480 sq km); its size is between Indiana and Kentucky.
Profile: Korea, a peninsula between China and Japan, was invaded many times by both countries. Japan ruled it from 1910 to 1945. Today, Korea is no longer one country. It is divided into North Korea, ruled by Communists, and South Korea, a republic. The Korean alphabet is considered highly scientific. The Korean lifestyle reflects the teachings of Confucius. South Korea, which has twice as many people as North Korea, is a modern, industrial, democratic nation. South Korea's chief crops are rice, barley, vegetables,

legumes, chickens, pigs, and cattle. Its natural resources include coal, tungsten, and graphite. Major industries include electronics, automobiles, chemicals, and shipbuilding.

Sweden (Kingdom of Sweden)
Population: 8,865,051 (1997). **Nationality:** noun: Swede(s), adjective: Swedish. **Ethnic groups:** homogenous white population; small Lappish minority; about 12% foreign-born or first-generation immigrants (Finns, Yugoslavs, Danes, Norwegians, Greeks, Turks). **Languages:** Swedish, small Lapp- and Finnish-speaking minorities. **Religions:** 94% Evangelical Lutheran, 1.5% Roman Catholic, 4.5% other. **Area:** 173,731 sq. mi. (449,964 sq km); slightly larger than California.
Profile: The earliest Swedes were the Svear. They dominated a trading empire in the 900s. Sweden is long and narrow. Its terrain is mostly flat or gently rolling lowlands; there are mountains in the north and west. Nature is special to the Swedes. While Sweden has different climates, it tends to be cool in the summer and cold in the winter. The country's chief crops are grain, sugar beets, potatoes, meat, and milk; its natural resources include iron ore, zinc, lead, copper, silver, timber, uranium, and hydropower. Swedes are industrious and work hard to improve their society.

Switzerland (Swiss Confederation)
Population: 7,240,463 (1997 estimated). **Nationality:** noun: Swiss (singular, plural), adjective: Swiss. **Ethnic groups:** German, French, Italian, Romansch, other. **Languages:** total population: 63.7% German, 19.2% French, 7.6% Italian, 0.6% Romansch, 8.9% other. **Religions:** 46.7% Catholic, 40% Protestant. **Area:** 15,942 sq. mi. (41,290 sq km); its size is between Maryland and West Virginia.

Profile: Switzerland is a landlocked country in the middle of Europe. It is famous for its neutrality in the two world wars and for its mountains, the Alps. In its early years, Switzerland was a Roman province called Helvetia. It came into its present form around 1300, with the formation of the Swiss League. Now the league numbers twenty cantons (states) and six half-cantons. Switzerland has one of the highest standards of living in Europe. Its major industries are machinery, chemicals, and watchmaking.

Ukraine (Republic of Ukraine)
Population: 50,447,719 (1997 estimated). **Nationality:** noun: Ukranian(s); adjective: Ukranian. **Ethnic groups:** Ukranian, Russian, Jewish. **Languages:** Ukranian (official), Russian, Romanian, Polish, Hungarian. **Religions:** Christian: Ukranian Orthodox, Ukranian Autocephalous Orthodox, Ukranian Catholic, Protestant; Judaism, Islam. **Area:** 233,089 sq. mi. (603,700 sq km); about twice the size of Arizona.
Profile: The Ukraine is the third largest country in the Commonwealth of Independent States (Russia) and the most densely populated of the former Soviet republics. Established in the 800s, Ukraine is the heartland of ancient Russia and the center for Ukranian Orthodox religion. Its people are called East Slavs or "Little Russians." Kiev, the capital and cultural center of the Ukraine, is considered the Mother of Russian cities. It is an ancient Christian city with many cathedrals and monuments that date back to the eleventh and twelfth centuries. The Ukraine contributes beets, grain, coal, and iron to the Commonwealth.

Student Passport to World Cultures

United Kingdom (United Kingdom of Great Britain and Northern Ireland)
Population: 57,591,677 (1997 estimated).
Nationality: noun: Briton(s), British (collective plural); adjective: British. **Ethnic groups:** English, Scottish, Irish, Welsh, Ulster, West Indian, Indian, Pakistani, other.
Languages: English, Welsh, Scottish form of Gaelic. **Religions:** 27 million Anglican; 5.3 million Roman Catholic; 2.0 million Presbyterian; 760,000 Methodist; 450,000 Jewish. **Area:** 94,525 sq. mi. (244,820 sq km); slightly smaller than Oregon.
Profile: Many factors have shaped British culture. Its four countries (England, Scotland, Wales, and Ireland) share a varied geography and a mild, wet climate. The rich British culture has roots in invaders' cultures. These include Celts, Romans, Vikings, and French. Britain has shared its culture with many other countries. This includes the United States and other former colonies. Many countries use the principles of law and government developed in Britain. The Industrial Revolution begun in Great Britain changed most world cultures. Many British writers are loved all over the world. Today, Britain has emerged from two world wars as a modern industrial power. The British enjoy a high level of social support from the government. Everyday life in Britain includes typically British sports like rugby and cricket, unique customs, and excellent schools.

United States of America

Population: 267,954,764 (1997 estimated).
Nationality: noun: American(s); adjective: American. **Ethnic groups:** white, black, Asian or Pacific Islander, American Indian, Eskimo, or Aleut. **Languages:** English; large Spanish-speaking minority. **Religions:** 56% Protestant, 28% Roman Catholic, 10% none, 2% Jewish,

4% other. **Area:** 3,618,770 sq. mi. (9,372,610 sq km); fourth-largest country.
Profile: The United States is one of the largest and strongest countries in the world. Its geography changes greatly from the Pacific Ocean on the west coast to the Atlantic Ocean on the east coast. Deserts, forests, mountains, and plains are all included. The United States is an international economic leader. It is the world's second-largest producer, and number-one exporter, of grain. Other natural resources include coal, copper, lead, uranium, gold, iron, nickel, silver, crude oil, natural gas, and timber. Major industries in the United States include petroleum, steel, motor vehicles, aerospace, telecommunications, chemicals, electronics, food processing, consumer goods, fishing, lumber, and mining.

Vietnam (Socialist Republic of Vietnam)

Population: 75,123,880 (1997 estimated).
Nationality: noun: Vietnamese (singular, plural); adjective: Vietnamese. **Ethnic groups:** Vietnamese, Chinese; ethnic minorities include Muong, Thai, Meo, Khmer, Man, Cham, other mountain groups. **Languages:** Vietnamese (official), French, Chinese, English, Khmer, ethnic languages (Mon-Khmer and Malayo-Polynesian). **Religions:** Buddhist, Confucian, Taoist, Roman Catholic. **Area:** 127,243 sq. mi. (329,560 sq km); about the size of Virginia and North and South Carolina combined.
Profile: The Chinese first ruled the Vietnamese by the year 111. In the 1800s, the French ruled them. With the French withdrawal in 1954, Vietnam was divided into North and South. The two countries fought for over a decade. The United States and the Soviet Union were also involved. In 1975 North and South Vietnam were reunited

under Communist rule. The Vietnamese people have borrowed traditions from China, France, and India. They tend to be shy. They greet people with a slight bow and with the palms of their hands open. The teachings of Confucius have influenced the rural people, and they live simply. Vietnam's chief crops are rice, corn, potatoes, rubber, soybeans, and coffee. Its major industries are food processing, textiles, and machine-building.

Wales (Constituent Principality of the United Kingdom of Great Britain and Northern Ireland)

Profile: The history of Wales involves many struggles. Some invaders came from inside Britain and some from outside. The land has been controlled by Romans, Saxons, Picts, Vikings, and Norman French. Finally, in 1536, the Act of Union made it a principality within Britain. Wales's climate is temperate. Its terrain includes high plateaus with mountain ranges cut through by river valleys. It is a land of small farms. In the mountains and moors, sheep farming is a major occupation. Along the coast, dairy and mixed farming are the rule. Among Wales's old heavy industries, even coal mining has almost ceased in Wales. *See also* United Kingdom.

Zimbabwe (Republic of Zimbabwe)

Population: 11,423,175 (1997 estimated). **Nationality:** noun: Zimbabwean(s); adjective: Zimbabwean. **Ethnic groups:** African (Shona, Ndebele, other), white, mixed and Asian. **Languages:** English (official), ChiShona, Si Ndebele. **Religions:** 50% syncretic (part Christian, part indigenous beliefs), 25% Christian, 24% indigenous beliefs, 1% Muslim. **Area:** 150,803 sq. mi. (390,580 sq km); slightly larger than Montana.

Profile: In 1880 Englishman Cecil Rhodes forced the Matabele, a Bantu ethnic group, to surrender ownership of their land to the British. These lands were combined with what is now Zambia. Together they were called Rhodesia. At the end of the 1800s, the countries were divided into Northern and Southern Rhodesia. After black Africans defeated Rhodesia's white supremacy regime in 1980, Southern Rhodesia became the independent country of Zimbabwe. (Northern Rhodesia became Zambia.) The middle of Zimbabwe is a high plateau; the edges are lowlands. The climate is mild and the soil rich. Most people farm. Since the tsetse fly is not a problem, herders raise cattle and sheep for meat. Zimbabwe's chief crops are tobacco, corn, tea, sugar, and cotton. Its natural resources are coal, chromium ore, asbestos, gold, and nickel. The major industries are mining, steel, clothing, and footwear manufacturing.

Handbook of Literary Terms

A

act the separate sections of a play

action what goes on in a story

alliteration the repetition of initial consonant sounds

allusion something referring to a historical event, a person, a place, or a work of literature

almanac a calendar and date book

anecdote a short, funny story

animal imagery a literary device that uses animal-like descriptions to tell about a person

antagonist a person or thing in the story struggling against the main character

aphorism a wise and clever saying

assonance the repetition of vowel sounds

autobiography a person's life story written by that person

B

ballad a simple song that often uses a refrain and sometimes uses rhyme and is passed from person to person

biography a person's life story told by someone else

blank verse unrhymed iambic pentameter

by-line a line in a news article that tells who wrote it

C

character a person in a story

characterization the way a writer develops characters by revealing personality traits

chorus a group of actors who comment on and explain the action in a play

classical drama the rules that define the form of a play

climax an event that triggers the comic or tragic ending of a play

column a regularly appearing article in a periodical

comedy a play with a nontragic ending

coming-of-age story a story that tells how a young person matures

conflict a struggle the main character of a story has

connotation images or emotions connected to a word

consonance the repetition of consonant sounds usually within the context of several words

contemporary current or recent literature

couplet a rhyming pair

D

denouement the resolution to a story

detective story a story in which the main character solves a crime

dialect a regional variety of a language

dialogue the conversation among characters in a story; the words that characters in a play speak

diary a record of personal events, thoughts, or private feelings

drama a play

dramatic monologue a poem in which a character talks to the reader

E

editorial a news writer's personal opinion about an event or topic

elegy a poem that mourns someone's death

end rhyme a feature of a poem or song in which the last words of two lines rhyme with one another

epic a long story written in verse

essay a written work that shows a writer's opinions on some basic or current issue

exaggeration a use of words to make something seem worse than it is; stretching the truth to a great extent

excerpt a short passage from a longer piece of writing

expressionistic drama a play that may seem realistic but that changes some elements for dramatic effect

F

fable a short story or poem with a moral, often with animals who act like humans

fantasy stories in which wizards and other creatures participate

feature story a news story that analyzes the effect and importance of an event

fiction writing that is imaginative and designed to entertain

figurative language language that makes a comparison and is not meant to be taken literally

first person written as if someone is telling the story

flashback a look into the past at some point in a story

folktale a story that has been handed down from one generation to another

free verse poetry that does not have a strict rhyming pattern or regular line length, and uses actual speech patterns for the rhythms of sound

G

genre a kind of literature

ghost writer someone paid to write a person's autobiography and let that person take the credit

H

haiku a Japanese poetry form, made of seventeen unrhymed syllables

Harlem Renaissance a literary movement within modern literature that focuses on African American pride

historical fiction writing that draws on factual events of history

humor literature created to be funny

humorist someone who writes funny works

hyperbole a gross exaggeration

I

iambic pentameter five two-beat sounds in a line of poetry

image a word or phrase that appeals to the senses and allows the reader to picture events

imagery pictures created by words; the use of words that appeal to the senses

immediate news stories on TV and in newspapers as the event happens

Internet a worldwide network of computers that speak a common language

irony the use of words that seem to say one thing but mean the opposite

J

joke a short story that ends with a punchline

journal writing that records a writer's first impressions about a subject

journalism the gathering and communicating of news to the public

L

legend a traditional story that once was told orally and was handed down from one generation to another

letter impressions and feelings written to a specific person

limerick a humorous five-line poem

local color a kind of writing that reflects the way people speak, dress, and behave, and the customs popular in certain places

lullaby a soothing song or poem sung to a baby

M

metaphor a figure of speech that says one thing *is* another; a figure of speech that makes a comparison

modernism a literary movement in the twentieth century that focuses on trying to explain the many changes of the modern world

monologue a longer story told in person

mood the feeling that writing creates

moral a message in a story

myth a story that explains how some things in the natural world came to be

N

narrator the teller of a story

naturalism a literary movement that focuses on the survival of the fittest against nature and features characters as being helpless against events that are beyond human control and understanding

neoclassical recent plays written in the classical form

news cycle the length of time between the publishing of a news item and an update or reaction to the item

news story the first reports of an event; mainly covers the bare facts

nonfiction writing about real people and events

novel fiction that is book-length and has more plot and character details than a short story

O

onomatopoeia the use of a word to imitate a sound

P

pamphlet a short printed essay about a specific problem; it has no cover or has a paper cover

parody an exaggerated look at a situation

pen name a false name used for writing

personal essay a kind of writing that explores the author's opinion of a topic in a light and often entertaining way

personification giving human characteristics to a nonhuman object

persuasive meant to influence

playwright the author of a play

plot the series of events in a story

poem a short piece of literature that usually has rhythm and paints powerful or beautiful impressions with words

point of view the position from which the author or storyteller tells the story

proclamation letters about important events meant to be read aloud

prop piece of equipment used on stage during a play

prose written language that is not verse

prose poem an open form of poetry that is written as prose rather than as traditional poetry

protagonist the main character in a story

pun humorous use of words or phrases

Handbook of Literary Terms

R

realism a literary movement in which authors write about life as it is, not as they wish it to be

realistic drama a play that tells a story just as it might happen in real life

refrain the repetition of words or phrases to create mood or emphasis

regionalism a word or phrase that comes from a particular area

requiem a prayer for the dead; a work that has been written in honor of the dead

rhyme words with the same vowel and ending sounds

rhyme scheme a pattern of end rhymes in a poem

rhythm a regular pattern of stressed and unstressed syllables

rising action the buildup of excitement in a story

romanticism a literary movement marked by the excitement of learning, the sense of hopefulness, the spirit of individual freedom, strong morals, deeply personal thoughts, emotional sincerity, an interest in nature, and an interest in the unusual and the original

routine a longer story that a storyteller uses over and over in a live performance

S

sarcasm a heavy, sometimes mean-spirited kind of irony

satire humorous writing that makes fun of foolishness or evil

"sci-fi" a kind of science fiction that predicts what the future might be like

science fiction a type of literature that deals with people, places, and events that could not happen in our reality

semiautobiography a story based on a person's life written by that person, with some events changed

sequence the order of events in a literary work

setting the time and place in a story

short story a brief prose narrative

sidebar research and analysis of a news story

simile a figure of speech that makes a comparison using the words *like* or *as*

sketch a brief writing that often runs from subject to subject and is often humorous

sonnet a fourteen-line poem divided into four sections, in iambic pentameter

speech a written work meant to be read aloud

spiritual a religious and emotional song developed among enslaved Africans in the South during the middle of the 1800s

stanza a group of lines that forms a unit and often has the same rhythm and rhyme pattern

stereotype a simplified idea about another person or group

stream of consciousness a writing technique that develops the plot by allowing the reader to see how and what the characters are thinking

style an author's way of writing

subtitle a second, less important title under the first that gives more information about the writing

surrealism a writing style that is meant to be understood by a reader's subconscious

symbol a person, place, or thing that represents an idea or thought

symbolism the larger meaning of a person, place, or object

T

theme the main idea of a literary work

third person a point of view that refers to characters as "he" or "she" and expresses some characters' thoughts

tone the attitude an author takes toward a subject

tragedy a play in which the main character is destroyed

transcendentalism a literary movement in which the spiritual world has greater value than the material world and the individual is of great importance

turning point a story about an experience that changes a literary character's life

V

verse word patterns that follow definite rhythm and rhyme

villanelle a nineteen-line poem with several repeating rhymes

W

Web site a place on the Internet where information is published

Glossary

abandoned no longer lived in, 127

abhor to dislike intensely; to find disgusting, 268

abject humble; without self-respect, 114; miserable, 212

abolish to put an end to, 338

abreast side by side; in an even line, 181

abruptly suddenly; all of a sudden, 89, 132

abstinence stopping oneself from doing something; self-denial, 96

abstract not practical; not related to real life, 112

acclaim to praise, 331

accordance agreement, 169, 322

accost to approach and speak to in challenging way, 186

adamant refusing to change or move, 38

addicted controlled by a bad habit, 256

adequately well enough, 163

administer to manage, 68

admirable worth admiration, 357

admonish to warn; to scold with a warning, 180

adolescent a teenager or young person, 146

adversary an enemy, 339

aerial an antenna for receiving radio or TV, 354

affected artificial; assumed to impress others, 146

affectionate showing loving, fond feelings for someone, 144

affectionately with love and tenderness, 241

affections emotions or feelings, 273

affluent rich; having plenty of money, 111

aflame burning, 48

agenda a list of things to be done, 210

agitation strong emotion; disturbance, 25

ailment a sickness; an illness, 45, 245

air to discuss in public, 217

alarming frightening, 218

alms charity; a hand-out, 372

ambling slow-moving, 93

amiable friendly, 53

amniotic sac a pouch that holds a developing baby before it is born, 357

ample enough to satisfy, 186

amusement entertainment, 63

analysis a study of how parts fit together, 329

analyzing examining; studying the parts of, 40

anew again, 339

antedate to come before, 60

anthology a collection of writings, 329

anticipated expected, 210

aphrodisiac a food or drug that brings about sexual desire, 359

apology an expression of regret for something one has done, 261

appalled filled with horror or dismay, 256

apparent easily understood, 171

appliance a piece of household equipment, such as a toaster, stove, or microwave, 391

application a way to use something, 215

appropriations public money to be spent on certain things, 57

aptitude a natural ability or talent, 72

aquatic living in or on water, 386

archduke a royal rank equal to that of a prince, 395

aright correctly, 97

aristocratic of high social class, 27; noble or superior in appearance, 204

armaments weapons, 226

arms weapons, 222

arrogant overly proud in a self-important way, 41

arsenal a storehouse for weapons, 218

artillery branch of the military armed with large guns, 27

askew to one side, 95

assault to attack, 47

assimilate to take in, 322

assimilation being taken in by a group, 109

associating being with; keeping company, 113

asunder into separate parts, 339

at loggerheads an expression meaning "quarreling," 270

audacity boldness; daring, 253

austere stern and serious, 182

averted looking away, 26; turned away, 131

babble to make a low, quiet sound like water, 385

baboon a large monkey, 28

backbreaking very difficult, 217

backtrack to go back the way one came, 188

baffled confused, 166

balk to stop and refuse to go, 177

banality the quality of having little meaning, 359, 380

bandy to talk back and forth, 406

bantam a small barnyard fowl, 302

bathrobelike like a robe worn after a bath, 385

battalion a large group of soldiers, 398

bawling crying loudly, 180

beckon to summon by gesturing, 178

begone a command meaning "go away," 245

behalf interest, 239

belaboring going over again and again, 340

belligerent marked by hostile or warlike behavior, 189

belongings personal possessions, 404

beneficial doing good; helpful, 121

benzene a colorless, flammable liquid, 176

bequeath to give to, as in a will, 27

betel an Asian plant whose leaves are chewed, 292

bewitch to fascinate, 272

bigoted stubbornly holding a belief and disliking those who disagree, 324

billiards a game similar to pool, played with a cue and solid balls on a large oblong table with raised edges, 267

blanch to turn pale, 30

blockade something that stops movement in and out of an area, 212

blurt to say suddenly and without thinking, 179

boarding house a place to live where one pays for a room and meals, 253

bosom the breast of a human, 192

bottleneck something that slows progress, 62

boutique a small shop that sells special, often expensive, goods, 355

Glossary

brandish to wave about in a threatening way, 331, 408

breach a failure to live up to a promise, 241; a break, 332

breadth width; extent, 130, 404

breakthrough a major accomplishment, 61

breeching strap of harness behind a horse's rear legs, 95

brood to think moodily about something, 245

buffet a restaurant in which people serve themselves from a counter, 407

bugger a slang word meaning companion or chap, 253

burr a rough or prickly covering around a nut, 128

cadence a rhythm of speech, 58

calculate to plan, 48

calculation a mathematical process or answer, 67

calligraphy fine handwriting, 70

candelabra a candle holder with several branches, 44

capability the ability to do something, 211

capillary a tiny blood vessel, 386

capricious acting on impulse; hard to predict, 59

captivate to fascinate; to interest deeply, 176

caress a gentle touch, 101

caste a social class, 330

catastrophic terrible, 58

celestial heavenly, 36

ceremoniously with formal ceremony, 44

certify to confirm that standards have been met, 72

champagne a sparkling white wine made in France, 45

charitable generous, 109

cheetah a wild spotted cat, 28

cherished kept fondly in mind, 147

chestnut a type of tree that has nuts enclosed in a prickly casing, 127

chiffonier a high chest of drawers, often with a mirror, 269

Christendom all Christianity; the land in which most people are Christians, 318

christening a ceremony for naming and baptizing a child, 271

chronic constant; continuing for a long time, 114, 245

cicada a type of large insect; the males make a loud, humming noise, 385

cipher a zero, 53

circumstance an event; a situation, 374

circumstances conditions, 63; the way someone lives, 145

circumstantial depending on the surrounding conditions, 46

civil service civilian workers of the government, 166

civility courtesy, 340

clanging ringing, 30

cleansed clean; free of dirt, 349

cliché an expression or idea that has been used over and over, 357

client a customer; a person for whom one does a professional service, 24

clod a lump or chunk of dirt, 160

coincidence an accident that makes events seem related, 46

collective grouped together, 326

commentary an explanation; a series of remarks, 378

commiserate to express sorrow and sympathy, 120

commit to do or perform, 42, 243

commonwealth the community as a whole; the nation, 372

communion a sharing of feelings, 163

compass limited area, 94

compatriot a person from one's own country, 326

compel to force, 63

compelling forceful, 186

compensate to repay, 345

competitive involving the effort to win, 169

compile to put together information into a record, 75

completion ending, 210

compliance yielding to a demand, 184

complicated not simple; not easy to understand, 56, 78, 395

complicity state of being involved in a wrong action, 332

compose to make quiet or calm, 38

comprehensive knowing, 25

compulsion the force or reason behind an action, 212

compute to find a number; to work mathematical problems, 54; to count, 373

concealment a state of being hidden, 39

concede to give up, 42

conceive to form in the mind, 336

conception an idea; a mental picture, 329

concisely briefly, 331

concussion a shock; an injury, 322

condescension an attitude of being better than someone else, 37

confidential meant to be secret, 402

confirm to give proof, 203

conflict a battle; the fighting, 127

confounded confused; puzzled, 181

congregate to collect or gather, 187

conjecture a guess, 44

conscientious careful to do things right, 70, 102

consecrate to dedicate to a serious purpose, 336

consequence importance, 29

consequently as a result, 53

conservative not liking change, 59

constellation a pattern of stars that form a picture, 72

constitute to make up, 330

constraint force that limits freedom of thought or action, 323

constructively helpfully, 221

consumption the process of eating or drinking, 70; buying, 380

contemplate to look at thoughtfully, 180

contemporary living at the same time, 326

contemptuous showing scorn, 268

contemptuously with scorn, 46

context the setting or situation, 216

contorted twisted; hard to follow, 151

contradict to say both one thing and its opposite, 57

contrivance a mechanical device, 60

convent a community of nuns, 110

convey to bring or carry, 160

convict to find guilty, 42

convulsed shaken or pulled jerkily, 30

convulsively shaking violently, 321

coolie an unskilled worker who does odd jobs, 171

cope to manage successfully, 166

coppice a dense growth of bushes; a small wood, 96

cormorant a water bird, 386

coroner the official who decides the cause of death, 32

correlate to show a relationship, 331

corrugate to wrinkle, 55

corrupt dishonest, 210

corrupt to spoil; to make less honest or moral, 112

cosmopolitan including people from many places, 117

coterie a group of people who meet often, 180

counterbalance to use one act to make up for another, 345

couple to attach; to link together, 407

courtesy an act of politeness, 169

courtyard an open space surrounded by buildings or walls, 43

coverage the way something is reported in newspapers or on television, 68

cowed frightened by threats, 129

credence belief; proof, 186

criminologist a person who studies crime and criminal behavior, 38

criticism a judgment that finds fault, 397

cruelty something that causes pain or suffering, 148

crusty gruff; stern in manner, 298

cubicle a small room, 182

currency the form of money a country uses, 349

curry a food dish seasoned with curry powder, 169

curtail to cut short, 325

dash to run quickly, 128

data information, 57, 68

deadening making less intense or lively, 151

debark to get off, as from a ship, 80

debased lowered in worth, 379

decade a period of ten years, 352

deceit a trick, 321

decrepit worn out, 332

deduction an answer found by reasoning, 24

defensive done to defend oneself, 211

deference courteous respect for another's wishes, 122, 374

definitively finally; completely, 378

defray to pay the costs, 26

degenerate to become much worse, 328

deliberately slowly; with care, 43; carefully considered; on purpose, 215, 253

delicacy a rare or special food, 45; a special, enjoyable food, 188

delicious delightful, 154

delusion a false or imaginary belief, 247

depart to leave; to go away, 288

deplorable terrible, 372

deployment the spreading of troops or weapons in a larger area, 218

depravity a wicked act, 328

depression a state of sadness, 359

deserted empty, 172

designate to select for a role, 71

despise to look down on, 261

despite in spite of, 212, 396

destiny fate; a person's fate or future, 105, 192

detached not connected, 328

detachment a small military unit of soldiers, 128

deterrent something that prevents or discourages an action, 217

detonation an explosion, 222

detract to take away, 336

detrimental harmful, 325

development growth; progress, 215

dictatorial having the powers of a strong, single ruler, 380

differentiate to show a difference between, 324

dilapidated shabby from neglect, 350

dilemma a situation that requires a difficult choice, 327

director a person who directs or manages a business, 404

disability a weakened physical or mental condition, 245

disastrous causing disaster, 325

disbelief a refusal to believe, 253

disburse to pay out or hand out, 72

disciplinarian a person who strictly carries out rules, 380

discipline punishment given as a correction, 185

disciplined trained to act according to certain rules, 338

discomfort the feeling of being uneasy or not comfortable, 353

disconcertingly in an upsetting way, 119

disconsolate very sad, 267

discord arguments, disagreements, 205

discordance a harsh, confused sound, 322

discordant unpleasant; disturbing, 270

discourse to discuss, 374

discrepancy a difference; a conflict, 321

disembark to get out of a craft, such as a boat or plane, 349

disfigured marred or spoiled, 188

disinfection getting rid of germs that can cause diseases, 78

dismissive in a manner that discards or sends away, 323

disoblige to go against the wishes of, 375

disparity difference, 324

dispatch to send out, 78; to send off quickly to a place, 402

dispel to make disappear, 32

dispensable not necessary, 63

disperse to scatter in different directions, 332

displacedness a state of being out of place or in the wrong place, 357

disputation a discussion or debate, 151

disrupt to upset or interfere, 112

dissolute wicked; of bad character, 26

dissuade to persuade someone not to take a certain action, 212

dissuasion discouraging someone from an action, 120

distinguished appearing important or famous, 203

distorted twisted, 38

divergent drawing apart; differing, 322

diversion something that entertains, 387

divert to turn aside, 59

divine coming from a god, 163

dog-cart a cart pulled by one horse with room for two passengers, 25

domination control or rule of one person or group by another, 353

draught (Amer. draft) a current of air, 269

dubious causing doubt as to worth or truth, 396

dumbfounded stunned into silence, 324

dunce a stupid person, 118

duration the period of time that something lasts, 379

dynamic full of energy; changing, 328

dystrophy illness caused by poor nutrition, 71

eavesdrop to listen secretly, 113

ebbing fading away; becoming less, 260

eccentrically oddly, not in an expected way, 71

ecliptic circle formed where the plane of earth's orbit and another object cross, 71

effective having the desired result, 285

electric eel a long, thin fish that can produce an electric current, 198

eliminate to get rid of, 62

embalm to preserve, 179

embattled locked in a struggle, 53; ready for battle, 341

embrace to adopt; to welcome, 190

emit to send out, 102

emotionally with strong feelings, 204

enclosure an area inside a fence or wall, 43

encroached gradually entered or occupied, 321

endeavor a sincere attempt, 341

endow to provide with a talent or quality, 403

engulf to swallow up; to surround completely, 339

enlarge to make larger, 285

ensign a flag, 379

entailing resulting in, 375

enthuse to show excitement or interest, 114

entice to tempt, 327

epithet an insulting word or phrase, 380

epoch a long period of history, 321

equality state of being equal, 62

equalize to make equal, 345

equivalent something that is equal, 58

eradicate to get rid of, 340

escalation an increase or rapid growth, 226

essence the basic quality of something, 330

esteem to think highly of, 374

etherealization making things lighter, 60

eucalyptus a tall tree with strong-smelling leaves, 171

evader a person who avoids doing something, 210

evaluate to judge the worth of, 322

evenly without a change in tone, 255

exaggerate to make something greater or more serious than it really is, 146

exasperating annoying, 323

excessive too much, 122

excursion a trip; an expedition, 74, 104

executive the branch of government that carries out the laws, 217

exigency something demanding immediate attention, 63

existential based on real experience, 205

expectantly eagerly waiting to hear or see something, 259

expenditure spending, 211

expletive a curse, 155

explicitness a very frank or clear statement, 113

exploitation the unfair use of a person or resource for selfish purposes, 323, 353

exportation being sent to another country for sale, 375

extinguish to put out, 151

extraneous not necessary, 73

extraordinary remarkable; very unusual, 167, 354

facet one part or angle, 326

faltering hesitating in movement, 48

famine a severe lack of food, 408

fancy imagination, 95

federation an association of states, 57

feign to pretend, 102

fervent showing deep feeling, 109

fiancé a French term meaning a man engaged to be married, 268

fiasco a complete failure, 254

fickle not faithful; not reliable, 159

filth foul matter; dirt, 260

financial having to do with money, 111

finery elegant, dressy clothing, 197

finite limited, 58

fit a sudden violent outburst, 243

fitful restless, 38

flamethrower a military weapon that sends out a stream of burning fuel, 387

flawless perfect; without any marks, 239

flicker to give off unsteady light, 47

fluently using language easily, 119

fodder dry food for farm animals, 129

footwear anything worn on the feet, 384

foppishly vainly; overly proud of one's looks, 182

fore the front part, 374

forebear an ancestor, 338

formalise (Amer. formalize) to make official; to sign an agreement, 221

formalities official rules; customs, 80

formulate to plan, 340

forsaken abandoned; left alone, 123

forthwith immediately, 211

fortnight a period of two weeks, 28

foyer an entrance hall, 43

fragrance sweetness of smell, 171

frank bluntly honest, 349

frenzy a wild excitement, 88

fricassee a dish made with cut-up pieces of meat in gravy, 373

frivolously not seriously; playfully, 327

function a normal use or activity, 358

function to work properly, 73

fundamentals the basics, 62

futon a thin mattress usually used on the floor or on a frame, 385

gab a slang word meaning to talk; to chatter, 397

gangly tall, thin, and ungraceful, 298

garnish to add extras to a serving of food, 46

gash a long deep cut, 241

gemstone a jewel, 163

gendarme a police officer, 406

gender sex; male or female, 71

gild to cover with gold, 36

glimmer to give off a dim light, 54

global alliance an agreement among world nations, 341

global worldwide, 217

Glossary

glorified made to seem more important than is really true, 38

glorify to give honor or high praise, 111

Gold Mountain Chinese immigrants' name for the United States, 198

gory stained with blood, 241

gourd a kind of vegetable that grows on a vine, 127

graveyard a place where people are buried, 285

gravity seriousness, 47, 225

graybeards old men, 292

grievance something to complain about, 372

grieve to cause harm or sadness, 305

grubby dirty, 379

grudgingly unwillingly, 122

guarantor a person or thing that promises a certain result, 226

haggard looking worn because of worry, 25; looking thin and tired, 57

hallow to set apart as holy, 336

handpicked chosen carefully, 407

harmony agreement, 146; a pleasant agreement in feeling or actions, 358

hastily quickly, 90

hatred strong dislike or hate, 291

hazard something dangerous, 73

headmistress female principal of a school, 166

hearsay gossip, 406

heartfelt deeply felt; sincere, 259

heartily with enthusiasm, 267

hearty sincere, 239

hectic confused; full of fast activity, 177

heighten to make more intense, 161

heir person who inherits something from the person who once had it, 338

hence from this time, 185; from here, 318

herbalist a person who makes medicines from herbs, 121

heritage what is handed down from earlier generations, 338

hesitate to hold back, 131

Hindi languages widely spoken in India, 167

hoard to save for the future, 299

holster a case for a pistol, 100

holy writ a piece of religious writing; the Bible, 299

homily a sermon, 120

hooligan a troublemaker; a young man who does vicious or violent acts, 403

hornswoggling tricking someone, 56

hospitality the friendly treatment of guests, 28

hostile angrily opposed to, 122

hubbub confusion, 30

humidity the amount of moisture in the air, 69

humiliating causing shame or loss of dignity, 323

humiliation the state of being disgraced or shamed, 186

hydroponics a method of growing plants in water, 60

hyperactive very active, 386

hypothesis an idea that needs to be proved, 44

idealism belief that things can be perfect, 111

identical exactly the same, 47

illiterate not knowing how to read or write, 192

illusionist a magician, 54

immemorial beyond the limits of memory, 321

imminent about to happen, 324

immortal one who lives forever, 199

impaled speared; stuck on a sharp stick, 298

impasse a road with no way out, 45

impassive not moving; not showing any feeling, 37

impending about to happen, 30

impenetrable thick; not possible to get through, 39; not able to be pierced or broken, 58

imperative commanding, 54

impetuous hasty; quick to act, 36

impingement the act of intruding or disturbing, 59

implore to beg, 123

importuning begging, 372

impoverish to make poor, 326

improvise to invent or put together on the spur of the moment, 79

in earnest sincere, 154

inability lack of ability, 166

incalculable not possible to measure in advance, 58

incandescent glowing; very bright, 298

incapable without the ability, 121

incarnation the solid or human form of an idea, 46

incessantly continuing without stopping, 36, 145

incision a thin cut, 105

inclemency storms; discomforts, 375

inclination a leaning toward something, 327

incomprehensible not capable of being understood, 168

incomprehension lack of understanding, 324

incredible too unlikely to be believed, 349

incredulously in surprise; not believing, 112

incur to bring upon oneself, 375

indifferent not caring one way or another, 42, 68

indignity an insult; shameful treatment, 38

indistinct not clear, 95

indivisibility state of not being able to be divided, 328

indoctrination the teaching of a certain point of view, 330

induce to persuade, 37

ineligible not qualified, 184

ineradicable impossible to erase or remove, 104

inevitable sure to happen, 96, 375

inevitably in a way that can't be prevented, 43

inexorably in a way that can't be stopped, 40, 331

inexplicable not possible to explain, 129

infectious capable of causing infection, 205

infer to conclude, 205

infinitely without any limits, 120

inflexible stiff; rigid, 102

infuriating causing great anger, 253

ingenuity cleverness; inventive skill, 353

inkling a hint; a suggestion, 183

innermost most personal; deepest, 147

inscrutable mysterious; hard to understand, 37

insignificant small; not important, 151

insolence a rude or insulting attitude, 406

tangential a point or line that touches, but doesn't cross, another, 73

taro a plant grown for its edible, starchy root, 159

taxing tiring; difficult, 357

temerity foolish boldness, 328

tendency a pattern of doing things a certain way, 77

tension an uneasy or angry relationship, 221; the condition of being stretched, 329

tentatively with hesitation, 113

tepid slightly warm, 170

terrestrial referring to the earth and its people, 57

theological related to the study of religion, 121

thicken to become deeper or denser, 291

thrash to beat or strike, 199

threshold an entrance or beginning, 218

tiara a small crown, 26

ticked off a slang term meaning to be annoyed or angry, 387

till to make land ready for growing crops, 130

tirade a long, violent, scolding speech, 187

tirelessly constantly; without stopping, 40

to wit an expression meaning "that is to say," 154

toast a speech made along with a drink to honor someone, 241

togs clothes, 178

tolerable able to be endured, 323

tolerably sufficiently; enough, 374

tonga a wagon, 171

touched affected, 204

traditional referring to customs followed for many years, 384

trait a quality of character; a peculiarity, 177

tranquillity calm, 148

transcribe to make a copy of, 77

transplant to lift and replant in another area, 160

tribulation suffering, 341

tribune a platform from which to speak to a group, 325

trireme an ancient Greek or Roman warship, 60

trivial not important, 26

tuft a small clump of hair, 102

tussle to struggle; to wrestle, 179

tyrannous unfair; severe; cruel, 185

tyranny rule by a harsh, powerful government, 339

unaccountably mysteriously; without explanation, 94

unbearable painful; hard to endure, 203

uncluttered empty; not filled with things, 198

undoing the destruction of something already accomplished, 338

unfulfilled not finished; not completed, 352

ungodly wicked or outrageous, 178

ungovernable not possible to control, 380

unhealthy dangerous, risky, 206

unhindered not prevented or stopped, 205

unilateral involving only one side in an issue, 221

union a marriage, 396

unleashed let loose; released, 339

unlovable difficult to love, 298

unnaturally unusually; in an unexpected way, 397

unprovable not possible to prove, 399

unrealistic not likely to happen in real life, 399

unsolicited not requested, 181

unspeakable too bad to be described, 269

unspeakableness a condition too bad to be described, 353

unsuspecting trusting; not suspicious, 87

unworthy not deserving, 298

uphold to maintain; to keep, 148

usher to conduct; to escort, 182; to show people the way, 398

utility a household service, such as electricity, telephone, or water, 390

valid completely acceptable; genuine, 167; reliable, 324

veal cutlet a thin slice of meat, 45

vehemently with strong emotion, 120; forcefully; violently, 189

veld the South African grassland, 180

ventilate to put in motion; to blow away, 402

ventilator a passage in a house that air is blown through, 31

veranda a roofed porch extending along the outside of a building, 167

via by way of, 385

vindication proof that clears away blame or guilt, 378

vintage a crop of grapes grown for wine, 345

violate to ruin by force, 318

violent hard; with great physical force, 39; intense, 270

violently with strong physical force or rough action, 260

visa a paper that permits a person to enter a country, 398

visionary imaginary; not practical, 375

visualize to imagine, 40

vital very important and necessary, 76

void a feeling of emptiness, 190

vulgarly in bad taste; crudely, 358

waning growing smaller, as the visible part of the moon, 70

warhead the front part of a missile or bomb that contains the explosive, 218

waver to be unsure, 147

weaponry different types of weapons seen as a group, 216

wen a small growth on the skin, 127

westernized influenced by European or American ways, 384

wethers sheep, 96

whereas while at the same time, 109

wholesome healthful, 373

widower a man whose wife has died, 130

wiry slender yet muscular, 182

withhold to keep back, 318

wizened dried up; wrinkled, 170, 180

woe misfortune; great sorrow, 87

wolf to eat hungrily, like an animal, 299

wrench to jerk, 39

wretched worthless; seen with scorn, 29; miserable; very unhappy, 272

writhe to twist as in pain, 30

yearn to wish for deeply, 291

ziggurat an ancient tower built something like a pyramid, 60

Index of Authors and Titles

Index of Authors and Titles

Index of Selections by Country

Index of Selections by Country

Index of Fine Art

Index

Index

Index

Index

Index

Acknowledgments

Acknowledgment is made for permission to reprint or record the following copyrighted material. Every effort has been made to determine copyright owners. In the case of any omissions, the publisher will be pleased to make suitable acknowledgments in future editions.

Pages 24-32: "The Adventure of the Speckled Band" from *The Complete Sherlock Holmes* by Sir Arthur Conan Doyle. Reprinted by permission of Sir Arthur Conan Doyle Copyright holders.

Pages 36-48: "Death Arrives on Schedule" by Hansjörg Martin, trans. by Charles E. Pederson. From *Blut an der Manschette*, ©1974 Hansjörg Martin. Used by permission of Rowohlt Verlag, Reinbek, Germany.

Pages 53-63: "The Feeling of Power" From THE BEST SCIENCE FICTION OF ISAAC ASIMOV by Isaac Asimov. Copyright © 1986 by Nightfall, Inc. Used by permission of Doubleday, a division of Bantam Doubleday Dell Publishing Group, Inc

Pages 67-81: "The Expedition" ("Die Expedition") by Rudolf Lorenzen, trans. by Charles E. Pederson. Reprinted by permission of Herbach & Haase Literarische Agentur.

Pages 86-90: "The Cegua," From *Short and Shivery: Thirty Chilling Tales* by Robert D. San Souci Illus. by Katherine Coville. Copyright ©1987 by Robert D. San Souci. Used by permission of Bantam Doubleday Dell Books for Young Readers.

Pages 93-97: From "Master and Man" by Leo Tolstoy from *Master and Man and Other Stories* trans. by Paul Foote (Penguin Classics, 1977) copyright © Paul Foote, 1977. Reproduced by permission of Penguin Books Ltd.

Pages 100-105: "Just Lather, That's All" by Hernando Téllez, trans. by Donald A. Yates from *Contemporary Latin American Short Stories* edited by Pat McNees. Reprinted by permission of Donald A. Yates and the estate of Beatriz Téllez.

Pages 109-114: From *Nervous Conditions* by Tsitsi Dangarembga. (Seattle: Seal Press, 1988) pp. 178-183. Used with permission.

Pages 117-123: Text: "Marriage Is a Private Affair" from *Girls at War and Other Stories* by Chinua Achebe. Copyright ©1972, 1973. Used by permission of Doubleday, a division of Bantam Doubleday Dell Publishing Group, Inc. and Harold Ober Associates Incorporated. Audio: "Marriage Is a Private Affair" from *Girls at War and Other Stories* by Chinua Achebe. Copyright © 1972 by Chinua Achebe. Reprinted by permission of Harold Ober Associates Incorporated.

Pages 127-132: "Cranes," From *Shadows of a Sound* ©1990 by Hwang Sun-won. Published by Mercury House, San Francisco, CA and reprinted by permission.

Pages 144-148: From *The Diary of a Young Girl: The Definitive Edition* by Anne Frank. Otto H. Frank & Mirjam Pressler, Editors, translated by Susan Massotty. Translation copyright ©1995 by Doubleday, a division of Bantam Doubleday Dell Publishing Group, Inc. Used by permission of Doubleday, a division of Bantam Doubleday Dell Publishing Group, Inc.

Page 151: "Letter to Indira Tagore," from *Rabindranath Tagore: An Anthology*, Krishna Dutta and Andrew Robinson eds./trans. (New York, 1997, St. Martin's Press.) Reprinted by permission of Andrew Robinson.

Pages 158-163: Text: From *When Heaven and Earth Changed Places* by Le Ly Hayslip. Copyright © 1989 by Le Ly Hayslip and Charles Jay Wurts. Used by permission of Doubleday, a division of Bantam Doubleday Dell Publishing Group, Inc. Audio: From *When Heaven and Earth Changed Places* by Le Ly Hayslip. Copyright © 1989 by Le Ly Hayslip with Jay Wurts. Reprinted by permission of Le Ly Hayslip, Jay Wurts and the Sandra Dijkstra Literary Agency.

Pages 166-172: "By Any Other Name" from *Gifts of Passage* by Santha Rama Rau. Copyright 1951 by Santha Rama Rau. Copyright renewed ©1979 by Santha Rama Rau. Reprinted by permission of HarperCollins Publishers, Inc. "By Any Other Name" originally appeared in *The New Yorker.*

Pages 176-192: Text: Reprinted with permission of Simon & Schuster from *Kaffir Boy* by Mark Mathabane. Copyright © 1986 by Mark Mathabane. Audio: Reproduced with the permission of Fifi Oscard Agency, Inc., from *Kaffir Boy* by Mark Mathabane. Copyright © 1986 by Mark Mathabane.

Pages 197-199: "The Father from China" from *China Men* by Maxine Hong Kingston. Copyright ©1980 by Maxine Hong Kingston. Reprinted by permission of Alfred A. Knopf Inc.

Pages 202-206: From *The Last Seven Months of Anne Frank* by Willy Lindwer translated by Alison Meersschaert. Copyright © 1991 by Willy Lindwer. Reprinted by permission of Pantheon Books, a division of Random House, Inc.

Pages 210-212: "Account Evened With India, Says PM: Pakistan Opts to Go Nuclear" by M. Ziauddin from *The Dawn* (Pakistan) 29 May 1998. Reprinted by permission.

Pages 215-218: "Tests Are Nowhere Near India's: Fernandes" from *The Times of India*, June 1,1998. Reprinted by arrangement with The Times of India and The Press Trust of India. No part of this may be reproduced, reprinted, transmitted or stored in any form or medium without

Acknowledgments

permission of the publishers, Bennett, Coleman & Co. Ltd, New Delhi, India.

Pages 221-222: "Pakistan Nuclear Moratorium Welcomed" from BBC Online Network, Friday, June 12, 1998. Reprinted by permission of BBC News Online. www.bbc.co.uk/news.

Page 225: "The Frightening Joy" from *DeVolkskrant* as appeared in World Press Review Vol. 45, Issue 8, August 1998. Reprinted by permission.

Page 226: "Building Atomic Security" by Tomasz Wroblewski as appeared in *World Press Review* Vol. 45, Issue 8, August 1998. Reprinted by permission.

Pages 238-246: "Macbeth" Act 3, Scene 4 from *The Complete Works of William Shakespeare* by William Shakespeare, the Cambridge text established by John Dover Wilson. Copyright ©The Cambridge text of the complete works of William Shakespeare. Cambridge University Press 1921, 1922, 1923, 1924, 1926, 1928, 1929, 1930, 1931, 1934, 1936, 1939, 1946, 1947, 1949, 1950, 1952, 1954, 1955, 1956, 1957, 1960, 1962, 1966. Reprinted with the permission of Cambridge University Press.

Pages 239-247: From *Shakespeare Made Easy: Macbeth* by William Shakespeare, edited and translated by Alan Durband. Copyright © 1984 Alan Durband. Reprinted by permission of Hutchinson & Co. Ltd and Barron's Educational Series, Inc.

Pages 252-262: From *"Master Harold"... and the Boys* by Athol Fugard. Copyright ©1982 by Athol Fugard. Reprinted by permission of Alfred A. Knopf, Inc.

Pages 267-273: *The Stronger*, by August Strindberg, trans. by Ants Oras. Translation ©Ants Oras.

Page 285: "The Diameter of the Bomb" from *The Selected Poetry of Yehuda Amichai* by Yehuda Amichai edited and trans. by Chana Bloch and Stephen Mitchell. Copyright ©1996 The Regents of the University of California. Reprinted by permission of The Regents of the University of California and Chana Bloch.

Page 288: "Taking Leave of a Friend" by Li Po from *Personae* by Ezra Pound. Copyright ©1926 by Ezra Pound. Reprinted by permission of New Directions Publishing Corp.

Pages 291-292: "Thoughts of Hanoi" from *A Thousand Years of Vietnamese Poetry* by Nguyen Thi Vinh, trans. by Nguyen Ngoc Bich with Burton Raffel and W. S. Mervin, ©1974. Reprinted by permission of The Asia Society.

Pages 294-295: "Mindoro" by Ramón C. Sunico from *This Same Sky* by Naomi Shihab Nye. Reprinted by permission of Ramón C. Sunico.

Pages 298-299: "Ode to a Pair of Socks" from *Odes to Common Things* by Pablo Neruda. Copyright ©1994 by Pablo Neruda and Pablo Neruda Fundacion (Odes in Spanish); Compilation and Illustrations ©by Ferris Cook; Odes (English translation) ©by Ken Krabbenhoft. By permission of Little, Brown and Company.

Page 302: Japanese haiku translated by Harry Behn. From *More Cricket Songs*. Copyright ©1971 Harry Behn. Used by permission of Marian Reiner.

Pages 305-306: "Do Not Go Gentle Into That Good Night" by Dylan Thomas, from *The Poems of Dylan Thomas*. Copyright © 1952 by Dylan Thomas. Reprinted by permission of New Directions Publishing Corp. Also from *Collected Poems* by Dylan Thomas. Reprinted by permission of David Higham Associates.

Page 318: "Letter to the English," From *Joan of Arc In Her Own Words* translated by Willard Trask. Copyright ©1996. Reprinted by permission of Books & Co./Turtle Point.

Pages 321-332: "Nobel Lecture" by Alexander Solzhenitsyn. ©The Nobel Foundation 1970. Reprinted by permission of The Nobel Foundation.

Page 345: From "On Repentance" from *Essays* by Michel de Montaigne, trans. by J. M. Cohen (Penguin Classics, 1958) copyright © J. M. Cohen, 1958. Reproduced by permission of Penguin Books Ltd.

Pages 348-359: Text: Excerpt from *A Small Place* by Jamaica Kincaid. Reprinted by permission of Farrar, Straus & Giroux, Inc. Audio: Excerpt from *A Small Place* by Jamaica Kincaid. Copyright © 1988 by Jamaica Kincaid, recorded with the permission of The Wylie Agency, Inc.

Pages 378-380: "Cup Inanity and Patriotic Profanity" by Andrew Graham-Yooll, "On Thursday" column, July 2, 1998, *Buenos Aires Herald*, (Founded 1876). Reprinted by permission of the author.

Pages 384-387: "Japanese Inns: Peace, Tranquillity, Insects," From *Dave Barry Does Japan* by Dave Barry. Copyright © 1992 by Dave Barry. Reprinted by permission of Random House, Inc.

Pages 390-391: "Why Can't We Have Our Own Apartment?" From *If Life Is a Bowl of Cherries, What Am I Doing in the Pits?* by Erma Bombeck. Reprinted by permission of The Aaron M. Priest Literary Agency, Inc.

Pages 395-399: "Lohengrin" by Leo Slezak, trans. by Charles E. Pederson. From *Der Wortbruch* by Leo Slezak. Copyright ©1927, 1959 by Rowohlt Verlag GmbH, Reinbek bei

Acknowledgments

Hamburg. Reprinted by permission of Sanford J. Greenburger Associates.

Pages 402-408: "A Wedding Without Musicians," reprinted from *Tevye's Daughters* by Sholom Aleichem. Copyright ©1949 by the children of Sholom Aleichem and Crown Publishers, Inc. Copyrights renewed 1977 by Crown Publishers, Inc. Reprinted by permission of Crown Publishers, Inc.

Images
Page 10, David Young-Wolff/PhotoEdit; p. 16 (top), Tony Freeman/PhotoEdit; p.16 (bottom), Myrleen Ferguson Cate/PhotoEdit; p. 18, Private Collection/John Kaufmann/SuperStock; p. 21, Judy King; p. 23, Brown Brothers; pp. 28, 29, 31, Rachel Taylor; p. 35, Carl Purcell/Corbis; pp. 37, 42, 46, PhotoDisc ©1999; p. 52, Brown Brothers; p. 54, James Harrington/Tony Stone Images; p. 55 Biondo Productions/Gamma Liaisons; p. 66, Carl Purcell/Corbis; p. 68, ©Tony Stone Images; p. 71, ©PHOTRI; p. 85, Robert D. San Souci; pp. 87, 89 Jeff Spackman; p. 92, The Granger Collection, New York; p. 94, Josef Mensing Gallery, Hamm-Rhynern/Bridgeman Art Library, London/SuperStock; p. 99, Gran Enciclopedie de Colombia; p. 100, ©Estate of Ilya Bolotowsky/Licensed by VAGA, New York, NY; p. 103, Kactus Foto/SuperStock; p. 108, The Women's Press, U.K.; p. 110, Reuters/Corbis-Bettmann; p. 111, ©Mark Peters/Gamma Liaison; p. 116, ©Steve Miller/New York Times; p. 118, Mike Wells/Tony Stone Worldwide; p. 126, Courtesy of the Korean Cultural Center, NY; p. 127, Underwood & Underwood/Corbis-Bettman; p. 132, Christie's Images/SuperStock; p. 138, Private collection/Beth Hinckley/ SuperStock; p. 141, Judy King; p. 143, ©SuperStock; pp. 145, 148, Associated Press/Worldwide; p. 150, The Granger Collection, New York; p. 151, Ben Edwards/Tony Stone Worldwide; p. 153, Brown Brothers; p. 155, Joel Iskowitz; p. 158, ©Alain Buu/Gamma; p. 159, Associate Press/Worldwide; p. 160, UPI/Corbis-Bettmann; p. 165, Archive Photos; pp. 166, 170, Sandy Rabinowitz; p. 175, Musee des Arts Africains et Oceaniens Paris/Explorer, Paris/SuperStock; pp. 177, 180, Hajima Ota; 183, Private Collection/Mathabane; 187, Jeanne Montassamy-Ashe; p. 196, Nancy Crampton; p. 199, Associated Press/Worldwide; pp. 201, 202, 205, 206, H. Pick-Goslar Foundation; p. 209, Rachel Taylor; p. 210, Saeed Ahmed/Associated Press/Worldwide; p. 214, Rachel Taylor; p. 218, Ajit Kumar/Associated Press/Worldwide; p. 220, ©Bob Clarke/Liaison International; p. 222, Agence France Presse; p. 224, Rachel Taylor; p. 225, Ajit Kumar/Associated Press/Worldwide; p. 232, Michelle Puleo/SuperStock; p. 235, Judy King; p. 237, National Portrait Gallery, London/SuperStock; p. 238, ©Victoria & Albert Museum, London/Art Resource, NY; p. 241, A.K.G., Berlin/SuperStock; p. 242, Corbis-Bettmann; p. 251, ©Archive Photos; p. 255, ©1983 Gerry Goodstein; p. 257, Archive Photos; p. 266, Brown Brothers; p. 269, National Museum of American Art, Washington DC/Art Resource, NY; p. 272, ©Stock Montage, Inc.; p. 280, David David Gallery, Philadelphia/David David Gallery/SuperStock; p. 283, Judy King; p. 284, Nancy Crampton; p. 285, Ian O'Leary/Tony Stone Images; p. 287, Liang Kai, by permission of China Span; p. 288, ©Bill Mitchell; p. 290, ©SuperStock; p. 291, Mark Lewis/Tony Stone Images; p. 292, Hugh Sitton/Tony Stone Images; p. 293, S. Vilder/SuperStock; p. 294, Randa Bishop/Tony Stone Images; p. 297, UPI/Corbis-Bettmann; pp. 298-299, From "ODES TO COMMON THINGS" by Pablo Neruda. copyright ©1994 by Pablo Neruda and Pablo Neruda Foundation (Odes in Spanish); 1994 by Ferris Cook (Compilation and illustrations); 1994 by Ken Krabbenhoft (Odes in English-Translation). by permission of Little, Brown and Company; p. 301, ©T. Iwamiya/PPS; p. 302, from "A Haiku Garden" by Stephen Addiss with Fumiko and Akira Yamamoto, 1996/Weatherhill; p. 304, The Granger Collection, New York; p. 306, Terry Vine/Tony Stone Images; p. 312, Giraudon/Art Resource, NY; p. 315, Judy King; p. 317, Christie's Images/SuperStock; p. 318, Stock Montage/SuperStock; p. 320, The Granger Collection, New York; p. 322, George Haling/Tony Stone Images; p. 327, Lori Adamski Peek/Tony Stone Images; p. 328, Ron Sangha/Tony Stone Images; p. 331, Paul Chesley/Tony Stone Images; p. 335, Brown Brothers; pp. 336, 337, The Granger Collection, New York; pp. 339, 340, Associated Press/Worldwide; p. 344, The Granger Collection, New York; p. 345, Christie's Images/SuperStock; p. 347, ©Neal Boenzi, New York Times; p. 348, Allan Aflack Courtesy of the Antigua Tourism Board; p. 351, Cosmo Condina/Tony Stone Images; p. 356, Allan Aflack Courtesy of the Antigua Tourism Board; p. 366, ©1999 Artists Rights Society (ARS), New York/ADAGP, Paris; p. 369, Judy King; p. 370, The Granger Collection, New York; p. 371, ©Stock Montage, Inc.; p. 375, Stedelijk Museum, Amsterdam, Holland; p. 377, Rachel Taylor; p. 379, Agence France Presse/Corbis-Bettmann; p. 383, ©SAGA 1991/Frank Capri/Archive Photos; p. 385, ©Adrian Bradshaw; p. 389, Frank Capri/Archive Photos; p. 391, Guy Porfirio; p. 394, Brown Brothers; pp. 396, 397, 399, Karen Lafoya; p. 401, ©Archive Photos; pp. 406, 407, 408, Carole Katchen